FORGING A REGION

SOAS Studies on South Asia

Stuart Blackburn	*The Fatal Rumour: A Nineteenth-century Indian Novel*
Terence J. Byres, ed.	*The State and Development Planning in India*
Terence J. Byres, ed.	*The State, Development Planning and Liberalization in India*
Indira Chowdhury	*The Frail Hero and Virile History: Gender and the Politics of Culture in Colonial Bengal*
Nigel Crook	*India's Industrial Cities: Essays in Economy and Demography*
Dagmar Engels	*Beyond Purdah? Women in Bengal 1890–1939*
Michael Hutt, ed.	*Nepal in the Nineties: Versions of the Past, Visions of the Future*
Sudipta Kaviraj	*The Unhappy Consciousness: Bankimchandra Chattopadhyay and the Formation of Nationalist Discourse in India*
William Radice	*Swami Vivekananda and the Modernization of Hinduism*
Peter Robb, ed.	*Rural India: Land, Power and Society under British Rule*
Peter Robb, ed.	*Society and Ideology: Essays in South Asian History*
Peter Robb, ed.	*Dalit Movements and the Meanings of Labour in India*
Sanjay Sharma	*Famine, Philanthropy and the Colonial State*
Ujjwal K. Singh	*Political Prisoners in India 1922–1977*
Subho Basu	*Does Class Matter? Colonial Capital and Workers' Resistance in Bengal (1890–1937)*
Avril A. Powell and Siobhan Lambert-Hurley, eds	*Rhetoric and Reality: Gender and the Colonial Experience in South Asia*
Ronald Inden	*Text and Practice: Essays on South Asian History*
Rochelle Pinto	*Between Empires: Print and Politics in Goa*
Jason Hawkes and Akira Shimada (eds)	*Buddhist Stupas in South Asia: Recent Archaeological, Art-Historical, and Historical Perspectives*

SOAS Studies on South Asia

FORGING A REGION

Sultans, Traders, and Pilgrims in Gujarat, 1200–1500

Samira Sheikh

OXFORD
UNIVERSITY PRESS

OXFORD
UNIVERSITY PRESS

Oxford University Press is a department of the University of Oxford. It furthers the University's objective of excellence in research, scholarship, and education by publishing worldwide. Oxford is a registered trademark of Oxford University Press in the UK and in certain other countries

Published in India by
Oxford University Press
22 Workspace, 2nd Floor, 1/22 Asaf Ali Road, New Delhi 110002, India

First Edition published in 2010

ISBN-13 (print edition): 978-0-19-806019-2
ISBN-10 (print edition): 0-19-806019-x

ISBN-13 (eBook): 978-0-19-908879-9
ISBN-10 (eBook): 0-19-908879-9

Typeset in Giovanni Book 9.5/12.7
by Eleven Arts, Keshav Puram, Delhi 110 035
Printed in India by Repro India Limited

Contents

Map and Tables

MAP

TABLES

Acknowledgements

The book that follows is based on doctoral work completed at Oxford. I have accumulated many debts in the writing of the thesis and in the years that followed. This is an opportunity to acknowledge some of them. My supervisor was David Washbrook whose vision, acuity and patience never failed me. I was privileged to have Sanjay Subrahmanyam and Dirk H.A. Kolff as thesis examiners. Their detailed comments helped me refine and revise this work.

Much of the direction of my research owes its origins to Muzaffar Alam's teaching and writing. I take this chance to acknowledge my wonderful teachers at the Centre for Historical Studies in Jawaharlal Nehru University, New Delhi, in particular Harbans Mukhia. S. Hasan Mahmud was the teacher who first interested me, as an undergraduate, in studying the history of medieval Gujarat. Also at the Maharaja Sayajirao University of Baroda, I am grateful to Gita Bajpai for her kindness in facilitating my research.

Daud Ali recommended this work be published in the SOAS Studies on South Asia series. At different times, my research has benefitted from comments by Daud Ali, Judith M. Brown, Francesca Orsini, Mahesh Rangarajan, Ramya Sreenivasan and Romila Thapar. Rachel Dwyer has always been generous with her time, expertise and collection of Gujarat-related books. Zawahir Moir introduced me to the intricacies of Ismā‘īlī history and opened her home and library to me. I am grateful to Françoise Mallison for her consistent support and enthusiasm, and for reading parts of this work. Thanks are also due to Joya Chatterji, Françoise 'Nalini' Delvoye, Dominique-Sila Khan and Amrita Shodhan for their friendship and scholarship. Zulfikar Hirji's interest in my work led me to the Institute of Ismaili Studies, where I worked between 2003 and 2009. I am grateful to my colleagues at the Institute and in particular, to Farhad Daftary, for his support and the example of his scholarship.

It is heartening to be part of two small but growing communities of scholars: those who work on Gujarat and those who study medieval South Asia. Colleagues from both areas of study have been a constant source of encouragement and advice. My friends—each one a wonderful scholar and interlocutor—have always been at hand. Rochana Bajpai, Nandini Bhattacharya, Aparna Kapadia, Prashant Kidambi, Bhavani Raman, Nilanjan Sarkar and Shalini Sharma have put up with my Gujarat obsession for years now. Kaushik Bhaumik taught me to see the bigger picture. This book relies heavily on his insights. My family has always shared and supported my interests: here's my chance to acknowledge my parents, my brother Kabir Sheikh and sister-in-law Deeksha Nath, my grandfather Dr P.C. Dhanda, and my late grandmother Leila Dhanda. My special thanks to Tony K Stewart: for listening, reading, responding, and for keeping my head above water.

I am grateful to Ratan Parimoo, Director, L.D. Museum and N.C. Mehta Gallery, Ahmedabad, for permission to reproduce the cover image. Robert Skelton was kind enough to comment on the manuscript painting on the cover. Tina Bone in Cambridge produced the map of Gujarat. The editorial team at Oxford University Press India have been very patient with me. Prashant Kidambi and Amrita Shodhan have read the manuscript and I have benefited greatly from their critical judgement. All errors are of course mine alone.

Parts of Chapter 3 have appeared in the *Medieval History Journal*, 11:1 (2008), and parts of Chapter 4 in my article in *Gināns: Texts and Contexts. Essays on Ismaili Hymns from South Asia in Honour of Zawahir Moir*, edited by Tazim Kassam and Françoise Mallison, Delhi, Matrix (2007). I am grateful to the editors for permission to reproduce this material.

Growing up in Gujarat helped me negotiate identity, language and belonging. But there were always questions: who belonged and who was left out? Why did people speak and write and live the way they did? Why were there some boundaries I could see, in brick and stone, and others that were no less solid for being invisible? Why did some histories disappear entirely and other memories persist over centuries? And where did the hatred come from that provoked 'riots', year after year? This is my first attempt to try to understand, and it is dedicated to my parents, Nilima and Gulam Mohammed Sheikh.

Abbreviations

ARIE	*Annual Report on Indian Epigraphy*
CE/ BCE	*Common Era/Before Common Era*
EI	*Epigraphia Indica*
EIM	*Epigraphia Indo-Moslemica*
HIG	*Historical Inscriptions of Gujarat*
IA	*Indian Antiquary*
IESHR	*Indian Economic and Social History Review*
IK	*Inscriptions of Kathiawad*
JAS	*Journal of Asian Studies*
JESHO	*Journal of the Economic and Social History of the Orient*
JMSUB	*Journal of the Maharaja Sayajirao University of Baroda*
JOIB	*Journal of the Oriental Institute, Baroda*
JRAS	*Journal of the Royal Asiatic Society*
MAS	*Modern Asian Studies*
MS	*Mir'āt-i Sikandarī*
PAEG	*Persian and Arabic Epigraphy of Gujarat*
RLARBP	*Revised List of Antiquarian Remains in the Bombay Presidency*
	Ṭabaqāt-i Akbarī
TMS	*Ta'rīkh-i Maḥmūd Shāhī*

Transliteration and Conventions

Place names are not transliterated, except when they are archaic or within a quote. Gujarati and Sanskrit words are transcribed according to the American Language Association-Library of Congress (ALA-LC) charts with one exception: 'ṛ' as in Kṛṣṇa, which is transcribed with a dot under the r. The final 'a' in Gujarati words is often omitted. Terms in Arabic follow the *Encyclopaedia of Islam* (3rd edition), with some modifications for Indo-Persian usage. The *marbūṭā* is generally not represented.

The use of terms from a variety of languages has led to some conflict. For example, 'ṭ' represents different phonetic values in Sanskrit and Arabic transliteration. The same goes for 'ṣ'. In Arabic and Persian words, I have used 'ch' for the unaspirated voiceless affricate, while in Sanskrit and Gujarati words, this is 'c'. Here 'ch' represents the aspirated version. 'Sh' sounds in Sk/Gujarati are transcribed as 'ś' and 'ṣ', respectively, following orthography, while in Arabic and Persian, this is invariably 'sh'. In certain cases, as in the use of Arabic/Persian words in Gujarati, or Indic words in Persian, I have followed the orthography in the text rather than the received vocalization. Thus the author of a Gujarati book is rendered as 'Imāmuddīn', rather than 'Imām al-Dīn'. The most obvious of such choices will be in my transcription of the name of the late-fifteenth century Gujarat sultan as Maḥmūd Bīgara. While the name is more familiarly rendered with Indic vocalization as 'Begaḍā', here I have used the Persian spelling as my guide. Most specialists will recognize these accommodations and, I hope, will work out the appropriate vocalization from the context.

Dates are rendered in the Common Era throughout the book. Compound words in Arabic, Persian, and Sanskrit have occasionally been broken up with hyphens. In modern Gujarati, possessive suffixes follow nouns without a break, as in *vāvno śilālekh*, but I have separated the suffix by a hyphen (*vāv-no śilālekh*) to aid those unfamiliar with Gujarati.

Non-European languages do not capitalize proper nouns, and book titles should correctly be rendered in lower-case throughout. But I have been reluctant to depart too far from familiar usage, thus readily recognizable proper nouns begin in upper case. Examples include *Śrī Bahucarājī-no itihās* and *Ṭabaqāt-i Akbarī*.

Introduction

GUJARAT: ORIGINS

The modern state of Gujarat is a recent creation. It was only in 1960 that Bombay state was divided into Maharashtra and Gujarat on the basis of the linguistic and cultural distinctiveness of each.[1] The movement for a separate state of Gujarat derived much energy from the writings and personal efforts of K.M. Munshi (1887–1971), an ardent Gujarati nationalist who made the campaign for statehood a cry for the restoration of the ancient *asmitā* or glory of Gujarat. Munshi was a popular and prolific novelist in Gujarati who wrote on historical and cultural themes. He was also a politician, a close associate of Vallabhbhai Patel, and a prime mover in the construction of a new temple at Somanath. In 1950 this oft-vandalized medieval temple was demolished after a cursory archaeological survey and a modern temple built at the site as a symbolic foundation stone of the new Gujarat. Indeed, for Munshi, Patel, and their adherents on the right wing of the Congress Party, the new temple was a symbol of newly independent India.[2]

As the founding father of the state of Gujarat, Munshi's writings cast a long shadow over all those who write on its past. For him, Gujarat denoted, first, 'the mainland between Mount Ābu and the river Damaṇagaṅgā, distinguishing it from Kachchha or Saurashtra on the one side and Marwar and Malava on the other.'[3] Echoing the nineteenth-century poet Narmad who affirmed the integrity of the Gujarati-speaking region, Munshi continued: '... it [Gujarat] connotes modern Gujarati is spoken at the present time.'[4] More contentiously, he affirmed that Gujarat emerged as a culturally cohesive region in a the Solaṅkī (Caulukya) period *circa* 1100. The golden age of the Solaṅkīs was followed by the 'Muslim' and 'British' periods, which he saw as predominantly painful episodes of occupation that needed to be swept away from popular memory in order to regain pride in Gujarati identity. Thus, he had three criteria to justify the existence of the modern state of Gujarat: a modern linguistic area, a clearly delimited topographical area bounded by natural features such as rivers and mountains, and, as the clinching argument, the assertion that the political and cultural unity of Gujarat was wrought about eight hundred years ago by the Caulukyas.[5] This last contention has not been systematically questioned by historians.

There has been an attenuation of historical and anthropological inquiry on Gujarat in the last generation, both within and outside the region, which is only now beginning to be redressed. The violence in Gujarat in 2002 left scholars scrambling for academic work to explain Gujarat's peculiar caste and community configurations. The lack of reliable historical scholarship on the state is made more glaring by the regular evocation of history in Gujarati cultural and political debate. Since the nineteenth century, Gujarati political discourse has evolved a complex web of narratives of inclusion, traditional rights, and customary practice, many of which depend on establishing 'historical' precedents. Caste groups employ historical narratives to justify their place of residence, local contacts, religious networks, and occupations in Gujarat. The Levā Pāṭīdār farming community of central Gujarat, for example, has a tradition of having migrated there from the Ganga region in the early medieval period in search of military service.[6] The Girnārā and Unevāl brahmins maintain that they were invited to Saurashtra by twelfth-century rulers.[7] The historical invocation of the temple of Somanath and its history of vandalization and renovation translates as a potent political narrative of defeat and regeneration for some Hindus. While modern Gujarat is, of course, a product of recent events, there can be little doubt that Gujarat's medieval history continues to have considerable bearing on contemporary politics.

This neglect of history is puzzling because Gujarat is a region that has been continuously settled for almost four millennia. It is the quintessential land of the immigrant, subject to continual waves of invaders, traders, pastoralists, and peasants. Located at the intersection of a variety of ecological zones, Gujarat's history reflects the dynamics of all these. It has far-flung maritime links from its long coastline, desert and scrublands suitable only for nomad pastoralists in the north-west, good agricultural lands in the east and north-east, and dense hilly forest cover in the centre of the Saurashtra peninsula and the eastern hill tracts. It also lies at the intersection of cultural and economic worlds: it is marginal to classical brahmanical texts yet contains important places of pilgrimage; it has trade links with both north and south India; it was from the eleventh century at the edge of the moving frontier of Turkic expansionism; and, of course, it has long belonged to the world of Indian Ocean trade.

The primary reason for the present book, therefore, must be this neglect in the existing historiography. Even a cursory familiarity with the institutions, texts, and remains of medieval Gujarat that survive into the present throw up questions that the available literature cannot answer. The literature on other contemporary medieval regions too is inadequate to explicate Gujarat's history. While political formations in Gujarat exhibit some commonalities with the polities described in recent literature on south India, they are significantly different in other ways. Similarly, descriptions of the agrarian polities of hinterland north India are insufficient for our purposes; politics in Gujarat combined the effects of an expanding agrarian frontier with the vital presence of merchants and martial pastoralists.

In the decades since the state of Gujarat was inaugurated, 'Gujarat' and 'Gujarati' have become commonplace terms with familiar images and values attached to them. But these have not always been constant. What *is* Gujarat? If we accept Munshi's contention that Gujarat can be traced back to the political unit forged by the Caulukyas c.1200, how did this unit survive the intervening years ruled by sultans, Rajputs, Mughals, Marathas, the East India Company, and scores of princely states? What is the Gujarati linguistic region? How did it come into being and who propagated it? Who are Gujaratis, where did they come from, and where did they settle? How was religious and social life organized? What are Gujarat's geophysical characteristics and what influence did they have on its history? Who named the region and what were the consequences of this naming?

This book tackles some of these questions within a specific time period: from the late twelfth to the end of the fifteenth century. The twelfth century had seen the establishment under the Caulukyas of what has elsewhere been called a 'vernacular polity'. The Caulukyas gradually extended a contested form of political control over most of the territory of modern Gujarat including Saurashtra and Kachchh. They patronized a variegated intellectual elite, most prominently Jains who produced a large body of biographical, ritual, and aesthetic texts in Sanskrit and Apabhraṃśa.[8] Although Caulukya patronage of Apabhraṃśa texts did not lead to the elaboration of a vernacular polity—regional political statements were expressed in Sanskrit and Apabhraṃśa, both transregional languages—nevertheless, the dominions of the Caulukyas came to be identified as the land of the Gurjaras, Gurjaradeśa.[9] 'Gurjara' was not at this stage a linguistic category. Apabhraṃśa was used as a literary language over large parts of northern and western India, especially by the Jains, and was not specifically identified with Gujarat or the Caulukyas. By the twelfth century Gurjaradeśa was the land of the Gurjaras, that is, all those who inhabited Gurjaradeśa, not merely members of the Gurjara tribe. Thus, the Caulukyas presided over the invention of a regional entity that far outlasted them.

This study begins from the point when the Caulukya-dominated regional entity had already come into existence and its political control was in decline after the death of Kumārapāla in 1174. By 1201, the Caulukya ruler Bhīma was back in his capital after a devastating attack by a general from the Ghūrid army of Mu'izz al-Dīn Muḥammad in 1197. Although Bhīma recovered his capital after the retreat of the Turks, Caulukya power was now clearly on the wane. The flourishing court society and region-wide control of the twelfth century was in disarray as the Caulukyas continued to suffer military defeats. By the mid-thirteenth century they were edged out by former subsidiaries, the Vāghelās, who ruled a small strip of eastern Gujarat in the Caulukya name for the remainder of the century.

The decline of Caulukya rule inaugurated a period of sub-regional political elaboration, one feature of which was the rise of groups who later came to call themselves Rajputs. Martial pastoralist clans battled each other all over the region to establish small local patrilinies, some of which went on to ally themselves to the Rajput status hierarchy emerging in Rajasthan. Pastoralist clans were also moving into Gujarat from Sind and Rajasthan to enter the fray. There was unprecedented movement of populations throughout Gujarat and new areas were cleared for agriculture or grazing.

Meanwhile, trade along the coastline and overland continued unabated. This was the era of the merchant magnate who dabbled in politics. Merchants, especially those who could manipulate the trade in items of military value such as horses and weaponry, made bids for influence at court or even claimed local sovereignty. The thirteenth-century Vāghelās were controlled by powerful Jain merchant families. Other merchants, such as a horse trader in Kachchh whose life will be discussed in Chapter 3, set themselves up as local rulers. The port towns housed large colonies of Arab, Persian, and Indian Ocean merchants, many of whom had business and political interests in the hinterland.

Revenues from trade made a crucial difference to the finances of whatever group was in power in Gujarat. This may be as true of the Gujarat of the twenty-first century as of the twelfth. The continuing importance of trade tended to impose checks upon inter-group violence. Merchant groups periodically entered politics to help control policy. As during Vāghelā rule in the thirteenth century, and also when power was concentrated in the hands of pastoralist chieftains, the necessity of promoting trade was quickly brought home to rulers. Warfare and disruption were inevitable, but were generally checked by the need to safeguard trade.

Historically, the most important groups in Gujarat were merchants and pastoralists. Rulers were usually former pastoralists, transforming themselves from cattle rustlers, bandits, or pirates into patrons and enforcers of security. 'Merchant' and 'pastoralist' were overarching and at times interchangeable identities: merchants could be itinerant and pastoralists could engage in trade. It was the interaction between the two that fuelled the history of the region. Between them was created the immense productivity and mobility that attracted producers, peasants, and religious specialists. The mutual reliance of the two groups was constantly reinforced in the literature of the period; texts put out by rulers referred to the security they enforced to facilitate trade, while merchant texts highlighted the influence and security they enjoyed in the kingdom.

The settlement and sub-regional political activity of the thirteenth century were followed by another significant Turkic invasion, this time that of generals sent by 'Alā' al-Dīn Khaljī from Delhi, seeking to acquire control over the lucrative trade routes and manufacture of Gujarat. This time the Vāghelās were driven out, and by 1307 governors from Delhi controlled strategic fortresses across Gujarat. Peace was soon re-established and trade continued to flourish. New pastoralist incursions continued and the local Rajput lineages continued in their territories subject to the payment of tribute. For courtiers of the sultans of Delhi, the governorship of Gujarat became a much sought-after post and some were willing to pay substantial bribes to be appointed to Anhilvada or Cambay. But by the end of the fourteenth century the Delhi sultanate was in crisis. Tīmūr's sack of Delhi in 1398–9 had left the sultans in no position to control their regional governors. After a period of negotiation and uncertainty in Delhi, the last governor of Gujarat, Ẓafar Khān, declared his sovereignty in 1407.

The descendants of Ẓafar Khān ruled Gujarat for the next century and a half, and were responsible for the invention of institutions of governance and political articulation that had a remarkable longevity and resilience. Over time, the sultans came to exert military and political control over almost the whole of the territory of modern Gujarat. They patronized scholarship and literature in Arabic, Persian, and Sanskrit. During sultanate rule in the fifteenth century, scholars and poets began to write in early Gujarati and Gūjarī, a Gujarati-inflected version of early Urdu. The region was no longer just an administrative division; it was identified with the local language in its diverse forms. This was, I argue, the high point of the elaboration of the Indo-Muslim vernacular regional state.

WHY STUDY GUJARAT?

In terms of the evolution of a political culture, the period studied here was crucial for the invention of long-lasting institutions of religion, language, administration, and trade. Administrative divisions, revenue arrangements, and political units established in this period persisted in the face of Mughal and British attempts to overhaul them. With the decline of the early medieval state represented by brahmin-legitimized kings, sacrifice, and royal cults, we begin to see the emergence of more familiar castes, sects, and religious groups: Vaiṣṇavas, Ismāʿīlīs, Jains, Rajputs, *vāṇiā* merchant groups, and Kaṇbī Pāṭīdārs. This was also the period of the development of new languages—written and spoken.

Sheldon Pollock's account of the vernacular millennium fails to take into account the role played by the Indo-Muslim polities of north India. For all its limitations, the Delhi sultanate was an attempt to establish transregional rule over the larger part of South Asia, at least partly in a vernacular idiom.[10] After its decline, the actual task of vernacularization was taken up by the regional sultanates of north India, most notably in Bengal.[11] Thus, while the preliminary articulation of the vernacular, albeit in Apabhraṃśa, was inaugurated in Gujarat by Jain intellectuals at the Caulukya court, it was further elaborated by Muslim and non-Muslim intellectuals in the fourteenth and fifteenth centuries under sultanate rule. This was the period when a plethora of writings were produced in Apabhraṃśa and Sanskrit, early Gujarati, gal, and Gūjarī, coexisting with literature in Arabic and Persian. While there was a lot of writing commissioned by the sultans and their courtiers, we also begin to get the first evidence of compositions, especially sectarian and religious ones, from non-court sources.

The period described is thus one in which language and literary culture were elaborated to a considerable extent. This was also a period that saw an expansion in manifestations of religion—with state patronage and outside it. As the Caulukyas expanded in the twelfth century, a number of local deities were incorporated into the transregional religious vocabulary. This is particularly evident in inscriptions, many of which mention local deities assimilated as versions of Śiva or Viṣṇu. When royal patronage shrank in the thirteenth century, there was a proliferation of cults and religious figures, all struggling for patrons and resources. Several immigrant pastoralist groups brought their own deities to Gujarat. They also revered warrior-heroes and women who were sanctified for their valour and sacrifice. As sacrificial manifestations of royal religion declined, we see the evolution of practices of *bhakti* or personal worship. Some temples continued to be built and endowed, but by merchants and courtiers rather than by rulers. These tended to be Jain or Vaiṣṇava in denomination after the Śaivite dominance of the Caulukya years.

This was also when Muslim religious figures first began to make inroads into the hinterland. The early conversions to Ismāʿīlī Islam in Gujarat date from this period, and branches of Ismāʿīlī practice continued to gain ground even during the Sunni-dominated sultanate. The sultanate ostensibly inaugurated a period of orthodox Sunni observance presided over by rival Sufi orders, but there is little evidence that Sunni beliefs penetrated widely outside court or urban circles. Nor is there much evidence of conversion to Sunni Islam, while there are indications that Ismāʿīlī preachers continued to attract converts throughout the sultanate period.

While exploring the politics of the period, I provide a broad picture of settlement, the extension of agriculture and the development of trade routes in a land that was at once a frontier region and one of the longest-settled regions in South Asia. Medieval polities need to be mapped with reference to religion and trade, as well as war and agrarian relations. It has repeatedly been established that medieval states—least of all Gujarat—were not de-urbanized or de-monetized. This was not a period of economic decline, and moreover, politics were inextricably intertwined with trade.[12] Arrangements for agriculture, commodity production, and trade in Gujarat led to unique political arrangements and negotiations. While Gujarat had features in common with both south and north India, its location and diversity led to complex and unique political elaborations that offer emendations to the accepted historiography of medieval south Asia.

Over the three centuries when Gujarat was emerging as a political and linguistic region, the political landscape was differentiated by a variety of religious and sectarian groups competing for resources and followers. Settlers struggled over territory and the evolving networks of trade, adapting to the terrain, the climate, and natural resources. Itinerancy and mobility were as crucial to the polity as settlement. Patterns of political formation were related to the tension between mobility and sedentarization.

The study of medieval Gujarat, and of medieval South Asia in general, has suffered from the assumption that texts from the period are scanty. But there is considerably more source material than one might be led to believe. From Gujarat the sources that are strictly contemporary with our period include several Persian chronicles and literary works, about four hundred published inscriptions in Sanskrit, Arabic, Persian, and Old Gujarati, travellers' accounts, and scores of historical ballads, plays, biographies, and poems in Sanskrit and Apabhraṃśa. In addition are works in Arabic, Persian, and Sanskrit on religious traditions and rituals, many of which contain incidental historical information. There is a large body of texts from Jain and other religious communities. Chronicles and accounts from later periods also have a wealth of information.

A number of buildings from the period still exist and there are archaeological reports of varying accuracy on many of them. An estimate of the coins from Gujarat in various collections may be derived from the information that a single hoard of eleventh- to thirteenth-century coins found in Bhinmal contained over a hundred thousand specimens.[13] *Pāḷiyā*s or hero-stones are found in every village, and some of the early ones have been published and studied.[14] Information on Gujarat trade has been found in the Geniza records, and in the Fāṭimid and Mamlūk chronicles of Egypt. There is similar information in the Yemeni chronicles and those from the Persian Gulf. Princely state histories based on local documentation, and clan genealogists and genealogical and historical material collected in the nineteenth century

Five histories dealing with Gujarat were written during the Mughal period. It has been these, rather than the strictly contemporary sources that modern authors have used to reconstruct the history of the Gujarat sultanate. The mainstay of our knowledge about medieval Gujarat has been the *Mir'āt-i Sikandarī* which was completed in 1611 (and revised a few years later).[15] It was written at least twenty years after the death of the last nominal sultan, Muẓaffar III, when Mughal authority was well entrenched in Gujarat. Although the author was the son of a sultanate official, his account is not an eyewitness one, nor can it be said to reflect accurately the kind of history that the sultans would have liked to have had composed. Nevertheless, the *Mir'āt*, based as it is on earlier histories, such as the lost *Ta'rīkh-i Bahādur Shāhī* and traditions transmitted by word of mouth, is one of the most comprehensive texts available for a study of the Gujarat sultans. It is perhaps also a more 'objective' account, since it was not encumbered by having to flatter or eulogize reigning monarchs.

The *Mir'āt* or 'mirror' of Sikandar was written by a middle-ranking official who lived in Mughal Ahmadabad. Sikandar b. Muḥammad Manjhū b. Akbar worked for the Bukhārī Sayyid family of Vatwa and Dholka as steward of their estates. He joined imperial service about 1610. Four years later, he journeyed to Agra and presented a copy of *Mir'āt-i Sikandarī* to Jahāngīr's minister I'timād al-Dawla.[16] Jahāngīr (r. 1605–27) himself visited Ahmadabad during Sikandar's last years, and called on him there.

Sikandar's account manifestly reflects his allegiance to his patrons, the Bukhārī Sayyids, and their role in the fortunes of the sultanate. He describes at length the implicit rivalry and contestation of influence between the sultans and the main branch of the Bukhārī family at Vatwa. He relates the exploits of the early sultans in a matter-of-fact and brief way. Understandably, he is much more voluble on the later sultans, relating tales of the court, the Sufi families and their intrigues and interactions.

Another book that includes abundant information about the Gujarat sultans, and was written at almost the same time as the *Mir'āt* is the *Ẓafar al-wālih bi muẓaffar wa-ālihi*.[17] This work is unique in that it is the only known secular history in Arabic written in pre-modern India. The author, 'Abd allāh Muḥammad al-Makkī al-Āṣafī al-Ulugh nī, known as Ḥājjī al-Dabīr, was born in Mecca, and came to India in 1554. In Ahmadabad, he entered the service of an Abyssinian general ḥammad Ulugh Khān, as a *dabīr* or scribe. After Akbar's conquest

Later he was assigned to carry *waqf* (endowment) money to the Hijaz and to distribute it among the poor there. He returned to India in 1575–6, and served in the Deccan in 1605–6, after which he seems to have returned to Mecca where he wrote his book. The first section of his work is a detailed narration of the era of the Gujarat sultans interspersed with numerous digressions, anecdotes, and moral and religious discussions on prevalent topics. The rest of the work is a general account of the other important Muslim kingdoms of north India, which is partly paraphrased from earlier writers but also contains some previously unknown information.

The *Ta'rīkh-i salāṭīn-i Gujarāt* of Sayyid Maḥmūd b. Munawwar al-mulk Bukhārī and the *Ta'rīkh-i Gujarāt* of Mīr Abū Turāb Walī were both written in the reign of Akbar.[18] Sayyid Maḥmūd Bukhārī, whose work is a brief account of the dynasty from Aḥmad Shāh (1411–42) to the conquest of Gujarat by Akbar (1572), belonged to the family of the Bukhārī Sayyids of Rasulabad, near Ahmadabad, who, like Sikandar's patrons, had close links with the Gujarat sultans.[19] In fact the Sufi Makhdūm-i Jahāniyān, ancestor and founder of the Bukhārī lineage, had prophetically granted the kingdom of Gujarat to Ẓafar n in gratitude for services he had performed (see chapter 5 for details). Branches of the Bukhārī family figured prominently in court activities and intrigues.

The *Ta'rīkh-i Gujarāt* of Mīr Abū Turāb Walī, on the other hand, is a history of the reign of Bahādur Shāḥ (1526–37) and the subsequent years, ending with the revolt of Muẓaffar Shāh III (1561–73) against the Mughals.[20] The author belonged to the Maghribī Sayyid family who had long served the sultans. In the reign of Akbar, Abū Turāb ī was appointed Mīr-Ḥajj—the leader of pilgrims—and he brought back from the pilgrimage a stone tablet with the impression of the Prophet's foot.[21]

The general histories written in the Mughal period, most notably *Ṭabaqāt-i Akbarī* of Niẓām al-Dīn Aḥmad, contain considerable information about the Gujarat sultans, as does Firishta's *Gulshan-i hīmī*, written in the Deccan. Another important source of information is the *Mir'āt-i Aḥmadī* and its supplement, which were written by the last Mughal governor of Gujarat, 'Alī Muḥammad Khān, around 1762.[22] This work is less valuable for its account of the sultans, which is largely based on earlier works, than for its information about Gujarat in the second half of the eighteenth century, and the preservation of legends and traditions regarding the sultans and various saints. The *āt-i Aḥmadī* is known to have been compiled after extensive surveys of the landholdings, agriculture, and trade of the era.

In addition to the Mughal-period accounts, there are seven surviving contemporary accounts of the Gujarat sultans in Persian. These include five texts written in the reign of Maḥmūd Bīgara (r. 1459–1511). The earliest of these texts (if we ignore the possibility of a *Ta'rīkh-i Muẓaffar hī* written in the reign of the first sultan Muẓaffar Shāh I[23]), is the *kh-i Aḥmad Shāhī*, a verse panegyric to Aḥmad Shāh I, by a poet named Ḥūlwī Shīrāzī. This work has not survived, but extracts are quoted both in the *Mir'āt-i Sikandarī* and in the *Ta'rīkh-i ṣalāṭīn-i Gujarāt*.[24]

The best known of these contemporary texts is the work that has been published as the *Ta'rīkh-i Maḥmūd Shāhī*.[25] There has been considerable confusion over the name and authorship of this work, but investigations by S.A.I. Tirmizi and Jean Aubin have plausibly cleared up the question.[26] According to them, the work published as *Ta'rīkh-i Maḥmūd Shāhī* by an unknown author was known alternatively by the title *Kītab-i ma'āthir-i Maḥmūd Shāhī*, and was compiled at the court of Maḥmūd Bīgara in the last years of the fifteenth century. This work was compiled in two parts, the first of which was written by a Persian immigrant named 'Abd al-Ḥusayn b. ī Tūnī. The book begins with the foundation of the Muẓaffarid dynasty of Gujarat but the history of the Timurids and of Persia occupy the maximum space. The author was probably born in Iran. His father served in the Deccan in the army of 'Alā' al-Dīn Aḥmad Shāh Bāhmanī, and came to Gujarat to seek his fortune. At the time of his death in 1489–90, his work was not complete and the narrative ends rather suddenly. The writer who completed the work began his account with the year following the death of the first writer. Aubin surmises that *Ma'āthir* was completed by a certain Mawlānā Shams al-Dīn Zīrak āzī. His observation is based on the fact that the *Gulzār-i abrār* of Mawlāna Ghawthī (seventeenth century) attributes the authorship of *Ma'āthir-i Maḥmūd Shāhī* to Shīrāzī.[27]

Another work of the reign of Maḥmūd Bīgara has not yet been published. This is the *Ṭabaqāt-i Maḥmud Shāhī* of 'Abd al-Karīm Nīmdihī, who has also been the subject of some confusion.[28] Since the publication of the lithographed edition and translation of the *Gulshan-i Ibrāhīmī* of Firishta, it had been assumed that a certain courtier of the Bāhmanīs, Mullā 'Abd al-Karīm Hamadānī, wrote a chronicle on the reign of ḥmūd Bīgara that was presumed to be lost. Aubin, however demonstrated that the editors of the *Gulshan-i Ibr h* had misread the name 'Hamadānī'. The correct reading revealed that the author of this work was none other than the well-known secretary of Maḥmūd wān, 'Abd al-Karim Nīmdihī, and that 'Hamadānī' did not exist.

Nīmdihī was born in Laristan and studied at Shiraz, after which he came to India to find employment. After a sojourn at Mandu, then ruled by either Maḥmūd or Ghiyāth al-Dīn Khaljī, where he failed to find a job, Nīmdihī proceeded to Muhammadabad-Bidar and entered the Bāhmanī chancellery. Around 1472–3, Maḥmūd Gāwān took him on as his personal secretary (*dabīr-khāna-yi khāṣṣ*). Nīmdihī is likely to have composed much of Maḥmūd Gāwān's correspondence, some of which is conserved in the collections of letters of the famous minister. After Maḥmūd Gāwān's execution in 1481, Nīmdihī seems to have lost his job and proceeded to Ahmadabad and thence to Hormuz. In 1487, the king of Hormuz dispatched him to Gujarat to mediate a dispute with Maḥmūd Bīgara. The boat that carried Nīmdihī was wrecked and he reached Gujarat only after considerable hardship. It is likely that he remained in Gujarat until 1499–1501, and compiled a universal chronicle commissioned by Maḥmūd Bīgara, the *Ṭabaqāt-i Maḥmud Shāhī*.[29]

The other two accounts from the reign of Maḥmūd Bīgara are the *īkh-i ṣadr-i jahān* of Fayḍ allāh Binbānī, and the *Ṭabaqāt-i Gujarāt* of Sharaf al-Dīn Bukhārī. Both these chronicles, like Nīmdihī's work, are in the *ṭabaqāt* or 'layered' format. Fayḍ allāh Zayn al-'Ābidīn b. ām Binbānī was a scholar with the Bāhmanīs who moved to Gujarat in the reign of Maḥmūd Bīgara. His universal history, dealing with the entire Islamic world and only peripherally with Gujarat, was written in 1501–2 when the author had been sent as ambassador to Ahmadnagar, and was dedicated to Maḥmūd Bīgara.[30] Sharaf al-Dīn ḥammad Bukhārī was a scholar of the reign of Maḥmūd Bīgara and his son Muẓaffar II, whose ancestors had emigrated from Bukhara and settled in Ahmadabad.[31]

The next Persian chronicle to be commissioned at the Gujarat court was the *Ta'rīkh-i Muẓaffar Shāhī* by a poet named Qāni' who wrote in the reign of Muẓaffar Shāh II (1511–26).[32] The author of this short chronicle was a native of Kashan whose full name was Mīr Sayyid 'Alī. The work itself, 'the most ornate, florid, and verbose of all chronicles', describes only one campaign of Muẓaffar Shāh II: his attack on Malwa to rescue Maḥmūd Shāh II from the besieging Pūrbiyā Rājpūts led by Medini Rāi.[33]

The incumbency of Bahādur Shāh (1526–37) was chronicled twice, of which one verse history, the *Ganj-i ma'āni*, by a poet named Muṭī' survives. The other was the *Ta'rīkh-i Bahādur Shāhī* by Ḥusām Khān Gujarātī, which was the most definitive source-book for the history of the Gujarat sultans until it was superseded by the *Mir'āt-i Sikandarī* after 1611. The author was a grandson of the famous minister of Maḥmūd gara, Muḥāfiz Khān, and is referred to by Sikandar as *al-mu'arrikh* (the historian). The *Bahādur Shāhī* survived until the eighteenth century, but has not been heard of since then.[34] Most writers of the seventeenth century, including Sikandar, Hājjī al-Dabīr, Niẓām al-Dīn Aḥmad, and Firishta used the *Bahādur Shāhī* and extracts appear in their own works.

The last contemporary chronicle of the dynasty is the lost *Tuḥfat al-sa'ādāt* written by Ārām Kashmīrī, who was a follower of Sayyid Mubārak Bukhārī (also the patron of Sikandar's father) in the reign of ḥmūd Shāh III (1537–54). The book was not very well known, and is quoted only by Sikandar and Hājjī al-Dabīr.[35]

Although the history of Gujarat has been relatively neglected in recent years, this was not always the case. Its history and ethnography were among the chief interests of Orientalist scholars in western India, as evidenced in the high proportion of studies on Gujarat in scholarly periodicals such as the *Indian Antiquary* [henceforth *IA*] and the journal of the Bombay branch of the Royal Asiatic Society. This followed from the earlier writing of British officials such as James Macmurdo, Alexander Walker, and Alexander Kinloch Forbes in the early nineteenth century.[36] Until the early years of the twentieth century, there was considerable ethnographic research carried out in Gujarat, taking up from where Forbes had left off. While the latter had confined himself to the histories of ruling Rajput clans, largely based on information made available by court historians and genealogists, later Indian and British ethnographers consulted village elders, and the bards and genealogists of other castes [37] Some of the information they gathered went into district-wise surveys to list and characterize every contemporary community for the *Bombay Gazetteer* and the census. Separate volumes were published on the Hindu and Muslim tribes and castes of Gujarat. Meanwhile, 'native states' in Gujarat began to publish histories of their dynasties or regions, although early versions of these usually regurgitated information already published in the *Bombay Gazetteer* or by Forbes.

While it might be argued that information from colonial sources is too 'late' and 'Orientalist' to be of value for our period, they nevertheless record some historical processes which may be corroborated with contemporary sources. The use of nineteenth-century sources is particularly useful in Gujarat where the colonial state (and, indeed, the

Mughal state before it) never managed to overhaul completely the pre-existing administrative and political structure, and often reinforced it.

In the wake of colonial scholarly efforts and in response to the classifying demands of the decennial census from 1871, caste groups and communities began to publish historical, mythological, and descriptive information to claim separate and historically validated status in the eyes of the British administration. Some of this material can be assessed against with similar traditions recorded earlier. In other cases, historical corroboration with other kinds of sources is possible. Mythical and legendary materials often provide clues to social processes that would not be available from Persian historical sources.

Brahmin subcastes produced historical accounts or 'translated' parts of the Sanskrit Purāṇas or religious narratives for the benefit of those of their fellows who were losing pride in their tradition and falling prey to divisive forces. These narratives often provided accounts of migrations, patrons, family feuds, and divine blessings from manuscript sources and family tradition. Many of the originary claims set out by brahmin groups were based on the authority of the *Skanda Purāṇa*.[38] Sections dealing with origin myths and praises (*māhātmya*) of places of pilgrimage (*tīrtha*), and cities were published as deriving from the *Skanda Purāṇa*. Other publications recorded migrations, sectarian divisions, patronage, and the adoption of different religious practices, coded in the form of mythological stories. It is likely that the caste-based claim-making literature of the early twentieth century was in emulation of caste and shrine claims that were made much earlier. Much of Purāṇic literature may thus represent claims made by groups of brahmins and the custodians of cults and shrines for the notice of their patrons and the state, and to be competitively integrated into the network of Sanskritic civilization.

Among the 'lower castes', Gujarati ballads and martial epics glorifying deified heroes were sometimes called *purāṇas*.[39] The Rajput princely states on occasion commissioned ministers or prominent court figures to write state histories. This class of accounts was distinct from the Purāṇic literature, which was usually written by brahmins in Sanskrit or in emulation of Sanskrit literary devices. The princely states also employed professional genealogists and record-keepers, usually, if inaccurately, referred to as bards, whose records ran parallel to the brahmanical Purāṇic one. Genealogists such as the Cāraṇs, Vahīvancās, and Bhāṭs were also employed by other groups to record genealogies and chronicles, and to arrange marriage, military, and business alliances.

Brahmins performed similar functions at times, but professional bards possessed sacral properties that made them indispensable to the political and economic system prior to about 1810.[40] Even when their role as guarantors was superseded, the bards retained their role as genealogists and chroniclers, and some of them participated in the caste-claim literature to press their own claims or those of their patrons.

When the defining criterion for admission to Rajput status for a martial/pastoralist group became its descent hierarchy, the 'bards', in their role as genealogists, played a significant part in the consolidation of Rajput identity. Legitimate descent usually required a mythological or historical hero as lineage ancestor, and the bards, as ritual or sacral guarantors, could provide the necessary genealogies. Brahmins were only peripherally involved in this process of the compilation of genealogies; in the early stages of assimilation into Rajput identity, bards performed many of the functions of ritual priests and genealogists while older established or prestige groups tended to have a brahmin as clan priest who was distinct in status and role from the bard.

This differentiation has links with the increasing brahminization of the Rajput groups from the fifteenth century and their gradual distancing from the goddess worship that was intrinsically connected with the bards. This evolution of identity also owed something to the interface with Muslim rulers. It is possible to speculate that the valorization of the Rajputs was a consequence of the attempts of Muslim as well as bardic chroniclers to make their antagonists or protagonists out to be proud kings instead of livestock-herding chieftains. The advent with the Indo-Muslim courts of new forms of literacy, new languages, and new ways of disseminating information—the chronicles, the administrative structure, and the role of propagandists such as the Sufis or Ismā'īlī missionaries—could also have influenced the rise to prominence and, indeed, the idiom of the bards.

Less prominent martial or pastoralist groups who called themselves Rajput commissioned histories to prove their links to established Rajput clans or to publicize charters or grants that gave them control over their lands. In the early twentieth century, farming communities such as the bīs and Pāṭīdārs of the fertile lands of eastern Gujarat were prolific with pamphlets, both to carve out separate *jñāti* (sub-caste) identities among themselves and to claim an ancient *kṣatriya* past. Such groups employed professional genealogists to write their histories or put together information in the form of historical pamphlets. The employment of such record-keepers was itself an attempt to emulate Rajput practice.

Even 'lower' caste communities who claimed an ancient kingly past possessed affiliated 'bards' to record their histories and traditions.

There were, thus, four main strands of historical recording in medieval Gujarat. Rajput clans and groups claiming kṣatriya status were remembered in genealogies, ballads, and chronicles preserved by professional bards and poets in the form of manuscripts, oral testimonies, or performative tradition. Brahmins and groups that relied on brahmanical legitimation such as certain merchant groups, tended to employ the Purāṇa genre, which coded the rights and claims of groups of people, shrines, or sects in the form of mythological stories. Next was the biographical tradition of the Jains, which recorded the exemplary lives of important Jains and their patrons. The fourth was the Persian tradition of history writing. This was still practised in the nineteenth century, as in the *Ta'rīkh-i Sorath* written by the Nāgar brahmin minister of Junagadh. Persian histories have generally been considered the most reliable source of political information and were employed for corroborative purposes by Forbes and the compilers of *Bombay Gazetteer*, and, in emulation of them, by many of the writers of caste pamphlets.

These traditions were not mutually exclusive, and at times relied on one another's authority, coexisting for several centuries. Thus, Persian writers often used the tag-line, 'It is written in the books of the Hindus that...', while Jain writers made occasional references to Hindu works. From the twelfth to the fifteenth centuries, genealogists and guarantors brokered a transition from a predominantly pastoralist society interspersed with merchant-dominated towns to a genuine court society in which the sultan of Gujarat was the overlord of a number of subsidiary chieftains who now had courts and priests. In the heyday of the Gujarat sultanate and during Mughal rule, such groups served many of the same functions as under British government, the most important of which was to record group histories and present claims for favour or patronage to the state. The details of this transition are recorded in the 'bardic' accounts collected in the nineteenth and twentieth centuries, and from some of the caste and princely state histories. In the present study an attempt has been made to juxtapose major sources in order to get a composite idea of territory, settlement, and politics.

HISTORIOGRAPHY

The literature on medieval Gujarat is scanty and outdated, and at times politically contentious. For Hindu nationalist writers such as K.M. Munshi and A.K. Majumdar, the Turkic conquest of Gujarat in the late thirteenth century was the end of civilization.[41] The subsequent ignominious period of Hindu 'defeat' was considered best forgotten. The works of these writers have formed the basis of subsequent Gujarati history as well as of school and university textbooks, and continue to dominate local historiography.

After A.K. Forbes' *Ras Mala* (1878) and J.M. Campbell's historical section of the *Bombay Gazetteer*, M.S. Commissariat's monumental *History of Gujarat* (1938) is still the indispensable starting point for inquiry into the period. The next major works on medieval Gujarat were monographs by S.C. Misra and S.A.I. Tirmizi.[42] Misra, a north Indian scholar trained in the nationalist historiographical tradition of Allahabad, recognized the primary importance of the Persian chronicles for political history and made thorough use of them for his study of political factions and military campaigns in Gujarat under the Delhi sultans and the early independent sultans. Although he used Jain and published bardic works for corroboration, he could ignore the Gujarati nationalist project of privileging the 'Rajput period' and its source materials, and align himself with the larger nationalist history-writing effort. Tirmizi also relied heavily on Persian chronicles to construct his narrative of the Gujarat sultanate.

Other accounts have treated the beginning of the European trading interface with India as the beginning of their story. The arrival of the Portuguese off the western coast of the peninsula *circa* 1500 seemed a convenient beginning to sketch the backdrop of colonialism in India. M.N. Pearson's *Merchants and Rulers of Gujarat* (1976) reflected the growing historical interest in the 1970s in the Indian Ocean trade and the economic effects of European incursions. This work was also part of the effort to sideline political history in favour of studies of trade and exchange—it denied, for example, that the Gujarat sultans were much concerned with the trade off their coasts—and used largely Portuguese material from the sixteenth century. This work was part of a trend in coastal studies of trade which had the unfortunate effect of marginalizing political history.[43]

Another reason for the neglect of medieval Gujarat, and, indeed, of medieval studies in general, is the fact that the period is not seen to have a direct bearing on present-day politics, except in its appropriation by retrogressive and socially divisive agencies. Medieval history as a whole, especially periods of encounter with the Muslims, is seen as inherently problematic. Issues such as conversion, violence, and religious identity are still politically fraught and do not receive much attention, or are treated with careful political neutrality.[44]

In some important ways, this study draws on Richard Eaton's work, which attempts to explain the phenomenon of the rise of Islam in Bengal over a six-hundred-year span by linking it with the extension of rice cultivation over the region. Here, I do not have a comparable singular proposition to offer. Although the rise of Muslim political rule is examined, Islam and Muslims had been present in Gujarat for about five hundred years before the starting point of this study. Second, there is no singular and traceable phenomenon such as the extension of rice cultivation in Gujarat. Instead, we have much messier incursions of waves of pastoralists and subsequent internal quarrels to document.

Cynthia Talbot has examined the relationship between agrarian expansion, settlement, and religion through an exploration of Kākatīya temple inscriptions.[45] In Andhra, temple inscriptions made up a representative sample, in that endowments to temples were the regular mode of signalling settlement and prosperity, at least for a clearly differentiated part of the population. However, for Gujarat there is no comparable corpus of temple inscriptions to analyse. Further, donations to temples tailed off in the thirteenth century and did not pick up until the Vaiṣṇava temple-building movements in the sixteenth and seventeenth centuries. There were still inscriptions on pāḷiyās, wells, and other secular structures, but Muslim rule and religious redefinition meant that large-scale legitimatory temples were no longer being built by merchants or rulers.

In terms of method, one the most instructive analyses of western India is found in B.D. Chattopadhyaya's collection of studies on early medieval Rajasthan.[46] His accounts of the rise of the Rajputs and the relationship of trade and periodic markets with political developments were among the studies that contested the Indian feudalism theory through a careful study of contemporary sources. Unfortunately for the purposes of the present work, his studies end around 1200, leaving subsequent political and economic developments unexplored.[47] D.H.A. Kolff's study of the military labour market in north India is equally instructive.[48] It also explains the Rajputs' rise to political prominence in terms of the transformation of pastoralist groups into militarized chieftaincies. Another study of Rajput kinship, albeit in the Mughal period, is Norman Ziegler's exposition of the complex web of marriage alliances, inheritance patterns, and political power.[49] This offers several pointers for the analysis of similar patterns in Gujarat. Simon Digby's analysis of the importance of military supplies to the Delhi sultanate has contributed to my understanding of the relationship between trade and politics while his sweeping survey of fourteenth century north India is vital reading for any analysis of that much-neglected period.[50]

Works on south India by Burton Stein, David Ludden, Cynthia Talbot, and others, and on Bengal by Richard Eaton have shown the way for the historical geography of medieval India.[51] All these are exercises in mapping territory and its occupation by various groups and attempt to understand the nature of politics in these circumstances. However, each of them works with a particular central question. While Eaton's book attempts to tackle the problematic of conversion to Islam in the Ganga delta region, Talbot's explores the Kākatīya polity through a study of temple endowment inscriptions. Ludden's work on the other hand is a long-term study of settlement and agriculture in a single district.

The present research uses aspects of all these approaches, but there are significant differences. First, the Gujarat economy and sultanate were more complex than Talbot's Kākatīyas in terms of the size of the economy, the diversity of cultures, and the importance of the region. While Talbot attempts to evolve a complete picture of a small elite engaged in political intervention partly through the act of building or making endowments to temples, this is not my aim here. Chattopadhyaya's work is focused solely on Rajputs and bypasses the interactivity of cultures, although the processes he identifies form the core of the present study. Nor do I attempt to explain a single remarkable phenomenon, such as that of conversion to Islam. Like Eaton, I study an Indo-Muslim polity, but here it is engaged in complex negotiations with locally evolving pastoralist polities. The crucial difference with Eaton is the focus on the relationship between politics, the economy, and religion. While Eaton takes a long-term approach to his problematic, I study the politics that led up to the establishment of the Gujarat sultanate. This is, therefore, a broad-brush picture of a medieval polity in a period of transition, which led up to the formation of a regional rulership.

OUTLINE OF THE STUDY

The political region of Gujarat, with frontiers roughly similar to modern ones, had an independent existence from the twelfth century onwards. There was a continually contested relationship between the prosperous eastern mainland and the Saurashtra peninsula, in which the former usually held the advantage. Saurashtra was an arid, largely pastoralist peninsula and the east was a fertile agricultural and trading plain. The consistently prosperous region between the Caulukya capital of Anhilvada Patan and the coastal port of Cambay became the most sought-after political territory in Gujarat between the thirteenth and fifteenth centuries. Overseas and overland trade, and local manufacture were inextricably bound up with local political authority, which both exploited and safeguarded them. Political power did not rely solely on the exploitation of a sedentary peasantry, but was also dependent upon the smooth running of trade. As new patterns of urban and rural settlement in eastern Gujarat stabilized, a balance between settlement and mobility was achieved, which suited both sultans and merchants.

In the thirteenth and fourteenth centuries pastoralist groups migrated into Saurashtra and Kachchh from the north and north-west. These groups struggled against each other to carve out territories, exploit the pilgrim traffic to shrines such as Somanath and Girnar, and tax the trade from the numerous ports of the region. This struggle resulted in a political order with many similarities with those of neighbouring Rajasthan and Sind. By the fifteenth century many of these groups had settled down and their loosely-formulated pastoralist kinship organization began to give way to little states, in which the genealogical legitimation provided by bardic communities and ritual roles performed by brahmins became increasingly important. As these pastoralists began to claim a higher, more courtly status in the fifteenth century, the more successful groups began to shed aspects of their pastoralist past, excluding ambiguous religious identities and affiliations to varieties of Islam in favour of reconstructed Sanskritic legitimation. Although most of Saurashtra and Kachchh were conquered by the sultans of Gujarat by the late fifteenth century, local chieftains were often allowed to retain virtual autonomy in return for nominal subject status and payment of tribute. Over time, most of them were absorbed into the political system of the sultans based in eastern Gujarat.

Religious affiliation had considerable importance in the political system. This was a period when Sanskritic religion was spreading out to encompass various immigrant groups from the north-west, while simultaneously, many of the same groups were approached by Muslim—especially Ismā'īlī—missionaries. There is evidence that affiliation to Buddhism, solar worship, and other religious practices were over time being replaced by brahmanical Śaivism, which itself, by the late fourteenth century, received a challenge from emergent neo-Vaiṣṇavism. Brahmin groups migrated to Gujarat in search of patrons from amongst local chieftains and merchants. Meanwhile, Jain communities continued to play an important part in the economic and political networks of Gujarat, especially in urban areas. Several Sufis and Muslim scholars found their way to Gujarat, more so after the foundation of the Gujarat sultanate. Local cults, deities, hero-figures, and saints also arose from a non-Sanskritic matrix of practices and beliefs. Many groups and individuals changed their religious affiliations in this period, a process that inevitably had political consequences. The sultanate was deeply concerned with the administration of religious groups and the role of religious groupings in the organization of trade. 'Conversion' or religious reaffiliation led to religious manifestations that have often been studied under the rubric of 'syncretism', a term that evokes the mingling of self-contained religious traditions in an atmosphere of generalized goodwill.[52] When more closely examined, such manifestations of 'syncretism' often show strategic choices employed by groups for historically contingent reasons.

The second half of the fifteenth century is dominated by the figure of Maḥmūd 'Bīgara'. The present study will end with his death in 1511, coincidentally also the time when the Portuguese began to pose a serious challenge to the political and economic system of Gujarat. The political and administrative measures of the sultanate have considerable implications for our understanding of pre-colonial states. Some of the measures instituted by the sultans in a distinctive balance of alliance and compromise proved very tenacious and persisted through Mughal rule and even into the nineteenth century. Further, the formation of a prestigious kingly identity sought by non-Muslim chieftains in this period was not an autonomous Hindu search for identity, but was forged out of a reciprocal relationship of legitimation between the sultans and local chieftains, which anticipated a similar relationship between the Rajputs and the Mughals in the seventeenth century.

NOTES

1. John R. Wood (1984), 'British Versus Princely Legacies and the Political Integration of Gujarat', *Journal of Asian Studies* [henceforth *JAS*], 44(1). See also Achyut Yagnik and Suchitra Sheth (2005), *The Shaping of Modern Gujarat: Plurality, Hindutva and Beyond*.
2. See K.M. Munshi (1952), *Somnath: The Shrine Eternal*; J.M. Nanavati, R.N. Mehta, and S.N. Chowdhary (1971), *Somnath, 1956: Being a Report of Excavations*.
3. K.M. Munshi (1958), *Glory That Was Gurjara-deśa*, p. 10.

5. Wood, 'British Versus Princely Legacies,' pp. 67–8.
Ḍāhyābhāi Lakṣmaṇdās Paṭel (1906), *Vaḍnagarā kaṇbīnī utpatti ane temno ācār-vicār (The Origin of the Vaḍnagarā Kaṇbīs and their Customs)*, p. 14.
7. Revāśaṅkar Śāstrī (1922), *Unevāl jñyātino itihās, (History of the Unevāl Caste)*, p. 12, Jīvarām Durlabhajī Śukla and M.M. Vyās (1917), *Śrī girinārāyaṇ jñyātinī unnati tathā utpatti (The Progress and Origins of the Girinārāyaṇ Caste)*, p. 32.
8. Sheldon Pollock (1998), 'India in the Vernacular Millennium: Literary Culture and Polity, 1000–1500,' *Daedalus*, 127(3), p. 71, fn.9. Gujarat under the Caulukyas saw a great elaboration of Apabhraṃśa literature, but Apabhraṃśa did not articulate regional identity in the way that Tamil did in the Cola country or Telugu under the Kākatīyas. See Richard J. Cohen (1999), 'The Apabhraṃśa *Cariu* as Courtly Poem', in Alan W. Entwistle, et al., eds, *Studies in Early Modern Indo-Aryan Languages, Literature and Culture*. On the transformation of *nāgara* Apabhraṃśa into local variants of western Indian languages from the thirteenth century, see also C. Vaudeville (1999), *Myths, Saints and Legends in Medieval India*, pp. 274–5.
9. Although the name is usually traced to the Gurjara pastoralist clan, branches of which settled in Gujarat in the early centuries of the first millennium, it is not clear whether this was yet an ethnic category. M.R. Majmudar (1965), *Cultural History of Gujarat (From Early Times to Pre-British Period)*, pp. 18–20. See also Chapter 1 in this volume.
10. The Mughals made a deliberate choice to use Persian as the language of state and literature. At the sultanates of Delhi and other regions, on the other hand, local literary dialects were often promoted. See Muzaffar Alam (1998), 'The Pursuit of Persian: Language in Mughal Politics', *Modern Asian Studies* [henceforth *MAS*], 32(2), p. 318.
11. See Richard M. Eaton (1993), *The Rise of Islam and the Bengal Frontier, 1204–1760*, pp. 66–9.
12. For a discussion of the limitations of 'Indian feudalism', see B.D. Chattopadhyaya (1993), *The Making of Early Medieval India*, Introduction.
13. John Deyell (1990), *Living Without Silver: The Monetary History of Early Medieval North India*, p. 125.
14. Varṣā Jānī (1992) *Saurāṣṭra-nā pāḷiyā* (*Hero-stones of Saurashtra*); Romila Thapar (1981), 'Death and the Hero', in S.C. Humphreys and Helen King, eds, *Mortality and Immortality: The Anthropology and Archaeology of Death*.
15. Sikandar b. Muḥammad (1961), *Mir'āt-i Sikandarī* [henceforth *MS*] ed. S.C. Misra and M.L. Rahman.
16. Misra, 'Introduction', *MS*, pp. 46–50.
17. Hajjī 'Abd Allāh al-Dabīr (1921–28), *Ẓafar al-wālih bi muẓaffar wa-ālihī*, ed. E. Denison Ross; trans. M.F. Lokhandwala as *An Arabic History of Gujarat* (1970–74). This title has been translated by Lokhandwala (p. xxiii) as 'Bewildering Victories Connected with Muzaffar and his

18. Sayyid Maḥmūd Bukhāri, *Ta'rīkh-i salāṭīn-i Gujarāt* (1964), ed., S.A.I. Tirmizi; Mīr Abū Turāb Walī (1909), *Ta'rīkh-i Gujarāt*, ed., E. Denison Ross.
19. Misra, 'Introduction', *MS*, pp. 39–40.
20. M.H. Siddiqui (1985), *The Growth of Indo-Persian Literature in Gujarat*, p. xiv.
21. Nabi Hadi (1995), *Dictionary of Indo-Persian Literature*, p. 38.

    'Alī Muḥammad Khān, *Mir'āt-i Aḥmadī*, and *Khātima* (1927–30), ed. Syed Nawab Ali.

23. Misra, 'Introduction', *MS*, pp. 12–13.
24. Ibid., pp. 14–15.

    'Abd al-Ḥusayn Tūnī (1988), *Ta'rīkh-i Maḥmūd Shāhī* [henceforth *TMS*], ed. S.C. Misra.

26. S.A.I. Tirmizi (1968), *Some Aspects of Medieval Gujarat*, pp. 24–6; Jean Aubin (1966), 'Indo-islamica I. La vie et l'oeuvre de Nimdihi', *Revue des Etudes islamiques*, 34, pp. 61–81, and (1964), 'The Secretary of Maḥmūd Gāvān and his Lost Chronicle', *Journal of the Research Society of Pakistan*, 1:2, pp. 9–13.
27. Jean Aubin, 'Nimdihi', p. 77.

    'Abd al-Karīm Nīmdihī, *Ṭabaqāt-i Maḥmūd Shāhī*, Cambridge University Library, Ms. Eton (Pote) 160.

29. Jean Aubin, 'Nimdihi', p. 77.
30. See Nabi Hadi (1985), 'Ta'rīkh-i Ṣadr-i Jahān or Ta'rīkh-i Maḥmūd Shāhī', in M.H. Siddiqi, ed., *Growth of Indo-Persian Literature in Gujarāt*, pp. 46–51, p. 49.
31. Sharaf al-Dīn Bukhārī (1985), *Ṭabaqāt-i Gujarāt*, ed. M.H. Siddiqi.
32. Mīr Sayyid 'Alī Qāni' (1943), *Ta'rīkh-i Muẓaffar Shāhī*, ed. and trans. into Gujarāti by Sayyid Abū Ẓafar Nadwī and C.R. Naik.
33. Misra, 'Introduction', *MS*, p., 19.
34. Ibid., pp. 21–6.
35. Ibid., pp. 26–9.
36. Alexander Kinloch Forbes (1878), *Ras Mala: Hindoo Annals of the Province of Goozerat in Western India*, Vol. 1; James Macmurdo (1977), *The Peninsula of Gujarat in the Early Nineteenth Century*.
37. James McNabb Campbell and Bhimbhai Kirparam, eds (1901), *Gujarát Population: Hindus*.
38. A sprawling accretive text, parts of which may have been composed in the fifth–sixth centuries CE, but whose current form bears little resemblance to the earliest manuscripts. R. Adriaensen, H.T. Bakker, and H. Isaacson, eds (1998), *The Skandapurāṇa*, pp. 2–3.
39. Veena Das (1977), *Structure and Cognition: Aspects of Hindu Caste and Ritual*, p. 87.
40. Neil Rabitoy (1974), 'Administrative Modernization and the Bhats of British Gujarat 1800–1820', *IESHR*, 11(1), p. 49.

42. S.C. Misra (1963), *The Rise of Muslim Power in Gujarat: A History of Gujarat from 1298 to 1442*; S.A.I. Tirmizi (1968), 'Gujarat and Khandesh', in Mohammad Habib and K.A. Nizami, eds, *The Delhi Sultanat (AD 1206–1526), A Comprehensive History of India*, Vol. 5, Part 2, S.A.I. Tirmizi, *Some Aspects of Medieval Gujarat*.
43. A notable recent exception is Farhat Hasan (2004), *State and Locality in Mughal India: Power Relations in Western India, c. 1572–1730*.
44. There are now significant exceptions to this trend, including Romila Thapar (2004), *Somanatha: The Many Voices of a History*, a wide-ranging analysis of the histories and memories around a contested medieval site. Another recent intervention that examines the contentious histories of medieval mosques in Gujarat is Alka Patel (2004), *Building Communities in Gujarāt: Architecure and Society During the Twelfth through Fourteenth Centuries*.
45. Cynthia Talbot (2001), *Precolonial India in Practice: Society, Region and Identity in Medieval Andhra*.
46. Chattopadhyaya, *Making of Early Medieval India*, see especially Chapters 3, 4, 8.
47. Recent scholars who have picked up the threads in Rajasthan include Nandini Sinha Kapur (2002), *State Formation in Rajasthan: Mewar During the Seventh-fifteenth Centuries*; Nandita Prasad Sahai (2006), *Politics of Patronage and Protest: The State, Society, and Artisans in Early Modern Rajasthan*; and Ramya Sreenivasan (2007), *The Many Lives of a Rajput Queen: Heroic Pasts in India 1500–1900*.
48. Dirk H.A. Kolff (1990), *Naukar, Rajput and Sepoy: The Ethnohistory of the Military Labour Market in Hindustan, 1450–1850*.
49. Norman P. Ziegler (1998), 'Some Notes on Rajput Loyalties during the Mughal Period', in J.F. Richards, ed., *Kingship and Authority in South Asia*.
50. Simon Digby (1971), *War-horse and Elephant in the Delhi Sultanate: A Study of Military Supplies* and (2004), 'Before Timur Came: Provincialization of the Delhi Sultanate through the Fourteenth Century', *Journal of the Economic and Social History of the Orient* [henceforth *JESHO*], 47(3).
51. Arjun Appadurai (1977), 'Kings, Sects and Temples in South India, 1350–1700', *IESHR*, 14(1); James Heitzman (2000), *Gifts of Power: Lordship in an Early Indian State*; David Ludden (1985), *Peasant History in South India*; George W. Spencer (1968), 'Temple Money Lending and Livestock Distribution', *IESHR*, 5(3); Burton Stein (1977), 'Circulation and the Historical Geography of Tamil Country', *JAS*, 37(1).
52. For an analysis of 'syncretism' to explain medieval South Asian religion, see Tony K. Stewart (2001), 'In Search of Equivalence: Conceiving Muslim–Hindu Encounter through Translation Theory', *History of Religions* 40(3).

1

The Regions of Gujarat, c. 100–1200

Gujarat is a political region cobbled out of a number of topographical and climatic zones, from fertile plains and forested hills to arid desert lands. The overarching political formations of the Caulukyas and sultans were interspersed by and coexisted with scores of smaller subdivisions. These units were bounded by a long coastline dotted with port towns, many of which were independently governed by merchants. People constantly migrated into Gujarat; at times the north and north-west were virtually a moving frontier of immigration. Groups of different kinds made their way into and around the region, settling in the countryside, populating towns, clearing agricultural lands, and establishing routes for trade and pilgrimage. Although it is not possible to estimate figures, the increase in the number of settlements indicates that the population must have grown considerably from the eleventh century onwards. By the end of the twelfth century, the Caulukyas had established a symbolic sovereignty over most of the territory, large tracts of the region were settled and cultivated, and its roads were familiar to travellers, soldiers, and traders.

ETYMOLOGY AND THE REGION

The term Gujarat is widely acknowledged to derive from the Gurjaras or Gujjaras, clans of 'cattle-rearers, husbandmen and soldiers' who settled in or passed through north and north-western India from about the first century CE.[1] It is a version of the Prakrit Gujjara-raṭṭa or

Gurjaras.[2] Branches of these clans settled in eastern Rajasthan, Malwa, and Gujarat, possibly as subsidiaries of the Guptas. The term Gurjara as an ethnic prefix came to be used by the sixth century, as with the Gurjara brahmins.[3] It was also used as a regional marker for several separate territories. Early Chinese travellers mention the land of Kü-che-lo (Gūjara/Gurjara) to the north of Valabhi and north-west of Ujjain, with its capital at Pi-lo-mi-lo (usually read as Bhīnmāl/Bhīlmāl).[4] A Gurjara kingdom was established in Nandipuri in southern Gujarat, which flourished from 589 to 735 CE. The 'Gurjara' Pratihāras rose to prominence in the eighth century. Their territories in central and eastern Rajasthan were sometimes called Gurjaratrā-*bhūmi*.[5] Contemporary Arab travellers knew the territory of the Pratihāras as al-Juzr or al-Jurz, recognizable transliterations of Gurjara.[6]

Most texts from this period refer to the hinterland of modern Gujarat Ānartta, southern Gujarat as Lāṭa, and the peninsula as Saurāṣṭra. The Arabs knew Gujarat largely from its great ports, Kanbāya or Cambay being the most prominent of them. They also recognized the term Lāṭa: al-Bīrūnī mentions 'Lārdesh' in south Gujarat.[7] The Arabs' term for the sea between western India and Oman, Baḥr al-Lārwī, was derived from Lāṭa.[8] The territory of Gujarat was variously classified as belonging to al-Hind and al-Sind. Later, the interior of Gujarat was referred to by its capital—Nahrwāla, a version of Anhilvada.

The term Gurjara as a prefix to describe the territories occupied by Gujarat was not widely used until the rule of the Caulukyas. It is not clear why they should have adopted the Gurjara clan name to describe their territories, although one possibility is that they saw themselves as the successors of the Pratihāras.[9] From the reign of Siddharāja Jayasiṃha (1094–1143), the terms Gurjara-*maṇḍala* or Gurjara-ūmi signified territories in which Caulukya political control had been established. These included north Gujarat, parts of Mevad, and the eastern strip of territory from Anhilvada Patan to Cambay. After Siddharāja's wide-ranging conquests in the early twelfth century, Gurjara-maṇḍala included Malwa and southern Rajasthan in addition to Kachchh and the peninsula of Saurashtra.[10] These were incorporated into the administrative structure as maṇḍalas (provinces). While Malwa and southern Rajasthan were later lost, the Caulukyas continued to exercise political control over the Saurashtra peninsula, at least nominally, until 1296.

The terms Gurjara or Gūjar persisted in community and occupational names, such as those of the Gūjar vāṇiās or traders, potters, carpenters, or goldsmiths. These indicated the region inhabited by the groups rather than claims to descent from the 'original' Gūjars. The Caulukyas' use of 'Gurjara-bhūmi' and 'Gurjaraṭṭā' for their dominions outlasted them. These became the standard terms used by administrators to refer to the entire region, occasionally including the provinces of Saurashtra and Kachchh. In the Persian records of the Delhi sultanate, the terms Gujarāt and Nahrwāla (for Anhilvada Patan, the Caulukya capital), are both used.

By the time of its incorporation as a province of the Delhi sultanate in the early thirteenth century, 'Gujarāt' had been accepted as a convenient expression for the entire administrative unit, usually including south Gujarat.[11] This unit was largely based in eastern Gujarat with tenuously held outposts in Saurashtra and the eastern hills bordering Malwa. The governors sent out from Delhi ruled for a little over a century (1297–1402), after which the political unit of Gujarat became distinct and independent under the sultans of Gujarat. It was only in the 1480s, well into the rule of the seventh sultan, Maḥmūd gara 'Gujarātī', that military and political control was re-established over the whole of the territories of modern Gujarat, with the addition at times of parts of Malwa, southern Rajasthan, and the southern coastal lands stretching almost all the way to Bombay.

THE TOPOGRAPHIC REGIONS OF GUJARAT

In terms of land use and patterns of settlement, the modern region of Gujarat falls into four categories—mainland, peninsula, coast, and desert. It is not surprising that these physiographic divisions coincide with its broad political units. Each of these regions has had different histories of settlement and consequent political organization.

The Gujarat Mainland

The Nal lake in central Gujarat is the remnant of a water body that used to stretch in the rainy season from the Little Rann to the Gulf of Cambay, virtually separating the Saurashtra peninsula from the mainland. It was only after the earthquake of 1819 that the channel was closed. The physical division imposed by the water body had implications for the political organization of eastern Gujarat and Saurashtra. To the west of the Nal creek is the peninsula: arid, scrub-forested, and cultivable only in parts. To the east lie the fertile plains of Gujarat drained by the Sabarmati, Mahi, Narmada, Tapi, and their tributaries descending from the rocky plateau of central India and becoming wide and sluggish in the plains as they flow towards the Arabian Sea.

Eastern Gujarat is a corridor region—a fertile, populous space carved out between natural boundaries to facilitate trade and mobility. It is part of one of the most important trade routes from north India to the coast. While there is an alternative route through Malwa, the Gujarat route tended to be favoured in the period in question, and a string of urban settlements sprang up along the way. A traveller from the north would enter Gujarat through the Abu hills, which roughly separate it from Mevad. The settlements and fertile areas are edged on the east and south by heavily forested mountain regions which cut them off from the Malwa plateau.

Although central Gujarat around Ahmadabad and Kheda is highly fertile, it does not seem to have been widely cleared and cultivated before the tenth century when step-wells and reservoirs began to be constructed to aid agriculture. Thereafter, the chief crops were cotton, indigo, and foodgrains. Cotton was also grown in the Sabarmati valley and in the black soil region north of Cambay. Arab travellers from the tenth century onwards paint a rosy picture of coastal Gujarat. Al-ʿūdī (915) remarked that the Gulf of Cambay had 'towns, villas, cultivation, gardens, palms, cocoanut trees, guinea-fowls, parrots and other Indian birds.'[12] In the mid-tenth century a Persian visitor listed the great towns of the coast: Samur, Sindān, Subāra, and Kanbāya (Cambay), in which he said Muslims and Hindus lived. There was a Friday mosque (*mazgit-i ādhīna*) and an idol-temple in each. In Cambay, shoes were produced for export. Nearby, he said, was a mountain where bamboo, rattan palms, pepper, and coconut were to be found.[13] Ibn Hawqal (968–996) also remarked upon the local fruit—mangoes, coconuts, and lemons. About 1300, ʿAbd Allāh Waṣṣāf waxed eloquent about the region:

> Gujarat, which is commonly called Kambayat, contains 70,000 villages and towns, all populous, and the people abound in wealth and luxuries. In the course of the four seasons of the year seventy different species of beautiful flowers grow within that province. ... The air is healthy and the earth picturesque, neither too warm nor too cool, but in perpetual spring. The winter cultivation is brought about only through the moistness of dew, called *barasi*. When that harvest is over they begin summer cultivation, which is dependent upon the influence of the rain. The vineyards in this country bring forth blue grapes twice a year; and the strength of the soil is so great that the cotton

plants spread their branches like willows and plane trees, and yield produce for several years successively.[14]

The main rivers, the Narmada, Tapi, and Mahi, cut narrow gorges through hillsides and widen out near the coast. They were not easy to navigate and the land route was preferred for trade. Nevertheless, a significant volume of trade moved along the Narmada from the hinterland of Malwa to the port of Bhrigukaccha, the greatest port of western India in the early centuries CE. Bhrigukaccha, at the mouth of the Narmada, gradually became unnavigable because of excessive siltation which left it several kilometres inland. By the tenth century it was replaced as the chief port of the region by Cambay, located at the head of the Gulf at the mouth of a wayward branch of the Indus.

The territorial control of the Caulukyas began about 942 when a chieftain named Mūlarāja I acquired control over some districts in north Gujarat, the *Sārasvata-maṇḍala* including parts of Mehsana, Radhanpur and Palanpur districts. By the time of his death, the kingdom stretched from Lāṭa or south-east Gujarat to Mount Abu in the north. According to later chroniclers, Mūlarāja also defeated the kings of Saurashtra and Kachchh but the nature of the control he exercised after the victory is not clear since his descendants are again found fighting these chieftains. Mūlarāja had his capital at the Cāvaḍā city of Anahilapataka or Anhilvada, and his dominion included the modern districts of Viramgam, Chansana, Patan, and Mehsana. In the south, he conquered the whole of Lāṭa up to the Narmada river.

From Persian records, we know that Mūlarāja's descendant Bhīma faced, within a year of his accession in 1025, the famous invasion of the Ghaznavid ruler Maḥmūd.[15] The latter's army was hardly challenged in the march towards Somanath, either in Anhilvada, Modhera, or Delvada. After the sack of Somanath, Maḥmūd quickly retreated, again meeting with no resistance. Bhīma's son Karṇa is credited in the bardic accounts with defeating the Bhīls of central Gujarat between the Rann of Kachchh and the Sabarmati river and thus extending Caulukya control in this area.

His son Siddharāja Jayasiṃha, crowned in 1094, was the most famous king of the dynasty. He defeated the king of Girnar, Rā Kheṅgār, and enforced tribute payments from the Cāhamānas of Naddula and kambharī. He also achieved decisive victories in Malwa, over the Paramāras of Bhinmal, Sindhurāja of Sind, and an unidentified ruler named Barbaraka. The large number of conquests increased Siddharāja's territories and the Caulukya kingdom acquired its maximum span, with Saurashtra, southern Rajasthan, the Sambhar area, and parts of Malwa including Dhar and Ujjain coming within the kingdom.[16]

The next ruler was Kumārapāla (1143–74) who achieved renown not for his conquests, but for his adoption and propagation of Jainism. Kumārapāla's territories extended in the south to the Vindhyas and at least as far as the Tapti, to the west, to Saurashtra, to the north roughly from Chitor to Jaisalmer, including parts of Udaipur and Jodhpur, and to the east beyond Bhilsa.

Kumārapāla's grandson, Mūlarāja II came to power in 1176. The Caulukya records single out his reign for the defeat that he handed out in 1178 to Hammīra (Amīr), the lord of the Turuṣkas, that is, the Ghūrid sultan, Mu'izz al-Dīn Muḥammad bin Sām who was routed near Anhilvada (Nahrwāla in the Persian chronicles) and had great difficulty in returning to Ghazna.[17]

In spite of this victory, the Caulukyas lost territory over the years and faced internal conflict. In 1197 Mu'izz al-Dīn's slave general, Quṭb al-Dīn Aybeg, avenged his master's defeat by sacking Nahrwāla. Soon after, the kingdom passed into the hands of the Vāghelā family, formerly Caulukya courtiers. In the course of the thirteenth century, ghelā control over the sprawling Caulukya territories shrank to a small region of eastern Gujarat, although nominal sovereignty continued to be exercised in parts of Saurashtra and north Gujarat.

Political upheaval and military conflict do not appear to have retarded trade and towns continued to expand along the trade routes. Around the new settlements there was an expansion of cultivation, as is made clear by land grant inscriptions that mention agriculture and the building of wells and step-wells.[18]

From north India, there were several routes into Gujarat of varying commercial and strategic significance. During his invasion in 1025, ḥmūd took a difficult desert route via Multan, Jaisalmer, and Barmer, entering north Gujarat through the Palanpur Gap between the Aravalli outcrop of Mount Abu and the Rann of Kachchh.[19] He brought with him an immense army that carried provisions of water and food on thirty thousand camels. The route through the Palanpur Gap towards the north-east was the most popular one for traders and pilgrims. Going north, an Anhilvada trader would pass through Siddhpur, Chandravati, Nadol, Jalor, and Palli towards Ajmer in Rajasthan, and thence towards Delhi, Mathura, and Kanauj. A little to the east was the route into

Rajasthan from Idar and Ahada (modern Udaipur). As we have seen earlier, in 1197 Aybeg defeated Bhīma II who was encamped near Abu to defend the route into Gujarat. Moving onwards, he sacked the city of Anhilvada and then returned to Delhi by way of Ajmer. Some years later, in 1234, Vīradhavala Vāghelā returned to Dholka from Delhi via Abu, Chandravati, Siddhpur, Anhilvada, and Karnavati.[20]

From Ajmer or Naraina, one route went towards Delhi while another went west towards Multan and Sind, and to the north towards Ghazna. According to al-Iṣṭakhrī (951), the distance between Anhilvada and Mansura in Sind was eight days of travel, while it took four days to get from Cambay to Anhilvada.[21] The route to Mansura passed through Palli and Kiradu, both of which were within the Caulukya dominions. An alternative route to Sind was through eastern Kachchh, skirting the Rann towards Nagar Parkar and thence north to Mansura.

Another route linking Gujarat with north India was through Malwa into south Gujarat via Godhra and Dohad in the Panchamahal hills. It linked western India with Dhar and Ujjain, from where the road split towards north and south India. The northern road was the main route towards the Ganga basin too. The early fourteenth-century writer Merutuṅga tells us that the Caulukya king Durlabharāja (c.1009–1024) took this route to Varanasi on pilgrimage, passing through Malwa.[22] This was also the route that the Moroccan jurist and globe-trotter Ibn ṭṭūṭa took in the fourteenth century, travelling south from Delhi to Cambay. The Caulukya kings and their successors took considerable pains to keep their part of the route secure for traders and pilgrims.

The increase in traffic along the northern route through Rajasthan from the tenth century saw new towns springing up along the trade routes and minor villages growing into important staging posts or towns.[23] The first of these was Anhilvada, established by Mūlarāja in the tenth century, which soon became a prosperous trading town. Al-sī (c. 1100) referred to Anhilvada as one of the towns of the second climate 'on the confines of a desert between Sindh and Hind, the home of the sheep-grazing and horse and camel-breeding Meds.'[24] Over time, the town and the region around it became a trade hub, a site for the production of goods, the locus of successive royal cults and an important stop on the trade and military route from north India to the coast.

Siddhpur, also built in the tenth century, came into prominence under Siddharāja, who completed the royal Śaiva temple complex of Rudramahālaya there and invited families of north Indian brahmins to settle in its vicinity. In southern Rajasthan, towns like Nadlai, Nadol,

Bali, Kiradu, and Jalor came into prominence and inscriptions show that they housed merchants, customs posts, and warehouses. Bhinmal rīmāla, which lay on the land route to Sind from western India, was also an important town in spite of large-scale migrations of merchants and brahmins into Gujarat from the tenth century onwards. An inscription of 1219 mentions that Karmasiṃha, 'in charge of the export and import departments' of Bhinmal gave gifts for the worship of Mahāvīradeva.[25]

Along the eastern route towards Malwa, the chief towns were Dabhoi, Kapadvanj, Godhra, and Dohad. All these lay on the route between the Malwa hinterland and Cambay and the other Gujarat ports, and are mentioned as the 'chief towns' in the Girnar inscription of 1231.[26] Dabhoi or Darbhāvati was developed as a frontier fortress by Siddharāja in the twelfth century.

For the south-bound traveller, there was a road towards Konkan, but this was made difficult by river crossings and hilly terrain, and traders tended to take the easterly route through Malwa instead. Alternatively, they could sail down the coast to the Konkan ports.

While the hinterland towns of Gujarat became prosperous and were important centres of trade and manufacture, they did not receive as much attention as the great ports such as Cambay or Somanath in the accounts of travellers. Asaval and Dholka were said to be 'populous, commercial, rich, industrious and productive of useful articles.'[27] Anhilvada, the Caulukya capital, was even less impressive. In 1100 it was reported to be a staging point: 'a town of moderate importance on the route from Sindh to India, a place of little trade, producing small quantities of fruit but numerous flocks'.[28]

As new towns came up along the trade routes, epigraphic references to tanks, ponds, and wells show that there was corresponding expansion of agriculture too. Parts of the central forested region that stretched from the eastern Rann of Kachchh towards Anhilvada, and between Anhilvada and Cambay remained uncultivated, heavily wooded, and inhabited by ls. It was not until the fifteenth century that parts of these territories would be cleared and brought under the plough.

SAURASHTRA AND THE COAST

The Saurashtra coastline, by and large, has narrow beaches and low cliffs, with only a few indentations.[29] In spite of its length, its only good natural harbour is in the north-east corner of Okhamandal. The Gulf of Cambay coast on the other hand is deeply indented, providing sites for the many estuarine ports of Gujarat where commerce was carried out, including Mangrol, Veraval, Diu, Ghogha, and Cambay. The mouths of the rivers Sabarmati, Mahi, Narmada, and Tapi, which open into the Gulf of Cambay, are dotted with small islands called s. These include the island of Piram, which was the stronghold of the piratical Gohil chieftains in the fourteenth century.

The distinction between the coast and the hinterland seems to have been particularly marked in medieval Gujarat, and each had a distinct historical trajectory. While mainland Gujarat was regularly invaded from the north, the sea route to the Gujarati ports led to the development of a vast regional trading complex that was largely independent of hinterland political activity. The coast appeared to occupy a different political status and was never more than nominally subject to a hinterland power, whether administered from Anhilvada, Delhi, or Ahmadabad. From the tenth century onwards the coastal ports were self-administered for the most part, with the merchant colonies having their own representatives and a supervising official as overseer.

Saurashtra projects into the Arabian Sea to the south of Kachchh. The salt-encrusted Rann stretches along its northern border, while the east of the peninsula is marked by a long fault line that once cut it off from the mainland of Gujarat and is now known as the Nal lake. We know from the testimony of al-Mas'ūdī and others that a tributary of the Indus used to discharge itself into the Gulf of Cambay passing through the Rann, bisecting Saurashtra from mainland Gujarat and joining the Sabarmati as it drained into the Gulf.[30] Later travellers also remarked that Saurashtra was virtually an island for part of the year because of a branch of the Indus that emptied into the Gulf of Cambay. Varthema who visited Gujarat in 1503–8 mentioned that the city of Cambay lay three miles (approximately 5 km) inland, close to the mouth of the Indus.[31] James Macmurdo stated in 1813 that a tract similar to the Rann connected the Gulf of Kachchh and Cambay, cutting Saurashtra during the rains.[32] It was the earthquake of 1819 that cut off the old Indus distributaries into the Rann, and the consequent silting up of the eastern branch of the Indus and other rivers helped join north-eastern Saurashtra to the Gujarat mainland. All that is left of this channel of water is the marshy Nal lake south-east of the Little Rann. Even now during the monsoon the Little Rann gets waterlogged and water drains into the Gulf of Cambay through the Nal lake.[33]

In the rainy season it was easiest to enter Saurashtra from the low plateau in the north near Dhrangadhra and Vadhvan, both of which had considerable strategic importance for this reason.[34] Before the eleventh century the main route from Gujarat to the peninsula was by the coastal route from Cambay to Bhavnagar, along the coast to Somanath and thence to the north-western corner of the peninsula at Dvaraka. This is the route that most pilgrims and traders took as the central part of the peninsula was hazardous and uncharted, and believed to be inhabited by 'wild' tribes. During his campaign in 1025, Maḥmūd seems to have taken the coastal route from Anhilvada to Somanath, returning along the arid northerly route through Kachchh and Sind.[35] It was in the twelfth century that Siddharāja built a new road cutting through the peninsula on his campaign against the Cūḍāsamā chieftain of Junagadh. This passed through Munjapura, Jhinjhuvad, Viramgam, Vadhvan, Sayla, Gondal, Jetpur, and Vanthali on to the coast at Somanath.[36] New settlements and wells were constructed along this road, which soon became the regular route from north Gujarat to the Saurashtra ports.

The peninsula of Saurashtra is radially drained towards the coast by rivers arising from a central plateau, to the south of which is the Girnar range. The seventeenth century writer Sikandar described the Girnar region while narrating Maḥmūd Bīgara's expedition to the region:

> Be it known that there is a mountain surrounding Girnar on all sides but the northern. On the south there is a pass between two mountains, twelve *kos* in extent, and in this valley there is a jungle so dense that a horse cannot pass through it; it has numerous caves and it is uninhabitable, except for birds and beasts and a tribe of infidels, called Khants, who bear a greater resemblance to wild beasts than men.[37]

Saurashtra and Kachchh possess an arid climate, a fact that is attested by early observers. There is little rainfall, especially in Kachchh (average 305–81 mm), and the main vegetation is dry thorn forest.[38] This led to the dominance of a pastoralist and semi-pastoralist economy over most of the region. The northern coast of the peninsula around Dvaraka and Halar shade into the Kachchh region where agriculture is scarce and livestock pastoralism is the norm. Water is a scarce commodity in the entire region and settlers made considerable efforts to conserve it in agricultural areas by building wells, tanks, and bunds. This process was a slow one and the expansion of agriculture and settlement in the region may be traced through inscriptions and remains of water-bodies.

The two most fertile regions are the elevated area around the Girnar mountains where rainfall tends to be higher, and the well-drained eastern region of Gohilvad along the Nal depression.[39] Accordingly, some of the earliest settlements in the peninsula were in these regions. There is an Aśokan inscription at Girnar from 257 BCE, and a tank was built by the local governor during the Gupta period, who also commissioned a long inscription. The next significant settlement was that of the Maitrakas in the Valabhi region. Xuan Zang visited the region in the seventh century and remarked on the monasteries established for the benefit of Buddhist recluses. The inhabitants of the land were indifferent, he said, and not given to learning, but profited by the proximity of the sea and engaged much in trade and barter.[40] It is generally believed that the rule of the Maitrakas ended after a sea-borne Arab raid in the late eighth century.

According to one account, the chief inhabitants of the peninsula at the end of the seventh century were the Jeṭhvās, Cāvaḍās, Vālās, Āhīrs, ārīs, Mers, Bhīls, and Kolīs.[41] On the evidence of their legends and motifs, it has been suggested that the first three groups were converts from Buddhism.[42] The Jeṭhvās, who trace their origin to a mythical crocodile, were sun-worshipping pastoralists who made their way to Gujarat from the north-west and controlled the region of modern Porbandar by the seventh century. The Cāvaḍās settled successively in Dhank, Okha, and then Prabhas Patan, the latter the eventual site of the Somanath temple. The Cāvaḍas, often stigmatized as plunderers and pirates, controlled Somanath at the time of Maḥmūd's invasion in 1025. Although they were early custodians of the Śaivite Somanath temple, they may also have been sun-worshippers.[43] The third clan that was significant in this early period was that of the Vālās, who claimed descent from the Maitrakas of Valabhi.

The next three clans—Āhīrs, Rabārīs, Mers—were pastoralist groups who were already resident in the peninsula. It is possible that these groups suffered military defeats against the dominant clans, as a result of which they accepted subsidiary positions. This can be seen in the relationship of the Mers with the Jeṭhvās wherein the installation of a new Jeṭhvā ruler can only be completed by a blood-mark on his forehead from the finger of the Mer leader.[44] It may be that the Mers, having been defeated at some point, became the allies and symbolic granters of the throne to the Jeṭhvās. A similar relationship is seen between the Āhīrs and the Cūḍāsamās of Junagadh.[45]

At this time, the northern part of the peninsula was largely uninhabited. The Jeṭhvās and Mers ruled along the western coast, the vaḍās along the south-western coast, and the Vālās controlled a territory from Vanthali in the centre of the peninsula to the south-eastern coast bordering the Gulf of Cambay. Around 875, the Vālās were displaced from Vanthali by the Cūḍāsamās, migrants from Sind who went on to control the surrounding territories until well into the fifteenth century.

During the Caulukya reign in mainland Gujarat the peninsula was divided between various clans including the Jeṭhvās in western Saurashtra (in the vicinity of modern Porbandar) and the Jhālās in northern Kathiavad. The Gohils entered the peninsula from Marwar in the thirteenth century while the Jāḍejās and Kāṭhīs came from Kachchh.[46] The prominent threat to the Caulukyas of eastern Gujarat were, however, the Cūḍāsamā rulers with their stronghold at Vanthali, near Junagadh.

While the pastoralist clans lived in the countryside, the towns were inhabited by merchants, religious establishments, and occupational groups. Chieftains such as the Cūḍāsamās or the Vājās did not exercise direct control over towns such as Somanath although they clearly had interests in the trade and pilgrim traffic to and from the towns. It is rare, however, to find inscriptions of the pastoralist clans within the towns.

The fabled wealth of the temple of Somanath in southern Saurashtra became an attraction for a succession of iconoclastic plunderers beginning with Maḥmūd of Ghazna. Its wealth did not only attract Muslim invaders: even Mokhḍājī, the Gohil chieftain of the late fourteenth century is believed to have plundered it.[47] Somanath was also a prominent port where Arab sailors regularly docked to trade and even build mosques, one of which was built by a Muslim ship-owner from Hormuz on land bought from the temple property.[48] Earlier, in the tenth century, the Caulukya ruler Mūlarāja of Gujarat had a long tussle with the Cūḍāsamā ruler of Vanthali near Junagadh who was accused of harassing pilgrims on their way to Somanath, the route for which lay in his territories. Although Mūlarāja defeated the chieftain, the Cūḍāsamās went on to become one of the prestigious Rajput clans of the area until the fifteenth century. This was the first instance in a long series of conflicts between the rulers of the peninsula and the hinterland of eastern Gujarat.

Kachchh and the Rann

The land of Kachchh itself is now almost cut off from the Indian subcontinent. The marshlands of the Rann and the Little Rann stretch to the north and east, while the Gulf of Kachchh to the south joins the Arabian Sea. The land is rocky, treeless scrubland with infrequent intervals of fertile and cultivated plain and pastureland. Possibly in the eleventh or twelfth century the course of the Indus began to move to its western branch. As a result of this, aided by one of the seismic disturbances common in Kachchh, a lagoon dried up and was salinated by seeping sea water to form the Rann.[49] Another earthquake in 1819 resulted in the sinking of a large portion of the western part of the Rann, so that a large marshy area became an inland sea.[50]

The Rann of Kachchh and the contiguous Little Rann are 'an extensive country of naked tidal mud flats transected by dead and live creeks'.[51] They are partly inundated during the monsoon when they are dotted with little islands that surround the sparsely populated Kachchh, separating it from Sind and the Thar desert to the north, and Radhanpur and Kathiavad on the east and south. Both the south and west Kachchh coastlines have a marshy zone dotted with mangrove into which sea water flows at low tide. In ancient times the Rann is believed to have been an arm of the Arabian Sea, so that Kachchh was an island, more accessible from Sind than from Gujarat. The Rann is believed to have been a navigable lake at the time of Alexander's invasion (325 BCE) and a shallow lagoon at the date of the Periplus (first century CE), and there are local traditions of seaports on its borders.[52] Since then it has been a salty desert populated only by wild animals.

Kachchh has an identity and language quite distinct from that of Gujarat, and its history also demonstrates that it has at least as much in common with Sind as with Gujarat.[53] Traces of the Indus valley civilization have been found in Kachchh and it has been surmised that the civilization penetrated into Saurashtra and western India through Kachchh. Kachchh was intermittently part of subsequent kingdoms, such as those of the Indo-Bactrians, the Śakas, and the Maitrakas. If the place called K-i-ta or Ki-c'ha mentioned by Xuan Zang refers to Kachchh, then the region in the seventh century was prosperous with trade and contained, apart from eighty Buddhist convents, several Hindu temples.[54] From the eighth century onwards, parts of Kachchh were settled and occupied by pastoralist groups such as the Sammas, Kāṭhīs, and Cāvaḍās. Arab and Persian merchants arrived along the coast to trade and remained a consistent presence through the subsequent centuries. Trade already ranged from East Asia to Africa, and the coast of Kachchh is notorious in the accounts of Arab travellers for being infested with pirates.

In the following years, there is a legend of the incursion of the Jakhs, a band of 'white-skinned, horse-riding foreigners from Central Asia', or, in another version, from Byzantium, who delivered the people from a tyrant in Kachchh. These curious figures—seventy-two men and a woman—are revered as hero-gods and there are several shrines dedicated to them in Kachchh.[55]

Branches of a pastoralist clan, the Sammas, began to enter Kachchh from the tenth century and later achieved control over the area. The eleventh century also saw the establishment of the rule of the Sūmrā clan in lower Sind and the beginning of a tradition of enmity with the Sammas. In the twelfth century the Sammas fled from Sind into Kachchh and were granted land by the ruling Cāvaḍās. The Sammas, under a ruler named Lākho, soon supplanted the Cāvaḍās and came to be known as the Jāḍejās. Branches of the Jāḍejā clans joined forces in the thirteenth century to drive out the Kāṭhīs from Kachchh. The conquest of Gujarat by 'Alā' al-Dīn Khaljī in the early fourteenth century and the appointment of governors at Anhilvada does not seem to have affected ejā fortunes in Kachchh.

The Sūmras continued to rule lower Sind until the mid-fourteenth century when Muḥammad bin Tughluq, the sultan of Delhi, invaded Sind in pursuit of the rebel Taghai who was harboured by the last of the Sūmrā Jāms. After their defeat, many Sūmras fled to Kachchh.[56] The sultan died near Sind and his forces were worsted by the Sammas. His successor, Fīrūz Shāh, marched to Thatta with cavalry and elephants to avenge this defeat. The enterprise did not succeed and he was obliged to retreat to Gujarat, marching through Kachchh to chastise the Kachchhi branch of the Sammas. On the way his army was stranded for weeks in the Rann. Shams-i Sirāj 'Afīf described the difficulties of z Shāh's army in the *Ta'rīkh-i Fīrūz Shāhī*:

> Grain rose to one *tanka* and two *tanka*s a ser and even at that price was not to be obtained. Men, through craving hunger and helpless nakedness, could not pursue their way, and in their extreme distress gave up in despair. As no corn was to be procured, carrion and raw hides were devoured; some men were driven by extreme hunger to boil old hides and to eat them. A deadly famine reigned and all men saw death staring them in the face. All the horses were destroyed and the *khan*s and *malik*s were compelled to pursue their weary way on foot. ... The guides who led the way and conducted them had maliciously misled them into a place called Kunchi-ran [the Rann of Kachchh]. In this place all the land is impregnated with salt to a degree impossible to describe and if the water was held upon the tongue it crystallised.

> When the army was thus reduced to the extremity of despair, the Sultan had one of the false guides beheaded. Then the others came honestly before him and said: 'We have dealt falsely toward you and have led you into a place where none but you could have survived; not even things which could fly in the air and drive along like the wind. This place is called Kunchi-ran and the sea is near. The saltness of the water arises from this proximity, and the district is deadly'. ... The water, indeed, was so excessively salt that all men were in amazement and despair. As far as the eye could reach, all was salt water. ... When with great difficulty and exertion they escaped from that salt country they came into a desert where no bird laid an egg or flapped its wing, where no tree was to be seen, and where no blade of grass grew. If even a lethal weed had been wanted it could not have been found. No other desert, however fearful, could be compared with this.[57]

Fīrūz Shāh returned to Sind by a safer route in 1363. The Samma m of Thatta was soon afterwards confirmed in his position on condition of paying tribute to Delhi and his descendants remained in control until the sixteenth century.

After Fīrūz Shāh's death and Tīmūr's sack of Delhi in 1398–9, the rulers of Delhi were unable to control provincial governments, many of which became independent. With the crumbling of imperial control, Gujarat's last governor Ẓafar Khān took over as Muẓaffar Shāh, the ruler of Gujarat. In his last campaign in 1410, Muẓaffar compelled the ejā ruler of the fort of Kanthkot in eastern Kachchh to submit and pay tribute, thereby reopening the old connection between Kachchh and Anhilvada.[58] The rest of Kachchh does not seem to have come under the control of the new capital Ahmadabad until the late fifteenth century. The Jāḍejā rulers were, from Maḥmūd Bīgara's reign, subservient to the Ahmadabad sultans; they paid no tribute but were liable for military service.

MERCHANTS AND PASTORALISTS

In order to map settlement, trade, and the development of political authority in this period, it may be useful to trace the overlapping spheres of the merchants and the pastoralists. The most important feature of the politics of Gujarat from the first century onwards was the incursion of pastoralist groups, often highly militarized. Waves of such incursions continued until the fourteenth century and on a smaller scale, even later. These pastoralists came from Sind, Rajasthan, and Punjab, and often, as in the case of the Śakas and Hūṇas, originated much further away. Many of these pastoralists sedentarized and took control of territories in Saurashtra, Kachchh, and Gujarat. The fact that they were often castigated as robbers or pirates suggests that their livelihood depended upon exploiting the trade and pilgrim traffic through their territories. There is little evidence that these groups practised large-scale agriculture. Other such groups retained an itinerant lifestyle, periodically migrating across north India with cattle and goods.

Certain individuals from such pastoralist groups seem to have set themselves up as merchants. For example, a merchant named Wāsa Abhīr, whose name suggests his membership of the pastoralist Ābhīra clan, lived in Ghazni in the eleventh century.[59] Such merchants, along with other inhabitants of the urbanized belt of north Gujarat, became important players in the widening web of trade networks. As the trade of Gujarat linked up with wide-ranging networks over land and sea, intricately regulated sets of trading arrangements evolved which had remarkable longevity and often functioned independently of political changes. The expansion of trade also meant that political authorities were obliged to take into account the needs of traders and at times make political accommodations with them. For example, the twelfth-century Jain merchant Jagaḍū of Bhadreshvar in Kachchh wielded considerable local power because of his interests in the militarily vital horse trade from the Persian Gulf.[60] By the end of his life Jagaḍū was a merchant prince with Caulukya backing.

Merchants and their agents had to be mobile and communities able to transport goods acquired great importance. Nomadic communities marched with their cattle and laden carts across north India to the ports of the coast. Nomads and merchants also met at periodic markets and fairs where livestock and commodities were bought and sold, information exchanged, and, often, religious duties fulfilled. Rural produce—foodgrains, raw cotton, and metal—was collected at village fairs or small periodic markets to be taken to the towns for resale or processing, and urban or imported goods such as textiles, wine, and sweets were brought to the village fairs for sale.[61] Access to information was vital to trade. Merchants needed privileged information in order to be able to plan trade strategies, and mobility became the key to information. All those who sought power or wealth had to be constantly mobile or had to patronize mobile groups such as nomads, wandering ascetics, bards, and other privileged repositories of information.

From the tenth century onwards periodic markets were often held near temples or pilgrimage sites. In fact, most such markets and fairs had ritual significance. It is not unlikely that the temples themselves functioned as redistributive agencies on these occasions. Later, fairs were also associated with local cult shrines, sacred rivers or ponds, and Muslim grave shrines. While references may be found to fairs pertaining to the larger, more Sanskritized shrines, accounts of the pastoralist and 'lower' caste fairs, which must have been the more numerous, are hard to come by and must be reconstructed from later, even modern, accounts. Fairs were often held for the exchange of livestock, but many other goods changed hands on these occasions. With some of the fairs attracting large numbers, elaborate arrangements were made by local authorities. A tenth-century text describes a fair covering an area of two miles, furnished with tents, stalls for cattle, eating houses, water supply, warehouses, and a toll house, 'which was free from the presence of jesters, gamblers etc.'[62] Evidently jesters and gamblers frequented fairs, as did musicians, genealogists, mendicants, soothsayers, healers, and preachers. Fairs often attracted people from a specific mix of castes. Modern census accounts suggest that 'lower' castes and 'tribals' were often the chief participants.[63] In the past, fairs and large markets were looked upon as potentially disruptive and leading to the intermingling of castes. The fair organized by the priest Śrībhūti was closely guarded by soldiers and had an assembly to settle commercial disputes.[64] In *Kīrtikaumudī* of the thirteenth century, the merchant-minister Vastupāla is credited with controlling *varṇasaṃkara* or the intermingling of castes in the markets of Cambay.[65]

Gujarat and Saurashtra were home to a variety of pastoralist groups. By the twelfth century most of Gujarat was apportioned between chieftains, some related to older clans in Rajasthan, others who had migrated from Sind and the north-west and yet others like Bhīls and s who already lived in the hills and forests. This was a period in which the process of caste and religious group formation intersected with 'state' formation in the whole of north India, especially Sind, Rajasthan, Gujarat, and central India. Several communities who later came to be known generically as Rajputs were at this time in the process of making the alliances and networks that would eventually emerge as an overarching Rajput identity from the sixteenth century.

The term *rājpūt* was not in common use in Gujarat in this period. Chieftains and kings are referred to in Sanskrit inscriptions by more general terms such as *rājā, mahārājā, rauta, rāṇaka,* and others, although *japutra* (son of a king) to denote royal claims was common in Rajasthan. In the fifteenth century, a Sanskrit verse play composed by a court-poet of the ruler of Champaner does not refer to the king as a

Rajput. In the play, which includes an account of the conflict between Sultan Muḥammad II of Ahmadabad and Gaṅgadāsa of Champaner, the sultan in a letter to the rāja demands that he stop sheltering *garāsiyā/siyā* chiefs.[66] Chieftains in Persian sources were also generally referred to as garāsiyas or by the specific name of their community or lineage group. It would, thus, be erroneous to assume a homogeneity of status or even of political intent among the various 'indigenous' ruling groups prior to the fifteenth century. There was considerable diversity in political status, position in the caste hierarchy, and ethnic origin.

According to Chattopadhyaya, inscriptions from Rajasthan from the seventh to the fourteenth centuries demonstrate that the emergence of the Rajputs needs to be seen essentially as 'a political process in which disparate groups seeking political power conformed to such norms as permeated the contemporary political ideology'.[67] He links the rise of the Rajputs in this period to a pan-Indian phenomenon: the formation of dynasties seeking legitimation by linking themselves to mythical kṣatriya lineages. Conversely, he also links their rise to local social phenomena which drew in groups as the Medas and the Hūṇas and incorporated them into local caste hierarchies.[68] The Rajputs then underwent a process by which sub-clans claiming affinity to a major clan proliferated in Rajasthan (as also in Gujarat). Sub-clans were formed not necessarily through the segmentation of the larger clans, but often as the result of the absorption of local groups as subsidiary or junior clans.[69]

This absorption was carried out by marriage or political alliance, the former being a process by which groups such as the Hūṇas, who had acquired substantial political power, could also acquire social legitimacy. By the end of the thirteenth century, the term rājaputra, which had hitherto been used to denote the 'son of a king', gradually changed in connotation and 'came to denote descent groups and not necessarily a particularly exalted political status'.[70] Fourteenth-century texts such as *Prabandhacintāmaṇi* also seem to suggest that descent was the most important factor in the identification of the rājaputra.[71] Rajput status, therefore, became one in which descent—real or invented—was the single most important factor to legitimize political authority, and a variety of groups came to adhere to this requirement in order to find place in the political hierarchy. The oldest layer of Rajputhood was, thus, 'an open status group of warrior-ascetics in search of patronage and marriage'.[72] The idea of descent was also related to the invention of royal cults and the construction of royal temples by many of these chieftains. The Turkic Muslims who arrived in Gujarat at the end of the thirteenth century were the first ruling group that did not immediately aspire for 'Rajputization'. They challenged the 'contemporary political ideology' that had made a range of pastoralist groups such as the Medas, ūṇas, Bhīls, and Kolīs in Gujarat—who had pretensions to political power but were marginal to the brahmanical order—conform to descent hierarchies.[73] The Turks had no need for legitimation from the local chieftains. Situated as they were in towns and forts, they were confident of support from powerful traders and, most importantly, of being able to mobilize military resources to back up their governance.

SETTLEMENT AND TRADE ON THE COAST

The reason for the great success of the ports of the Gulf of Cambay has never been entirely clear. The Gulf has a long and broken coastline, there are shoals, siltation, high tides, and many hazards for the sailor. Navigation there was notoriously difficult and treacherous due to sandbanks and quirks of the tide, to the extent that coastal merchants and rulers often had to send out pilot ships to guide vessels to safety. The heavy deposits of silt brought down by the rivers were always a difficulty. In spite of these drawbacks, the Gujarat ports have been active for millennia.

An account from the Periplus of the Erythraean Sea (c. 50 CE) gives a sense of the hazards a sailor could expect while entering Barygaza, the ancient port of Bhrigukaccha, near modern Bharuch:

> This gulf is very narrow to Barygaza and very hard to navigate for those coming from the ocean. ... And even if the entrance to the gulf is made safely, the mouth of the river at Barygaza is found with difficulty, because the shore is very low and cannot be made out until you are close upon it. And when you have found it the passage is difficult because of the shoals at the mouth of the river.[74]

Additionally, the tides were very strong and the unwary navigator could get into serious trouble. 'For the rush of waters at the incoming tide is irresistible and the anchors cannot hold against it; so that large ships are caught up by the force of it, turned broadside on through the speed of the current and so driven on the shoals and wrecked; and smaller boats are overturned.'[75]

Bhrigukaccha was abandoned after excessive siltation rendered it completely inaccessible. It was succeeded by ports on the Konkan coast such as Thana and Sopara. By the tenth century Cambay had become the pre-eminent port of the region. But again, by the mid-fourteenth century, it was inaccessible to ocean-going ships. Goods had to be unloaded on to smaller boats, which would then make the trip through the shallows to the port.[76] Later, the auxiliary ports of Gandhar or Ghogha functioned as the loading points for Cambay. Eventually a combination of severe natural difficulties and political changes meant that Cambay was supplanted by Diu and then Surat as the main port of Gujarat.

The long coastline of Gujarat often had a divergent history from the mainland. As its ports became the hub of the Indian Ocean trade from the eighth century onwards, patterns of settlement and political organization were distinct from those of the mainland, although hinterland politics were affected by the necessity of controlling the revenues and resources of the vast trade. With the consolidation of city-based Islam by the end of the seventh century, the ports of the Gujarat coastline became a vital point in the fast-developing Asian trade system from Africa and the Mediterranean to south-east Asia and China. It was as early as 636 that a naval expedition was sent by the governor of Bahrayn to attack Thana and then Bharuch in the following year. Although neither expedition seems to have met with much success, these early sorties revitalized the route to India that continued to expand for the next millennium.

Commerce between the Arabs and local trading groups made up the trading activities that stretched in a long chain from the Mediterranean to Malacca. Gujarat, with the abundant resources of its productive hinterland, became crucial to this chain, and large colonies of merchants of disparate origins—from the Arabian peninsula, Iraq, Central Asia, Abyssinia, Andalusia, and even Sicily—settled in its port towns. When al-Masʿūdī visited Cambay in 916, he found a large Muslim population consisting of settlers from Siraf, Oman, Basra, Baghdad, and other places. Many of the coastal cities had mosques where Friday prayers were observed. Al-Iṣṭakhrī recorded that at 'Sambil, Sindan, Saymur', and Cambay there were cathedral mosques for public prayers. At the time of the visit of al-Bīrūnī (1022–64) Cambay was the chief town of the Gujarat kingdom, and its markets were supplied with cotton and ginger from the surrounding region. Cambay was connected by an overland route to Multan and to Kachchh by sea. North Indian products, palm from Kachchh and sugar from Malwa, all found their way to Cambay.[77] Al-Bīrūnī also mentioned a great trading centre, Asaval, on the Anhilvada Patan route from Cambay. Idrīsī reported that many of the merchants of Cambay were Arabs and Persians and that some had their own mosques. They were said to be well treated by the king.[78]

The Gujarati port towns were largely autonomous, with colonies of foreign merchants administered by their own representatives. An official was appointed to administer the affairs of the port in general. Gujarat had a unique position in the trade network as a site for both production and redistribution of goods. Here the overland network of trade intersected with and became crucial in the formulation of the oceanic trade. From the tenth century onwards the Caulukyas stimulated agricultural expansion as well as internal and external trade. They built step-wells, water reservoirs, and a 'military road' connecting Anhilvada with the Saurashtra peninsula.[79]

Merchants also travelled farther afield. In *The Travels of Sulaimān* (916), Abū Zayd related that Hindu merchants visited Siraf in large numbers and maintained cordial relations with the Muslim merchants of that region. 'When the Indian merchants of Siraf were invited by one of the principal merchants of the place, the latter out of regard for the susceptibility of the Hindus served them food in separate plates.'[80] Buzurg b. Shahriyār in the tenth century referred to Hindu merchants *baniās*) aboard Muslim-owned ships as passengers visiting the ports of the Persian Gulf. 'Awfī (1211) mentioned Wāsa Abhīr, a Hindu merchant of Nahrwāla, who had a flourishing trade with Ghazni with the help of his agents. After the defeat of Mu'izz al-Dīn's army in Gujarat, the latter was advised by one of his councillors to replenish his treasury by confiscating the property of Wāsa Abhīr. 'But this Mu'izz al-Dīn refused to do, stating that had Nahrwāla fallen into his hands the appropriation of Wāsa Abhīr's property would have been lawful, but to seize his property at Ghazni would be contrary to justice.'[81]

Cotton was the leading agricultural product in Gujarat, along with indigo, oilseeds, sugarcane, and hemp. From the tenth century onwards we see a shift in the Arab trade from Gujarat from merely luxury trade to bulk goods, which supported the expansion of local production, including cotton and leather goods, timber, sugar, dyes, spices, and semi-precious stones.[82] Silk cloth and velvet were also produced, using raw silk from China and Bengal. Drugs and medicinal products, such as opium, spikenard, arrowroot, lac, borax, and Indian wormwood were fabricated, as were handicrafts such as iron weapons, furniture, and jewellery.[83] Large and increasing quantities of cotton, refined indigo, and hemp were required for the growing textile industry that supplied utilitarian and luxury fabrics for domestic and overseas markets. Although figures for production are not available, textual evidence indicates a wide use of Indian textiles for purposes of dress, furnishing, and ritual.[84]

Gujarati block-printed cotton from the eleventh century onwards has been recovered from Cairo, sites on the Red Sea, and up the Nile in Nubia, and seems to have been used for utilitarian clothing, bedding, and furnishing.[85] Similar block-printed material dating to the fifteenth century was put to ritual use in Indonesia. Textual evidence indicates that better-quality woven and embroidered fabrics of silk, cotton, and leather, were also exported from Gujarat, but excavated or preserved fragments cannot be conclusively proved to be Gujarati in origin.[86]

Trade from the Gujarat ports, however, did not include only items produced locally. The transit trade dealt in commodities from as far afield as China and Europe. Imports into India, handled again by both Arab and local merchants, were more limited and depended to a greater degree on demand. Commodities that were imported included furs, wines, and dates.[87] Barbosa, writing before 1518, refers to the sea-borne transport of Sinhalese elephants to Gujarat. Elephants from Ceylon and even Burma were shipped to Cambay and other ports for the use of the sultans of Gujarat and Delhi, among others.[88] Of the imported goods, some were intended to be sold locally. In Geniza letters from the twelfth century, the commodities sent to India from the Red Sea included coral, textiles such as Russian linen, drugs, gold coins, and silver and copper vessels. In Gujarat these goods were to have been traded for a consignment of lac. Some items were intended for the use of the Jewish merchant families settled there, or—like damaged bronze utensils—were sent to be re-made by artisans in south India.[89] Many imports were re-traded at the Gujarat ports.

A vital item of trade was horses, required by most Indian rulers since locally-bred horses were not of the quality required for war animals. The only areas where Indian horses were found were Kachchh, Kathiavad, Rajasthan, and along the Indus to the Himalayas—linked to the Central Asian breeding grounds. Relatively cheaper cross-bred horses from this area and Afghanistan were imported overland—the Turki or Tātāri horses.[90] Horses were also exported from the Gujarat ports. When Muḥammad b. Tughluq wanted to send a hundred horses to China, they were dispatched from Gandhar, near Cambay.[91] In Caulukya Gujarat imported horses were virtually the monopoly of royalty. The claim of the merchant Jagaḍū of Bhadreshvar to a horse ordered for the king was tantamount to a challenge of authority.[92] In the fifteenth century most rulers required horses 'for show and for wars' as a priority of military survival.[93] Horses also had symbolic significance, standing in for royalty, heroism, and the warrior ethos.

Merchant ships, as well as those owned by the sultans of Gujarat and Delhi, which sailed between the ports of Gujarat and the Persian Gulf, were engaged in the import of horses.[94] Large numbers of costly Arab horses were imported annually. Many died on the voyage, the cost for which would be borne by the client kings. Marco Polo reported that the Gulf merchants refused to let horse doctors travel to India, so that large numbers of the animals died each year and the demand for them was kept up. Consequently, 10,000 horses were imported every year at Maʿbar, Kanbāyat (Cambay), and other western Indian ports.[95] The horse trade also attracted small 'peddlers' like the Russian Afanasio Nikitin, who embarked at Hormuz with his horses in a *tava* boat bound for India. With the rise of the Red Sea–Malabar link, the Konkan ports were deprived of Arab horses, which led the ruler of Thana to resort to piracy to procure them.

The Red Sea ports consistently gained in importance from the tenth century. The Malabar and Coromandel trade was initially more important, but the Gujarat and Konkan ports soon regained a share.[96] By the thirteenth century, the Arab trade was increasingly diverted towards the ports of south-west India, and Calicut grew to be the greatest spice emporium while Cambay saw an imperceptible decline. The growing European demand for goods from the East made the Red Sea ports the transit centre, importing from the East and selling to the West. The rise of the Red Sea ports and the increasing demand for spices also resulted in a reorganization of the Gujarati ports. Smaller ports began to share in the trade, and Cambay was no longer the largest or most important of them. At the same time, smaller ports such as Veraval, Diu, and Mangrol were developing along the Gujarat coastline, in almost every creek or inlet. Ports also began to specialize in specific commodities, and ships from Aden and Fustat came bound for specific destinations. Ships did not go from port to port on the coast because of the high import duties levied on the goods. As new ports came up, others were abandoned and the tenor of trade changed. Bharuch gave way to Cambay, which was supplanted by Diu, Somanath, Mangrol, and a host of smaller ports, which in turn gave way to Surat.

A RELIGIOUS GEOGRAPHY

Gujarat itself, especially the peninsula of Saurashtra, had long been considered a 'frontier region' from the point of view of brahmanical civilization. The incursions and assimilation of outsiders from Central

Asia, Persia, and the north-west from an early historic period gave the region the stigma of impurity in brahmanical texts. In early texts, it was a frontier zone, not quite within the brahmanical fold. The *Viṣṇu* *āṇa* (eighth century or later) says: 'He who goes to Anga, Vanga, Kalinga, Surāṣṭra or Magadha, unless it be for pilgrimage, deserves to go through a fresh purification.'[97] Peninsular Gujarat was thus grouped with Bengal, Bihar, and Orissa as a ritually impure marginal area.

Part of the reason for the stigmatization of Gujarat may have been the popularity of Buddhism, Jainism, and other non-brahmanical sects. Like eastern India, Gujarat and Sind had been strongholds of Buddhist (and in the case of Gujarat, Jain) settlements. In the seventh century Xuan Zang found Buddhist monasteries well established in Saurashtra and Sind although, as in Bengal, their links with the lay populace were beginning to shrink.[98] Buddhism never again became a state-sponsored religion in Gujarat. On the other hand, Jainism had been on the rise since the Valabhi conference in the fifth century when the great schism between the Jain orders took place. Gujarat became the centre of Śvetāmbara (white-clad) Jainism, which found increasing adherents among the merchant groups of Saurashtra and north Gujarat.

After the death of Skandagupta in 470, the Guptas lost control over Gujarat. Saurashtra, Kachchh, and north and central Gujarat came under Maitraka control. They were ardent worshippers of Śiva as Maheśvara, but the Vaiṣṇava Bhāgavata *dharma* continued to some extent in a subsidiary position. However, there is no evidence that Vaiṣṇava temples were built in this period, and there are no epigraphic references to temples dedicated solely to Viṣṇu or his incarnations.[99]

In most of north India the early medieval period was one of the invention of royal cults presided over by brahmins, such as those of iva, Viṣṇu-Nārāyaṇa, and Devī. Gujarat and Saurashtra were important centres of the Nāga and Yakṣa cults which had also spread over north-west India in the post-Gupta period. Many of these were the totemic or family deities of the pastoralist groups coming into Gujarat from the first century CE. The Purāṇas became the literary manifestation of the expansion, rooting, and patronage of the cults of various deities.

In addition, Gujarat saw the advent and success of a solar cult, introduced by the Magas from the north-west. Evidence of the introduction of sun worship into India comes largely from the *Sāmba* *āṇa* and part of the *Bhaviṣya Purāṇa*. The *Sāmba Purāṇa*, one of the āṇas mentioned by al-Bīrūnī, is believed to have been written between 500 and 800 CE, probably in north-western India.[100] It records the advent of the *maga-brāhmaṇas* to India from Śakadvīpa, usually identified as Persia or Afghanistan. The sun was believed to have the ability to destroy sins and to cure certain diseases, particularly leprosy.[101] The evidence that solar worship was common in north Gujarat and Saurashtra is suggested by the construction of several important sun temples such as those at Modhera and Than, and the fact that the Kāṭhī clan, who also entered Saurashtra from Sind via Kachchh, worshipped the sun.[102] Several inscriptions from the eleventh and twelfth centuries also mention sun temples, particularly in the southern part of Saurashtra.

The Purāṇas and inscriptions record the defeat and subjugation of local deities at the hands of the reinvented royal brahmanical deities from the seventh or eighth centuries. However, the advent of these transregional brahmanical practices into Gujarat was a slow and keenly contested process. In the eighth century, a Gurjara Pratihāra king was the first to adopt Śaivism as the royal cult and appoint brahmins as royal priests, rewarding them with land grants.[103] In south Gujarat the āṣṭrakūṭas had adopted Vaiṣṇavism, although they also made grants for the construction of solar and Jain temples. The Cāvaḍās, who succeeded the Gurjara Pratihāras in controlling north Gujarat by the eighth century, seem to have resisted brahminization. Later Jain writers claimed that Vanarāja (lit., lord of the wilderness) Cāvaḍā was a devotee of Jainism and endowed a local Jain temple, but there is no contemporary confirmation of this.

In spite of the fact that Gujarat was considered a ritually impure area, it housed several important shrines that became vital to expanding brahmanism from the eighth century onwards. The majority of these temples were Śaiva shrines, many of which incorporated or superseded local deities. Across most of north India claims to royalty were usually backed by the construction of royal temples and invitations to brahmins to reside in the area. In Gujarat most such attempts at legitimation involved the construction of Śaiva shrines and land grants offered to brahmins. Vaiṣṇava temples were also built in this period, but were usually subsidiary to the Śaiva shrines.[104]

The rule of Mūlarāja in the tenth century is associated with a flurry of brahmanical activity. His reign is the first time that the famous Śaiva temple of Somanath, to the far south-west of Saurashtra, appears as the royal temple with a royal champion, although this may be a retrospective claim made by later writers. Mūlarāja is said to have made a pilgrimage to Somanath in the late tenth century and cleared the way for pilgrims. On his return, he built a Śaiva temple in Anhilvada, thus bringing to his own capital the blessings of the deity and reducing the necessity of pilgrimage to distant Somanath. He is also credited with granting land to brahmins from the north to settle in the region.[105]

Somanath—dedicated to Soma, the moon deity—may be identified Śaiva temple in the eleventh century in the descriptions of writers who accompanied Maḥmūd of Ghazna on his campaigns in Gujarat. This temple had already acquired considerable notoriety in the Muslim world as an embodiment of idolatry. In Maḥmūd's period its care was in the hands of local merchants and possibly chieftains. Later Caulukya rulers continued to make sporadic visits to the temple and possibly contributed to its upkeep. By the time of the Veraval inscription of 1264, the temple and the town were regulated by a committee of five important citizens.[106]

One of the oldest sacral sites, first marked out by an Aśokan inscription and, several centuries later, in the fourth century CE by the inscription of Skandagupta, is the sacred mountain of Girnar. It is dotted with some of the most important shrines of Gujarat, including Jain, Muslim, Nāthpanthī, and mother goddess shrines. The mountain itself was worshipped and is a sacred site of great antiquity.

BUDDHISM AND JAINISM

There is considerable evidence for the spread of Buddhism in Gujarat from about the third century BCE. Apart from Aśoka's rock edicts in Girnar and Sopara (on the coast), there is material evidence in the form of *stupas* and *vihāras* from the Kṣatrapa period in the first century CE. Records pertaining to the Valabhi kingdom also indicate the substantial prevalence of Buddhism. By the time of Xuan Zang's visit in the mid-seventh century, Buddhism had a widespread but waning influence in the Valabhi territories of southern Saurashtra. The vihāra of Duddā, a woman belonging to the ruling family, was a well-known centre of Buddhist learning. The Buddhist university of Valabhi was also renowned in the eighth century, and Buddhist scholars from Valabhi are known to have travelled to China where they were received with respect.[107]

Buddhism waned along with the Valabhi kingdom. The reasons may have been similar to those in contemporary Sind, where the monastic orders lost the support of the laity. Those of late Buddhism may have taken on other patrons and forms, transforming themselves in the process. For example, it has been suggested that the structure and hierarchies of the Aghorī order of renouncers is similar to that of Buddhists, and they retain certain practices, such as begging for food only in the mornings.[108] Similarly, it is noticeable that the Nāthpanth began to be influential in Gujarat in the years following the decline of Buddhism, and, again, its monastic hierarchies are similar to Buddhist ones. Whether a product of declining Buddhism or not, monastic orders, especially those affiliated to Śaivism, continued to exert a considerable influence on the religious landscape of Gujarat in the subsequent period.

The monastic non-brahmanical religious practice that came to have a much greater influence in Gujarat was Jainism. When Jains moved westwards from the Ganga basin from about the third century CE, one of their chief settlements was the cosmopolitan city of Mathura. Jain tradition relates that two monks converted a local goddess who became a devout lay-woman and built a golden stupa there, in imitation of one on Mount Meru. This stupa became a contested site, claimed also by local Buddhists and Hindus, but it was miraculously proved to belong to the Jains. By the first century CE, the Jain laity included prosperous traders, craftspersons, and courtesans. This was also the time when the cult of Kṛṣṇa Vāsudeva at Mathura was gradually being eclipsed, to return only in the seventeenth century.[109] The strong local tradition of Kṛṣṇa at Mathura was also adopted by the Jains, who linked him with the twenty-second *tīrthaṅkara* Neminātha.[110] This intertwining of the story of Kṛṣṇa with Nemi became popular later in Gujarat.

By the fourth and fifth centuries Jain groups were moving away from Mathura and the centre of the Gupta kingdom towards the territories of the Maitrakas of Valabhi in south-west Gujarat. The Jain *tras* or scriptures were first committed to writing in the early fifth century during a convention of Jain preceptors in Valabhi. This council was attended exclusively by Śvetāmbaras (the White-Robed), an indication that western India was henceforth the domain of this sect, while the Digambaras (or Sky-Clad) became influential in south India. By the late seventh century Jains had acquired a considerable following in Gujarat, especially among urban merchant groups.

Although the great Jain conference took place in Valabhi in Saurashtra in the fifth century, later concentrations of the community were more in north Gujarat. The mountain of Girnar in Saurashtra had already acquired a sanctity for the Jains by this time. There are references in the *Kuvalayamālā* (c. 788 CE) to a Jain named Śivacandragaṇi who settled at Bhinnamāla (Śrīmāla or modern Bhinmal, southern Rajasthan) in the seventh century. His disciple Yakṣadattagaṇi caused Gujjara-deśa (Gujarat) to be adorned with Jain temples. Ś ī āli merchants, both

Jain and Hindu, did indeed fan out over Gujarat, acquiring considerable influence and wealth over time.[111] By the Caulukya period small settlements of Jains were to be found in most of the towns of the region.

There is a legend in the *Kuvalayamālā* that Vanarāja Cāvaḍā (eighth century), the founder of Anhilvada, was assisted in acquiring his kingdom by a Jain renouncer.[112] While Jains were reluctant, by and large, to assume actual political power, from the tenth century onwards they are to be found close to the centres of power in various capacities. After gaining considerable, though contested, political influence at the court of the Caulukyas, they retained an economic and moral influence out of proportion to their actual numbers throughout Gujarat's subsequent history. Correspondingly, the wealth and influence of the Jain community resulted in the construction of a network of monumental Jain shrines at various places in Saurashtra and Gujarat. Most of this building took place during the period when Jainism was patronized by the Caulukyas from the mid-eleventh century. A prolific textual tradition also grew to regulate and prescribe rituals for the new shrines. This variant of royal and merchant-sponsored Śvetāmbara Jainism privileged the worship of icons and spectacular shrines—such as those at Shatrunjaya and Mount Abu—were created for the purpose. The Caulukyas' patronage of Jainism ensured that their activities were recorded in great detail in the Jain chronicles.

THE MOVING FRONTIER OF ISLAM, c. 650–1200

Muslims reached Gujarat along the trade routes from the north and north-west, and also by sea, perhaps as early as the late seventh century. The Arabs in Sind mounted raids into Gujarat and central India in the eighth and ninth centuries, but these did not give rise to sustained settlement or conversion of local communities. References to Muslims settled in western India come up from the ninth century. One epigraph records that a Muslim official of the Rāṣṭrakūṭas in the Sanjan region of south Gujarat endowed a rest-house for pilgrims and travellers.[113] It has been argued that the expansion of the Turkish–Muslim empire in north India from the twelfth century took place concurrently with the development of commercial operations on the coast:

> These developments—of the interior and the littoral—were closely linked and part of the wider process which characterized these centuries, the fusion of the world of sedentary agriculture with the frontier world of nomads, overland and maritime long-distance traders, of movable goods and precious metals.[114]

All through this period Muslim traders and religious figures had settled in the ports of Gujarat. By the time ʿAlāʾ al-Dīn Khaljī's generals conquered parts of north Gujarat in 1297, Muslims had lived in Gujarat for six hundred years. There was significant activity by Muslim holy men and preachers of different denominations, but in this period, there are few stories of the *ghāzī*, the Muslim warrior-preacher. Most stories and biographies of early Muslim proselytizers in Gujarat relate narratives of conversion by stealth and persuasion.

One of the first denominations to get a foothold in Gujarat was that of the Ismāʿīlīs, who entered Gujarat through two routes. The first was the sea route from the Ismāʿīlī Fāṭimid caliphate in Egypt and its outposts, and, after its decline in the eleventh century, from Ṣulayḥid kingdom of Yemen. The other was along the trade routes from Sind and Multan through Kachchh and Rajasthan. Ismāʿīlīs had played a significant part in the politics of Sind from the late ninth century. A Fāṭimid Ismāʿīlī mission was set up in Yemen in 883 from where a propagandist or *dāʿī* was sent to Sind.[115] By the time of the imid Qāḍī al-Nuʿmān in the tenth century, the *daʿwa* (mission) had penetrated Multan, Gujarat, and Punjab.[116]

In the reign of the Fāṭimid Caliph al-Muʿizz (953–75), a dāʿī of Sind was accused of heresy. While he was given credit for converting a large number of *majūs* (identified with sun-worshipping maga-hmaṇas), he was accused of permitting them to 'follow their earlier practices, taking no notice of those prohibitions of God that did not exist in their former religion', with particular reference to dietary and matrimonial practices.[117] The Ismāʿīlī missionaries who were later sent to Gujarat seem to have carried out conversions in a similar way. Convert communities in Gujarat were often not required to relinquish their former dietary and marriage practices, and were encouraged to keep their Ismāʿīlī affiliations secret.[118] As a result, these conversions fitted into former practices.

The Ismāʿīlīs in Multan secured political power early in the eleventh century, but their rule was destroyed by Maḥmūd of Ghazna in 1010–11. Nevertheless, the mission in Multan remained in existence and āʿīlī revolts occurred here in 1041 and then against the Ghūrids in 1175. After the Nizārī-Mustaʿlī schism of 1094, the Nizārī variant of āʿīlism was introduced into Sind with its main centre at Uchch, south of Multan. This time, proselytization was aimed at the trading communities and sections of the Lohāṇā caste were converted.

Ismāʿīlī missionaries spread their faith along the 'frontier', among peasant, trading, and pastoralist groups. They influenced some of the pastoralist and seafaring communities of the coast of Kachchh and Saurashtra, often using versions of Hindu mythology and ritual, local hero-tales and cults. Many of the convert communities still practise versions of the belief, or retain memories of it in their legends, rituals, and burial practices.[119]

In 1068, a Fāṭimid dāʿī named ʿAbd Allāh arrived in Gujarat with two Indian assistants. Less than a decade later, official Fāṭimid letters mention a flourishing Ismāʿīlī community in Gujarat. The earliest Islamic structures in India have been identified as belonging to the āʿīlī community.[120] These are a set of buildings in the town of Bhadreshvar in Kachchh, which possess inscriptions dating from the late twelfth century. One of these epigraphs refers to a dignitary named hīm who has been identified with Ibrāhīm b. al-Ḥasan al-Ḥāmidī, the contemporary Ismāʿīlī dāʿī then living in Yemen.[121] Further evidence of an Ismāʿīlī settlement in twelfth-century Kachchh is provided by the *Jagaḍūcarita*. This verse biography of a Jain merchant magnate of the twelfth century mentions that among Jagaḍū's good works was his construction or renovation of the mosque of the local āʿīlī community.[122]

CONCLUSION

The early history of the territory of Gujarat already saw political divisions corresponding to eastern Gujarat, Saurashtra, and Kachchh. Any history of Gujarat must deal with the interactions between these three regions and their contiguous areas. One way to view the history of the period before 1200 CE is in terms of three major arenas of transformation. The first of these is pastoralism. Politics were dominated by the pastoralists entering the region from the first century CE. As they sedentarized, they became part of larger networks and Rajput hierarchies in which descent emerged as the primary source of status. The second feature was the merchant ethos. Merchants and merchant-pastoralists rose in significance since the eighth century as Gujarat became the primary point where the trade networks radiating out from north India met the rapidly expanding trade of the Indian Ocean. Many of these merchants settled along the great trade route running north to south, especially between south Rajasthan and north Gujarat. As trade flourished, a merchant could become a prince.

The third frontier was that of the extension of Hinduism and hmanical texts and practices into Gujarat. Aspirations to royalty and membership of Rajput descent hierarchies were usually accompanied by the adoption of one or another reinvented Vedic deity. In Gujarat this deity was usually Śiva in myriad localized forms. Meanwhile, Muslims, especially Ismā'īlīs, were settling in Gujarat and recruiting converts. The Jainism practised by many of the crucially important merchant groups often found royal favour. By the twelfth century, networks of both Jain and brahmanical sites of pilgrimage had spread all over Gujarat.

NOTES

1. J.M. Campbell, ed. (1896), *Gazetteer of the Bombay Presidency*, Vol. 1, Part 1: *History of Gujarat*, p. 2: 'The rise of Gurjara power appears to represent a shift from pastoral nomadism and a predatory way of life to agriculture and a more settled state.' See also Andre Wink (1990), *Al-Hind*, Vol. 1. *Early Medieval India and the Expansion of Islam, Seventh to Eleventh Centuries*, p. 279.
2. M.R. Majmudar (1965), *Cultural History of Gujarat*, p. 19. The etymology of the term is debatable, but the Sanskrit Gurjara-rāṣṭra of Caulukya texts post-dates the Prakrit Gujjaraṭṭā found in Gurjara Pratihāra inscriptions such as the inscription of 859 CE of Kakkukā at Ghatiala. D.C. Sircar (1942), *Select Inscriptions Bearing Upon Indian History and Civilization from 6–18th Century AD.*, Vol. I, No. 12.
3. B.N. Puri (1986), *The History of the Gurjara Pratiharas*, p. vii.
4. Samuel Beal (1884), *Si-yu-ki: Buddhist Records of the Western World, Translated from the Chinese of Hiuen Tsiang (AD 629)*, Vol. 2, pp. 269ff. Beal reads Pi-lo-mi-lo as Barmer, but this has been discredited. See Campbell, *Gazetteer*, Vol. 1, Part 1, p. 3, fn. 5; Wink, *Al-Hind*, Vol. 1, pp. 277–80.
5. Puri, *Gurjara Pratiharas*, pp. 8–9. Several inscriptions from the eighth and ninth centuries use the term Gurjaratrā-bhūmi for part of the Pratihāra territories.
6. S. Maqbul Ahmad (1969), *Indo-Arab Relations: An Account of India's Relations with the Arab World from Ancient upto Modern Times*, p. 96.
7. E. Sachau (1910), *Alberuni's India*, p. 205.
8. Ahmad, *Indo-Arab Relations*, p. 144.
9. The first Caulukya ruler, Mūlarāja (c. 941–996), may have been in the service of the Gurjara Pratihāras.
10. H.D. Sankalia (1949), *Studies in the Historical and Cultural Geography and Ethnography of Gujarat*, p. 30.
11. Majmudar, *Cultural History of Gujarat*, p. 19.

12. Abu'l-Ḥasan 'Alī al-Mas'ūdī (1841), *Murūj al-dhahab wa ma'ādin al-jawhar*, trans. Aloys Sprenger as *El-Mas'údí's Historical Encyclopaedia*, p. 279.
13. V. Minorsky (1937), *Ḥudūd al-'Ālam: 'The Regions of the World': A Persian Geography, 372 AH–982 AD*, p. 88.
14. Waṣṣāf, *Tajziyat al-amṣār wa tazjiyat al-a'ṣār*, trans. in H.M. Elliot and John Dowson (1867–77), *The History of India as Told by its Own Historians*, Vol. 3, p. 32.
15. Interestingly, this raid is nowhere mentioned by the 'Hindu' sources, thus, the campaign has to be gleaned entirely from the Persian chronicles. See Romila Thapar (2004), *Somanatha: The Many Voices of a History*, pp. 78–9.
16. Majumdar, *Chaulukyas of Gujarat*, pp. 82–3.
17. Peter Jackson (1999), *The Delhi Sultanate: A Political and Military History*, p. 10; Majumdar, *Chaulukyas*, pp. 131–2.
18. Chattopadhyaya, *Making of Early Medieval India*, Chapter 2.
19. Ibn al-Athīr, *Kāmil al-tawārīkh*, trans. in Elliot and Dowson, *History of India*, Vol. 2, p. 469; Abu'l-Qāsim Firishta (1829), *History of the Rise of the Mahomedan Power in India till the year AD 1612*, trans. John Briggs, Vol. 1, p. 69; M. Nazim (1931), *The Life and Times of Sultan Mahmud of Ghazna*, p. 215.
20. C.D. Dalal, ed. (1920), *Hammīramadamardana of Jayasiṃha Sūri*, Act V.
21. Campbell, *Gazetteer*, pp. 506ff.
22. Merutuṅgācārya (1901), *The Prabandhacintāmaṇi or Wishing-Stone of Narratives*, trans., C.H. Tawney, p. 30.
23. For a discussion of South Asian towns in this period, see André Wink, *Al Hīnd*, Vol. 3, pp. 67–78.
24. Al-Idrīsī, *Kitāb nuzhat al-mushtāq*, trans. in Elliot and Dowson, *History*, Vol. 1, p. 77.
25. V.K. Jain (1990), *Trade and Traders in Western India, 1000–1300*, p. 120.
26. James Burgess (1876), *Report on the Antiquities of Kutch and Kathiawar*, pp. 170, 218.
27. Al-Idrīsī, trans. in Elliot and Dowson, *History of India*, Vol. 1, p. 87.
28. Ibid., p. 84.
29. Saurashtra was called Sorath in medieval times and was later called Kathiavad by the Marathas (the name deriving from the horse-breeding Kāṭhīs who entered the peninsula from Kachchh).
30. al-Mas'ūdī, *Kitab murūj al-dhahab*, trans. in Elliot and Dowson, *History of India*, Vol. 1, p. 23.
31. R.E. Enthoven and S.M. Edwardes, eds. (1909), *Imperial Gazetteer of India: Provincial Series—Bombay Presidency*, Vols. 1 and 2, p. 105.
32. James Macmurdo (1834), 'Dissertation on the River Indus', *Journal of the Royal Asiatic Society* [henceforth *JRAS*], 1, p. 41.
33. O.H.K. Spate and A.T.A. Learmonth (1967), *India and Pakistan: A General and Regional Geography*, p. 646.

34. Ibid., p. 645.
35. Nazim, *Maḥmūd of Ghazna*, p. 215.
36. Jain, *Trade and Traders*, p. 110.
37. Sikandar b. Muḥammad (n.d.), *MS*, trans. F.L. Faridi (n.d.), p. 53, Sikandar b. Muḥammad (1961), *MS*, p. 114.
38. Spate and Learmonth, *India and Pakistan*, p. 646.
39. Ibid., pp. 646–7.
40. Enthoven and Edwardes, *Imperial Gazetteer*, p. 351.
41. H. Wilberforce-Bell (1916), *History of Kathiavad from the Earliest Times*, p. 48.
42. Ibid., p. 49.
43. Ibid., pp. 51–2.
44. There was a similar relationship between the Bhīls and the Guhilas in Mevad. See B.D. Chattopadhyaya (1993), 'Origin of the Rajputs: The Political, Economic and Social Processes in Early Medieval Rajasthan', in *The Making of Early Medieval India*, p. 62.
45. Harald Tambs-Lyche (1997), *Power, Profit and Poetry: Traditional Society in Kathiawar, Western India*, pp. 32–3.
46. Enthoven and Edwardes, *Imperial Gazetteer*, p. 352.
47. M.I. Dar, *Literary and Cultural Activities in the Sultanate of Gujarat*, p. 30, citing inscriptions found on Mount Girnar, source not mentioned.
48. Sircar, *Select Inscriptions*, Vol. 2, pp. 402–6. The accompanying inscription is discussed at length in Ranabir Chakravarti (2002), 'Nakhuda Nuruddin Firuz at Somanath: AD 1264', in *Trade and Traders in Early Indian Society*, pp. 220–42 and Thapar, *Somanatha*, pp. 88–102.
49. L.F. Rushbrook Williams (1958), *Black Hills: Kutch in History and Legend*, pp. 57–9.
50. Ibid., p. 58.
51. K.R. Dikshit (1970), *Geography of Gujarat*, p. 121.
52. Enthoven and Edwardes, *Imperial Gazetteer*, p. 185.
53. For a recent study of Kachchh and its identity, see Farhana Ibrahim (2009), *Mobility, Territory and Memory: The Making of a Region in Western India*.
54. Beal, *Si-yu-ki: Buddhist Records of the Western World*, p. 51.
55. Williams, *Black Hills*, p. 84. F. Mallison (2003), 'Saints and Sacred Places in Saurashtra and Kutch: The Cases of the Naklaṃkī Cult and the Jakhs', in Phyllis Granoff and Koichi Shinohara, eds, *Pilgrims, Patrons, and Place: Localizing Sanctity in Asian Religions*, p. 332–49.
56. U.M. Daudpota (1970), 'Sind and Multan', in Mohammad Habib and K.A. Nizami, eds, *The Delhi Sultanat: AD 1206–1526, A Comprehensive History of India*, Vol. 5, Part 2, p. 1122–3. For the pursuit of Taghai, see Simon Digby (1979), 'Muḥammad bin Tughluq's Last Years in Kāthiāwār and his Invasions of Thattha', *Hamdard Islamicus*, 2(1), pp. 78–9.

57. Shams-i Sirāj 'Afīf, *Ta'rīkh-i Firūz Shāhī*, trans. in Elliot and Dowson, *History of India*, Vol. 3, pp. 324–5.
58. Sikandar, *MS*, trans., p. 10.
'Awfī, *Jawāmi' al-hikāyat*, trans. in Elliot and Dowson, *History of India*, Vol. 2, pp. 200–1.
60. Sarvāṇanda (1892), *Jagaḍūcarita*, ed. Georg Bühler. See Chapter 3 in this volume for further discussion on this.
61. Jain, *Trade and Traders*, p. 139.
62. Ibid., p. 139, citing Somadeva's *Yaṣastilakacampu* (959 CE).
63. R.K. Trivedi (1965), *Census of India: 1961*, Vol. 5, *Gujarat*, Part VII-B: Fairs and Festivals, p. 27.
64. Jain, *Trade and Traders*, p. 140.
65. More accurately, 'the mixture of castes through intermarriage'. Ibid., p. 139.
66. The Sanskritized term used is '*grāsino-rājānah*'. Gaṅgādhara (1973), *Gaṅgadāsa-pratāpa-vilāsanāṭakam*, eds B.J. Sandesara and A.M. Bhojak, p. 40.
67. Chattopadhyaya, *Making of Early Medieval India*, p. 88.
68. Ibid., p. 87.
69. Ibid., pp. 87–8.
70. Ibid., pp. 79–80.
71. Ibid., p. 80.
72. Kolff, *Naukar, Rajput and Sepoy*, p. 84.
73. Chattopadhyaya, *Making of Early Medieval India*, p. 88. It is interesting that the chronicler of the Gujarat sultans, Sikandar, writing in the seventeenth century, attributed to the sultans a respectable Rajput genealogy and descent from Rāma. Eventually, even the sultans needed the legitimation offered by descent.
74. Arrianus (1912), *The Periplus of the Erythraean Sea*, trans. W.H. Schoff, p. 22.
75. Ibid., p. 23.
76. Ibn Baṭṭūṭa (1953), *Riḥla*, trans. Mahdi Husain, p. 172.
77. Sachau, *Alberuni's India*, pp. 208–9.
78. Al-Idrīsī, trans. in Elliot and Dowson, *History of India*, Vol. 1, p. 87.
79. Jain, *Trade and Traders*, p. 110.
80. Sayyid Sulaymān Nadwī (1929), *Arab-o-Hind ke ta'alluqāt*, p. 49.
'Awfī, trans. in Elliot and Dowson, *History of India*, Vol. 2, p. 200; Majumdar, *Chaulukyas of Gujarat*, p. 267.
82. Jain, *Trade and Traders*, pp. 12–20, 105–6.
83. M.N. Pearson (1976), *Merchants and Rulers of Gujarat: The Response to the Portuguese in the Sixteenth Century*, p. 13.
84. Ruth Barnes (1997), *Indian Block-Printed Textiles in Egypt: The Newberry Collection in the Ashmolean Museum, Oxford*, Vol. 1, p. 80. Gujarati block-printed textiles were used in ceremonies and as funeral shrouds in

85. Ibid., p. 31.
86. Ibid., p. 32.
87. M. Zaki (1987), *Arab Accounts of India (During the Fourteenth Century)*, p. 27.
88. Simon Digby (1971), *War-horse and Elephant in the Dehli Sultanate: A Study of Military Supplies*, pp. 71–3.
89. S.D. Goitein (1954), 'From the Mediterranean to India: Documents on the Trade to India, South Arabia, and East Africa from the Eleventh and Twelfth Centuries', *Speculum* 29(2–1), pp. 192–3.
90. Andre Wink (1997), *Al-Hind*, Vol. 2, *The Slave Kings and the Islamic Conquest, 11th-13th Centuries*, pp. 83–84.
91. Ibn Baṭṭūṭa, *Riḥla*, pp. 58–9.
92. Sarvāṇanda, *Jagaḍūcarita*, p. 22.
93. Pearson, *Merchants and Rulers*, p. 13.
94. Digby, *War-horse and Elephant*, p. 25.
95. Ibid., p. 31. Waṣṣāf says that during the time of Atābeg Abū Bakr, 10,000 horses were exported to western Indian ports including Cambay, and 2.2 million dinars were paid for them out of the Hindu temple revenues and taxes on courtesans attached to temples.
96. Wink, *Al-Hind*, Vol. 2, p. 22.
97. Campbell, *Gazetteer*, p. 13 fn. 1. The Anuśāsanaparvan of the *Mahābhārata* mentions Lāṭas among the kṣatriya tribes who became outcastes from seeing no brahmins. There is also a mention of the robber Saurāṣṭras.
98. Eaton, *Rise of Islam*, p. 13; Derryl N. MacLean (1989), *Religion and Society in Arab Sind*, pp. 52–61.
99. Haripriya Rangarajan (1990), *Spread of Vaiṣṇavism in Gujarat up to 1600 AD*, p. 6.
100. Some opinions locate the origin of the *Sāmba Purāṇa* in Orissa, which was associated with the sun cult, but as Gujarat, Sind, and Multan also have evidence of sun worship and as most of the holy places and rivers mentioned in the text refer to northern India, it is more likely that the text originated there. Ludo Rocher, ed. (1986), *The Purāṇas: A History of Indian Literature*, Vol. 2, p. 238. See also Heinrich von Stietencron (1966), *Indische Sonnenpriester Sāmba und die Sākadvīpiya–Brāhmaṇa*.
101. R.C. Hazra (1958), *Studies in the Upapurāṇas*, Vol. 1, p. 30, fn. 6.
102. J.W. Watson (1875), 'Sketch of the Kathis. Especially Those of the Tribe of Khachar and House of Chotila', *IA*, 4, p. 105.
103. Campbell, *Gazetteer*, p. 33.
104. Rangarajan, *Spread of Vaiṣṇavism*, p. 21.
105. Uttamarām Durlabharām (1877), *Ṭoḷakanibandha* [*Essay on the Ṭoḷakas*], Narasiṃhadās Durlabharām Purohit (1877), *Audicya ṭoḷakiya jñātinī sthiti* [*The Condition of the Audicya Toḷakiya caste*]. See also Campbell, ed., *Gazetteer*, p. 161.

107. Majmudar, *Cultural History of Gujarat*, p. 205.
108. Ibid., p. 203.
109. C. Vaudeville (1999), 'Braj Lost and Found', in Vasudha Dalmia, ed., *Myths, Saints, and Legends of Medieval India*, p. 48.
110. Paul Dundas (2002), *The Jains*, p. 236.
111. B.M.N. Parmar (1990), *Cultural and Critical Study of Srimala Purana*, p. 12.
112. Majmudar, *Cultural History of Gujarat*, p. 165.
113. Sircar, *Select Inscriptions*, Vol. 1, p. 55.
114. Wink, *Al-Hind*, Vol. 2, p. 269.
115. W. Ivanow (1948), 'Satpanth', in W. Ivanow, ed., *Collectanea*, p. 6.
116. Abbas H. al-Hamdani (1956), *The Beginnings of the Ismā'īlī Da'wa in Northern India*, p. 16.
117. MacLean, *Religion and Society*, p. 132. MacLean convincingly argues that the *majūs* should be identified as sun-worshippers.
118. Farhad Daftary (2007), *The Ismā'īlīs*, p. 444.
119. For such practices in Rajasthan, see D.-S. Khan (1997), *Conversion and Shifting Identities: Ramdev Pir and the Ismailis in Rajasthan*. For Gujarat, also see F. Mallison and Z. Moir (1976), '"Recontrer L'Absolu, O Ami": Un Hymne Commun aux Hindous Tantriques et aux Musulmans Ismaeliens du Saurashtra (Gujarat)', *Puruṣārtha* (19), and Nirañjan Rājyaguru (1995), *Bījamārgī gupta pāṭ-upāsana ane mahāpanthī santonī bhajanvāṇī* [*The Secret Worship of the Bījamārga and the Devotional Compositions of Mahāpanthī Saints*].
120. Mehrdad Shokoohy, Manijeh Bayani-Wolpert, and Natalie Shokoohy, (1988), *Bhadreśvar: The Oldest Islamic Monuments in India*, Vol. 2, pp. 54–5.
121. Ibid., p. 54.
122. Sarvāṇanda, *Jagaḍūcarita*, p. 18.

2

Settlement and Authority in Eastern Gujarat

From the twelfth to the end of the fifteenth century and even later, Gujarat was still in the process of being 'settled'. Many led unsettled lives in this period, either moving here or travelling from place to place within it. By the twelfth century several large towns were in existence, and manufacture and long-distance trade, both overseas and overland, were well established. The coastal towns were particularly prosperous, and housed sizeable and entrenched colonies of local and itinerant merchants. In the hinterland, however, migration and mobility were the norm for all those engaged in trade, pilgrimage, and politics.

While settled agriculture was well established in parts of Gujarat, it was not the only source of revenue for local political hierarchies. A general assumption of Indian economic history has been that pre-colonial states were reliant upon the exploitation of the labour of a sedentary peasant class and its agricultural productivity. While this may have been the case in other parts of north India, the situation seems to have been different in Gujarat. During the period of this study, the eastern strip of Gujarat was already urbanized, and trade and even agriculture were largely monetized.[1] Cash crops such as cotton, indigo, and sugarcane were a priority, while foodgrains were grown on a subsistence basis or imported for cash from grain-surplus regions such as Malwa. The peasantry, defined either in caste or occupational terms, did not exclusively engage in agriculture; nor were agriculturists strictly sedentary. Agriculture consisted largely of cash crops such as indigo

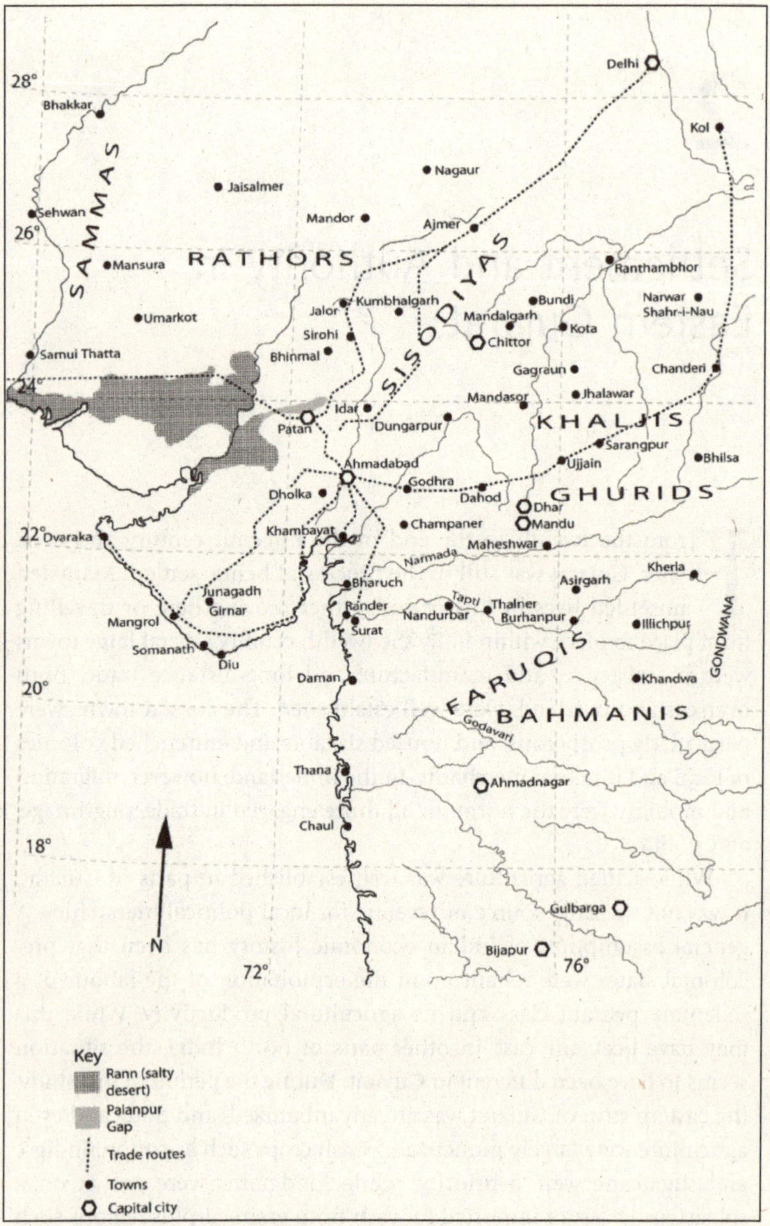

Map 2.1: Routes in Western India*

*This is a historical map. This does not imply any judgement concerning the legal status or the endorsement or the acceptance of such boundaries. For present

groups who also engaged in some kind of commodity production, trade, or haulage. Economic or political circumstances often impelled the migration and resettlement of populations. Even agriculturists were thus obliged to be mobile. The case of Gujarat in this period may revise our ideas about the nature of pre-colonial economies in South Asia.

There is also evidence to indicate that political authority in central Gujarat was bound up with the trading activities of the region. It is now possible to challenge the traditional thesis that trade had little to do with the politics of the hinterland, and that the rulers, in particular the sultans of Gujarat, did not derive significant benefit from it.[2] This view emerges from the idea that pre-colonial hinterland empires were primarily based on the exploitation of land resources in relation to which trade was largely autonomous. But it is clear that the repeated invasions of Gujarat, and the contestations for power within it, took place for a share in its fabled riches. It is also clear that the repositories of these riches were its temples and merchants. It is then difficult to understand the assumption that political strife in Gujarat was primarily to do with the control of *agrarian* resources. The historiography of Gujarat bears out this assumption, so that political histories of the region take little interest in its trade, and the numerous histories of the Indian Ocean trade, especially of the role of Gujarati traders and products, assume that political authority on land was irrelevant to it. However, settlement patterns in Gujarat and corresponding local political authority clearly indicate the extent to which settlement and administration were governed by the necessities of trade. Most of the campaigns of the sultans were to safeguard trade for their own benefit and secure their supplies of resources.

After the establishment of rule by governors sent by the Delhi sultans in the early years of the fourteenth century, urban settlements grew around the new forts in response to new patrons and political alignments. However, it was only after the establishment of the Gujarat sultanate in the early fifteenth century that rulers began to invest in the long-term economic and political stability of the region. The sultans personally supervised the construction of several new forts, city walls, and even entire towns. They ruled from three capitals in the course of the century, of which two, Ahmadabad and Champaner, were built by them. Building and settling towns did not only mean the construction of buildings suitable for the court. Provision was also made for merchants, traders, artisans, and agriculturists to settle and cultivate the surrounding areas. Merchant families became well entrenched within the inner citadels of the important cities, and in some cases continued to live there for several centuries. In the case of Ahmadabad, courtiers were encouraged to build similar suburbs of their own outside the city walls.

During the fifteenth century the sultanate progressed from operating out of a series of fortified garrisons to evolving an overarching structure ensuring the safety of settlements, and even more importantly, the security of the roads. While it was important to provide secure settlements for merchants and producers, it was vital to ensure that the routes they traversed were safe. This facilitated the movement of goods, pastoralists with their animals, pilgrims, and most importantly, the army. One of the most important criteria recorded by chroniclers to signify good government was the safety of the roads. According to the chronicler Sikandar, during Maḥmūd Bīgara's rule (1458–1511), *faujdār* of Ahmadabad, Muḥāfiẓ Khān, 'made such excellent arrangements that thieving and high-way robbery became extinct ... and the merchants opened their loads on the roads and stages'.[3]

Thus, while settlement and resettlement were important themes in the history of Gujarat, political power was still associated with mobility and the control of resources such as horses, military equipment, and warriors. The Delhi governors and then the sultans had to maintain close contacts with merchants and carrier communities to remain informed and supplied with sufficient resources. Their survival over rival chieftains depended upon the superior patronage and protection they could offer merchants, which set up a reciprocal system of dependence. The rulers needed arms, boats, horses, precious metals, and luxury goods, while in turn they could provide the merchants with security, a stable currency, and regular custom.

While the sultans made every effort to encourage settlement and the growth of towns and agriculture, it was, paradoxically, equally necessary for them to safeguard the very mobility of Gujarat that had enabled its prosperity. Their efforts had to be directed towards a more effective regulation of that mobility. The extension of political control and settlement meant that roads were more secure and Gujarat attracted a growing trade and pilgrim traffic. Groups of artisans, traders, and priests gravitated towards the towns in search of security and patronage. By the early fifteenth century the sultans had acquired regular access to arms supplies, horses, elephants, and ships through their patronage and safeguarding of trade. It was this superior access to military resources that enabled them to enforce tribute collection from subordinate chiefs. Although the last two governors of the Delhi sultanate, Farḥat al-Mulk

Ẓafar Khān, had been able to manipulate immigrant politics and relations with merchants to form long-term political alliances, it was only in the second half of the reign of Maḥmūd Bīgara (r. 1453–1511) that a stable and indisputably paramount court society emerged. The effective compromise that was achieved in sultanate Gujarat between settlement and mobility may thus indicate a new model of settled civilization in the fifteenth century.

Traditions of migration are often helpful in the reconstruction of political events or economic changes. Migration and settlement can be traced through inscriptions, land grants, and the traditions of the communities or their representatives. Such traditions were often preserved by genealogists, vital members of the social infrastructure for many communities that were upwardly mobile and, therefore, required records in written or oral form. For other communities these traditions were recorded by community members or priests in the āṇa genre, at times in Sanskrit but later, often in Gujarati.[4] The caste Purāṇas are an important form of information about the histories of communities, and their manuscript versions have not yet been systematically collected or interpreted. However, several caste traditions and claims were published by the communities in the early part of the twentieth century as efforts to unite their members (often by exclusion), codify their customs, make claims to status, territory or antiquity, or simply to declare their separate existence. Many of them drew upon manuscript caste Purāṇas or recorded oral tradition within the community. Most of the communities for whom records exist, either in the form of contemporary inscriptions and grants or traditions recorded later, indicate practices of migration. Migration and settlement are among the chief motifs of the caste Purāṇas. Other chronicles, such as the fourteenth-century *Jagaḍūcarita,* also mention the migration of the protagonist's ancestors from Śrimāla in Rajasthan to eastern Kachchh. Other accounts record migrations in search of economic opportunity, in response to invitations by rulers or legendary figures, in response to famine or political tumult, and so on.

Governments inevitably encouraged settlement of 'wild' areas and invited aspirants for state favour to conquer territories and then 'settle' or 'populate' them, typically with peasants, merchants, and religious figures. They offered inducements in the form of land control or tax relief to peasants to clear scrub or forest and cultivate such areas after their former inhabitants had been pacified or defeated. For example, the Ka bīs were induced by Aḥmad Shāh to settle in the Charotar after the local Kolīs had been defeated.[5] This region soon became the most agriculturally productive in Gujarat.

Some people settled in Gujarat after achieving military success. Apart from the Turkic invaders and their camp followers, several local or immigrant chieftains and bands of adventurers captured lands, towns, forts, and routes in eastern Gujarat in this period. In some cases chieftains were accompanied by their entire clans who settled and defended the captured or granted territory. Adventurers and mercenaries attached themselves to patrons and received grants of land and military or administrative offices.

Others found economic reasons to settle in Gujarat: for cultivation, manufacture, or trade. Artisans and traders flocked to the manufacturing towns of eastern Gujarat from the eleventh century onwards. Traders and brahmins from Śrīmāla in southern Rajasthan began to enter eastern Gujarat at this time. Many of them achieved prominence as priests, bankers, and merchants. Brahmins came from even further afield in search of patrons. The Kaṇbī peasants have a tradition of migration from Punjab. Within Gujarat they settled along the major trade routes and moved into the new towns such as Adalaj, Champaner, and Ahmadabad. 'Foreign' traders settled in the coastal ports in this period, particularly at Cambay.

The third important category of settlers in Gujarat were religious figures. As mentioned earlier, brahmin groups moved into the region and found patrons among the scores of local chieftains seeking to legitimize their status as they sedentarized and established courts. Other brahmins attached themselves to merchants anxious to patronize places of worship and cash in on the flourishing pilgrim traffic. Some were even patronized by the Gujarat sultans.[6] Religious endowments were also a good way to invest money for spiritual and temporal gain. In the thirteenth century, the brothers Vastupāla and Tejahpāla acquired much wealth from trade. When a Muslim trader named Sayad was arrested at Cambay, his wealth was confiscated and much of it passed to the brothers. Their wives advised them thus: 'Spend your wealth on a hill top. All can see it; no one can carry it away.' Accordingly, the brothers adorned the summits of Abu, Girnar, and Shatrunjaya with magnificent temples.[7] Sufis and Muslim scholars went to Gujarat, especially after the foundation of the sultanate, as the sultans were eager to attract prominent Muslim scholars to their court. Many of them received r ent-free lands or stipends. The estates of the Bukhārī Sufis at Vatwa and that of Shaykh Aḥmad Khattū at Sarkhej became important counterpoints to the sultans' court at Ahmadabad—with some parallels to the Chishti Sufis' relations with the sultans of Delhi.[8] Ismā'īlī preachers had also been prominent in Gujarat and one of them, Imām h, was granted territory close to Ahmadabad.[9]

CONQUEST AND SETTLEMENT

The sultanate of Gujarat was established in the early fifteenth century, in an area of eastern Gujarat that had been sought after and contested since the late tenth century when Mularāja established the Caulukya dynasty. With the rise of the Caulukyas, a strip of territory extending north to south, roughly from the area north of Patan to Cambay on the coast, became the core area from where Gujarat was ruled in the subsequent centuries. This eastern strip included, by the twelfth century, most of the prosperous towns, manufacturing centres, and agriculturally productive territories, and was the 'productive hinterland' that supplied goods for the wide-ranging trade from Gujarat's ports. From the tenth century onwards the Caulukyas stimulated internal and external trade. They constructed a 'military road', connecting Anhilvada with the Saurashtra peninsula.[10] Eastern Gujarat was also on the most popular trade route that connected northern India with the ports. Most caravans to and from the north and north-west were obliged to pass through eastern Gujarat through the Abu–Palanpur ingress into southern Rajasthan.

The territories ruled by the Caulukyas included most of the eastern area. Their decline and replacement by their erstwhile subordinates, the Vāghelās, in the thirteenth century, led to incursions of other groups from the north and north-west towards the core eastern territory. For example, the Jhālās, first heard of in eastern Kachchh, were driven further east by the incursions of branches of the Sūmrās from southern Sind. They took refuge with Karṇa Vāghelā around 1290, receiving land in reward.[11] After 'Alā' al-Dīn's conquest, they took control of the area to the west of the Vāghelā territories. Similarly, the Gohils who ruled an area west of the Sabarmati at the end of the thirteenth century, moved south-east into the coastal area of Valabhi with the help of the Mers.[12] By the time of Muḥammad bin Tughluq's campaign in 1351, the Gohils were a well-known threat to shipping and controlled the strategic island of Piram at the mouth of the Gulf of Cambay from where they preyed on both merchant caravans and ships.[13]

The Rāṭhoḍs of Idar, to the north of Patan, rose to prominence only after the rule of Arjunadeva Vāghelā (1267–80) whose inscriptions show that Idar was within his territories.[14] The Rāṭhoḍs, once Caulukya subsidiaries, took the mountain fortress of Idar from a Kolī chieftain in the early fourteenth century. The story is that they were bribed with the revenues of Idar by the dissatisfied Nāgar brahmin minister of the Kolīs.[15]

Large pastoralist groups moved into Gujarat in the wake of famine, persecution or loss of political control, or simply in search of opportunity. The Soḍhās, for example, were driven south from Sind by famine in the late thirteenth century and were employed by the Vāghelās to suppress the Bhīl chieftains of the Sabarmati valleys. The attraction to enter eastern Gujarat was the lure of its considerable commercial and pilgrim traffic, as well as the unsettled political conditions in the late thirteenth and fourteenth centuries when territory and patronage were up for grabs. It does not seem that the incoming clans made agriculture their main occupation. They possibly continued as armed pastoralist clans whose cattle or animal wealth was their main livelihood. Local clans presumably regulated, taxed, protected, and on occasion robbed the trade and pilgrim caravans passing through their territories.

The decline of Vāghelā rule followed by the invasion by 'Alā' al-n Khaljī's army allowed various groups to stake claims to political control of parts of the eastern strip up to the prosperous coast. Khaljī's generals invaded eastern Gujarat in 1299 and captured Asaval, Anhilvada Patan (which was abandoned by the Vāghelā ruler), Somanath, Vanthali, and Cambay. They gained large spoils from looting the prosperous Jain and foreign merchants of Cambay, and then returned to Delhi. Another invasion was sent out in 1304–5, following which the Vāghelā ruler again abandoned Patan and fled to Deogir. By 1306 the first governor sent out from Delhi, Alp Khān, former governor of Multan, was in residence in Patan.

Immigration continued throughout the period of the governors of the Delhi sultanate (1297–1407). Trade seems to have carried on unabated, seemingly unaffected by political vicissitudes.[16] The governors sent from Delhi employed the same tactics as their predecessors, the ghelās and Caulukyas, of inviting armed bands or pastoralist clans to settle and pacify territories in return for the local revenues and the promise of protection. According to S.C. Misra, at this point, 'The Turks succeeded in breaking down the apex of the Rajput power-structure but not its lower echelons.'[17] He suggests that local landholders and chieftains offered nominal submission to the Delhi governor but remained powerful in their own territories. Delhi's power was maintained through garrisons in Patan and the main cities while the countryside remained unsubdued. Misra's analysis suggests that the Delhi governors replaced the Vāghelās in a smooth transfer of power, while the positions of the other players in local politics, the Rajputs, remained essentially unchanged.

This analysis cannot be supported. The decline of Vāghelā power and the Delhi invasion combined to create a virtual free-for-all in the eastern plains. Even before the Khaljī army came to Gujarat, Vāghelā control was seriously reduced and the latter were hardly more powerful than neighbouring chieftaincies such as the Jhālās or Cūḍāsamās.[18] Central and eastern Gujarat in the early fourteenth century was prime territory for migrant bands of warriors in search of patronage, alliance, or marriage as described by Dirk Kolff.[19] The Jhālās, Gohils, and hoḍs, all powerful chieftaincies by the mid-fourteenth century, moved in to snatch territory in eastern Gujarat. The eastern hill fortress of Champaner with its strategic position between Malwa and Gujarat was also built in this period.[20]

Other minor chieftains of the Narmada and Mahi river valleys, as well as Bhīl and Kolī chieftains, acquired significant territory and resources. The Godhra region in the eastern hills was controlled by a cattle-herding chieftain named Ghughula in the mid-thirteenth century who had to be chastised for plundering the caravans that passed through his territory on their way to the coast.[21] The central region around Asaval and the plains of Charotar, the main agricultural area of the fifteenth century, were still uncleared and controlled by Bhīl and Kolī chiefs.[22] The Bhīls repeatedly appear as a threatening force: the sultans called on immigrants such as the Gohils and the Soḍhās to suppress Bhīl threats in return for refuge and vassalage. Bhīls operated from hilly and forest areas such as the ravines of the Sabarmati, the forests of Banswara and Dungarpur, and the forests around Junagadh.

Although Bhīls were considered to be of lower status than many other pastoralist clans, they were well within the pale of the acceptable as allies or even marriage partners. The Kolīs seem to have functioned as an intermediate caste. A Gohil chief contemporaneous to Maḥmūd gara is said to have married the daughter of a Bhīl from Sihor who assisted him in his battle against the *mleccha*. Their descendants were referred to as Gohil Kolīs.[23] In addition, the Bhīls had political power in their own right and were allies worth having if necessity arose. This probably indicates that the overarching 'Rajput' identity that later developed was able, in this period, to assimilate certain powerful Bhīl clans and chieftainships. The distance between the Bhīls and the Rajputs is not so great as might be assumed from the 'Great Tradition' of Rajput identity in which 'Rajput' is equated with 'aristocrat'. Before the fourteenth century and on occasion even later, political power and corresponding status were available to Bhīls and similar groups.

During the rule of Muḥammad bin Tughluq, Cambay and Gujarat were administered by Khwāja Jahān who commanded the loyalty of the inhabitants. 'Most of them were infidels and some were rebels who would fortify themselves in the mountains.'[24] When a rich Cambay merchant, Malik al-Tujjār al-Kāzarūnī was granted the *iqṭā*' (military assignment) of Cambay in his stead, Khwāja Jahān incited his 'infidel' followers to attack and kill Malik al-Tujjār. Several Afghan adventurers who had accompanied the invasion similarly entered the fray to acquire strongholds for themselves.[25] They quickly acquired powerful local status and their support or lack of it could tilt the balance for any governor sent out from Delhi.[26] In 1344 a group of Afghans in the vicinity of Cambay and Baroda defied the local governor and entered Cambay where they 'plundered the royal treasury and the property of private individuals and that of Ibn al-Kaulami, the merchant'.[27] The rebellion proved serious for the sultan as Afghans in Multan and Daulatabad also rebelled, and in Cambay other 'turbulent and disaffected people' joined the rebels. The Afghans took charge of much of central Gujarat, besieging the sultan's advance guard at the fort of Bharuch and dispersing only when the sultan himself arrived. After their defeat, many of the Afghan *amīr*s were executed, while others escaped to Khandesh or took refuge with local chieftains.[28] Soon after this episode, the Afghans again assisted the rebel Taghai, in whose pursuit the sultan spent the last years of his life.[29]

The Delhi governor was thus obliged to negotiate with and keep the upper hand over a large number of belligerent local interests. In the thirteenth century land revenue had not been the most significant source of income for the Caulukyas and Vāghelās; the greater part of the revenues came from taxes on trade.[30] There are no indications that the situation changed with the advent of the Delhi governors in the fourteenth century. Taxation of trade, octroi, pilgrim taxes, and tribute from subsidiary chieftains continued to be the main source of income.

By the 1390s, reports reached Delhi that Farḥat al-Mulk had failed to remit the revenues of the *khāliṣa* (crown) lands to the central treasury and was 'oppressing' the locals. Subsequently, Ẓafar Khān, the son of a peasant convert who had become a confidant of Fīrūz Shāh, was to Gujarat was the shortest possible. En route he halted at Nagaur, where he received a delegation from Cambay who complained about Farḥat al-Mulk's 'tyranny'. They were reassured and Ẓafar Khān proceeded towards Patan. After preliminary negotiations failed, Ẓafar Khān met ḥat al-Mulk's army, 'consisting mostly of Hindus', at Kambhoi near Patan.[31] Farḥat was decisively defeated and killed while fleeing from the field.

Ẓafar Khān then dispatched agents to take control of the country and purge the area of officials who may have had loyalties to the former governor. He installed himself in the name of the Delhi sultan at Patan, conducted formal ceremonies, and bestowed robes and distinctions.[32] Thus, having pacified the crucial urbanized eastern strip of Gujarat, afar Khān was, for the rest of his life, engaged in a struggle against the chieftains and confederacies that threatened his frontiers.

BUILDING FORTS AND CAPITALS

At the end of the fourteenth century power was concentrated around the area of Cambay, although the seat of the governors was nominally at Patan. Subsequently, power shifted inland. Within the eastern territory, centres of influence changed and shifted depending upon political circumstances. The sultans used three capitals in the fifteenth century, all within the core eastern region. For most of the century, the sultans were obliged to be mobile in order to be prepared for threats from different directions and this led to rapid but massive construction of forts and citadels.

In the fourteenth century the main threat was from the north and north-west, that is, from Delhi, and the capital was accordingly in Patan in north Gujarat. Aḥmad Shāh then built Ahmadabad, south of Patan, after the northern frontier had been largely pacified. Now the main threats were from Saurashtra, not far to the west, and from the hill chieftains from the east. After his decisive military victory at the end of a long and expensive military campaign over the Māṇḍalik ruler of Junagadh in 1470, Maḥmud Bīgara built an alternative or subsidiary capital in Junagadh, renamed Mustafabad. Later it was in response to the threat of invasion from Malwa and allied hill chieftains in the eastern hilly region between Gujarat and Malwa that Maḥmūd Bīgara built a capital for himself in Champaner, at the edge of the mountainous region, which possessed a lookout hill from where aggression from the east could easily be spied. Champaner was also the site of his greatest military victory against the Paṭāi Rāval who had, from his mountain here represented taking over the military advantages that the Paṭāi val had enjoyed.

The region of Ahmadabad, Kheda, Bharuch, Cambay, and parts of the northern regions around Patan and Siddhpur were among the few areas ruled directly by the sultans. At the outset, they did away with the top rung of the local ruling hierarchy, the bulk of the revenue-sharing hierarchy remaining intact on condition of payment of tribute. But even in these areas, such as the district of Ahmadabad, large tracts remained in the hands of Bhīl and Kolī chiefs.[33] Further south, in Surat, the chief at Kanrej had submitted to the Muslim rulers in the fourteenth century and was allowed to remain autonomous. In 1373, Fīrūz h built a fort there as a safeguard against the Bhīls. Another small chieftain of the region was that of Sunth, probably related to the Panwārs of Malwa. The region of Reva Kantha, by the banks of the Narmada, was largely controlled by the Bhīls and Kolīs, except for the fort of Champaner and its Cauhāṇ chieftain. To the east, the region of Mahi Kantha was also dominated by Bhīl and Kolī chieftains. Rajpipla was ruled by the Gohils after 1470, but had an arrangement with the Ahmadabad sultans to provide 1,000 foot and 300 horsemen whenever necessary.[34]

Before Aḥmad Shāh became sultan, his first campaign was against the Kolīs of the village of Asaval who, 'having thrown off their allegiance, took to brigandage and highway robbery'.[35] Soon after he became the ruler in 1411, the first challenge to his authority came from a confederacy based at the other important manufacturing centre of Baroda. The instigators of this conspiracy included his cousin or uncle z Khān, the *muqṭa*ʿ (right-holder) of Baroda, assisted by his brothers, and Jīvandās and Prayāgdās Khatrī, and later by Raṇmal, the ruler of Idar. In this conflict Aḥmad was supported by the former muqṭaʿ of Baroda, Malik Bektars, an Afghan chieftain.[36] It would thus seem that at least part of the still-powerful Afghan lobby of Gujarat supported mad's claims to rule Gujarat.

Aḥmad Shāh subsequently founded Ahmadabad in the vicinity of Asaval, on the eastern bank of the river Sabarmati. Asaval was at a strategic place for the transportation of goods to Cambay, and the former chieftain had evidently derived considerable benefit from the goods passing through his territories. Its conquest thus secured Aḥmad a site that was conveniently located for the safe transport of goods to Cambay, and by its location would help effectively subdue and safeguard the entire surrounding region. It was also conveniently located against days march of the main threat, the eastern frontier with Malwa and the chieftains of the eastern hills.

The establishment of Ahmadabad as the capital began with the building of the Bhadra citadel in 1411. This was soon followed by the royal palace and the Jāmiʿ mosque. The city was built in a planned way. Aḥmad Shāh diverted the course of the Hathmati river to the Sabar to increase the water supply to Ahmadabad.[37] Separate quarters were built for different kinds of artisans and tradespeople. He also settled weavers, craftsmen, and merchants in the city. Religious figures were given yearly stipends, and arrangements were made for the recipients of rent-free lands and their descendants.

Aḥmad then continued with strategic fortification in his territories: after completing the citadel of Ahmadabad, he built and repaired forts along the eastern border with Malwa. He constructed 'fortified *thānas*' in the eastern hills and repaired the century-old fort of Kareth.[38] Later he founded the northern town of Ahmadnagar (now Himmatnagar) on the banks of the Hathmati river in order to have a nearby fort from which to take on the chieftain of Idar.

Aḥmad's reign was the period when the *vānṭā* tenure system, peculiar to Gujarat, was first elaborated.[39] During the sultanate period land control was farmed out and tribute payments were the major source of income from subordinates. Large parts of Gujarat had not yet been cleared and settled for agriculture. Gujarat's most productive agricultural zone at present is the Charotar region, now associated with the prosperous agricultural Kaṇbī Pāṭīdār community. The Kaṇbīs settled here and cleared the land only after Aḥmad Shāh subdued the turbulent Mehwāsīs of the region probably in the 1420s.[40]

The sultans gradually promoted settlement and agriculture in their territories, often through courtiers who were granted lands and encouraged to develop them. A Persian inscription of 1452 from the Ahmadabad suburb of Rakhyal relates the terms of a royal grant made by Quṭb al-Dīn Aḥmad Shāh to the courtier Malik Shaʿbān:

> Upon a petition being made in our world-refuge royalty and august kingly court, by our favourite servant and special well-wisher, Malik Shaʿbān ....; we, in compliance with the request of the said Malik, through the plenitude of our Royal bounty and abundance of Imperial favours, endow upon him, his children and descendants to their remotest generation, six ploughs [*juftwār*] of land, out of the Mauza' Rakhyal, a dependency of the circuit of the renowned city of Ahmadabad, in which the said Malik has caused wells to be dug, trees to be planted and channels to be made—aforesaid being included in the

circuit of the renowned city that they leave the said land together with the gardens, the wells and the trees, to the posterity and progeny of the said Malik, and make no change or variation in the grant so that they fall not under the condemnation of the verse—'And he who changes it after he has heard it, the wrong of this shall be on those who change it.' (Qur'ān, 2: 181).[41]

ARCHITECTURE AND POLITICS

The decline of Caulukya power in the late twelfth century led to a century of changes in the religious landscape of Gujarat and the development of a religious marketplace as missionaries and propagandists poured into the region in search of patrons and converts. It also coincided with a fall in patronage to monumental temple building, largely associated in Gujarat with Śaiva temple complexes. Meanwhile, Jain structures continued to be built. A major contributor to Jain building was the minister-merchant Vastupāla and his brother Tejahpāla, who built or renovated widely in this period. There was also an increased emphasis on civic buildings, in particular water structures, usually built in arid areas to aid agriculture or along trade routes for the benefit of travellers and pilgrims.

The patronage of religious structures in medieval Gujarat served several purposes for donors. Constructing or renovating religious structures was a source of merit, whether Hindu, Jain, or Muslim. It could also be a way of investing surplus wealth, which could bring returns in the form of increased pilgrim revenues. It also earned the donor respect and political influence. Many donations signalled the donor's bid for political recognition or local significance, spelt out in accompanying inscriptions.

The tradition of building monumental Hindu temples began to decline from about 1250, even before the Khaljī invasion from Delhi. However, this did not affect networks of pilgrimage, which continued to develop under sultanate rule. Wealthy Hindus, especially chieftains, could no longer make monumental temples in the Caulukya style, but more people were now being attracted to extant shrines, saints, tombs, and ancient religious sites such as Dvaraka and Girnar. On the other hand, Jains could still, if not build new temple complexes, keep the older ones in good repair and make donations towards their upkeep. This bears out the argument that after the initial iconoclasm and plundering of invading armies died down, the sultanate was concerned with controlling only those temples that were seen to be associated with local chieftains and their political power.[42] As the Jains pragmatically stayed away from political association in the fourteenth and sultans went on repeated campaigns to put down recalcitrant chieftains and their regnal temples.

Monumental public architecture in Gujarat in this period consisted of fortifications and town walls, water structures, and religious buildings such as temples, mosques, tombs, and shrines, all of which were built to last, usually in stone. It is significant that there is little evidence throughout the period for solidly built permanent marketplaces. One of the rare commercial structures that appears in an epigraph is a customs building from 1387 in Cambay.[43] The inscription actually records the construction of a water-shed inside the customs office by one Shaykhzāda Badr. Here, while the meritorious act of providing water has been recorded by the donor, there is no epigraph for the customs building itself. We have accounts of lofty and grand merchants' dwellings in cities like Cambay and Patan, but very little survives of domestic architecture. Some of the oldest sections of the walled cities may date back to the fifteenth century. Houses in these areas were usually wooden and have survived because they were constantly occupied, renovated, and rebuilt. According to Baṭṭūṭa, the great Cambay merchants competed against each other to build the most impressive homes, and a detailed archaeological survey of the town may reveal traces of these residences. But on the whole, even the dwellings of rulers and sultans have not stood the test of time.[44]

According to accompanying inscriptions, fortifications and town walls were usually constructed on the orders of local or supra-local rulers. A bilingual inscription in Persian and Sanskrit from 1395 from Mangrol records that a fort with iron and steel gates was constructed during Ẓafar Khān's governorship by Malik Ya'qūb, the governor of Soraṭh, under the supervision of his brother Malik Mūsā, *kotwāl* of the region.[45] In 1404 Ẓafar Khān built a fort in Kapadvanj on the request of a local official.[46] Religious structures, on the other hand, were rarely attributed to direct royal commands. Even important royal temples such as Somanath or Rudramahālaya in Patan do not carry surviving inscriptions identifying the ruler as the instigator of the construction.[47] In most cases it was local merchants or courtiers who built or renovated religious structures, hoping to earn favour in the eyes of the rulers. In the case of Islamic structures, while there are examples of mosques being constructed on the orders of a ruler, accompanying inscriptions usually mention that the actual execution was carried out by a courtier.[48]

For Muslim donors, the building of a mosque brought religious merit as it denoted exceptional piety and enabled the local community to congregate. The merit that would accrue to the builder was usually indicated by a Qur'ānic verse. For conquerors, the building of a mosque signalled the establishment of Muslim rule in infidel territory. Although several mosques built in the wake of conquest employed the raw materials of demolished temples, very few accompanying inscriptions take note of such reuse.[49] One exception is an inscription of 1505 from Amod, which records the construction of a mosque on the site of a temple by Khalīl Khān, the future Muẓaffar II.[50] However, as most religious constructions—Hindu, Jain, or Muslim—were built by highly skilled local architects and builders, there is a distinct similarity in architectural styles.

Certain mosque inscriptions from the thirteenth and fourteenth centuries are bilingual, that is, in Arabic or Persian, as well as Sanskrit or Gujarati. Bilingual inscriptions would suggest that the information in the text was intended to reach both the Muslim and non-Muslim elite. The most famous are the twin Veraval inscriptions of 1264 in Arabic and Sanskrit.[51] These texts state that a Hormuz ship-owner named r al-Dīn Fīrūz bought a piece of land outside the town of Somanath with the consent of its *pañcakula* or town committee, built a mosque on the land, and made donations for its maintenance.

Another bilingual inscription—in Persian and Sanskrit—is dated 1323 and is from Petlad, referring to the construction of a well for public use by Ismā'īl b. 'Uthmān Shīrāzī on land donated by the local governor.[52] In 1340 a step-well and mosque were built by Mokhā Mahetā, son of Ketā Mahetā the Indian (Hindī) near Baroda. The accompanying inscriptions in Sanskrit and Persian record that the structures were built following an order issued to Malik Muẓaffar, the local ruler. The Persian text concludes with a Qur'ānic imprecation (2:181) against whoever abrogated or altered the endowment.[53]

Water structures—primarily step-wells, but also wells and tanks—were almost always built by merchants or courtiers. While one might have assumed that rulers would have some hand in the provision of water in an arid region such as Gujarat, it was in fact subordinates and merchants who were usually responsible. Supplying water along the trade routes or in unirrigated villages was a source of merit, and donors were anxious to make clear their generous intentions towards all humanity and animals. Malik Hājī, a courtier, declared in 1460 that his fine garden house, with its lofty porch, four painted walls, fruit-bearing trees, and a well and a tank, had been constructed for the benefit of all men and animals.[54] Water architecture is thus not entirely it was a merit-generating act of philanthropy. Although most step-wells were associated with Hindu donors and embellished with Hindu iconography, several were built by Muslims too. (There are virtually no

sponsors of step-wells.) One view has it that from the fourteenth century onwards, with Muslim influence, the religious nature of step-wells changed, and from being sacred public buildings they became private retreats for the elite during the hot summer.[55]

Going purely by extant and published epigraphs, Tables 2.1 and 2.2 give some sense of the patterns of patronage to religious structures of different denominations.[56]

Table 2.1: Building Patterns in Gujarat[a] as Reflected in Epigraphs, 1200–1509

	Step-wells, wells, tanks	Jain temples and images	Hindu temples	Mosques/ tombs	Civic architecture
1200–9	1				
1210–19		1	1	1	
1220–29		1	1		
1230–39		1	2		
1240–49			1		
1250–59					
1260–69		1	2	1	
1270–79		2	1		
1280–9				1	
1290–9		2	2	1	
1300–9		1	3	1	1
1310–19	2	1		3	
1320–9	2			6	
1330–39	1	1		4	1
1340–9	1	2		2	1
1350–9				2	
1360–9				7	
1370–9			1	4	
1380–9	5		2	13	
1390–9	2	1	2	3	1
1400–9	3		1	3	4
1410–19	4		2	8	
1420–9		1		9	
1430–9				9	
1440–9	2		1	6	
1450–9	1	2		7	3
1460–9	6	1		8	1
1470–9	1	2	1	7	
1480–9	4		1	6	2
1490–9	4			6	1
1500–9				5	
Total	39	20	24	123	15

Note: [a]Here Gujarat refers to the territory covered by modern Gujarat, unified

Table 2.2: Women Builders

	Year	Building	Place	Epigraph	Language
1.	1331	Step-well[a]	Petlad	This bounty (step-well) was constructed for public use by the late Kadbānū, wife of Irānshāh.	Arabic and Persian
2.	1368–9	Mosque[b]	Somanath	Built by Varū, daughter of 'Abd al-Raḥmān, widow of Ismā'īl bin Amīr Dā'ūd Shāh.	Persian and Arabic
3.	1380	Step-well[c]	Mahuva	Built by Sahajaladevī, daughter of Rāṇ whose husband worked for the Cūḍāsamās.	Sanskrit
4.	1385	Step-well dedicated to Someśa[d]	Somanath Patan	Step-well and other buildings by Yamunā, daughter of a Yādava king Bhīma and his wife Māṇikya-devī, and wife of Dharma of the Rāṣṭrakūṭa clan.	Sanskrit
5.	1389	Step-well[e]	Dhandhusar	Built by Hānī, wife of Vaijyanāth, son of Gadādhar, minister to the Cūḍāsamā ruler.	Sanskrit
6.	1397	Jain image[f]	Parnala (Surendra-nagar district)	Bhāvaldevī, wife of Guhilrāj Pratāpmal had the statue consecrated.	Sanskrit
7.	1401	Pond[g]	Bhuva-timbi (Junagadh district)	Nāgubāī, daughter of Bharam of the Bārad caste and his wife Megati, built a pond in the village.	Sanskrit
8.	1418	Step-well[h]	Khed (north Gujarat)	Construction of a well by Māyāpurī, wife of Maliryaka.	Sanskrit
9.	1443	Pāḷiyā (hero-stone)[i]	Lodhva (Junagadh district)	Records the death in battle of a Vājā warrior Godhā. Installed by his dejected wife Sāgaman.	Sanskrit
10.	1446–7	Mosque[j]	Ahmadabad	Construction of the mosque by Bībī Buddu, wet-nurse of Malik al-Sharq 'Imād al-mulk	Arabic

(contd)

Table 2.2 (contd)

	Year	Building	Place	Epigraph	Language
11.	1454	Mosque and tomb[k]	Ahmadabad	Jāmiʿ mosque built by Makhdūma-i Jahān, the sultan's mother, in memory of Bībījī, wife of Sayyid Buddha and mother of the Sufi Khwandamīr.	Arabic
12.	1461	Mosque[l]	Ahmadabad	Mosque built by a woman named Barman (Baḍī mān)	Arabic and Persian
13.	1462	Step-well[m]	Jegadva (Surendranagar district)	The queen of Rāṇā Śrī Raṇvīr of the Jhālā clan, Bāī Ramādevī had a step-well built.	Prakrit/ Old Gujarati
14.	1468	Pāḷiyā[n]	Jegadva (Surendranagar district)	Records the death of someone (name erased). Set up by Bāī Kāmelāsat, Bāī Kākālā.	Sanskrit
15.	1475	Digambara Jain images[o]	Himmatnagar	Lakhanahārani, daughter of Hrṣa offered perpetual obeisance to the image.	Sanskrit
16.	1478	Mosque[p]	Ahmadabad	Construction of a mosque by Bībī Daulat, daughter of Shaykh Malik and wife of Khān-i Aʿẓam ʿĀdil Khān.	Arabic
17.	1482	Step-well[q]	Rampura (Surendranagar district)	Rāṇībāī and Valhāde, the wives of Sheth Vīṇā of the Śrīmāla caste constructed a step-well.	Sanskrit
18.	1499	Step-well[r] (Ahmadabad)	Asarva	Bāī Harīr, a female official of Maḥmūd I, built a step-well at Asarva	Sanskrit and Persian
19.	1499	Step-well[s]	Adalaj (Ahmadabad)	Rāṇī Rūḍādevī's inscription mentions both her father's and husband's lineages.	Sanskrit, last 3 lines in Gujarati

Notes: [a] Z.A. Desai (1999), *Arabic, Persian and Urdu Inscriptions of West India: A Topographical*, No. 1868.

(contd...)

Table 2.2 (contd)

V.G. Oza, ed. (1889), *Corpus Inscriptionum Bhavanagari: Being a Selection of Arabic and Persian Inscriptions Collected by the Antiquarian Department, Bhavnagar State*, p. 6.

D.B. Diskalkar (1938–41), *Inscriptions of Kathiavad* (hereafter *IK*), No. 40; H.G. Shastri (1979), *Historical Inscriptions of Gujarat* (hereafter *HIG*), Vol. 4; No. 59.

James Burgess and Henry Cousens (1897), *Revised List of Antiquarian Remains in the Bombay Presidency* (hereafter *RLARBP*, p. 252.

Ibid., p. 245, Diskalkar, *IK*, No. 48; Shastri, *HIG*, No. 61.

Diskalkar, *IK*, No. 56; Shastri, *HIG*, No. 85.

Diskalkar, *IK*, No. 60; Shastri, *HIG*, No. 50. Unusually, this donor cites only her parents. There is no mention of a husband.

K.G. Krishnan, ed. (1987), *ARIE 1978–79*, App. B, No. 67.

Diskalkar, *IK*, No. 72; Shastri, *HIG*, No. 52.

Desai, *Arabic, Persian and Urdu Inscriptions*, No. 10, K.G. Krishnan, ed. (1986), *ARIE 1977–78*, App. D, No. 63, p. 148.

Desai, *Arabic, Persian and Urdu Inscriptions*, No. 15.

Ibid., No. 19.

Diskalkar, *IK*, No. 79; Shastri, *HIG*, No. 91–2.

Diskalkar, *IK*, No. 81; Shastri, *HIG*, No. 93.

Krishnan, *ARIE 1978–79*, App. B, No. 59.

Desai, *Arabic, Persian and Urdu Inscriptions*, No. 25.

Diskalkar, *IK*, No. 86.

James Burgess (1875), *IA*, Vol. 4, pp. 367–8.

Burgess and Cousens, *RLARBP*, pp. 301–11; Hariprasād Śāstrī (1955), 'Aḍālaj-nī vāv-no lekh, vs 1555 [The Adalaj step-well inscription, vs 1555], *Buddhiprakāś*, 104, pp. 19–23.

Until the 1350s we see endowments to Hindu (largely Śaiva) and Jain religious structures. From about 1300 onwards, coinciding with sultanate political control, there are more endowments to Islamic structures, although some mosques and tombs were built earlier by Muslim merchant families. Of the trends that emerge from this table, the most striking is the rise in the number of step-wells, many of which were built by women and by sultanate officials. As to the Jain figures, patterns of donation (often of an icon) seem to remain constant throughout the period of our study. Most of the Jain epigraphs record small-scale donations—of an icon or a sum of money—by families. While there was large-scale building in the thirteenth century, this is not reflected in accompanying epigraphs.

The epigraphs show a remarkably large number of women as donors and significant relatives. Women were the sole donors in nineteen epigraphs during the period studied here, erecting step-wells, mosques, Jain images, and hero-stones. In six other epigraphs (not listed here) they are mentioned by name as donors along with their husbands. Several other epigraphs mention the names of women donors or relatives. There are at least four instances of donations to temples or Jain images made for the spiritual welfare of a female relative, a mother, or wife. There are also gravestones of some prominent Muslim women.

It is no accident that several water structures were built with donations made by women, including two by Muslim women (Table 2.2, Nos. 1, 18). First, water sites were often linked to goddess worship and the granting of fertility. Perhaps women were more frequent users of these sites, especially step-wells. Second, this was a reflection of the economic importance of women in the merchant and pastoralist societies that predominated in Gujarat, whether Hindu or Muslim. Women contributed to other kinds of building too; unusually for the period, they also made several endowments to mosques.[57]

While there had been widespread temple building under the Caulukyas in the eleventh and twelfth centuries, there was a decided fall-off in patronage to Hindu temples from the thirteenth century onwards and particularly so from about 1310. In common with many early medieval states, Caulukya temple complexes and those of their imitators were political institutions designed to link the ruler's sovereignty with that of the deity.[58] In the Caulukya case the deity was usually iva in various manifestations and the main royal temples were those at Somanath, Anhilvada Patan, and Siddhpur.

However, the link between late Caulukya and Vāghelā rulers and their temples is not so clear in the epigraphic material. Thirteenth-century Jain epigraphs are usually assertions by private individuals of specific donations: to build temples, restore them, or to pay for the installation of icons. Non-Jain epigraphs from the same period, on the other hand, usually record local administrative hierarchies as well. For example, the Bharāṇā grant of a well in 1270 was made by two officers of Bharāṇā (near modern Jamnagar) who were subordinate to lha and Sāmantasiṃha, the governors of Saurashtra during the rule of Arjunadeva Vāghelā (r. 1262–74) in Anhilvada.[59] While epigraphs always cite the line of authority from the local chief to the Caulukya overlord, the actual grant was not made by the supreme ruler or even in his name, but at the local level by local chieftains, governors, or subjects. According to Chattopadhyaya: 'State formation, among the Rajputs and in general, was inevitably linked with the practice of grants of land to Brahmanas, temples, Buddhist monasteries (*vihāras*) and Brahmanic monasteries (*ṭhas*).'[60] This linked royal and sacred authority within a reciprocal system of legitimation. However, the grants we encounter in thirteenth-century Gujarat were almost invariably made by subordinates and only exceptionally did they directly link rulers with their royal temples.

This suggests that in the thirteenth century the Vāghelā rulers were not instigating building activity themselves. Local temples and shrines continued to be built and supported, but monumental royal shrine complexes were already a thing of the past. While the rulers still had ideological links with certain temples, new ones were not being built. This was now a shrinking political sphere.

As the Caulukyas and Vāghelās lost influence over many parts of Gujarat, other chieftains, some of whom were later assimilated into emerging Rajput status hierarchies, consolidated their hold over their territories. However, most of them did not go in for temple building on a grand scale. What epigraphs we have from regions of withdrawing Caulukya control do not show clear signs of brahmanism either—they are mostly hero-stones written in local dialect. Nevertheless the vast majority of the Sanskritic grant-recording epigraphs of the thirteenth century continued to invoke the distant Caulukya/Vāghelā overlords in Anhilvada although their actual authority was now only in name.

By the end of the thirteenth century, no new royal temples had been built for a century or more. The new Rajputizing pastoralist chieftains had not yet fully adopted the early medieval logic of deriving legitimacy from brahmins and large temples. Thus, when the Turkic invasion, backed by carefully targeted attacks on royal temple establishments, led to the setting up of sultanate political control by about 1310, the link between royalty and the royal temple was swept away. There was, correspondingly, an abrupt cessation of the Caulukya model of grant-making epigraphs in Sanskrit. Although imitative Śaivism of the Caulukya kind was gradually adopted by the smaller Rajput courts, it was in a rudimentary form. We have little evidence, for example, that there were elaborate courtly rituals at the Cūḍasamā court prior to the mid-fifteenth century.

URBAN SETTLEMENT IN THE HINTERLAND

ḥmūd Bīgara conducted some of the most spectacular building and settlement activities in Gujarat. In 1470, after the capture of the fort of Junagadh, he founded the city of Mustafabad at the foot of the hill.

After this [victory], the Sultan summoned from the cities and towns of Gujarat, ḥammad, and officers to enforce the laws of Islam, and settled them in Junagadh and in the towns around it, and he himself remained there, and began to populate the town, and to repair the fort-walls of Jahān-panāh, and built lofty palaces, and ordered his amirs to each of them build himself a residence.[61]

Soon after this, Maḥmūd, reaching a spot on the banks of the Vatrak where highway robberies often took place, ordered the construction of another city on that spot which was named Mahmudabad, the present suburb of Mehmedabad to the south-east of Ahmadabad. A stone embankment was built on the river and 'lofty palaces' were erected there. After the conquest of Champaner in 1483–4, he built what became his capital for the rest of his reign. Champaner was on a plain rich in wheat, barley, millet, rice, gram, chickpeas, lentils, and other pulses. People reared sheep and goats and it had an abundance of fruit:

The climate of Champaner was very pleasing to the Sultan, and he made it his capital, and built there a large city which was named Muhammadabad, and a lofty mosque was constructed, and the Sultan also erected a fort around Champaner and called it Jahān-panāh, and the *amīrs*, *vazīrs*, merchants and petty traders [*saudagār wa baqqāl*], each one, built for himself lofty dwellings.[62]

Thus, provision was made for the sultan's entire entourage, including his merchants and financiers.

The rapid and large-scale construction carried out across the span of their territories on the orders of the sultans had the additional purpose of stimulating settlement. Settling is a common theme in the chronicles. It connotes clearing land for cultivation, building towns, mosques, and gardens, patronizing religious figures, and cultivating a sedentary, prosperous, civic ambience. From the description of Champaner it is evident that merchants and traders were encouraged to settle within the central citadel. The presence of the court would further attract the entire network of production and supply, which customarily followed the court around, to settle and populate that location. While an entourage of traders, financiers, and suppliers customarily accompanied the sultans even to temporary encampments, the actual construction of a citadel provided the security necessary for them to put down roots, cultivate the surrounding territory, engage in production, and activate trade routes.

Similarly, the sultans encouraged prominent courtiers and religious figures to establish suburbs around Ahmadabad, many of which were named after them. These included Daryā Khān who established the suburb of Daryapur to the north of the citadel; Shaykh Raḥmat All h who settled Shaykhpura;[63] Khudāvand Khān ʿĀlim who built the southern suburb of Alimpur, ʿImād al-Mulk Asās of Asaspur, Tāj Khān r of Tajpur, Qiwām al-Mulk Sārang of Sarangpur; and Hājī Kālū of Kalupur—all of whom 'beautified their lands with gardens and lofty mosques'.[64] Courtiers were usually granted *jāgīr*s or land rights in perpetuity, which would encourage them to invest in the long-term prosperity of the region. This was unlike the usual Delhi sultanate practice of granting iqṭāʿs as transferable administrative assignments liable to resumption at any time. In the mid-fifteenth century, Malik Abd al-Laṭif Maḥmūd Dāwar al-Mulk was assigned a jāgīr near Morvi, which became proverbially prosperous. The Malik, in addition, acquired a reputation as a healer, and after he was killed by a local chieftain his tomb became a major place of pilgrimage.[65] Malik Ayāz was granted the territory of Diu and was largely responsible for making it an important port and naval centre, which eventually supplanted Cambay by the end of the fifteenth century.[66]

The basic architectural patterns of the oldest parts of the towns of Gujarat, including their road systems and neighbourhoods, did not change much as a result of political fortunes, the influx of migrants, or changes of rulers. In an important study of settlement patterns in Gujarat, V.S. Pramar found that the 'wards' in the older parts of Ahmadabad and Baroda had been intact for the last 250 years, that is, since about 1750, and that their foundations dated back to the fifteenth century. The fortified citadel was built for the use of the ruler or administrator and attendants. In Ahmadabad and Patan the central and most prized parts of the town had been consistently occupied by Hindu and Jain merchants. In Radhanpur and Palanpur, ruled by Muslim nawabs, 'the Hindu areas begin virtually at the citadels ... and stretch into the central parts of the town.'[67] A similar scenario was observed in Surat, Baroda, Kapadvanj, and Cambay.

> The presence of entrenched Hindu and Jain merchants in central areas even under Muslim rule would clearly indicate that the former were not merely tolerated but were encouraged to settle, or remain settled, in areas most valuable for commercial purposes and most secure from plunder. The reason is obvious: these merchants were an important source of revenue.[68]

Pramar found that Hindu citadels, such as those in Saurashtra, were invariably located in the centre of the town, which gave them added security from invasion. Muslim citadels, like those in Ahmadabad, Baroda, Surat, Radhanpur, and Palanpur, were usually to be found on the peripheries of the town. The problem of security was solved by placing the citadel next to a water body: a river in Ahmadabad, the sea at Cambay, or next to artificial lakes as at Baroda and Radhanpur. In some cases, moats were dug to ensure security, as around the fort of Morasa.[69] The outer fortification was the city wall enclosing the entire civic population, as at Ahmadabad and Baroda. This again was to defend the large commercial civilian population.[70]

As the city wall imposed limitations on horizontal expansion, there was no option but to grow vertically. Thus, multi-storey buildings were constructed, which required complex structural solutions. In Gujarat timber framing was used with brick walls, 'in such a manner that the woodwork held the walls together as a kind of horizontal and vertical bracing'.[71] Although Gujarat was a region notably lacking in good structural timber, superior teak was imported by sea for the purpose. Thus, several aspects of the profile of urban Gujarat, 'namely a high level of urbanization, numerous fortified towns, and a multi-storied architecture in wood, ... are directly related to the trade and commerce for which Gujarat was famous'.[72] The *Mir'āt-i Aḥmadī* bears out the fact that teak was used for the ceilings and pillars of houses. Important buildings were then covered with lime, quarried from near Idar. Lime was used 'in stucco work; for the walls or terraces of buildings; and for fine edifices, pleasurehouses and mausoleums. ... The mausoleums of the Mohammedan saints, the temples of the Hindus, and other public works... are erected with this lime; as are also numerous canals, water reservoirs, wells and other like buildings.'[73]

Such buildings were already common in fourteenth-century Cambay, where Baṭṭūṭa was struck by the 'fine mansions and magnificent buildings', and the 'excellence of its construction and the architecture', and ascribed it to the settling of foreign merchants. 'Among the grand buildings of the city is the house of Sharīf as-Sāmirī... I have never seen stronger pieces of timber than those used in this house. Its gate is like the gate of a town, and adjacent to the house is a large mosque which is named after as-Sāmirī.'[74] Varthema (1508) found Cambay a walled town and Barbosa a few years later found 'many fair houses, very lofty, with windows and roofed with tiles in our manner, well laid out with streets and fine open places, and great buildings of stone and mortar'.[75]

On Ahmadabad, Barbosa said:

> In the inland country going forward from this city of Champanel there is another much greater than it, called Andava [Ahmadabad], in which the kings

of this kingdom held their courts of old, inasmuch as it is very rich. Both of these towns are girt with strong walls and have fine stone and mortar houses roofed in our fashion. They have large courtyards in which there are tanks and wells of sweet water. ... In this city and in many other inland towns the King of Cambaya keeps his Governors and Collectors of Revenue.[76]

Significantly, the Gujarat towns had few buildings designed for commercial use. There are hardly any remains of markets, warehouses, courts, or other institutional buildings. There were caste buildings and occasionally *sarā'īs*, or resting-houses for travellers. In the texts as well, there are descriptions of city walls, forts, palaces, colleges for scholars, 'īs for travellers, and substantial residences for amīrs and merchants, but hardly any mentions of shops or civic buildings. As commerce was heavily dependent upon the personal patronage of the rulers and their courtiers who were very mobile, traders often travelled with them. Transactions were usually carried out in domestic spaces: traders carried their wares to the residences of their patrons. Most large houses had *ānkhānu*s or audience halls for audiences and other public activities. As civic disturbances were common, it was risky to display costly wares in the open market: the death of a ruler or a courtier's fall from favour could lead to looting and plunder by local mobs.[77] Public markets were usually temporary structures where merchants and hawkers set up stalls that could be quickly taken down.

One history of the Kaṇbīs says that they began to come to the city to engage in trade and to take up jobs after the establishment of Ahmadabad in 1413.[78] Large groups of Kaṇbīs settled in Unjha, Adalaj, Asarva, Idar, and Champaner. Those who lived in Champaner were skilled in silk and gold weaving, and dyeing, and were traders. After the fall of Champaner to Maḥmūd Bīgara, they also moved to Vadodara, Bharuch, Surat, and Valsad.

At the end of the fourteenth century, Adalaj, now a northern suburb of Ahmadabad, was an important town for some of the Sind and Kachchh trade. Most goods passed through Adalaj on their way to Cambay. Various groups from north Gujarat including Śrīmālī brahmins, traders such as the Moḍh vāṇiās, Kaṇbīs from the Patan region, artisans, and pastoralists had settled there. The Moḍh vāṇiās were from Modhera, but migrated to Adalaj and Ghogha near Cambay at the time of 'Alā' al-Dīn's invasion.[79]

In the fourteenth century, Adalaj was ruled by the Vāghelās, descendants of the erstwhile rulers, and was very prosperous, with reportedly 700 places for selling ghee and about 2,000 pack bullocks. It was a collecting point on the way to the port of Cambay. The pastoralists brought grain, cloth, leather, opium, and dry fruit from north India with their cattle and camels. A legend from the *Kaumārikā-khaṇḍa*, a part of the Māheśvara-khaṇḍa of the *Skanda Purāṇa*, has a legend that refers to the annual migration of pastoralist groups from Saurashtra and Kachchh.[80] The Moḍh vāṇiās who were middlemen and brokers, collected the goods and sent them on to Cambay. Bhāṭs, Cāraṇs, and

roṭs would go along with the caravans to safeguard them. The Kaṇbīs of the region, also known as Pāṭīdārs or Paṭels, farmed their lands in the monsoon and in the winter and summer took cartloads to Cambay. Barbosa also reported that there were men 'of low degree who act as messengers and go safely everywhere without molestation from any, even during war or from highwaymen; these men they call *Pateles*.'[81] When Cambay began to silt up, from the early fifteenth century onwards, Adalaj also began to decline and was replaced by the newly established Ahmadabad.

CAMBAY AND THE COAST

Ibn Baṭṭūṭa who visited Cambay in the fourteenth century found it a place of architectural glory where foreign merchants vied with each other to build beautiful mosques and mansions. He also visited Gandhar, Kavi, Piram, and Ghogha, where Muslims were settled. A fort was built in Cambay by the king for protection against the pirates of Kish, although in the fourteenth century Ibn Baṭṭūṭa reported that the city had no wall around it.[82] It had a cosmopolitan population. A Genoese merchant found 'Moorish merchants of Alexandria and Damascus' in Cambay at the end of the fifteenth century.[83] In the early sixteenth century Barbosa remarked of Cambay: '... in the city dwell substantial merchants and men of great fortune, both Moors and Heathen. There are also many craftsmen of mechanic trades in cunning work of many kinds, as in Flanders; and everything good cheap.'[84]

Cambay was the outlet for the trade from Patan and, by the fourteenth century, was the most important port in Gujarat. It was generally regarded as a safe harbour for merchants, although the seas around it were hazardous due to pirates and difficult sailing conditions. According to Marco Polo, Cambay was safe but the Arabian Sea was overrun by Kachchh and Somanath pirates. The India trade was harassed by Jats, Meds, Rajputs, Bāriās, and Kurks as far as Socotra. Afanasio Nikitin found that: 'The sea is infested with pirates, all of whom are Kofars, neither Christians nor Mussulmans; they pray to stone idols and know not Christ.'[85]

Indian merchants did little to protect themselves from the notorious pirates of the coast. Unlike Chinese and Arab ships, Indian traders did not travel in convoys and references to armaments aboard ship are few.[86] This apparent invulnerability to the pirates leads to the suspicion that the arrangement with them must have been monetary. Merchants certainly had links with pirates. A story of the thirteenth-century merchant Jagaḍū, in a text by a sixteenth-century Jain author ubhaśīlagaṇi, relates that coastal pirates once offered him a shipload of beeswax that had fallen into their hands. All the wax bricks were found to contain gold and thus Jagaḍū became richer by a further ten million *ṭankās*.[87] On land, forest communities were at times induced to police lonely routes, or were prevented from plundering by permitting them to levy tolls for passing through their territories.[88] It is not unlikely that pirates had similar arrangements with merchants on shore in order to restrict the activities of outsiders.

The colonies of foreign merchants in Cambay administered their own affairs and dealt with representatives of the hinterland government, usually a Jain merchant or one of the settlers. In the late fifteenth century Hieronimo di Santo Stefano remarked that the chief of Cambay 'is a Mahometan, and a great lord'.[89] The foreign merchants adapted to indigenous ways. A thirteenth-century bilingual inscription (in Sanskrit and Arabic) from Somanath demonstrates the close dealings that a trader-captain from Hormuz, Nākhuda Nūr al-Dīn Fīrūz, had with the local notables. The mosque that he endowed would be maintained by local Muslim communities, which included sailors, captains, oil-pressers, and lime-workers or masons.[90] By this time, evidently, Muslims numbered not just immigrant or itinerant merchants, but indigenous groups who, as in the case of the *ghāñcika*s or oil-pressers, even had their own *khāṭib* or leader of prayers. This is very significant, as it shows the earliest communities that must have converted to Islam in the region. The conversion to Islam of many of the coastal fishing and shipbuilding communities of Gujarat could date to this period. By the thirteenth century Muslim traders were settling and trading even in the hinterland as graves in Junagadh and Anhilvada show.[91] Jagaḍū Śāh of Bhadreshvar certainly had dealings with settler merchants, to the extent of making a donation towards a mosque for the local Ismā'īlī

Cambay was the place from where people embarked on the pilgrimage to Mecca in the fourteenth century. The *Kīrtikaumudī* mentions that the Delhi sultan's mother or, alternatively, his religious adviser, sailed out from Cambay. The minister Vastupāla ordered his men to plunder the vessel, and then had the men arrested and the property restored. The grateful travellers arranged for a friendly treaty between the Vāghelā king and the sultan.[92]

By the middle of the fourteenth century when Baṭṭūṭa visited it, Cambay was already subject to the difficulties of siltation and the uncertainties of the bore in the Gulf. Only small boats could come in at low tide. However, it remained important until the end of the fifteenth century.

INTERDEPENDENCE OF MERCHANTS AND THE STATE

The attractions of the prosperity of Gujarat were considerable. A Jain text tells of the migration of 18,000 people into Gujarat from the town of Śrīmāla in 953 CE. The *Śrīmāla Purāṇa* mentions that *śrī* or prosperity left Śrīmāla for Anhilvada in 1146.[93] Major merchants operated through far-flung networks. Apart from extensive settlements overseas, they had contacts in many parts of the Indian subcontinent. The merchant who persuaded Alp Khān to permit the renovation of the Shatrunjaya Jain temples in 1315, Samrā Śāh, had a brother in Deogir. Other important merchants were settled in Cambay, such as Jesal of the Ukeśavaṃśa who built the Stambhana-Pārśvanātha temple there in 1309–10.

The trade of Cambay had been strongly connected with the prosperity of the Caulukya kingdom. By the time of Bhīmadeva I, the Caulukyas had achieved control of the trade route between Patan and Cambay.

madeva's successor Karṇa had to send a force against the Kolīs of Asaval who menaced the trade route. He then built Karṇāvatī, a new town on the site of Asaval.[94] Evidently, the trade route was vital to the survival of Caulukya power. By the twelfth century Patan had become a large town. The *Kumārapālacarita* says that it had a population of 500,000, and there were eighty-four marts; export-import duties were 100,000 ṭankās a day.[95]

It was crucial for the governors to safeguard merchants and trade routes. 'Alā' al-Dīn's first governor Alp Khān actively conciliated the prosperous Jain merchant community by permitting Samrā Śāh to reconstruct a temple destroyed in the invasion and even contributing towards the renovation.[96] Another merchant Śāh Jesal was mitted to build a temple and hospital at Cambay in 1309–10.[97] Gravestones of Muslim merchants in Cambay attest to the benevolent rule of Alp n.[98] Meanwhile, Afghan, Turkic, and north Indian adventurers moved into strategic locations in Gujarat and established ties with the prosperous Arab and Persian Gulf merchants who lived and traded in Cambay. Others formed links with local chieftains or merchants—the allies of the amīrs of Baroda in the first challenge to Aḥmad Shāh included the merchants Jīvandās and Prayāgdās Khatrī.[99] The Delhi governors incorporated prominent merchants into the administrative structure or granted them honorific titles. Three inscriptions in Cambay provide information on the merchant Ẓakī al-Daulat wa'l-Dīn 'Umar ḥmad, entitled Malik Parvīz al-Kāzarūnī, who was granted the iqṭā' of Cambay and the title 'Prince among Princes of the East and the Ministers, Prince among Princes of the Merchants' by Muḥammad bin Tughluq.[100] Another Cambay merchant, Najm al-Dīn of Jilan, was appointed commandant of the city by Muḥammad bin Tughluq.[101]

At the beginning of the fourteenth century, Patan (Anhilvada in the Gujarati records and Nahrwāla in the Persian ones) was one of the most prominent manufacturing centres in Gujarat and, by extension, the most prominent seaport in north-west India and Cambay. In fact, the whole of Gujarat was customarily known to foreign visitors and traders as Cambay. Control of the Patan–Cambay belt thus ensured its rulers a share in the proceeds of arguably the most prosperous zone of trade and manufacture in the lands bounding the Arabian Sea. In addition, rulers in this region were assured access to a variety of goods and resources that would be hard to find in other regions. Merchants were eager to deal with local lords and potentates and networks, for the passage of goods and information was well organized and had been so at least since the rule of the Caulukyas. In general, it was in everyone's interest to preserve a state of peace and order for the successful continuance of trade. Of course, there were regular disruptions to peace in the form of invasions and local armed struggles, but these were usually succeeded by a rapid resumption of normal trade. In many cases 'normal trade' continued even alongside political upheaval.

A remarkable feature of the region and period was the stability of the currency, regardless of political circumstances. In the twelfth and thirteenth centuries, Caulukya silver alloy coins—*poruṭṭha drammas* or later *vīsalaprīya* and *bhīmaprīya* drammas—were struck at the Śrīmāla mint in southern Rajasthan.[102] These have been identified with the *gadhaiya* currency found in large quantities in central and western India.

They had a wide circulation in Malwa, Konkan, Sind, Rajasthan, Maharashtra, and even Afghanistan, suggesting that hinterland produce was completely dependent upon the Gujarat trade.[103] From 1064 to 1241 the Caulukya coins had a stable precious metal content. From the mid-thirteenth century, with much of Gujarat's commercial hinterland, that is, Sind and Rajasthan, passing into Turkic hands, there was chronic debasement of the currency, which could have been related to silver shortage due to the cutting off of silver supply from the north-west, inflation, or loss of trade revenues. From the time of Vīsaladeva ghelā, coins were increasingly devalued by reducing the silver content, and in this debased form the circulation of the gadhaiya shrank to the modern Kheda district and parts of the eastern Gujarat hinterland. It is suggested, therefore, that the later Vāghelās' 'economic horizons' became severely limited.

> It cannot be a coincidence that kingdoms that were most successful in maintaining the net precious metal content of their coins, were the most closely involved in trade. ... Such universal acceptability [of the *gadhaiya*] was conditional upon the preservation of the silver standard, and in fact for the better part of two centuries the net silver content of the *gadhaiya* was static. ... When stable billon coinage accepted in international trade began to slip in its actual or intrinsic value, its area of circulation contracted.[104]

After the Turkic invasion of Gujarat, the Delhi currency, the silver ankā, was immediately introduced, although it is likely that Śrīmāla continued to be an important mint. The mint master of the Delhi sultans (in 1318) was Ṭhakkura Pheru, a Jain of the Śrīmāla clan.[105] The movement outwards of Gujarati money was balanced by the import of foreign specie and bullion into Gujarat in the form of payment, which enabled the region to maintain a healthy currency. While the state could influence currency circulation in the administration and the military, non-governmental financial institutions, bankers, and bullion dealers were a necessary part of the financial system. In Gujarat, such activities were dominated by the Jains. The Delhi ṭankā was replaced by the local Gujarat coinage, the *maḥmūdī*, which again became one of the most stable and widely accepted currencies from the late fifteenth century onwards.

Links between the merchant magnates and inland political authority continued to grow through the fourteenth century. The sultans of Gujarat, and the Delhi sultans before them, invested in boats and possessed, by the late fifteenth century, some of the largest vessels then plying in the

Arabian Sea. They also safeguarded the sea trade: Muḥammad bin Tughluq fought a celebrated battle against Mokhḍājī Gohil, a chieftain who had snatched control of the strategic island of Piram at the mouth of the Gulf of Cambay, from where he harried and taxed shipping.[106] There is evidence that Muḥammad requisitioned boats for the invasion of Sind in 1350–1.[107] He came rushing to Gujarat and spent his last years and resources there because it was necessary to safeguard Gujarat and its trade from the local warlords and pirates. By 1361, his successor z was back in Gujarat and Kachchh to protect the local trade routes from the rebellious amīrs and Cambay from the pirates.

Prior to the arrival in Gujarat of Ẓafar Khān, the last governor sent out by the Delhi sultans, the previous governor had been based in Cambay and seemed to have fully exploited the commercial vitality of the port to his own advantage. An inscription of 1361 relates that Mufarriḥ Sulṭānī was deputy muqṭa' (right-holder) of the city of Khambhāt.[108] At this time, Shams al-Dīn Damaghāni was the *nā'ib* or governor of the province, appointed over the objections of the powerful Afghan landholders of Gujarat, the amīran-i ṣadah. After Damaghāni was killed by the disgruntled Afghan warlords, Mufarriḥ Sulṭānī, now entitled Farḥat al-Mulk, was appointed nā'ib in his stead. By 1380 Farḥat al-Mulk was being referred to as the muqṭa' of the iqṭā' of Khambhāt (Cambay) and the *ra'īs al-mamālik* (chief of the kingdom).[109] Until the advent of Ẓafar Khān in 1391, Mufarriḥ Sulṭānī had a span of thirty years in which to consolidate his local ties in and around Cambay and evidently enjoyed the support of the *ṣadah amīrs*.[110]

It is hardly true that the sultans were indifferent to the encouragement of trade and manufacture, or that they did nothing to promote it.[111] It was through the fifteenth century that large parts of Gujarat were cleared, settled, and urbanized, and a new set of relationships of patronage set up between merchants and the new elite. The polity presided over by the sultans proved to be the one of the greatest spurs to the local and international trade of Gujarat.

It was in the interest of the sultans not to antagonize the merchants and vice versa. Throughout this period, merchants as well as the cultivating and manufacturing classes rearranged themselves around the new set of patrons. Even pirates and robber bands accommodated themselves to the new networks. Merchants also needed to maintain good links with the sultans and their courtiers, who were vital patrons for their products and consumed quantities of luxury goods. On the eve of a decisive battle for the fort of Junagadh, Maḥ ūd Bī distributed among his soldiers 'fifty millions of ready money in gold', gold-handled Egyptian, Yemeni, Maghrebi, Khurasani, and Dailamani swords, Ahmadabad swords with silver hilts, daggers, and Arabian and Turkish horses with golden trappings. He also permitted his soldiers to ravage the 'country of Sorath' as a result of which 'countless plunder fell into their hands'.[112] Merchant princes in the fourteenth and fifteenth centuries seemed also to be able to bankroll the activities of warlords and chieftains. Similarly, traders were heavily dependent upon the patronage of courtiers and rulers, and could expect major profits.

> As the giving of presents has become an unfailing practice with the people (foreign visitors, travellers, officials), the merchants in Sind and Hind advance a loan of thousands of dinars to every new-comer intending to visit the Sultan; and they provide him with all that he needs for the purpose of presents to the king or for his personal use in the form of riding animals, camels and goods. They even render monetary and personal services to such persons and wait on them like attendants. When these persons reach the Sultan, he gives them magnificent gifts with which they pay off their debts and honour pledges. So the trade of the merchants thrives and they make enormous profits.[113]

While the aforementioned example was based on north Indian practice, it is likely that similar conventions obtained in Gujarat. The northern trade, especially the militarily vital trade in horses was very important to the sultans. When a party of merchants with four hundred Iraqi and Turkish horses were seized by the raja of Sirohi, Maḥmūd gara compensated them for their loss from the imperial treasury.[114]

Lands were cleared and grants made under the sultans to ensure agricultural production, particularly of cash crops. Many communities, including artisans and itinerant or carrier communities, engaged in agriculture for part of the year. For example, the Kaṇbīs of the region of Adalaj are reported to have cultivated one crop in the monsoon and spent the rest of the year carrying goods brought to Adalaj by western pastoralists to the great port of Cambay.[115] Cultivation in Gujarat, except perhaps for subsistence food products, consisted largely of cash crops, especially cotton and indigo.

Technologically proficient groups, such as weavers, dyers, printers, and leather-workers were given incentives to migrate to areas where they could be assured of work security. Thus, providing secure urban environments for the perusal of trade and manufacture was one of the most important priorities for any local authority, and the sultans were no exception. They depended crucially on the smooth continuance of trade and, in fact, most of their campaigns were not intended to disrupt local trade but to safeguard and fully exploit it.

The sultans invested in safeguarding of the coastal trade. Nicolò Conti, who visited Cambay in Aḥmad Shāh's reign, said that Cambay shared in equipping the fleet of the Gujarat kingdom and that Aḥmad h used his fleet against the Bahmanis.[116] He sent seventeen vessels to recover the island of Bombay and Salsette that had been seized by the Bahmani kingdom in 1429. Later, Maḥmūd Bīgara conducted several naval campaigns. In 1508, he defeated the Portuguese at Chaul. Nikitin (1468–74) said that the sea was infested with pirates, but the rulers of Gujarat paid attention to naval matters and kept the navigation channels into Cambay clear of silt, at a high cost. The sultan of Gujarat was called the 'Lord of the Sea' and had an efficient navy. The Sangars of Kachchh and Navanagar were known for their skill in ship-building during the sultanate.[117] Maḥmūd was able to call up boats from his ports for an expedition against the pirates of the Dvaraka region and made them 'chase and capture the vessels of the enemy'.[118] Soon after, he sent out vessels to punish Malabar pirates who had been harassing the ports of Gujarat.[119] He was thus able to secure boats even away from the areas of direct influence. Incidentally, Rā Māṇḍalik of Junagadh also made a sea expedition and was obviously able to call up some naval power when he needed to.

The interest in naval power increased over time. In 1490 Bahādur ānī from the Deccan, 'having collected many ships was committing piracies on the Gujarat coast and ... fear of his depredations had paralyzed the trade of the ports of Gujarat'.[120] The sultan sent a land expedition as well as 'three hundred boats with well-armed men furnished with both cannons and muskets' against him. In 1507–8 there was the famous naval battle in which the flotilla commanded by Malik Ayāz, assisted by boats sent by the last Mamlūk sultan of Egypt and the Ottoman governor of Bahrayn, defeated the Portuguese—their only defeat on Indian waters. The Gujarat kingdom under Bīgara eventually had under its control eighty-four ports. When Humayun secured Bahādur Shāh's jewelled belt in 1535, he declared: 'These are the trappings of the Lord of the Sea.'[121]

By the second half of the fifteenth century Cambay was silting up at the head of the gulf. The harbour had already ceased to be serviceable for large ships. Although Bīgara kept navigation open, it was running into difficulties. In the first years of the sixteenth century Diu was becoming the great port of Gujarat.[122]

NOTES

1. Jain, *Trade and Traders*, p. 137.
2. '... normally, rulers did not care what merchants did... it is the lack of political connections between ruler and merchant in Gujarati society which is crucial.' Pearson, *Merchants and Rulers*, p. 2.
3. Sikandar, *MS*, p. 126.
4. Several castes in Gujarat, including brahmins and traders, as well as occupational groups such as coppersmiths, barbers, and wrestlers, have their own Purāṇas. See, for example, B.J. Sandesara and P.N. Mehta, eds (1964), *Mallapurāṇam: A Rare Sanskrit Text on Indian Wrestling Especially as Practised by the Jyeṣṭhimallas*.
5. Gokaḷdās Somābhāi Paṭel and Aśokbhāi Gokaḷdās Paṭel (1986), *History of the Pāṭīdārs of Gujarat*, p. 21.
6. Gaṅgādhara (1973), *Gaṅgadāsa-pratāpavilāsa-nāṭakam*, pp. 17–18. The writer (c. 1450) mentions that he visited the court of the sultan (Muḥammad) at Ahmadabad and silenced all the scholars there. Maḥmūd Bīgara (r. 1458–1511) also had a Sanskrit eulogy, the *Rājavinoda*, composed by a brahmin poet, Udayarāja. Udayarāja (1956), *Rājavinodamahākāvyam or Mahmūda-suratrāṇa-carita*.
7. Someśvaradeva (1883), *Kīrtikaumudī: A Life of Vastupāla, a Minister of Lavaṇaprasāda and Vīradhavala Vāghelā*, pp. xviii-xx; B.J. Sandesara (1953), *Literary Circle of Mahāmātya Vastupāla and its Contribution to Sanskrit Literature*, p. 11.
8. See Simon Digby (1986), 'The Sufi Shaikh as a Source of Authority in Mediaeval India', *Puruṣārtha*, 9, pp. 57–77.
9. Sacedīnā Nāñjīyāṇī (1892), *Khojā vṛattānt* [*Account of the Khojas*], pp. 216–8.
10. Jain, *Trade and Traders*, p. 109.
11. Forbes, *Ras Mala*, Vol. 1, pp. 285–90.
12. Ibid., pp. 295–309.
13. Ibid., pp. 307–9.
14. Majumdar, *Chaulukyas of Gujarat*, p. 180.
15. 'Kolī' was a catch-all term for the mountain and forest chieftains of eastern Gujarat who were encountered by settlers and merchants in the region. Some of them intermarried with incoming clans, and later claimed 'degraded' Rajput status. Campbell, *Gazetteer*, p. 206.
16. On the stability of the Gujarat currency, see Deyell, *Living without Silver*, pp. 120–5, 240.
17. Misra, *Rise of Muslim Power*, p. 66.
18. During the late Vāghelā period the scope of the Gujarat currency and, by implication, Vāghelā political control, were constricted. Deyell, *Living without Silver*, p. 230.
19. Kolff, *Naukar, Rajput and Sepoy*, pp. 71–85.

20. Forbes, *Ras Mala*, Vol. 1, p. 354.
21. Jain, *Trade and Traders*, pp. 45, 48, citing the *Vastupālacarita* of Jinaharṣa.
Ḍiya al-Dīn Baranī (1860–62), *Ta'rīkh-i Fīrūz Shāhī*, pp. 396–402.
23. Enthoven and Edwardes, *Imperial Gazetteer*, p. 211.
24. Ibn Baṭṭūṭa, *Riḥla*, p. 68.
Ibid., p. 113.
26. The Afghan chiefs may be identical with or part of the *amīrān-i ṣadah*, a term used by Baranī and the later Tughluqid writers, but not used by earlier writers. Misra, *Rise of Muslim Power*, p. 98.
27. Ibn Baṭṭūṭa, *Riḥla*, p. 114.
28. Misra, *Rise of Muslim Power*, p. 111.
29. See Digby, 'Muḥammad bin Tughluq's Last Years', pp. 79–88.
30. Majumdar, *Chaulukyas of Gujarat*, pp. 256–9. In the thirteenth century agriculture seems to have been largely geared towards the production of goods for trade, and apart from certain foodstuffs, taxes and revenues were collected largely in cash (p. 253). While rice, wheat, and pulses were produced for subsistence, sugarcane, indigo, and cotton were the cash crops that played a vital economic role for Gujarat. Milk products such as ghee were also an important item of trade.
31. Firishta, *History of the Rise of Mahomedan Power*, Vol. 4, p. 2.
'Abd al-Ḥusayn Tūnī (1988), *TMS*, p. 6; Sikandar, *MS*, p. 17.
33. Sikandar, *MS*, pp. 23–24.
34. Forbes, *Ras Mala*, Vol. 1, pp. 230–45.
35. Sikandar, *MS*, p. 23.
36. Z.A. Desai (1982), *Persian and Arabic Epigraphy of Gujarat* (hereafter *PAEG*), p. 18.
37. V.A. Janaki (1980), *The Commerce of Cambay from the Earliest Period to the Nineteenth Century*, p. 20.
38. Sikandar, *MS*, p. 21.
39. For more discussion of land tenure, see Chapter 5.
40. Paṭel, *Vaḍnagarā kaṇbīni utpatti*, p. 22. The Mehwāsīs, or inhabitants of the Mahi river valley had the reputation of resisting central authority.
41. James Burgess (1900), *Muhammadan Architecture of Ahmadabad*, Vol. 1; Desai, *PAEG*, p. 21; Desai, *Arabic, Persian and Urdu Inscriptions*, No. 14; Ch. Mohammad Ismail and Munshi Fazil (1921–2), 'Two inscriptions from the Rauẓa of Malik Sha'bān in Rakhyāl near Ahmadabād', *Epigraphia Indo-Moslemica* (hereafter *EIM*), pp. 2–5.
42. Richard M. Eaton (2000), 'Temple Desecration and Indo-Muslim States', in *Essays on Islam and Indian History*, pp. 117–22.
43. Desai, *Arabic, Persian and Urdu Inscriptions*, No. 680.
44. There are some traces of sultanate domestic architecture in Champaner and Ahmadabád, as also garden pavilions and fountains, but these have not been studied systematically. See R.N. Mehta, *Cāmpāner* (1979). See

also section on 'Urban Settlement in the Hinterland' later in this chapter.

45. Desai, *Arabic, Persian and Urdu Inscriptions*, No. 1436; Mehta, *Cāmpāner*, p. xi.
46. Desai, *Arabic, Persian, and Urdu Inscriptions*, No. 1234.
47. There are often genealogies or praises of the king in the inscriptions installed by subordinates. The Thepavāpī step-well inscription of 1328 has a genealogy of the Cūḍāsamās as well as that of the builders, the Mehars or Mers of Talaja. Diskalkar, *IK*, No. 27.
48. The inscriptions in Aḥmad Shāh's mosques in Ahmadabad assign their construction to the king. Desai, *Arabic, Persian and Urdu Inscriptions*, Nos 6,8. However, many mosque inscriptions merely mention the name of the ruler.
49. On re-use of temple materials, see Alka Patel (2004), 'Architectural Histories Entwined: The Rudra-Mahalaya Congregational Mosque of Siddhpur, Gujarat', *The Journal of the Society of Architectural Historians* (63:2).
50. Ibid., No. 281, G.S. Gai, ed. (1990), *ARIE for 1974–75*, App. D, No. 13; M. Nazim (1933–4), 'Inscriptions from the Bombay Presidency,' *EIM*, Supplement, p. 36, XXIa.
51. The Sanskrit text is discussed in E. Hultszch (1882), 'A Grant of Arjunadeva of Gujarat, Dated 1264 AD', *IA* 11, p. 242f; Sircar, *Select Inscriptions*, Vol. 2, pp. 402–8; D.C. Sircar (1961–2), 'Veraval Inscription of Chalukya Vaghela Arjuna, 1264 AD', *Epigraphia Indica* [henceforth *EI*], 34(3), p. 141ff; Thapar, *Somanatha*, pp. 88–102. The shorter Arabic text is in Z.A. Desai (1961), 'Arabic Inscriptions of the Rajput Period from Gujarat', *Epigraphia Indica, Arabic and Persian Supplement*, pp. 12–14, IIb.

EIM (1915–16), pp. 17–18, No. XIVb; Desai, *Arabic, Persian and Urdu Inscriptions*, No. 1867; P.R. Srinivasan, ed. (1986) *ARIE for 1975–76*, App. D, 114.

ARIE (1961–2), App. C, No. 131, *ARIE* (1963–4), App. D, No. 85, Desai (1982), *PAEG*, p. 16; Desai, *Arabic, Persian and Urdu Inscriptions*, No. 2105; G. Yazdani and R. Gyani (1944), *Important Inscriptions from the Baroda State*, Vol. 2, pp. 1–2. The verse 2:181 from the Qur'ān goes thus: 'If anyone changes the bequest after hearing it, the guilt shall be on those who make the change. For Allah hears and knows [all things].' For a revised reading of the Persian text, see Z.A. Desai (1956), 'On Karakhdi Bilingual Inscription of 1340', *Journal of the Baroda Museum and Picture Gallery*, 12; Z.A. Desai (1985), *Corpus of Persian and Arabic Inscriptions in the Museums of Gujarat*, pp. 4–6.

54. Desai, *Arabic, Persian and Urdu Inscriptions*, No. 17.
55. Jutta Jain-Neubauer (1981), *The Stepwells of Gujarat in Art Historical Perspective*, p.xv.
56. It should be borne in mind that there are many buildings in existence, especially temples, that have no epigraphs attached to them. These have

not been included in the list. Correspondingly, there are epigraphs that mention buildings no longer in existence, which have been included, on the assumption that those buildings did exist once. The list also includes records of renovations. There are fewer epigraphs from the thirteenth century than subsequent ones, partly because of its greater antiquity and partly because Khaljī iconoclasm may have caused evidence to be scattered. It is also necessary to take into account a diversity of recording traditions—the Jains, for example, recorded virtually every renovation and donation to temples and images, which is not usually the case in Hindu temples.

57. M.A. Chaghatai (1942), *Muslim Monuments of Ahmadabad through their Inscriptions*, p. 5.
58. B.D. Chattopadhyaya (1993), 'Historiography, History and Religious Centers: Early Medieval North India, circa AD 700–1200', in Vishakha N. Desai and Darielle Mason, eds, *Gods, Guardians and Lovers: Temple Sculptures from North India, AD 700–1200*, p. 40. For Caulukya temples, see H. Cousens (1931), *Somanātha and other Mediaeval Temples in Kāṭhiawād*; M.A. Dhaky (1961), 'The Chronology of the Solaṅkī Temples of Gujarat', *Journal of the Madhya Pradesh Itihas Parishad*, 3, p. 45–8. The fact that even non-Hindus were aware of the ideological link between king and temple is demonstrated in the Ismā'īlī tradition of the conversion of Siddharāja, in which the dā'ī humbles the temple priest and then impresses the ruler. S.C. Misra (1964), *Muslim Communities in Gujarat: Preliminary Studies in their History and Social Organization*, p. 10.
59. D.B. Diskalkar (1938), 'Some Unpublished Inscriptions of the Chaulukyas of Gujarat (contd.)', *Poona Orientalist*, 2(4), pp. 232–3.
60. Chattopadhyaya, 'Historiography, History and Religious Centers', p. 44.
61. Sikandar, *MS*, p. 125.
62. Ibid., p. 137.
63. Ibid., p. 150.
64. Ibid., pp. 166–8.
65. Ibid., pp. 161–3.
66. Abdus Subhan (1960), 'Malik Ayāz', *Encyclopaedia of Islam*, Vol. 6, p. 269.
67. V.S. Pramar (1985), 'The Effects of Trade and Urbanization on the Architecture of Gujarat', in V.K. Chavda, ed., *Studies in Trade and Urbanization in Western India*, p. 86.
68. Ibid.
69. Sikandar, *MS*, p. 25.
70. Pramar, 'Effects of Trade and Urbanization,' p. 87.
71. Pramar suggests that the construction technique was borrowed from an almost identical procedure used in West Asia. Ibid., p. 87.
72. Ibid., p. 87.

'Alī Muḥammad Khan (1965), *Mir'āt-i Aḥmadī*, trans. M.F. Lokhandwala, p. 106.

74. Ibn Baṭṭūṭa, *Riḥla*, pp. 172–3.
75. Duarte Barbosa (1918–21), *The Book of Duarte Barbosa*, Vol. 1: *Including the Coasts of East Africa, Arabia, Persia, and Western India as Far as the Kingdom of Vijayanagar*, pp. 140–1.
76. Ibid., p. 125.
77. Pramar, 'Effects of Trade and Urbanization,' pp. 88–9.
78. Paṭel, *Vaḍnagara kaṇbīnī*, p. 11.
79. Majmudar, *Cultural History of Gujarat*, pp. 74–5.
80. R.N. Mehta and S.G. Kantawala (1973), 'Two Legends from the Skanda Purāṇa: A Study', *Purāṇa*. According to another view, the *Kaumārikā khaṇḍa* belongs, on internal evidence, to a period between the sixteenth and eighteenth centuries. R.N. Mehta (1965), 'Kaumārikā Khaṇḍa: A Study,' *Journal of the Maharaja Sayajirao University of Baroda* [henceforth *JMSUB*], 14, p. 45.
81. Barbosa, *Book*, Vol. I, p. 117.
82. At the time of the rebellion of the Afghan, Qāḍī Jalāl, the merchant Shams al-Dīn and the shipowner Iliyās, both eminent citizens, began to make a trench around the town to defend themselves against the rebel. Ibn Baṭṭūṭa, *Riḥla*, p. 173.
83. R.H. Major, ed. (1857), *India in the Fifteenth Century, Being a Collection of Narratives of Voyages to India in the Century Preceding the Portuguese Discovery of the Cape of Good Hope; from Latin, Persian, Russian and Italian Sources*, p. 46.
84. Barbosa, *Book*, Vol. 1, p. 132.
85. 'The Travels of Athanasius Nikitin of Twer', in Major, *India in the Fifteenth Century*, p. 11.
86. Jain, *Trade and Traders*, p. 89.
87. Sarvāṇanda, *Jagaḍūcarita*, p. 23.
88. See Stewart Gordon (1994), *Marathas, Marauders, and State Formation in Eighteenth Century Central India*, p. 112.
89. Major, *India in the Fifteenth Century*, p. 46.
90. Z.A. Desai (1960), 'Muslims in the 13th Century Gujarat, as known from Arabic inscriptions', *Journal of the Oriental Institute, Baroda* [henceforth *JOIB*] 10(4), pp. 353–64; Sircar, 'Veraval Inscription,' pp. 121–50.
91. Desai, 'Muslims in the 13th Century Gujarat', p. 356; Shokoohy, Bayani-Wolpert, and Shokoohy, *Bhadreśvar*, p. 55.
92. Someśvara, *Kīrtikaumudī*, pp. xxiv–xxv.
93. Hemacandra (1938), *Kāvyānuṣāsana*, Vol. 2, Part 1, p. cii.
94. A.S. Altekar (1925), 'A History of the Important Ancient Towns in Gujarat and Kathiavad,' *IA* 54, Supplement, p. 16.
95. Jayasiṃha Sūrī (1926), *Kumarapāla bhūpālacaritam mahakavyam*, p. 14.
96. 'Samrā-rasu', in C.D. Dalal, ed. (1978), *Prācīna gurjara kāvya-saṅgraha: A Collection of Old Gujarati Poems from the 12th to the 15th Centuries*, Vol. I, pp. 27–38.

97. Appendix VIII, 'Inscription of the Reign of Alapkhan in the Temple of Stambhana Pārśvanātha in Cambay', in ibid., p. 152.
98. Desai, *PAEG*, p. 13.
99. Sikandar, *MS*, p. 30.
100. Desai, *PAEG*, p. 16, fn. 37.
101. Ibn Baṭṭūṭa, *Riḥla*, p. 173.
102. Deyell, *Living without Silver*, p. 114.
103. Ibid., p. 125.
104. Ibid., pp. 240–1.
105. Ibid., p. 253. See also G.H. Khare (1966), 'Dravyapariksha of Thakkura Pheru: A Study', *Journal of the Numismatic Society of India*, 28, p. 25.
. Forbes, *Ras Mala*, Vol. 1, pp. 307–9.
107. Digby, 'Muhammad bin Tughluq's Last Years', p. 86.
108. Desai, *PAEG*, p. 17.
109. Ibid.
110. Yaḥyā b. Aḥmad b. 'Abd Allāh Sirhindī (1990), *Ta'rīkh-i Mubārak Shāhī*, trans. K.K. Basu, p. 146.
111. Majmudar, *Cultural History of Gujarat*, p. 69.
112. Sikandar, *MS*, trans., pp. 54–5, Sikandar, *MS*, p. 115.
113. Ibn Baṭṭūṭa, *Riḥla*, p. 5.
114. Sikandar, *MS*, trans., p. 72; Sikandar, *MS*, p. 143.
115. Patel, *Vaḍnagarā kaṇbīnī*, p. 18.
116. Major, *India in the Fifteenth Century*, p. 28.
117. Majmudar, *Cultural History of Gujarat*, p. xiv.
118. Sikandar, *MS*, p. 130.
119. Ibid., p. 131.
120. Ibid., p. 144.
121. E.C. Bayley (1886), *Local Muhammadan Dynasties of Gujarat*, p. 386.
122. Janaki, *Commerce of Cambay*, p. 21.

3

Pastoralism, Trade, and Settlement in Saurashtra and Kachchh

Trade and politics in Saurashtra and Kachchh functioned in a different physical environment from eastern Gujarat. Many of the important clans of Gujarat have a tradition of having migrated from elsewhere and of having moved from site to site before they finally settled down. Some of these groups took to sedentary lives and acquired in time the social and political systems of settled agrarian communities. Others stayed on the move, retaining their occupational flexibility and a certain adaptability in affiliation to religious traditions.

There were two kinds of migrations into Gujarat. One, as Kolff highlights, was the incursion of small bands of warriors, often dispossessed junior relatives of established lineages in Rajasthan who came in search of patrons and employers and offered their military services. The other kind, not always distinct from the first, was the incursion of entire clans with their cattle wealth and families, driven south by famine, local oppression or the hope of better pastures. These were accommodated as feudatories by host chieftains, given land to graze or inhabit and were expected to be loyal to their sponsor-clan.

In the fourteenth century the lands immediately west of the river Sabarmati were held by the Vāghelās, an offshoot of the same clan that had been ousted from Patan by the generals of 'Alā' al-Dīn Khaljī at the end of the thirteenth century. They controlled a larger region that is now called Jhalavad, as well as the Bhal, stretching from Patan almost to the Gulf of Cambay. The Vāghelās functioned as virtual overlords in much of this area, submitting only to the authority of

In the thirteenth century they had granted a part of their lands, the *chovīsī* or twenty-four villages of Than, Kandola, and Chotila to a branch of the Paramārs in return for suppressing the Bhīl chieftain Āso.[1]

In the late thirteenth century the region of Kanthkot in eastern Kachchh was controlled by the Jhālās.[2] Being driven out of there, they sought the protection of the Caulukyas of Anhilvada and were granted the territory now known as Jhalavad, between the lesser Rann of Kachchh and the Gulf of Cambay.

The sun-worshipping Kāṭhīs, who eventually gave their name to the region of Kathiavad, are mentioned as being in the service of the ūḍāsamās in the eleventh century.[3] Formerly vassals of the Sūmrās of Sind, they had to flee Sind and take refuge with the Vālā chief in Saurashtra. The Kāṭhīs were evidently outcastes at this period, since the ā chief was said to have lost caste after eating with them and was subsequently ousted from kingship by his brothers. He then cast in his lot with the Kāṭhīs and, with them, conquered several regions, including the Than–Chotila area, from the Soḍhās. Sons of the Kāṭhī–Vālā alliance were the founders of three Kāṭhī tribes named after them.[4] They also intermarried with local clans such as the Dhāndhal Rāṭhoḍs and Jhālās. They had a reputation as good fighters and as the best cattle rustlers available. They were also skilled horse breeders whose horses were among the hardiest in India. Kāṭhīs lent themselves out as military servants and did not subsequently acquire a high status as Rajputs. They 'exemplify, with their martial tradition, the continuum between warrior and robber as well as that between landlord and peasant.'[5]

The Kāṭhīs were driven out of Sind by the Samma Jām Abdā. In the fifteenth century, Kāṭhī branches also lived in Kachchh, where they founded the kingdom of Pavārgaḍh near Bhuj.[6] One tradition of their origin has it they were brought to Gujarat by the mythical hero of the Mahābhārata, Karṇa, since they were the best cattle lifters in the world.[7] They were then driven out of Kachchh by the Jāḍejās, and subsequently moved to the region of Than.

The Gohils were originally from the banks of the Luni river in Marwar, and settled in Saurashtra on land taken from the Bhīls.[8] This tradition is affirmed by a parallel one in Rajasthan. They were expelled from Marwar in the thirteenth century by the Rāṭhods and came to the region of Junagadh where they were granted villages by the Cūḍāsamā ruler with a commission to protect these lands against the depredations of the Khānt Bhīls. The Gohils expanded into several regions, finally conquering Valabhi from the Vālā

Mokhḍājī, a Gohil ruler who was a contemporary of Muḥammad b. Tughluq, became particularly notorious as a pirate chieftain. He took up strong positions on the hills between the Gulf of Cambay and Palitana for attacks on surrounding areas, including the island of Piram and the port of Ghogha. From these points, he was able to control the sea trade and engage in piracy: 'At Perumbh he kept many a ship, for the roads to many countries lay there, many a vessel did he plunder; in every port he was an object of terror. From all that sailed he exacted tribute did the raja seated upon the throne of Perumbh.'[9] Eventually, Muḥammad b. Tughluq had subdued this piratical chief to safeguard the Cambay trade. He was defeated and killed for plundering a merchant whose goods he had undertaken to protect. After his removal the island of Piram was deserted.[10]

Another tradition records the entry of a branch of the Soḍhā tribe into Gujarat from Sind, probably in the fourteenth century. In consequence of famine at Parkar, two thousand Soḍhā Paramārs with their wives and children are said to have entered Gujarat. They settled near Muli and were granted four districts of twenty-four villages each by the Vāghelās of Vadhvan in return for reducing the powerful Bhīls of the Sabarmati ravines. They evicted the Bābriās from the region of Than and Chotila, and founded the town of Muli. During the reign of ḥmūd I one branch of the family converted to Islam and settled at Ranpur, coming to be known as the Ranpur Molesalāms. The other branch remained at Muli until they were evicted from there in the sixteenth century by the Kāṭhīs. The Jats or Jāts of Bajana were vassals of the Paramārs of Than and played an important part in the army of ḥmūd Bīgara in the siege of Champaner in 1484. The sultan bestowed the region of Bajana upon them, which again they had to conquer for themselves. Assimilation was conditional on establishing military prowess and, as was the case in many medieval states, a 'vassal' who was able to conquer a territory was given control over it.

Several chieftains maintained a dual role as plunderers and landholders. In a province as commercially vibrant as Gujarat, large loads of goods proceeded through the interiors, protected on their journey by guards and bards. Kolff quotes Mundy (1619) as saying that caravans of goods were accompanied by armed guards such as Balūchīs āts, apart from professional carters and cameleers.[11] Professional guards such as these had multiple functions. The *Mir'āt-i Aḥmadī* in the eighteenth century describes them as a source of resistance against s, useful also in attacking villages, drawing away cattle, escorting notables, collecting tribute from *zamīndār*s, acting as recruits for armies, and so on. They supported themselves usually by their own fields.[12]

Certain communities such as garāsiyās and Kolīs, suggests Kolff, furnished military bondsmen. '[They] partook of the quality that "marginal peoples" generally have from a military point of view. Peasant robbers from the hills or forests make excellent skirmishers against their own kind and may well become a main element in established armies.'[13] Emphasis was also placed on agreements with chieftains who demanded cesses or taxes in return for guaranteeing the safety of caravans through their territories. While the Bhīls and Kolīs remained a constant terror for merchants, there are instances in which Bhīls were induced to police the forest areas they lived in, in return for autonomy.[14] In addition, Bhāṭs or Cāraṇs customarily accompanied merchant caravans, since their presence served as security. The curse of a Bhāṭ or Cāraṇ, traditionally sons of the mother goddess, was much feared. They also could commit a rite of self-mutilation to the point of suicide, called *trāga*, to further pressurize a plunderer, since the sin of injuring or killing a Bhāṭ was an extremely serious one.[15]

While some of these clans were groups of 'warrior-ascetics' in search of marriage alliances and patronage, others were owners of cattle wealth. Clans, then, need to be seen in terms not just of their political status, their roles as vassals, or the number of villages they controlled, but also differentially in terms of their changing occupations in the period. Groups that entered Gujarat as pastoralists could settle down to become cultivators while small bands of forest-dwelling cultivators could achieve military successes and become chieftains. In the agrarian landscape in the fifteenth century most activities were armed—even peasants were armed—and no one power was able to monopolize the immense armed manpower in the countryside.

The recurring threat of Bhīls as a disruptive force was not so much as destroyers of 'civilization' or a courtly way of life, but because they could drive off valuable cattle, forcibly harvest fields, or disrupt an agrarian/pastoralist order. However, most 'Rajput' chieftains in this period were not generally rulers of cities or palatial settlements, but prosperous agriculturists or herders living in wooden dwellings in small villages. While some chieftains were able to hire or rent labour to actually till their fields, in many cases it was the clan itself that carried out agriculture and transported goods. Life in the countryside was very different from that in the great port towns or commercial centres, few if any of which were controlled by these chieftains. Very little separated a chieftain from the neighbouring Bhīls or Kolīs who too were cultivators or pastoralists, or, on the coast, fishing, trading, or piratical communities.

'Garāsiyā', the term that came to be used in the period for landholders, did not specify the ethnic or community origin of the landholder (although Kolīs or Bhīls were generally singled out).[16] The term could be used for landholders of different grades—whether small zamīndārs, chieftains of hill fortresses, or major chieftains belonging to prestigious clans. This extensive differentiation of rural landholdings amongst countless claimants to the produce, cattle, and consequent social status led to a situation in which attempts at centralized revenue collection or even assessment were generally unsuccessful. The sultans of Gujarat were never able to enforce such a system. The most they could do was to demand a regular tribute from landholders. Attempts at imposing a jāgīr system generally failed: the early sultans usually asked a claimant for favours to conquer the granted lands in return for virtual autonomy subject to the payment of tribute. Few attempts were made to prevent right-holders from forming local roots; on the contrary, courtiers were encouraged to cultivate local power bases since that extended the reach of the sultanate into the countryside. As for the chieftains, they were left virtually free to administer their land, and it was by the threat of military force that revenues in the form of tribute were extracted from them.

There was also a continuity between chieftain and plunderer or pirate. Some of the coastal chiefs, often castigated as pirates, had access to trade goods, generally through plunder, an example being Mokhḍājī Gohil of Ghogha and Piram. Plunder was profitable only until it was regularized. When the state stepped in to control it, it could become an irregular and risky enterprise, and did not ensure regular income. Further, after the sultanate conquest of most of Sind by the late fourteenth century, military supplies for the Saurashtra chieftains were cut off and they were forced back on their agrarian or pastoralist resources. With only limited chances of securing larger alliances or military equipment, it was in the interest of most landed chieftains in Saurashtra either to offer tribute to the sultans or to make military arrangements with them. Although contravention of such arrangements could lead to conflict with immense armies and increased levies from the rest of the countryside, several communities did make such arrangements with the sultans. Sultanate forces depended heavily on such contributions, in addition to their levies of local peasant groups aided by itinerant mercenaries. Thus Maḥ ūd Bīgara's siege of

Champaner was much aided by the Jāts of Sind.[17] The chief of Rajpipla undertook to send horse and foot soldiers to the sultan's armies whenever necessary.[18]

STATUS AND REINVENTION: THE CŪḌĀSAMĀS OF JUNAGADH

An example of the process by which a pastoralist group originating in Sind became one of the prestigious Rajput clans of Saurashtra and Kachchh is that of the Sammas. Branches of this clan (who trace their descent to Kṛṣṇa) moved into Kachchh and Saurashtra, where they eventually became the important Rajput ruling houses of the Jāḍejās in Kachchh and the Cūḍāsamās in Junagadh. Latterday histories of these clans play down the fact that they had a pastoralist low-status past with significant links to Islam. Other branches stayed on in Sind where they were known as the Samma Jāms. The latter were Muslims and even had marriage links with the sultans of Gujarat in the fifteenth century.

Of these branches, the Cūḍāsamās were not Muslims. They became the most important rulers in Saurashtra and were the greatest threat in the peninsula to the Gujarat sultans. They also constructed their history in a Hindu religious idiom. In the fifteenth century a Sanskrit court chronicle of the last Cūḍāsamā ruler projected him as part-incarnation of Viṣṇu. They did, however, have ties with their Muslim clanspeople in Sind. As early as the twelfth century, the Cūḍāsamās were joined in a campaign against the Caulukyas of Anhilvada by a contingent of Sammas from Sind.[19] Perhaps significantly, the last ūḍāsamā ruler is said to have converted to Islam after his defeat at the hands of Maḥmūd Bīgara, in 1469.[20]

The Jāḍejās in Kachchh, on the other hand, were suspected of Muslim connections.

> These Jadejas, although generally spoken of as, and claiming to be Rajputs, appear originally to have been a tribe native to Sind and converts to Mohametism. They were probably expelled from Sind some 500 years ago, and settled themselves by conquest in Kutch. Thence in 1539 they spread into Kathiawar, and there, surrounded by Hindu Rajput tribes, viz., the Jetwas, Jhallas, and others, they reverted to Hinduism.[21]

They were also believed to have occasionally intermarried with Muslims and thus lost status. The Kachchh Jāḍejās in the early nineteenth century visited mosques and, in fact, were considered half Hindu and half

Muslim.[22] 'Political causes have disunited them from the Mahomedans, and they desire again to be considered as pure Rajpoots; but having been contaminated, no Rajpoot will intermarry with them.'[23]

The reiterated Muslim taint in the history of the Jāḍejā clan led them to a ritually degraded status and the practice of female infanticide as husbands of suitable status could not be found for their daughters. Scattered evidence for a proclivity towards Islam among the Jāḍejās and related clans, such as the Cūḍāsamās of Junagadh, emerges from the earliest period at which they can be traced and continues throughout their history. One of the Raos of Kachchh in the eighteenth century actually converted to Islam and is buried in the precincts of a mosque.

The ruling dynasty of the Cūḍāsamās of Junagadh ended in the fifteenth century, and their descendants were minor but prestigious Rajput landholders in the nineteenth century. It is more difficult to find whether the Cūḍāsamās had similar links with Islam, or indeed had anything but a 'proud' Rajput ancestry. As they achieved a settled court society, a clearly Hindu identity, and aspirations to prestige Rajput status in the fifteenth century, it became convenient for them to jettison traces of non-Sanskritic cultural practices. Shortly before the defeat and dethroning of the last Cūḍāsamā, Rā Māṇḍalik, a Sanskrit eulogy was written in his praise by an itinerant poet from Vijayanagara.[24] The *ṇḍalīka-mahākāvya* is also the only written text from the Cūḍāsamā court that has survived to the present.[25] The text is in the tradition of classical Sanskrit eulogy, and while it contains several interesting social details, it essentially represents the fact that the Cūḍāsamās in the fifteenth century needed the legitimation derived from patronizing Sanskrit literature. The text, therefore, represents the Cūḍāsamās as they would have liked to be portrayed, and contains few clues to a lower status or culturally ambiguous past.

The long-term history of a Rajput clan characterized by its 'pride of race' also throws up several features that are not strictly brahmanical and illustrates how brahmanism incorporates and codifies elements from the ideological world of politically powerful groups who, in this case, emerged on the fringes of brahmanical civilization. This historical process also clarifies how 'bardic' groups such as the Cāraṇs recorded and perpetuated information about groups like the Jāḍejās and ūḍāsamas with whom they had symbiotic relationships of patronage and legitimation. Before the fifteenth century Sind, Kachchh, and Kathiavad were frontier areas for Hindu civilization, albeit with great ritual significance. Many of the great centres of pilgrimage were to be found in these areas such as Dvaraka, Girnar, Somanath and Multan in upper Sind. Nevertheless, brahmanically sanctioned legal and customary systems had a tenuous hold on the ruling clans of these regions.[26]

The process of identity formation of many of the groups—who by the sixteenth century were beginning to claim the common identity of 'Rajput'—may be traced in the period under consideration. In the fourteenth and fifteenth centuries they still had considerable diversity in political status, position in the caste hierarchy, ethnic origin, and even occupation. Most were militarized nomad pastoralist groups with little or no evidence of a settled court society. For such groups, bards functioned as priests, genealogists, and guarantors. In return for patronage they provided religious legitimation, perpetuated or prepared suitable versions of their lineage, and arranged marriage and military alliances. Although groups such as the Cāraṇs depended on the Rajputs for patronage, they could also inflict harm on them by the withdrawal of their favour and thereby that of their goddess. For example, the ūḍāsamās do not appear in bardic accounts as unambiguously glorious rulers. They are inevitably to be found on the losing side of any conflict with the kings of Gujarat. Several of them are depicted as having a fatal fascination for women, a trait that eventually cost them their throne. When Rā Māṇḍalik, the last Cūḍāsamā ruler, made advances towards a Cāraṇ woman (Cāraṇīs are powerful embodiments of Śakti), she cursed him and foretold the loss of his kingdom. A version of the legend records that although a Muslim from Girnar, Jamial Shāh, attempted to intercede with the king on behalf of the Cāraṇī, he was unrepentant and the curse stood.[27] Any hereditary allegiance of the Cāraṇs to the Cūḍāsamās did not prevent them recording incidents in which they appeared in a less than positive light.

The Cāraṇs and the vocabulary of negotiation and alliance that they represented stood as guarantors of a mutually accepted legal system between clans. This was enforced by the sacrality of the mother goddess embodied by the person of the Cāraṇ. Any infringement of an agreement or alliance brokered by the Cāraṇs brought about the curse of the goddess. In order to maintain their credibility among different clans, the Cāraṇs were obliged to maintain a degree of impartiality. While genealogies and family histories preserved by them were, as with any other mechanism of recording, subject to subtle manipulation by the patrons, they did not always record versions preferred by their clients. Thus, genealogies and legends preserved by the bards, as also the esoteric traditions concerning the Cūḍāsamās in the oral tradition of 'lower' caste groups, contain traces of a past in which their religious and political identity was less certain. These traditions preserved and coded phases of a low-status, pastoralist origin, with evidence of patronage to and legitimation from religious groups that the later Cūḍāsamās would prefer forgotten. Even after the sedentarization and gradual brahminization of clans such as the Cūḍāsamās, the bards continued to have a great influence, right into the nineteenth century.

According to legends collected in nineteenth century Saurashtra, the Jāḍejās and the Cūḍāsamās trace their ancestry to a militarized herding clan, the Sammas, who inhabited Sind in the ninth century. The Sammas were pastoralists, probably a number of itinerant clans with large animal wealth consisting of camels, sheep, or cattle. One branch entered Saurashtra in the ninth century and wrested the principality of Vanthali from the local ruler, Vāḷārām Cāvaḍā.[28] They subsequently moved to the fortified Junagadh, from where they ruled a large part of the peninsula until the second half of the fifteenth century—a remarkable span of seven hundred years. The traditional etymology explains that this branch of the Sammas took its name from its leader, ūḍā or Candracūḍa, and came to be known as the Cūḍāsamā. Other branches of the clan settled in Kachchh, some of whom took their name from a common ancestor, Jāḍā, hence their name Jāḍejā. In the nineteenth century, the Jāḍejās, Sammas, Cūḍāsamās, and Bhaṭṭīs considered themselves related, however distantly, as Yādavas and descendants of Kṛṣṇa, and did not intermarry.[29]

The genealogy of the Sammas, Cūḍāsamās, and Jāḍejās records that mba, the son of Kṛṣṇa, was captured by pirates while on a sea voyage near Dvaraka, and was taken to the city of Śoṇitapur, the City of Blood.[30] There, Sāmba married Okhā, daughter of the local ruler. When the ruler died, he was succeeded by Sāmba and Okhā's son. A descendant, seventy-ninth in the line of succession, was Devavṛtta Yādava, the ruler oṇitapur in the sixth century CE who was killed in a battle against the armies of 'Alī.[31] Subsequently, his four sons Aspat, Gajpat, Narpat, and Bhūpat left Śoṇitapur and went to seek their fortunes, conquering Syria and Egypt. Aspat was defeated when the Muslim forces conquered Egypt and he accepted Islam. His descendants were the Sammas who went on to rule Sind. The other brothers then went to Afghanistan where Gajpat conquered the city of Gajna/Ghazna. However, the pursuing Muslim armies caught up with him and he was killed.

Bhūpat moved south, conquered the Silindrapur area of India and established the city of Bhāṭiyā-nagar (in Punjab). His clan later established the city of Jaisalmer. In Tod's account, the genealogy of the Bhaṭṭīs has a similar claim to Yadu or Yādava descent from Kṛṣṇa. After the death of Kṛṣṇa, his sons retreated to Multan, then proceeded to the Doab, passed into Zabulistan, founded Gajni (Ghazna), and had an influence as far as Samarkand. It is not known how they were driven back to India, but on their return they conquered Punjab, established Salbhanpur, then were driven out of there, and occupied the region of Jaisalmer.

The fourth brother Narpat came to Sind and established the city Nagar-Samoi which later came to be known as Thatta. He was the ancestor of Candracūḍa, the first Cūḍāsamā ruler of Vanthali. However, James Burgess encountered a slightly different version of the story.

> The Jâḍejâ or Jhâḍejâ princes of Kachh, who claim to be descended from ishṇa and the Yâdavas, trace their descent through a mythical line of eighty sovereigns of Sonitapura and Misr. ... We come to something more like a real personage in Jâm Narpat, though he is said to have fled with three brothers from Misr, 'embarking from the port of Urmârâ'[32] and to have gone to Ośam hill in Soraṭh,[33] where his eldest brother Ugrasena, became a Muhammadan and took the name of Aspat, while a younger brother, Gajapat, is the traditional ancestor of the Chuḍâsamâs of Soraṭh. Narpat is then said to have taken Gazni,[34] killing Firuz Shâh. He was succeeded by his son Sammâ, the ancestor of the Sammâs, who was driven from Gazni 'by Sulṭân Shâh the son of Firuz Shâh', and went to live at Kijarânand.[35]

A comparable genealogy of the Sammas of Sind, albeit with some token Islamization, is found in the *Tuḥfat al-kirām*, a history of Sind written in 1768–9. The primal ancestor here was the prophet Nūh whose son was Sām or Jām. The Sammas thus derive their name from the ancestor Sām (compare with Sāmba in the Hindu version), or, alternatively, from their origin in Syria or Shām.

> m whose father was Sambūt Rājā had a son called Jādam. Jādam had four sons. The first was Haibat whose descendants were the Sammas of Sind. The second was Gajpat, whose descendant was Chughda. The third was Bhūpat whose descendants are the Bhattī tribe (*qawm-i bhattī*), the fourth was rāsama whose son was Rā Diyāch, whose wife was Sorath.[36]

The four brothers, here Haibat, Gajpat, Bhūpat, and Churāsamā, were descended from Nūh through their father Jādam or Jādav (compare with Devavṛtta Yādava earlier), Rām, Daśarath and Bhagīrath. Correspondingly with the 'Hindu' genealogy, Haibat was the ancestor of the Sammas, Bhūpat of the Bhaṭṭīs, and Churāsamā, the ruler of Junagadh.

After the Ghurīd annexation of Sind, the Sūmrā clan ruled southern Sind, especially the region of Thatta.[37] They were harried regularly by the sultans of Delhi and were often obliged to move their capital. By the early fourteenth century there is evidence that they were being eclipsed in southern Sind by the Sammas who took over most of Sind and ruled from Thatta until the sixteenth century. It is not known when the latter converted to Islam. In the fourteenth and fifteenth centuries they appear to be Sunni Muslims. One of the Jāms sent two of his daughters to be married to the Sunni sultan of Gujarat and the Bukhārī Sufi Shāh 'Ālam respectively.

Returning to the Cūḍāsamās, we find that their first ruler to be mentioned in the chronicles of the Caulukya kingdom of eastern Gujarat was Graharipu (or Gārio in the bardic chronicles) of Vanthali, arch-rival of the Caulukya Mūlarāja of Anhilvada.[38] The *Dvyāśraya-kāvya* (c.1174) by a Jain teacher at the court of the twelfth-century Caulukya ruler Siddharāja offers a telling example of how the more Sanskritized Caulukyas characterized their enemies as barbarians and enemies of settled civilization. Here, the Cūḍāsamā ruler Graharipu was a demon *daityatallaja* and *dānavaśreṣṭha*: 5.92) born of a mleccha (outcaste or outsider) mother (4.25–33). 'He takes away the cows of the sages (2.65) ... kills Brahmanas, spoils sacrifices and hates oblations (2.76) and demands money and taxes of the ascetics (2.80) ... He consumes the meat of forbidden animals and hunts the *camarī* deer. (2.86–89) ... (He) kills pilgrims (4.25) ... captivates the wives of the sages and practises adultery (4.80–81).'[39]

The terms used to describe Graharipu, the Ābhīra or shepherd king, and his confederates—mleccha, *daitya*—are often used in Sanskrit texts to characterize or stigmatize Muslims.[40] Faced with this herder (*ābhīra*) king (6.25) who harassed pilgrims and traders travelling through his territories to the port of Somanath, the tenth-century ruler of Gujarat decided to wage war.[41] In the conflict that followed, the Cūḍāsamā chieftain was able to call up a formidable alliance. Chief among his supporters was his close kinsman, the ruler of Kachchh, who was as close 'as if they were sons of the same mother'.[42] He was supported by other allies including the king of Sind, a Bhilla (Bhīl) chieftain and a detachment of mlecchas from Turu ka (5.49).[43] In spite of the support of the king of Sind and his many horses (7.70), this decidedly non-Sanskritic alliance between 'barbarian' pastoralist chieftains and Bhils was defeated.

As was to be the pattern in every successive confrontation between Gujarat and the peninsula, the prosperous east Gujarat won and the pastoralist west was reduced to tributary status.

The antagonism with the Gujarat mainland continued in the story of Rā Dayās (traditionally dated 1003–1010) who was defeated by the Caulukyas. The history of Navghaṇ, Dayās' son, records the circumstances under which the pastoralist Āhīr clan, another group with an ambiguous cultural identity, was incorporated into the alliance structure that supported the Cūḍāsamās. A version of the tale also records the legitimation they received from the followers of Khoḍiyār and Śikotar, both non-Sanskritic medieval goddesses.

Navghaṇ survived the Caulukya conquest and was restored to power by an Āhīr chief who sacrificed his own son to save the prince, and thus compelling Navghaṇ's patronage and allegiance. The sacrifice of the son is reminiscent of the practice of the Cāraṇs to enforce political and commercial agreements by threatening to mutilate or kill their families or themselves, thereby making defaulters liable to the curse of the goddess. The Cāraṇs' moral and spiritual authority was, for these pastoralist clans, the only available guarantee of agreements.

Navghaṇ received the ceremonial allegiance of the Āhīrs at his coronation in 1025. In return, the Āhīrs called on the military power of the Cūḍāsamās to protect their sister clan in Sind from the Sūmrās.[44] In the wake of a great famine in Soraṭh, the Āhīrs had moved north towards Sind in search of pasture and there came into conflict with the Sūmrā ruler. Navghaṇ marched to their aid, defeated the Sūmrā, and secured at least nominal control over Sind.

Significantly, he also persuaded several Sindi Lohāṇā and Bhāṭiā merchants to move from Sind to Saurashtra.[45] In the Sūmrā's palace in Sind, his patron goddess Śikotar addressed Navghaṇ and expressed her wish to move to Soraṭh. She had withdrawn her blessing from the arrogant Sūmrā and extended it to Navghaṇ, who carried her to his capital in the form of water in a golden vessel. Here is evidence of additional legitimation from a deity of Sind. We know that Śikotar, the deified personification of the island of Socotra, is the patroness of sailors, fishermen, and traders in Sind and Kachchh, including the communities of Lohāṇās and Bhāṭiās.[46] Lohāṇās and Bhāṭiās themselves preserve a tradition of coming to Saurashtra in the reign of Navghaṇ. It may reasonably be inferred that the desire of the goddess to shift to Soraṭh signified the support and legitimation of the trading communities who settled in Saurashtra in this period.

One version of this legend incorporates the story of the entry of goddess Khoḍiyār as patron deity of the Cūḍāsamās. The Āhīrs are said to have been worshippers of Khoḍiyār who led them to buried treasure with which to arm themselves to overthrow the Caulukya viceroy. Also on Navghaṇ's campaign to Sind, he encountered a young raṇ girl who was the embodiment of the goddess. She caused the waters of the Rann to part to allow Navghaṇ's army to pass safely into Sind and rout the Sūmrā. The grateful Navghaṇ built a temple to Khoḍiyār on his return to Junagadh.[47] The goddess thus granted sovereignty to the Cūḍāsamā through the legitimation offered by the rs and the Cāraṇs in return for patronage.

Table 3.1: Cūḍāsamā Rulers

Legendary ancestor Gajpat, descended from Yadu	
ūḍācandra (the first ruler at Vanthạli)	875–907
Hamīr, Mūlarāja, Viśvavarāha	907–40
Graharipu (fought Caulukya ruler Mūlarāja)	940–82
Unbroken succession of rulers	....
Jayasiṃha II	1351–3
Mahipāla III	1373
Muktasiṃha	1373–97
āṇḍalik II	1397–1400
Melagadeva	1400–15
Jayasiṃha III	1415–40
Mahipāla IV	1440–51
āṇḍalik III	1451–72
'yzāda Bhūpat a.k.a. Melaga	1472–1505
Descendants were small landholders	....

Note: The table is adapted from a king-list in Rāyjādā, *Cūḍāsamā rājavaṃśa*, pp. 18–19.

THE LATER CŪḌĀSAMĀS

From the fourteenth century onwards the Rās of Junagadh take on a more concrete appearance in inscriptions commissioned by their subjects. Most inscriptions are pāḷiyās or hero-stones, placed on the outskirts of villages or near temples to commemorate clansmen who died fighting for the village, the king, or in the defence of their possessions. Many of them are dated and several mention the reigning ūḍāsamā king. The first pāḷiyā to mention a Cūḍāsamā king is dated 1377 and commemorates the death of an Āhīr who died fighting robbers during the reign of Rāya Jesanghade. Other inscriptions are set into step-wells, ponds, or temples and commemorate their builders, usually merchants, ministers, or their wives. Several of these include the names of the ruler and his ancestors.

An inscription of 1328, recording the building of a stepwell, is the first one known to claim descent within the prestigious lunar lineage *somavaṃśa*) for the Cūḍāsamās.[48] The lunar lineage of '*śrī candracūḍa-ūḍāsamā*' is reiterated in another stepwell inscription of 1389. This latter inscription records that the ruler Mokalasiṃha 'established his capital at Vāmanasthalī by the order of the Pātsāh' (the sultan of Delhi), confirming that Saurashtra was then controlled by governors sent out by the Tughluq sultans of Delhi who had established a military post in the Cūḍāsamā fort of Junagadh.[49] This signalled that Mokalasiṃha, who acknowledged the overlordship of the sultan, had been allowed to continue ruling after the Delhi governor's conquest, but was obliged to move his capital from Junagadh to the nearby town of Vāmanasthalī (modern Vanthali).

Subsequently, the fortress of Junagadh became a touchstone of success for the military commanders from Delhi who controlled Gujarat in the fourteenth century. When Delhi rule waned in the 1390s, the ūḍāsamās regained control of Junagadh, but in the fifteenth century, they were attacked by the newly independent sultans of Gujarat. In 1414, mad (r. 1411–42) defeated the Cūḍāsamā ruler but left the lineage in place in return for allegiance and the payment of tribute. Five pāḷiyās from 1413 record the death of warriors who died fighting for the ūḍāsamā ruler Melagade against the 'Turuṣkas', probably a reference to Aḥmad's campaign.[50] Three years later, an inscription dated 1417 from Junagadh claims that Dāmodar, a commander (*senāpati*) of the ūḍāsamās had defeated the Yavanas at Jhinjharkot (modern Jhanjhmer). *Turuṣka* and *yavana* were both contemporary terms for Muslims.[51]

The same inscription includes a long genealogy of the Cūḍāsamās, claiming for the first time that they were Yādavas, and hence descended from Kṛṣṇa (*maṇḍalīka-nṛpatiryadu-vaṃśe*). Significantly, this claim occurs just as Vaiṣṇavas were becoming more prominent and active in the area.[52] The influence of Vaiṣṇava and Jain traders and the power of their vegetarian ethos is demonstrated in an inscription of 1451 in which Rā Māṇḍalik declared at his coronation that animal slaughter would be prohibited on certain days of every month, in response to a petition by local traders.[53]

The *Māṇḍalīka-nṛpa-carita* (or *mahākāvya*) is the only written text commissioned by the Cūḍāsamās themselves that has survived to the present day. It is a long historical poem in 640 stanzas believed to have been written about 1460, at the height of the power of Rā āṇḍalik whose kingdom was annexed by Maḥmūd Bīgara in 1472.[54] According to the Persian chronicles, Māṇḍalik subsequently converted to Islam and died in Ahmadabad a few years later. His successors were given land and a title and continued to live in the region of Junagadh. They briefly came into prominence again during the struggle for power between the Mughals and the last of the Gujarat sultans in the 1570s.

The poet—Gaṅgādhara—gives no details about himself except that he was a 'conqueror of the poets of the Kali age'. However, he may be identical with the author of the *Gaṅgadāsa-pratāpavilāsa*, a historical play written at the court of Champaner in eastern Gujarat in the 1450s. If so, Gaṅgādhara was an itinerant poet from Vijayanagara who had visited the court of Sultan Muḥammad II and, having vanquished the poets of his court, proceeded to Champaner. It is reasonable to suppose that he next journeyed to Junagadh.

Gaṅgādhara relates that the family of Māṇḍalik derived descent from the moon and belonged to the Yādava clan.[55] In an account of āṇḍalik's marriage, he includes gestures of allegiance from his Yādava allies, the king of Sindhu (Sind) who held an umbrella over Māṇḍalik's head and the Vājā chief of the vicinity of Somanath who waved a pair of chowries over him. The king of Sindhu in this period was probably the Samma Jām, either Jām Sanjar (1454–62) or the famous Jām Nindo alias Niẓām al-Dīn (1462–1509).

At the beginning of the poem, he identifies Kṛṣṇa and Śiva, and pays obeisance to Śiva and Ambā. The family deity of the Cūḍāsamās was Rādhā Dāmodara to whom there is a temple on Girnar. Māṇḍalik also received favours from the deity Dattātreya whose temple is at the summit of Mount Girnar.

After a poetic description of the city of Junagadh, the *Maṇḍalīkapa-carita* continues with a summary of the exploits of Māṇḍalik's ancestors in which fighting the Yavanas (Muslims) figures prominently. āṇḍalik himself is celebrated for his kingly qualities, especially his equestrian skills, which resonate strongly with the lavish praise in the last canto, where the poet compares the king to Kalki, the tenth, anticipated *avatāra* of Viṣṇu:

When Māṇḍalika mounts his horse and brandishes his sword and stands up to kill the mlecchas, people begin to wonder: 'Is this Kalki, born as the destroyer at the end of the Kali age?' (10.4)

In days gone by [Nakula], the younger brother of Arjuna could be compared with Māṇḍalika in riding a horse; in the future there will be Kalki, but what kings of the present day can be called his peers? (10.7)

In spite of Māṇḍalik's avowed prowess against the mlecchas, the poet hints that the Cūḍāsamās occasionally collaborated with the sultans of Gujarat. One day an envoy from the king of the Yavanas, that is, the sultans, came to the court of Māṇḍalik's father Mahipāla (r. 1440–51). Significantly, this overture from the sultan to Mahipāla is nowhere indicated in the Persian sultanate chronicles. In this version, the envoy complained that the neighbouring Gohil chieftain Dudā, together with his friends, was wreaking havoc in the sultan's territories. Mahipāla took the decision to collaborate with the sultan against the Gohil, even though the two clans were related by marriage. He justified his decision thus:

On the one hand, a battle with the Yavanas, who had increased their strength owing to this Kali age, was not a happy thing. The king of the Yavanas had already deprived many kings of their kingdom. He however, has shown no open enmity towards the royal family of the Yādavas (i.e., the Cūḍāsamās), since on many occasions, my ancestors had put to flight the armies of the Yavana kings on the battle field. (3.34–35).

His decision was affirmed by his minister:

That Yavana king, who on the strength of his army of elephants and thousands of horses has courted your friendship, o King! What greater good and safety do you ask for? It would therefore be best for you to do what will be pleasing to him. On the other hand, if I were to recount the misdeeds of Dudā, I am afraid I shall incur the displeasure of the prince. These chiefs always seek shelter under you when they are harassed by the Yavanas and yet claim as their own the lands bordering on your kingdom. (3.40)

In this passage, Mahipāla's decision to collaborate with the sultan is justified as a strategic choice. Compliance with the sultan's request would secure a powerful ally for the Cūḍāsamās but would also elevate their own military standing among the chieftains of the region. Accordingly, āṇḍalik, then the crown prince, undertook to chastise Dudā, the uncle of his wife Kuntā, and killed him in battle for the sultan.

After being appointed crown prince, Māṇḍalik, possibly still functioning as an agent of the Gujarat sultan, defeated the 'king Sangana of the western ocean'. This 'king' can be identified as a pirate of the Vādhel clan who achieved control of parts of the coastal territory around modern Porbandar and Okha. The Vādhels, in common with many piratical and seafaring communities of the coast from Kathiavad to Makran, were adherents some form of Ismā'īlism.[56] Later, Māṇḍalik asked his minister whether any enemy remained to be laid low. The minister replied that the Yavana stood at a respectful distance and kings like Gohila sought shelter at his feet.

But the king of the western ocean, Sangana by name, whose fortress defended by water is very strong, is still showing himself insolent, even when he has been conquered by you in an open battle. ... May you therefore conquer this king who lives in the island where Lord Viṣṇu has taken his residence after killing the demon Śaṁkha, and plant a pillar of conquest there.

One of the villages in Okhamandal was still called Sangan Kotra in the nineteenth century. It was an island at high tide and was a refuge for pirates.[57] On seeing the approach of Māṇḍalik, Sangana escaped and his people surrendered. After planting the pillar of victory on the island and looting Sangana's palace, Māṇḍalik prepared to cross the sea on his way back to his capital. Just then Sangana reappeared and blocked his way with the help of a Pārasika (or Persian, possibly a Kachchhi or Makrāni pirate) chief, probably from one of the coastal islands. The Pārasika chief had a large army of horsemen and camel-riders, but Māṇḍalik's army defeated and captured him and Sangana. The latter was released by the chivalrous Māṇḍalik and soon returned to his piratical career. Maḥmūd Bīgara subsequently captured Sangana's son Bhīm and had him killed in Ahmadabad.[58]

The *Maṇḍalīka-nṛpa-carita* explicated the Cūḍāsamās' claims to royal status in the classical Sanskritic mode. It was produced in a milieu in which Sanskrit sophistication was highly prized and hard to find. The resilient Cūḍāsamā clan had made a long journey over the centuries: from Sind and Kachchh to Junagadh, from livestock herding and banditry to a settled court with an army, brahmins, bureaucrats, and poets, and from accusations of beef-eating outcaste status to the classical courtly image projected in the *Maṇḍalīka-nṛpa-carita*. By the time it was written, however, Māṇḍalik's days as a ruler were numbered.

The Cūḍāsamās had been allowed to retain their realms in return for submission to the sultans of Gujarat. But according to the sultanate chroniclers, Māṇḍalik's vainglory brought about his downfall. Soon after the completion of the eulogy, Maḥmūd Bīgara defeated Māṇḍalik after a siege and finally annexed the kingdom.

The Cāraṇs also seem to have withdrawn their support of Māṇḍalik. In the accounts of the bards, Māṇḍalik's downfall was destined. He had angered a Cāraṇ woman with his advances who cursed him to lose his kingdom. Earlier, Māṇḍalik's ancestor in the thirteenth century, Kheṅgār, was said to have ravished a Mer woman, but he received his just deserts when her kinsmen wounded him so badly that he died.[59] Māṇḍalik had committed further transgressions too. The *Ta'rīkh-i Sorath* relates that:

> The Raja had forcibly taken to himself Mohini, the beautiful wife of his minister Vishal. The injured husband, unable to show open resentment, schemed in secret for the downfall of his master. When the provisions in Girnar had given out, Vishal sent a messenger to the sultan that the opportunity was favourable for taking the fortress by assault. The king acted on the advice and before long the Rao came down to do him homage and handed up the keys of the fortress.[60]

Eventually, it would seem, both bards and courtiers withdrew their support to Māṇḍalik.

Maḥmūd made Junagadh a mint town and renamed it Mustafabad. āṇḍalik's life was spared, but he was made to convert to Islam and received the title Khān Jahān. Sikandar relates that Māṇḍalik was converted only after his arrival in Ahmadabad by the influence of the saintly Shāh 'Ālam.[61] Khān Jahān and his descendants occupied an honoured place at the Ahmadabad court. The *Ta'rīkh-i Sorath* mentions that the dynasty of Rā Māṇḍalik was allowed to continue for another century as tributary *jāgīrdār*s at Junagadh under the control of the governors of Sorath appointed by the Gujarat sultans. Later, they were a scattered network of small chieftains who controlled many of the areas around Junagadh.

In the nineteenth century the Cūḍāsamās did not suffer from a degraded status or the suspicion of a mixed Hindu-Islamic identity, unlike the related and neighbouring Jāḍejās. Nor did their kin, the Sammas in Sind, who, after their supercession in the sixteenth century, were able to project a clearly Sunni Muslim identity. The Jāḍejās, on the other hand, continued in power in Kachchh and Jamnagar, and evidence of their 'syncretic' identity was clearly visible to British observers in the nineteenth century. In spite of the bards' ambivalence towards the Cūḍāsamās and in spite of the fact that Māṇḍalik did not die fighting like the stereotypical Rajput, but capitulated and even converted to Islam, the image that persisted was of nobility and heroism in defeat. Eventually, the negotiated, mobile frontier world of alliance and genealogy represented and recorded by the bards was superseded and was replaced in the subsequent centuries by the brahmanical legal systems of the heartland. It would seem that the strategy of legitimation launched by the last few Cūḍāsamā rulers, of which the high point was the *Maṇḍalīka-nṛpa-carita*, was ultimately successful in catapulting their lineage to a high and untarnished status.

TRADE AND POLITICS IN KACHCHH: THE *JAGAḌŪCARITA*

One instance of the immigration, rise, and political significance of a merchant group is related in the *Jagaḍūcarita*. It is the verse biography in Sanskrit of a Jain merchant prince of Kachchh who lived in the thirteenth century. It consists of linked episodes from the life of Jagaḍū, most of which are intended to explain and celebrate his life as an exemplary philanthropist. Unusually for the *carita* form, it deals not with a royal personage, but with a 'simple' merchant.

Jagaḍū's ancestor Vīyaṭṭhu was a Śrīmālī Jain, a division of traders who trace their ancestry to the town of Śrīmāla or Bhillamāla in southern Marwad. Śrīmālīs are occasionally mentioned in the inscriptions of Gujarat of the eleventh century. His son Varaṇāga settled in Kanthkot in eastern Kachchh, which was within the Caulukya dominions since the beginning of their rule. Varaṇāga's grandson was Vīsala whose son Solaka emigrated to Bhadreshvar where his wife Śrī had three sons, ḍū, Rāja, and Padma.

After the death of Solaka, Jagaḍū became the provider for the family. He married Yaśomati and found wives for his brothers. Although he was generous by temperament, he came into possession of a talisman purchased from a shepherd that made him richer than ever and allowed him to indulge his generosity. Jagaḍū had no sons and his wife advised him to propitiate the gods to obtain a son. The god of the ocean declared that he would never have a son, but that fortune would be faithful to him and all his ships would come safely to port. He also presented ḍū with some excellent jewels from his treasury. Thereafter, the merchant went from strength to strength: 'the lamp of Sola's race, whose ships always arrived safely by virtue of the boon granted by the Ocean, shone in that town with increasing brilliancy, his glory being equal to that of Indra'.[62]

Having miraculously acquired wealth-generating properties from a herder of livestock and the ocean, Jagaḍū extended his business activities into another field. One of his assistants acquired at great cost a mysterious stone from the shore of a port in the Persian Gulf. Later, a Śaivite yogi advised Jagaḍū to split open the stone, which was found to be full of jewels. Again, Jagaḍū had enriched himself from a mysterious source and even acquired cooperation from the local aivites to exploit it.

A rich man, Jagaḍū now made a bid for political influence. He was not merely a munificent and exemplary merchant, but the saviour of his town. The tale goes as follows: Kachchh was invaded by king hadeva of Parkar, the Sūmrā chieftain Piṭṭhu, who destroyed the town wall of Bhadreshvar.[63] After returning to his own land, Pīṭhadeva heard that Jagaḍū was rebuilding the ramparts and sent him a messenger with a taunting message: 'The illustrious king Pīṭhadeva thus loudly speaks to thee through my mouth, "When two horns grow on the head of an ass, then thou will erect here a rampart!"' At this challenge, Jagaḍū vowed to set horns on the head of an ass and to build the ramparts too. The messenger rebuked him for destroying his race through excessive pride in his wealth. If he accepted the order of the king of Parkar, he might enjoy his riches in peace.

This is the first time that Jagaḍū made a political gesture beyond the normal accumulation of riches that might be expected of a merchant. He sent the messenger back, refusing to stop building the rampart, and thereby rejecting the sovereignty of Pīṭhadeva. He then visited the Vāghelā capital Anhilvada to seek the support of the ruler Lavaṇaprasāda (r. 1200–33) and represented to him that Pīṭhadeva's destruction of the ramparts was a challenge to Vāghelā sovereignty. He asked Lavaṇaprasāda for a protecting army of the 'thrice twelve' great kṣatriya tribes, which he duly received. Hearing of this, Pīṭhadeva fled his residence.

Jagaḍū then rebuilt the wall and above it built a 'dwelling of the god Bhadra who disguised appeared to him at night'. The rampart 'resembled Śiva's mountain and was beautified by an excellent encircling moat'. When the wall was completed, he sent the army back, 'keeping other warriors in his service'. He then triumphantly sent hadeva an obscene carving concerning his mother and an ass with golden horns. Pīṭhadeva died of horror on receiving the sculpture.[64] This dispatching of Pīṭhadeva also brought Jagaḍū the approval of the king of Sind, the Muslim Samma Jām who 'gladdened Jagaḍūka with gifts and honours'.

Jagaḍū had now made two important strategic moves for local political power: reasserted Caulukya sovereignty in the region and effectively pushed back the Sūmrā challenge from eastern Kachchh. He thereby achieved local representative status for himself. After having established his pretensions to political influence in the region, he made conspicuous demonstrations of Jain piety. He invited a senior Jain teacher and led a pilgrimage to the Jain holy sites with the permission of the new Vāghelā ruler Vīsaladeva. On his return, Jagaḍū carried out pious acts, which included the building and renovation of various Jain temples and images. He had wells, tanks, a hospital, and gardens constructed, as well as a brahmanical temple, that of Hariśaṅkara. In addition and most significantly, he built a *masīti* (*masjid*, mosque) called *ṣīmalī* (pertaining to the Ismā'īlīs) 'by reason of the wealth of the mlecchas'.[65] There is, indeed, a mosque identified as that of an ā'īlī community in Bhadreshvar that is also the earliest Islamic monument in India.[66] For Jagaḍū to consolidate his political base, it was necessary to keep the local trading communities happy.

Jagaḍū's political influence was next demonstrated during a great famine about which he had been warned by his Jain teacher. On the latter's instructions, he had stocked up on foodgrains so that he could exploit the coming time of want and hunger to 'gain great fame, brilliant like the waves of the milk-ocean, by saving the lives of men in the whole world'. When famine came, Jagaḍū was prepared. 'After two years of the famine had passed, the stores in the granaries of the kings were exhausted and prices rose to such a height that one dramma was paid for thirteen grains of gram.' The ruler of Anhilvada, saladeva Vāghelā, had reached the end of his resources and sent his minister Nāgaḍa to summon Jagaḍū who appeared accompanied by merchants, bearing presents but dressed austerely. Vīsaladeva asked him whether the report that he possessed 'seven hundred well-filled granaries' was true.

> ḍū smilingly replied that he possessed no grain of his own and that the king could easily convince himself of the truth of this statement, if he would send for the copperplates, hidden in the bricks of the granaries. The bricks were fetched and broken up and copperplates were found within, on which was written 'Jagaḍū stored this grain for the sake of the poor.' The merchant then declared that it would be his sin if the people died of starvation and he gave to Vīsaladeva eight thousand Mūṭakas of grain.[67]

Now even the king was in his debt. Jagaḍū then returned to Bhadreshvar and sent supplies of grain to other provinces: to Hammīra, the ruler of Sind, to King Madanavarman of Avanti, to the Garjaneśa Mojadīna of Delhi, to Pratāpasiṃha, king of Kāśī, and to King Skandhila. He also opened almshouses and helped the people through three years of famine.

After the famine was over, Jagaḍū was visited by Vīsaladeva's minister Nāgaḍa. During this visit, a ship with horses meant for the king was shipwrecked near Bhadreshvar and only one horse reached the shore alive. Nāgaḍa claimed the horse as royal property, but Jagaḍū claimed that it was his. Accordingly, a paper covered in skin was found attached to the neck of the animal, with Jagaḍū's name on it. Here Jagaḍū made his most audacious claim, for a prerogative usually reserved for rulers. Horses were an expensive and scarce commodity, and were imported at great cost from the Persian Gulf. By laying claim to the Caulukya horse, Jagaḍū was in effect making a claim to local sovereignty.

The tale ends with the death of Jagaḍū. 'When the neighbouring princes heard of his death, they all mourned for him. The king of Delhi [Garjaneśa] took off the turban from his head, Arjuna wept loudly and the king of Sindh did not touch food during two days.'

While there is no need to believe every detail of Jagaḍū's life, it demonstrates at least that in the thirteenth century it was possible for a merchant to stake claim to political power. The Vāghelās needed the allegiance of local chiefs, some of whom were merchants. While merchants in general and Jains in particular often took part in Gujarati politics at the Caulukya court, it was usually in a subsidiary position. In the case of Jagaḍū (or at least in the possibly wishful account of his life sponsored by his descendants), a claim was made to autonomous political power in a tellingly mercantile way—by an attempt to restrict and siphon off the ruler's supply of a scarce and continually required commodity—imported horses. A canny businessman who had risen to prominence by acquiring wealth, making pious donations, and conciliating the locals, could have made a kingdom for himself.

CONCLUSION

The history of Kachchh and Saurashtra prior to the fifteenth century demonstrates a political system that was marginal even to that of eastern Gujarat. While mainland Gujarat was dominated by a network of towns interspersed by agricultural lands, the peninsula was divided amongst struggling pastoralist clans with substantial cattle wealth. The main towns in the area were the ports from which a substantial local and oceanic trade was carried out. Agriculture in the region was largely for subsistence. The overwhelming dominance of pastoralist clans in the region and the transformation of their status created a polity that had its closest parallels in Rajasthan rather than mainland Gujarat. The chief difference from the situation in Rajasthan, however, was the connection between politics and trade, and the reciprocal struggle for the resources arising from trade.

Another feature of this polity, and its matrix of trading and pastoralist connections, was the religious ethos. This was a region where religious affiliations were largely pragmatic and were connected with the management of often scarce resources. Both trading and pastoralist communities tended to have pragmatic affiliations to religious belief, which could change or be modified to suit changing circumstances. Thus, one branch of a clan may have been Śaiva, another Ismāʿīlī, and yet another Sunni. Equally, as in the case of the magnate Jagaḍū, Jain religious affiliation was no barrier to building shrines for Śaivas and Ismāʿīlīs.

Towards the early fifteenth century, as a stable political system began to develop in eastern Gujarat under the sultans, the pastoralist-trading world also underwent some transformation. A political and mercantile system based on alliances and customary ties gradually gave way to a more settled court-based order, with concomitant bureaucratization and brahminization. Descent and genealogy rather than alliance became key factors in determining status. In the face of the overwhelming military dominance of the Gujarat sultans and their control over the trade routes for key military supplies such as arms, horses, and elephants, the erstwhile pastoralist clans entered into service or tribute-paying agreements with the sultans. This was accompanied by the establishment of courts, the employment of immigrant brahmins, the commissioning of Sanskritic chronicles, and so on. As a result of the new status hierarchies presided over by the sultans, evidence of pastoralist religious and occupational accommodations were sought to be erased or suppressed. However, even in the late fifteenth century, and indeed much later, the history of Kachchh and Saurashtra represented aspects of accommodation in the politics of the frontier.

NOTES

1. Forbes, *Ras Mala*, Vol. 1, p. 283.
2. Ibid., p. 229. According to Wilberforce-Bell, the date for this event was c. 1055. Wilberforce-Bell, *History of Kathiawad*, p. 66.
3. Wilberforce-Bell, *History of Kathiawad*, p. 67.
4. Forbes, *Ras Mala*, Vol. 1, p. 285.
5. Tambs-Lyche, *Power, Profit and Poetry*, p. 113.
6. Wilberforce-Bell, *History of Kathiawad*, p. 67.
7. Watson, 'Sketch of the Kathis', p. 321; Wilberforce-Bell, *History of Kathiawad*, p. 67.
8. Forbes, *Ras Mala*, Vol. 1, p. 295.
9. Ibid., p. 307.
10. Ibn Baṭṭūṭa, *Riḥla*, p. 144.
11. Kolff, *Naukar, Rajput and Sepoy*, p. 4.
12. Khan, *Mir'āt-i Aḥmadī: Supplement*, trans., p. 580, Kolff, *Naukar, Rajput and Sepoy*, p. 5.
13. Kolff, *Naukar, Rajput and Sepoy*, p. 18.
14. See Stewart Gordon (1994), 'Bhils and the Idea of a Criminal Tribe', in *Marathas, Marauders, and State Formation in Eighteenth Century Central India*, p. 152.
15. A.K. Forbes (1878), *Ras Mala, Hindoo Annals of the Province of Goozerat in Western India*, Vol. 2, p. 262n, A.M. Shah and R.S. Shroff (1975), 'The Vahīvancā Bāroṭs of Gujarat: A Caste of Genealogists and Mythographers', in Milton Singer, ed., *Traditional India: Structure and Change*, pp. 44–5.
16. Campbell, *Gazetteer*, p. 252, Sikandar, *MS*, p. 55.
17. Sikandar, *MS*, trans., p. 62.
18. Niẓām al-Din Aḥmad (1927–9), *The Ṭabaqāt-i Akbarī of Khwājah Niẓāmuddīn Aḥmad*, trans. Brajendranath De, Vol. 3, p. 71.
19. Forbes, *Ras Mala*, Vol. 1, pp. 58–60.
20. See section on Conversion in Chapter 4 of this volume.
21. H.R. Cooke et al. (1875), *Repression of Female Infanticide in the Bombay Presidency: A Compilation Report*, p. 5, fn.
22. Campbell and Kirparam, *Gujarat Population*, Vol. 1, p. 126.
23. James Tod (1829–32), *Annals and Antiquities of Rajasthan, or the Central*

24. H.D. Velankar (1953), '"Maṇḍalīka", The Last Great King of Independent Saurāṣṭra', *Bhāratīya Vidyā* 14, pp. 36–61; H.D. Velankar (1954), 'Maṇḍalīka Mahākāvya of Gangādhara Kavi', *Bhāratīya Vidyā,* 15(1), pp. 35–57; H.D. Velankar (1954), 'Śrī-gaṅgādharakavi-kṛt śrī-maṇḍalīka-mahākāvyam', *Bhāratīya Vidyā,* 15(2), pp. 13–40.
25. Several Sanskrit inscriptions, many with king lists, have survived from the reign of the Cūḍāsamās, but all of them were actually commissioned by local merchants or feudatories.
26. We hear of brahmins who were periodically imported into these regions. The history of the region by a minister of Junagadh relates that Nāgar, Girnārā, Sarasvati, and Soraṭh brahmins were invited into Saurashtra by the kings of Junagadh, especially by Rā Navghaṇ II in the twelfth century. Ranchodjī Amarjī (1882), *Ta'rīkh-i Sorath: A History of the Provinces of Sorath and Halar in Kathiawad,* trans. E. Rehatsek, pp. 26–7.
27. Ibid., p. 33.
28. One account says that the Cūḍāsamās came from Saminagar in Sind, now known as Thatta. J.W. Watson (1884), *Kathiawar: Gazetteer of the Bombay Presidency,* Vol. 8, p. 408.
29. Campbell and Kirparam, *Gujarat Population,* p. 124.
30. S.H. Desai (1991), *Saurāṣṭra-no itihās (History of Saurashtra),* pp. 222–3. Desai identifies Śoṇitapur with Babylon. Vikramsiṃh Rāyjādā suggests that it is to be identified with Sana in Yemen or with a place near Ukhimath in the Himalayas, on the banks of the Mandakini. V.B. Rāyjādā (1995), *Cūḍāsamā rājavaṃśa-no itihās, cūḍāsamā rajavaṃśa-nī praśasti kavitā (The History of the Cūḍāsamā Dynasty. The Cūḍāsamā Dynasty's Eulogy),* p. 11. The *Bombay Gazetteer* favours the identification with Sana. Watson, *Kathiawar,* p. 586.
31. Rāyjādā's variant has Garvagoḍ as the ruler of Śoṇitapur. Twenty-second in the line of descent from Garvagoḍ was Devendra who married Okhā. Their four sons were Ajpat, Gajpat, Narpat, and Bhūpat. Rāyjādā, *Cūḍāsamā rājavaṃśa,* p. 11.
32. Urmārā could be an indigenous term used for the port of Ormuz or Hormuz in the Persian Gulf.
33. A branch of the Cūḍāsamās, descended from the third son of Rā Navghaṇ (1067–98), did settle at Osam-Patanvav. Rāyjādā, *Cūḍāsamā rājavaṃśa,* p. 39.
34. James Burgess heard that Gazni was an ancient name of Cambay. Burgess, *Report on the Antiquities of Kutch and Kathiawar,* p. 43.
35. Ibid., p. 196.

'Alī Shīr Qāni', Thattawī, *Tuḥfat al-kirām,* in Elliot and Dowson, *History of India,* Vol. 1, pp. 336–9. The fact that there is a concordance between the 'Hindu' genealogies encountered by Tod, Burgess, Desai, and Rāyjādā, and the 'Muslim' one in the *Tuḥfat al-kirām,* suggest that they had a common

37. al-Hamdani, *Beginnings of the Ismā'īlī Da'wa*, p. 7.
38. Forbes, *Ras Mala*, Vol. 1, p. 53 fn.
39. Hemacandra (1915), *Dvyāśrayakāvya*, ed., A.V. Kathavate, Vol. 1, verses 2.65, 2.76, 2.80, 2.86–89, 4.25, 4.80–81. For a discussion of this text, see Satya Pal Narang (1972), *Hemacandra's Dvyāśrayakāvya: A Literary and Cultural Study*, and Majumdar, *Chaulukyas of Gujarat*, pp. 25–8.
40. See B.D. Chattopadhyaya (1998), *Representing the Other? Sanskrit Sources and the Muslims (8th–14th century)*, p. 30.
41. Narang, *Hemacandra's Dvyāśrayakāvya*, pp. 78–9.
42. The ruler of Kachchh was Lakṣa, son of Phulla who has been identified with one of the traditional ancestors of the Jāḍejās of Kachchh, Lākho Phūlānī. In Hemacandra's account, he was a powerful ruler who defeated the Turuṣkas (the Arabs of Mansura?). Majumdar's variant reading of the same verse suggests that Lakṣa saved the Turuṣkas from Kachchh. See Majumdar, *Chaulukyas of Gujarat*, p. 26, note 16.
43. Majumdar, *Chaulukyas of Gujarat*, pp. 25–7, notes 16, 26. Majumdar also cites the fourteenth-century writer Merutuṅga who refers to the ruler of Kachchh as an animal herder. Merutuṅga (1933), *Prabandhacintāmaṇi*, ed., Jinavijaya Muni, pp. 18–19. See also Forbes, *Ras Mala*, Vol. 1, pp. 58–60.
44. Although the Sūmrās are believed to have ruled from 1053 onwards, they could have been tributary chiefs for as long as 200 years before that.
45. Tambs-Lyche, *Power, Profit and Poetry*, p. 34–5.
46. Campbell and Kirparam, *Gujarat Population*, p. 520.
47. Tambs-Lyche, *Power, Profit and Poetry*, pp. 34–5.
48. Descent from the moon was a way of claiming Rajput status. The inscription here records that a well was built by one Kuntarāja of the Vallāditya clan on the order of the Mehar ruler Thepak, a tributary of the Cūḍāsamās. For the text of the inscription, see Vajeshankar G. Oza (1887), *Bhāvanagar prācīna śodha saṅgraha*, No. 84; Diskalkar, *IK*, No. 27.
49. Interestingly, this inscription, set into a step-well near Junagadh, also records that after Mokalasiṃha had moved his capital from Junagadh to Vanthali on the orders of the sultan, he fought and defeated the kings of Sind and Kachchh for the control of the town of Bhumbli (modern Ghumli). The well, dedicated to Viṣṇu, was built by Hānī, the daughter-in-law of Mokalasiṃha's minister Gadādhar. For the full Sanskrit text, see Burgess and Cousens, *RLARBP*, p. 245, Diskalkar, *IK*, No. 48 and Shastri, *HIG*, No. 61.
50. (i) 'Būbā' Pātāk, son of Venu son of Cūṇā of the Yādava clan died in battle against the Pātsāh's army, but children, elders and 18 Rājaputras reached Junagadh safely. (ii) Nūbhā, son of Bārad Nughaṇ died in battle against the Turuṣkas. (iii) Velāyulu son of Dāsā Cācā died in battle against the Turuṣkas. (iv) Meghā son of Jādav Merā died in battle against the

Turuṣkas. (v) Raut Cāmpā, son of Paḍhīārīyā Jhāṭā attained heaven fighting against the Yavanas. Diskalkar, *IK*, No. 64, Shastri, *HIG*, No. 65–69.

51. Chattopadhyay suggests that Turuṣka was originally an ethnic term that later became used as a generic term for Muslims. Chattopadhyay, *Representing the Other?*, p. 30.
52. The inscription was installed to commemorate the building of a *maṭha* (college or monastery for brahmins) by one Dāmodara and includes a genealogy of the ruling family. The genealogy indicates descent from Kṛṣṇa, in his role as the stealer of butter, and the Yādava lineage is mentioned for the first time. (*Maṇḍalīka-nṛpatiryadu-vamśe*). Diskalkar, *IK*, No. 68, Shastri, *HIG*, No. 74. The claim to Yādava ancestry coincides with an intensification of Kṛṣṇaite Vaiṣṇavism in the region. Françoise Mallison, drawing on the work of H.C. Bhayani, traces a diverse and refined culture of Kṛṣṇaite Vaiṣṇava literary production in Gujarat in the late fifteenth and early sixteenth century. F. Mallison (1995), 'Early Kṛṣṇa *Bhakti* in Gujarat: The Evidence of Old Gujarati Texts Recently Brought to Light', in A.W. Entwistle and F. Mallison, eds, *Studies in South Asian Devotional Literature, Research Papers 1988–1991*, pp. 59–60.
53. This long inscription, in Sanskrit and Old Gujarati, set into the fort wall of Junagadh is one of the few epigraphic examples of an official decree by the Cūḍāsamās. It relates that on the request of the trader Hāsā son of Devā of Stambhatīrtha (Cambay) and others, the Yādava ruler Maṇḍalīk decreed at his coronation that apart from *agiāras* (the 11th) and *amāvas* (no moon) when violence was forbidden, animal killing would also be prohibited on the 5th, 8th, and 14th of the months. Shastri, *HIG*, No. 78.
54. The ruler's name is recorded differently in different sources. In contemporary inscriptions and the *Maṇḍalīka-nṛpa-carita*, he is Maṇḍalīka, in the Persian sources, he is Rāy Mandalīk but in Cāraṇī accounts and in modern Gujarati, he is Rā or Rāh Māṇḍalik.
55. Soma-vaṃśa 2.8; Candra-vaṃśa 7.31; Vidhu-kula 8.62; Sudhākiraṇa-vaṃśa 9.3; Yadu-kula 1.66; 3.35; 8.25; 8.29. The name Cūḍāsamā is mentioned only once and does not seem to refer directly to the name of the royal house (10.3). Velankar, 'Maṇḍalīka Mahākāvya', p. 52.
56. Watson, *Kathiawar*, pp. 165, 287–8.
57. Ibid., p. 165, fn. 1.
58. Sikandar, *MS*, p. 78.
59. Watson, *Kathiawar*, p. 487.
60. Amarjī, *Ta'rīkh-i Sorath*, p. 117.
61. See section on Conversion in Chapter 4 in this volume.
62. Sarvāṇanda, *Jagaḍūcarita*, p. 10.
63. Bhadreshvar was overrun by Pīṭhadeva of Pāra, identified with Phitu or Phatu, a Sūmrā chief, a popular and powerful Muslim king of Sind (r. 1193–1226). Sayyid Muḥammad Ma'ṣūm Bakkarī (1938), *Ta'rīkh-i*

ma'sūmī, pp. 61, 290 and Mīr 'Alī Shīr Qānī' Thattawī (1971), *Tuḥfat al-kirām*, p. 69.

64. Carvings of this description to convey curses or maledictions are not uncommon in Saurashtra. They were also found in the eighteenth century: 'And sometimes during the rainy season silver coins with the image of an ass are found—said to have been struck in the name of Raja Gadhesingh, about whom strange stories are told.' Khan, *Mir'āt-i Aḥmadī: Supplement* trans., p. 211. A parallel tradition from Gedi in Kachchh demonstrates that Jagaḍū's is an archetypal story: A potter's ass, Gadhesingh, had the ability to assume human form at night, and in this form asked the potter to get him married to the daughter of the town's ruler. He was challenged to build a copper wall around the town, which he duly fulfilled and secured the princess' hand in marriage. After the wedding, the raja's daughter burnt the skin of the ass, and Gadhesingh and the copper wall disappeared. A similar legend was recorded about the origins of the city of Cambay. D.P. Khakhar (1879), *Report on the Architectural and Archaeological Remains in the Provinces of Kachh*, p. 39.
65. Sarvāṇanda, *Jagaḍūcarita*, p. 18.
66. Shokoohy, Bayani-Wolpert, and Shokoohy, *Bhadreśvar*, p. 33.
67. Sarvāṇanda, *Jagaḍūcarita*, p. 20, verses 71–90.

4

Religion, Politics, and Patronage in a Settling Society

With the decline of the Caulukyas at the end of the twelfth century, the continuing prosperity and diversity of Gujarat attracted priests and missionaries of a variety of denominations. Some of these secured powerful patrons in the shape of merchants or chieftains, others became the custodians of shrines or places of pilgrimage; and yet others became organizers of routes of pilgrimage. The increasing importance of pilgrimage ensured that the trade routes were regularly traversed and new sites enriched by pilgrims.

Although Gujarat is widely associated with Vaiṣṇavism in modern times, there is little evidence that it was particularly popular in this period. Various Vaiṣṇava streams, including the Bhāgavata, Kṛṣṇaite, and cults of Vāmana and Varāha found followers and patrons intermittently, yet Vaiṣṇavism was never the sole religion of the Caulukyas. From the fifteenth century onwards there is evidence that Dvaraka and sites associated with Kṛṣṇa were being incorporated into a trans-regional pilgrimage cycle.[1] Kṛṣṇaite Vaiṣṇavism gradually began to find popular appeal, this time not associated with the courts, but featuring bhakti or personal worship, particularly among merchant groups.

Ismā'īlī missionaries linked to the Fāṭimid caliphate had long been active in western India and Sind. Later, Sunni Muslim missionaries also achieved some success in Gujarat. However, unlike with the Ismā'īlīs, there is little indication of the mode of conversion employed by Sunni missionaries or what groups they first converted. By the thirteenth in the coastal towns, there were inland settlements in places like Anhilvada Patan, Bharuch, and Junagadh.[2] According to the Veraval inscription of 1264, local Muslim communities included oil-pressers, whitewashers, and other occupational groups.[3] Although large tracts of Gujarat were ruled by Muslims from the early fourteenth century onwards, conversion to Islam did not play an important role in state policy.

Since the fourteenth century Muslim rule and the separation of political power from the temple and its attendants resulted in a diversification of the patronage of religion. While certain sects were loosely appropriated into state-sponsored brahmanism, others continued to shift and evolve. The pastoralist clans who came from the north and north-west were gradually incorporated into military hierarchies and employment, becoming part of a trans-regional armed peasantry with its own sanctified heroes and deities. Some of the mother goddesses they venerated became *kul-devī*s or clan goddesses.[4] The goddesses coexisted with other deities, heroes, and preceptors, each of which played specific roles in religious life.

Many popular religious groupings in Gujarat originate in this period. Shrines increasingly became the centres of new sects. The shrines themselves were symbols of settlement, and the formulation of a sacred geography of closely packed shrines demonstrates the scale of settlement in Gujarat in this period. Far from stamping out religious diversity, sultanate rule in the fourteenth and early fifteenth centuries arguably opened up an unprecedented range of religious options, a veritable religious marketplace, as newly prosperous patrons sought legitimacy and divine assistance. It was only towards the end of the fifteenth century that dominant trends emerged out of the competing sects: Vaiṣṇavism among merchant groups, Sunni Islam among the Muslim rulers, and a combination of Śaivism and goddess worship among the genealogically hierarchized Rajput groups.

THE DECLINE OF THE ROYAL TEMPLE CULTS

In common with many contemporary lineages in north India, the Caulukyas' royal cult as indicated in their temples, epigraphs, chronicles, and titles was Śaivite. They built a far greater number of Śaiva temples than those of any other denomination. While temples to other deities—ṣṇu and his avatāras, Sūrya, and goddesses—were regularly built, these were usually either constructed by merchants or feudatories, or were subsidiary temples within predominantly Śaivite temple complexes.[5] However, the architectural form of the Gujarat temples did not differ according to sect, indicating that temples of all denominations were built by specialized architects.[6]

The Caulukyas built many temples and employed brahmins as priests and administrators. This was a period when it was vital to link the royal cult with larger north Indian networks of pilgrimage and Sanskritic legitimation. The Somanāth temple predated the Caulukyas but their patronage of this temple on the distant south-western coast of Saurashtra was an important indicator of their sovereignty in the region. The very first Caulukya king Mūlarāja is said to have been devoted to Somanath and to have worshipped there every week. Possibly tiring of this strenuous travelling, he built a temple of the moon god in Anhilvada.

He offered the post of administering the new temple to a senior ascetic named Kāṇṭhaḍī. As is usual between religious legitimators and governments, the Caulukyas had a contested relationship with the Śaiva ascetic orders. Kāṇṭhaḍī refused the job, but one of his disciples finally accepted on condition that he would be supplied with thirty-two women, a daily quantity of saffron, musk, and camphor for his massage, a white umbrella, and a grant of land.[7]

An important aspect of Śaiva religiosity at the court was animal sacrifice. Śaiva kings were regularly petitioned by their Jain subjects to restrict animal slaughter and sacrifice. Consequently, when the Caulukyas were influenced by Jainism, the most striking difference they introduced was to give up ritual sacrifice. When Kumārapāla became a Jain, his prohibition of animal slaughter was opposed by four sects.[8]

With the expansion of Caulukya power, local deities were incorporated into the royal idiom, often as junior members of the family of Śiva. For example, after defeating a Bhīl chieftain in the region of what is now Ahmadabad, Karṇa I built a temple to the local goddess Kocharabā on the instructions of Bhairavadevī, a consort of Śiva. Siddharāja Jayasiṃha built several Śiva temples of which the royal temple of Rudramahālaya (abode of Rudra, the fearsome form of Śiva) was most significant. Although his successor Kumārapāla was a convert to Jainism, he also built and restored several Śaiva temples.[9]

Besides kings, feudatories and merchants also constructed Śaiva temples. A wandering Śaiva ascetic built several temples from his own earnings after having travelled to Śaiva places of pilgrimage such as āranāth in the Himalayas and Rāmeśvaram in the south. On his arrival at Somanath he was offered the position of temple official. Interestingly, three of the five Śiva temples he built were named after the important women in his life—his mother and the wives of two of his benefactors.[10] As was to become common in Gujarat, women donors and supplicants figured prominently in inscriptions. Many Śaiva temples memorialized the names of their builders or their families: for example, Lavaṇaprasāda built the temples Ānaleśvara and Salakhaṇeśvara in the names of his father Ānala or Ānā and his mother Salakhaṇadevī.[11]

Apart from temples, there were Śaiva sectarian monasteries for the use of ascetics. These housed both celibate and householder ascetics and, in some cases, female ascetics as well.[12] The important Śaiva sect in this period was that of Lakulīśa-Pāśupata. Ascetics of the order became influential at the Caulukya court and administered most of the important royal temples such as those of Somanath and Anhilvada Patan.[13] Other Śaiva sects of the Caulukya period included the Kaula and Kāpālika ascetic orders, of which the latter were particularly influential among the pastoralist communities of Saurashtra.[14] As seen in the example of Kāṇṭhaḍī, ascetics often resisted becoming temple officials and preferred to stay within their own monastic orders.[15] Temple functionaries were generally considered lower in status and the Caulukyas had to invite brahmins from north India to take over ritual duties. These included the Gauḍas who were encouraged to settle around Patan.[16]

As shown in Chapter 2, significantly fewer new Hindu temples were built in the thirteenth century under Vāghelā domination. Monumental royal temple complexes were no longer being built. After the establishment of sultanate rule in the early fourteenth century, temple Śaivism, which played a political role by connecting the Hindu king to the divine, was no longer practised overtly. In territories outside direct sultanate control, however, there are signs that the new settling pastoralist polities took up the patronage of Śaivite monasteries and orders. The temple of Somanath continued to receive attention in this period and must have been kept up. An inscription of 1394–5 mentions a Paramār pastoralist worshipping at Somanath and making a donation of cows to the temple.[17] Another inscription of 1385 is dedicated to Someśa or Śiva at Somanath.[18] Such indicators continued throughout the Sultanate period.

ṢṆAVISM AND BHAKTI

ṣṇavism in Gujarat is a result of the mingling of several distinct sectarian traditions at various points in time. These include the separate cults of Bhāgavata or the Vedic Viṣṇu, Kṛṣṇa, Vāsudeva, and Baladeva, elements of which were conjoined within the Kṛṣṇaite neo-Vaiṣṇavism that became increasingly popular within Gujarat from the fifteenth century onwards, and subsequently became one of the most recognizable features of elite modern Gujarati religiosity. The synthesis of many of these traditions was first represented in a tenth-century Vaiṣṇava probably written in south India, the *Bhāgavata Purāṇa,* which subsequently became popular in Gujarat. In the light of its importance for Gujarat's subsequent history, it might be worthwhile to go over the antecedents of popular Vaiṣṇavism.

Although some aspects of Vaiṣṇavism were popular in Gujarat from the early common era, it fell out of favour as a royal cult by the tenth century. In the period of our study Vaiṣṇavism and its component sects were not an important feature of royal cults as manifested in texts or temples of which the overwhelming majority were dedicated iva. However, while the Vaiṣṇava and Kṛṣṇaite demoninations did not as a rule receive exclusive royal patronage, they continued to have some adherents among merchants and pastoralist groups in Gujarat throughout this period.

One of the most important components of the emergent bhakti ṣṇavism of the fifteenth century was the cult of Kṛṣṇa. The figure of Kṛṣṇa is generally understood to be a composite one. The heroic ṛṣṇa of the epic Mahābhārata is distinct from the pastoralist deity of north-west India.

> Historians of Hinduism ... agree in distinguishing the Kṛṣṇa of the epic, the dava prince of Dvaraka and ally of the Pāṇḍavas in their quarrel with the Kauravas, from Kṛṣṇa-Gopāla, the deified hero of the nomadic or semi-nomadic pastoralist tribes which in ancient times occupied the territory of the Surasenas on both banks of the river Yamuna.[19]

The warrior-king Kṛṣṇa who appears in the Mahābhārata is thus to be identified with Vāsudeva, the supreme deity of the Pañcarātra or gavata sect, and with the Vedic god Viṣṇu who was himself identified at a later date with Nārāyaṇa. The cowherd god Kṛṣṇa-Gopāla had little place in this synthesis. In the early Gupta period, Kṛṣṇa-Gopāla was gradually incorporated into the Viṣṇu tradition as the perfect incarnation of Viṣṇu. Gupta Vaiṣṇavism was thus a mingling of Bhāgavatism with the three elements of Vāsudeva-Kṛṣṇa, Nārāyaṇa, and Janārdana.[20] The gavata dharma was founded in the Mathura region in the early historical period and is seen in Gujarat from the Gupta period onwards.[21] The Girnar Skandagupta inscription, the only Gupta inscription in Gujarat, invokes the Vāmana avatāra of Viṣṇu and refers to the construction of a temple of Viṣṇu in 457 CE. The administrator Cakrapālita who built the Cakrabhṛt temple in Girnar was an ardent devotee of Govinda, that is, Kṛṣṇa the cowherd.[22] Another notable feature of Gupta Vaiṣṇavism was the worship of avatāras. In the gradual transformation of Bhāgavatism into Vaiṣṇavism, the doctrine of manifestations of Viṣṇu played an important role.[23] With the rise of the avatāra doctrine, Vāsudeva Kṛṣṇa was recognized as the most perfect incarnation of Viṣṇu. Other avatāras also became popular, as witnessed in the different Purāṇas and inscriptions, although no avatāra images from this period have been found in Gujarat.

From the post-Gupta period, in spite of the importance of the other āras of Viṣṇu, Vaiṣṇavite devotion became predominantly Kṛṣṇaite, focusing on the tale of the cowherd-god Kṛṣṇa-Gopāla at the expense of the supposedly older epic story that became secondary. In the *gavata Purāṇa* the legend of Kṛṣṇa-Gopāla in the erotic mode became the favourite theme of bhakti literature. The figure of Kṛṣṇa-Gopāla is itself composite and has been attributed a non-Aryan origin, a 'close connection with the pastoralist tribes, the Ābhīras, Gurjaras and others', and also an affinity with pre-Aryan earth divinities, primitive fertility cults, and forest, tree, and stream spirits.[24] In addition, early tradition would suggest that the cowherd-god was a minor figure associated with the deity of the plough, Halāyudha or Balarāma.[25]

However, during the rule of the Caulukyas (942–1242) the worship of Viṣṇu remained in a subsidiary position. Although the Caulukya rulers were mostly Śaivas, with some Jains, they seem to have taken a tolerant stance to other practices. Several rulers worshipped Lakṣmī, the consort of Viṣṇu and the goddess of wealth.[26] The worship of ṣmī by herself was a common feature even among non-Vaiṣṇava groups. She was particularly popular among merchant groups, including the Jains.

Several Caulukya officials and important merchants were Vaiṣṇavas. Both the Navasari inscription of Karṇadeva I's feudatory and the Dohad inscription from the reign of Siddharāja (1140 CE) begin with an invocation to Vāsudeva and the Varāha (boar) avatāra. In Kumārapāla's time too, some grants were given to Vaiṣṇavas although he was a Śaiva who became a Jain and had prominent Jain courtiers.[27] In the reign of ma II (1178–1242) a courtier built two Viṣṇu temples in Somanath.[28]

The successors to the Caulukyas, the Vāghelā family of Dholka, appear to have venerated Viṣṇu in the form of Nārāyaṇa. Vīradhavala ghelā built a temple to Vīranārāyaṇa (Viṣṇu in the heroic mode) in

1238. One of his courtiers also built Nārāyaṇa temples.[29] From the fourteenth century onwards there was a great proliferation of rulers and patrons in Gujarat. Several inscriptions from wells, memorial slabs, and temples in the fourteenth century mention Viṣṇu. The 1499 step-well inscription of Adalaj, set up by Rūḍādevī, the wife of a Vāghelā chieftain, indicates that she followed the Bhāgavata dharma. Images of Viṣṇu are found in the niches of the well.[30] However, Viṣṇu in the form of Kṛṣṇa, the cowherd-god, did not appear much in Gujarat after the eighth century CE.

Thus, the worship of Kṛṣṇa-Gopāla declined in north-western India (where it arose) from the end of the Gupta period. Meanwhile, the cults of Śiva, Sūrya, and later Viṣṇu made advances and found patrons among a range of new and aspirant rulers, the former up to the borders of Bengal and Orissa. The cowherd-god then reappeared in the south and in Bengal around the twelfth century, and was reintroduced to north India with the help of texts such as the *Bhāgavata Purāṇa*.[31] Although the legend of Kṛṣṇa-Gopāla arose among the pastoralist groups of the north Indian plains, it was in the south that it was assimilated into emergent Vaiṣṇava bhakti.

In Gujarat Nṛsiṃhāraṇyamuni composed *Viṣṇubhakticandrodaya* ('The Rising Moon of the Devotion of Viṣṇu') in 1416, an early manifestation of the renewed popularity of Vaiṣṇavism. The last leaf of a copy from Talaja states that it was prepared when Malik Śrī Usmān and Rāol Śrī Sārangajī were in power in Ghogha. It was recommended that it should be protected from oil, water, loose binding, and falling into strange hands.[32] In Girnar an inscription of 1417 commences with a prayer to Dāmodara or Kṛṣṇa as the butter-thief.[33] The turn towards Vaiṣṇavism and the translation of Puraṇic stories into the vernacular reached its height in the late fifteenth century with Bhālaṇ who translated numerous *akhyānas* (narratives) from the Purāṇas.[34] He also popularized Kṛṣṇa stories such as *Rukmiṇi-haraṇ, Satyabhāmā vivāha, Kṛṣṇa bālacarita* adapted from the *Bhāgavata Purāṇa*. There were also other poets such as Keśava Hṛdayarāma, a Kāyastha from Patan, and Bhīma, a Moḍha brahmin from Siddhpur, who translated cantos from the *Bhāgavata* and other Sanskrit Vaiṣṇava works into Gujarati.[35]

In Gujarat the transition to Vaiṣṇava bhakti seems to have happened in some important instances at the expense of Śaivism. This would bear out N.A. Thoothi's observation that Vaiṣṇavism had 'grown out of the struggle to supplant Saivism'.[36] This was also true of the rise of avism in other South Asian regions, for example, in Orissa.[37]

Even in the Dvaraka region, the only place where Vaiṣṇava shrines are in a majority, most of the shrines belong to the period of Vaiṣṇavite revivalism from the sixteenth century.[38] Many of these, such as the town of Dvaraka itself, were sacred sites earlier, but were not necessarily ṣṇava. Dvaraka was an important site from about the seventh century and was one of the four *pīṭha*s of Ādi Śaṅkarācārya, but the Kṛṣṇaite temple there belongs to the sixteenth century.[39] It is significant that in some of them, such as the temple of Kṛṣṇa as Raṇachoḍa in Dakor (built in 1556), the narrative of the installation of the icon indicates that the site was formerly a Śaivite shrine. The story of shifting the image of Dvārakādhīśa (Raṇachoḍajī) from Dvaraka to Dankapur reconciles the original Śaiva shrine with the new image. Ḍankarsī, the builder of the temple, propitiated Śiva and persuaded him to stay there permanently. Śiva then made Kṛṣṇa promise that he would also stay there forever.[40] The story also relates that the image of Kṛṣṇa was brought to Dakor four hundred years previously, but had to be hidden by his devotees until, presumably, it was safe to install it in the formerly aiva temple. This is an indication that while variants of Kṛṣṇaite belief may have existed prior to the building of important shrines, they did not usually find favour and patronage before the sixteenth century.

The history of Śāmalājī in Sabarkantha district, an important ṛṣṇaite temple popular from the sixteenth century, indicates Śaiva origins. Its legend says that Śiva permitted Brahma to do a *yajña* here. 'At the beginning of the *yajña*, Śrī Gadādhara Viṣṇu appeared before Brahma in a dark (Śyāmala or Śāmala) form and at the request of Brahma, Gadādhara Viṣṇu stayed in Karambuka kṣetra.'[41] Thus, the worship of Viṣṇu the mace-wielder was facilitated by the benediction iva who allowed Brahma to conduct the sacrifice in the first place. The tension between Śaivism and emergent Vaiṣṇavism is also seen in the life of the poet Bhālaṇ who began life as a Śaivite, but later seems to have transferred his allegiance to the Vaiṣṇava Ramānandī sect.[42]

By the mid-fifteenth century a Vaiṣṇava theme entered some texts that did not have a specifically sectarian orientation. The *Kānhaḍade prabandha*, written c.1456 in Gujarat sultanate-controlled Jalor, recalls for his descendants the heroic story of the Cauhan hero Kānhaḍade and his battles against the armies of 'Alā' al-Dīn Khaljī in the late thirteenth century. The brahmin poet Padmanābha dedicated his account to Vāsudeva although his own devotion, expressed later in the text, was to the Śaivite shrine of Somanath. However, Gujarat was already seen as a land of Vai avism:

> Where the *śāligrāma* (stone symbol of Viṣṇu) is worshipped and Hari's name is remembered; in the land where sacrifices are performed and donations (*tyāga*) given to the brahmins; where *tulasī* (holy basil) and *pīpal* (ficus) are worshipped *dharma* according to the Vedas and Purāṇas is understood; in the land where all go on pilgrimages and honour the *smṛtis*, the Purāṇas and the cow.[43]

According to this text, when 'Alā' al-Dīn's armies reached Somanath, the local chieftains—Vāḷā, Vājā, Jeṭhvā, and Cūḍāsamā—offered a united defence while 'the Khan's horsemen pillaged the town reminiscent of the sack of Lanka.'[44] In another episode, Kānhaḍade, whose very name indicates an allegiance to Kṛṣṇa (Kānhā), refused to pay obeisance to the sultan's general. His envoy declared: 'Should the world cool and the sun rise in the west, except to Nārāyaṇa, Kānhaḍade shall bow his head to none.'[45] This Vaiṣṇava orientation did not prevent nhaḍade from rescuing the Somanath idol of Śiva from the marauding army and worshipping it with full ceremonial.

In yet another episode, the Śaivite emphasis returns in an unexpected form. The sultan had now conquered all other territories, but Jalor remained a thorn in his side. He marched towards Jalor, first encountering nhaḍade's kinsman Sāntal. The latter called upon his family deity purī to help him defeat the enemy. In reply, the goddess granted ntal a tour of the sultan's army. He saw the king ('Alā' al-Dīn) fast asleep in the form of Śiva with three eyes, five faces, long matted hair, necklace of skulls, alms bowl and the Ganga in his top-knot. Sāntal was wonderstruck and bowed in awe.[46]

In this vision, the mleccha enemy appears in the form of Śiva-Rudra. A Vaiṣṇava pastoralist chieftain and devotee of Āśāpurī was thus pitted against the enemy as a manifestation of Śiva, throwing him into a quandary: 'The sultan was changed into the form of Rudra! How can the blow be struck?'[47] This is also the point at which the poet declares his own affiliations: 'Sāntal had seen the Lord of Padmanābha Paṇḍit.'[48]

The popularization of Vaiṣṇavism came from the south with mānuja (twelfth century) and Madhvācārya (thirteenth century). They were amongst the earliest propagators of the *Bhāgavata Purāṇa* and mystical ideas of abandonment to Kṛṣṇa based on the erotic aspect of the deity as the basis of bhakti.[49] It is likely that Gujarat was exposed to this form of neo-Vaiṣṇavism quite early. The first inscription of Kṛṣṇa worship, dated 1291, is from the reign of Sāraṅgadeva Vāghelā (1274–96) and records an instance of the communal worship of Kṛṣṇa at Palanpur. It contains a description of the offerings and theatricals performed for the worship of Kṛṣṇa.[50] However, bhakti Vaiṣṇavism does not seem to have taken on a popular form before the fifteenth century. Although there are several references to the practice of Vaiṣṇavism before the fifteenth century, this is when it began to become a popular and expanding sect in Gujarat.

Kṛṣṇa is associated primarily with the region of Dvaraka in the north-west of peninsular Gujarat. The legend recalls that a branch of ṛṣṇa's clan, the Yādavas, migrated from Mathura to Dvaraka, but their supremacy was brought to an end after disastrous infighting. The final feud took place in the region of Prabhasa, around Somanath, and Kṛṣṇa was killed by a hunter between Veraval and Prabhas Patan. According to Hermann Goetz, the sites of Mathura and Dvaraka, where the mythological Kṛṣṇa lived most of his life, were not incorporated into networks of pilgrimage until the fifteenth century.[51] Thus, while the site of Dvaraka may have been significant for the cult of the cowherd-god, he remained a local deity without pan-Indian significance. The influence of neo-Vaiṣṇava texts and propaganda did not immediately lead to the incorporation of Dvaraka in the pilgrimage network. This took off only after the proselytizing tours undertaken by Vallabhācārya in the first decade of the sixteenth century.

The visit of Vallabhācārya (1479–1532) to Gujarat in the early sixteenth century was immensely significant. He had remarkable success in converting several sections of people in Gujarat to his fold. He travelled to Siddhpur where he encountered orthodox Śaivas, Patan, a Jain stronghold, Vadnagar, and Visnagar, the base for the influential gar brahmins—followers of Śankara's monism—and Bharuch where the Bhṛgu brahmins questioned him on the distinction between Hari and Hara, that is, Viṣṇu and Śiva. He is said to have had success in all these places. Vallabhācārya is also claimed to have had Muslim devotees and impressed Sikandar Lodī and Maḥmūd Bīgara.[52] He established eighty four *baiṭhak*s—seats—all over India, of which some were in Gujarat. This is the chief Vaiṣṇava movement with relevance for modern Gujarat.

The fifteenth century Kṛṣṇaite poet Narasiṃha Mahetā—the 'first entirely monolingual Gujarati poet' predated the spread of the Vallabha movement in Gujarat.[53] His vocabulary came from a combination of the local cultic tradition in Saurashtra, prevalent Jain concepts of individual worship, and congregational devotion, and only latterly from the text-based brahmanical neo-Vaiṣṇavism from the south. It is significant that this early Vai avism in Gujarat tended largely to be non-brahmanical or even anti-brahmanical. There is little evidence in Gujarat of brahmins introducing it or engaging in its proselytization. While Narasiṃha Mahetā was a brahmin, he belonged to the Nāgar denomination that did not take up priestly or ritual duties, and in fact is comparable to scribal communities such as the Kāyasthas in north India.[54] Stories about Narasiṃha's battles with the Śaiva priesthood in Junagadh form the mainstay of his quasi-martyrology. Gujarati neo-ṣṇavism was adopted largely by traders and peasants (and by groups making a transition from agriculture to trade), and in some cases by women from Rajput communities (for example, the bhakti poet Mirā). The only function for brahmins in this Vaiṣṇavism was as temple priests—the so-called degraded brahmins of Dvaraka and Dakor.[55]

Interestingly, most of the pastoralist groups who gave rise to the idea of Kṛṣṇa and who claimed descent in his line did not adopt the new Vaiṣṇavism. The Cūḍāsamās, for example, claimed to belong to ṛṣṇa's Yādava clan in their inscriptions and texts, but did not respond to the neo-Vaiṣṇavism of figures such as Narasiṃha Mahetā. Several other Rajputizing groups similarly associated their lineage with Kṛṣṇa without adopting him as the clan deity.

JAINISM AND TRADE

The prevalence of Jainism was remarked upon by many travellers to Gujarat. They were especially struck by the Jains' reverence for animal life. Marco Polo, in the thirteenth century, was fascinated by the Jains:

> They could not kill an animal on any account, not even a fly or a flea or a louse or anything in fact that has life; for they say, these all have souls and it would be a sin to do so; for the same reasons they ate no vegetables in a green state and spread their food only on dry leaves.[56]

Al-Idrīsī remarked in the eleventh century upon the concern generally shown by the inhabitants of Nahrwāla for cattle: 'When their animals are enfeebled by age and are unable to walk, they free them from all labour and provide them with food without exacting any return.'[57]

In the twelfth century several Jains acquired powerful positions at court of Siddharāja Jayasiṃha (r. 1094–1143) and his successor Kumārapāla (r. 1143–74). This included the scholar and historian Hemacandra, the most important synthesizer of Śvetāmbara doctrine and practice. Hemacandra formed a close relationship with Siddharāja's nephew and successor Kumārapāla, who actually converted to Jainism and surrounded himself with prominent Jains, although he may have reverted to the Hindu fold later in his life.[58] Although Jain influence over the rulers ended with the death of Kumārapāla—his descendants were Śaivas, some aggressively so—the Jains continued to be a powerful and prosperous group who could not be ignored by rulers.

The surviving accounts of Kumārapāla's reign are marked by a curious tension since the two major chroniclers, Hemacandra and, later, Merutuṅga, both Jains, wished to emphasize Kumārapāla's conversion to Jainism and hence his adherence to non-violence. An attempt is thus made to present the wars of his reign as purely defensive. An incident related by both the chroniclers demonstrates how this tension worked. Once Kumārapāla was appointed head of the congregation of Jains and was about to start on pilgrimage when news came of the impending invasion of Dāhala. Full of fear, Kumārapāla consulted Hemacandra, who assured him that the gods of Jainism would look after him and that Dāhala would die before he could attack, which is what transpired. This episode was evidently related to demonstrate that 'by accepting non-violence, the king did not become weak and that the presiding deities of Jainism protected him by removing his enemies from the world', since obviously the king could not avoid fighting, even if only in self-defence.[59] Whether Kumārapāla was 'truly' a Jain or not, he engaged in plenty of warfare in his time, some of which was related without defensiveness by his Jain chroniclers too. Thus, we have several ideological statements of Jain kingship from this period—the only ones formulated when Jain rulers or ones heavily influenced by Jainism were actually in power. One of their important arguments was against ritual sacrifice.[60] However, the Caulukya kingdom was closely linked to Śaiva manifestations of religiosity, and the Jain-influenced control of slaughter during Kumārapāla's period did not persist under his successors.

In the thirteenth century, a prominent Jain figure close to the centre of power was the merchant Vastupāla (minister and strategist to the ghelā clan who succeeded the Caulukyas in most of their territories by about 1200), who was responsible for several military victories in spite of his Jain affiliation. This martial spirit was even celebrated by one of his biographers: 'Thy sword, illustrious Vastupāla, beautiful in rising and brandishing, valiant in deed.'[61] Along with his brother Tejahpāla, he became renowned as a great philanthropist and builder in the first half of the thirteenth century. The Vāghelā territories were by now greatly shrunk and beleaguered by attacks from all directions. āla, however, was loyal to his patrons, all the while carrying out a flourishing trade, the proceeds of which he invested in large-scale building of Jain edifices—temples, wells, hospitals, and rest houses—at Girnar, Abu, Cambay, and several other places. Another wealthy Jain businessman who surfaced into Vāghelā politics was Jagaḍū, the Śrīmālī merchant from Bhadreshvar in Kachchh who, as seen in Chapter 3, had intercepted the vital horse trade from the Persian Gulf to Anhilvada in a bid for local power. The biography commissioned by his descendants provides a graphic account of a provincial merchant's negotiations and dealings, all justified by his philanthropy during a famine in 1256–8, and his lavishness in supporting Jain and other religious institutions.

Pilgrimage was a theme that recurs in most medieval Jain chronicles. While there was no scriptural requirement for lay Jains to engage in pilgrimage, it was nevertheless seen as a merit-granting activity. Laypeople usually travelled in groups to the chief temples such as those of Abu, Shatrunjaya, and Girnar. Making donations to temples was also a meritorious activity, as was giving in other forms, such as food to wandering ascetics. While it was acceptable for laypeople to make money, wealth could generate merit for the individual only if it was donated towards religious building or upkeep, financing religious activities, or the care of animals. Moreover, the merchant was required to be financially stable and creditworthy, free from ostentation, temperate, vegetarian, and actively philanthropic towards his sect.

Jain merchants continued to build and renovate community structures throughout the thirteenth century. In 1299 came the invasion of Ulugh Khān and Nuṣrat Khān, the generals of 'Alā' al-Dīn Khaljī. While sultanate rule of Gujarat was being established, there were several more campaigns here. During one of them, in 1312–13, the Khaljī troops destroyed or desecrated some of the temples of the religious complex in Shatrunjaya. This caused widespread resentment in the Jain community until a rich Patan merchant, Samrā Śāh, undertook to carry out repairs. He applied to and received permission to do so from the governor Alp Khān who also, in a conciliatory gesture, gave him a casket of jewels to help with the costs.[62]

During sultanate rule Jains generally remained on cordial terms with the rulers. We do not come across further accounts of the desecration of Jain temples, and several inscriptions attest to the fact that temples within sultanate territories were still being used, endowed, and renovated.[63] In 1328 a Śvetāmbara scholar Jinaprabha Sūrī went to Delhi to meet the sultan Muḥammad bin Tughluq, and by his own account was received cordially. He and his successor Jinadeva Sū ī extracted an undertaking that the Śvetāmbaras and their shrines would henceforth be protected from further harm.[64] In many parts of Gujarat, Jains seem to have been free to practise their faith and engage in business, although names of prominent Jains in the administration are few. The production and patronage of Jain literary texts also continued throughout the sultanate period.

The present merchant-dominated composition of the Jain community has led scholars to believe that was always the case, but certain pastoralist and peasant groups also seem to have been influenced by Jainism in this period.[65] The Rabārīs of southern Rajasthan, for example, retain a reverence for the Dādās or teachers of the Kharatara *gaccha*. In modern times some Rabārī elders have become Jain renouncers, a practice that may date back to early contacts with Jain missionaries.[66] Another example of this process is the conversion of the Osvāls, inhabitants of the region of Osian in southern Rajasthan. The Osvāls were part of a wide range of sedentarizing pastoralist groups all over western India who were eventually assimilated at various levels into an emerging Rajput hierarchy. They claim kinship with the Paramārs and more specifically with the Caulukyas (Solaṅkīs). The story goes that the Osvāls were Solaṅkī Rajputs who converted to Jainism after their chief's son recovered from a snakebite.[67] In common with other pastoralist groups, they were adherents of a mother goddess, Sacciyā or Saccikā Mātā, a meat-eating goddess who demanded blood sacrifice. Sacciyā Mātā engaged in an epic struggle with a Jain teacher who finally subdued her and accepted her as a disciple along with the rest of the Osvāls.[68] Sacciyā Mātā is probably a version of Sancair Mātā, *kul-devī* (clan goddess) bestowed by legend upon the Paramārs during the Agnikula sacrifice at Mount Abu.[69]

Sacciyā Mātā remained the guardian deity of the Osvāls even after they accepted Jainism and the story is constantly reinvoked to underline the transformation of prior practice into Jain ritual.[70] Expanding Jainism similarly incorporated several other goddesses and guardians into its fold, some of whom were converted from their violent habits to become docile followers of the teacher. One tale relates how a recently converted layman was harassed by a goddess he had formerly revered to revert to his former faith. The layman stood fast and refused to do as she asked. Impressed by his resolve, the goddess asked him to show her a little respect. He agreed to do so if she would stand below the image of the tīrthaṅkara in the temple.[71] Jains also worshipped and installed icons of pan-Indian goddesses such as Sarasvatī and Lak ī in their temples.

One prominent set of Jains were the Śrīmālī vāṇiās or merchants who came to Gujarat in large numbers from southern Rajasthan, possibly from the eleventh century onwards. The Śrīmālīs, a successful trading group, contributed ascetics as well as a lay community to Śvetāmbara Jainism and fanned out over many parts of Gujarat. One of their skills was in handling currency. Several important mint-masters were Śrīmālī Jains, including Ṭhakkura Pheru, the master of the Delhi sultanate mint and author of the first numismatic manual, the *Dravyaparīkṣā*.[72] Similarly, the mints in Gujarat were often handled by Śrīmālī Jain merchants.

While the white-robed Śvetāmbaras had become the dominant sect in Gujarat since the council of Valabhi in the fifth century, Digambaras (the sky-clad) continued to live and find adherents in Gujarat until the twelfth century. An adversarial moment came in 1125 when the vetāmbara Vādideva and the Digambara Kumudacandra debated at the court of Siddharāja Jayasiṃha. One of the important issues at stake was whether women could attain *mokṣa* (liberation) without first being reborn as men. The Digambaras maintained that the perfect ascetic must conquer the emotions and be indifferent to worldly thoughts to the extent that clothes were irrelevant, whereas the Śvetāmbaras permitted the wearing of white garments for their renouncers. In addition, the stipulation on nakedness meant that women were barred from becoming renouncers in the Digambara order. The debate ended in victory for the āmbaras, and the Digambaras were obliged to migrate to the south. Although the debate was projected as being a ritual or doctrinal one, there may have been an underlying political flavour too.[73] Kumudacandra was from Karnataka, as was Siddharāja's wife, and this may have been a manifestation of a struggle between local Śvetāmbara interests against 'foreign' Digambara ones.

From about the eleventh century onwards the Śvetāmbara hierarchy in Gujarat was further divided into ascetic lineages or gacchas, each of which was led by a charismatic teacher and was supported by a lay community, usually of Hindu converts. The theme of the contest between the travelling teacher-missionary and local religious authorities, resolved when the missionary displayed superior magical powers and induced the locals to accept his guidance is a common one in medieval Gujarat. In Bhadreshvar, for example, evidently a Śaiva stronghold, a Jain preacher was confronted by a Śaiva yogi who began an argument with him. While the debate was going on, the yogi caused a poisonous snake to bite Śrīṣeṇa, the Jain teacher. He used his powers of meditation to draw out the poison, a miracle that caused the yogi to sing his praises.[74] There were also contests over particular sites. A Jain minister who wished to build a temple at Abu was rebuffed by the Hindu authorities of the region and proved his claim only when an image of abha was miraculously discovered there. This was not enough for the Hindus, who only permitted him to acquire the land he needed after he covered it with gold coins. Miraculous legitimacy sometimes had to be backed with hard cash.[75]

The chief ascetic lineages in our period were the Kharatara gaccha and the Tapā gaccha, both image-worshipping sects. The Tapā gaccha, later to become the most popular Śvetāmbara sect, was founded in 1228, its founder rejecting 'laxness' of practice in the community. There were other gacchas too, as well as subdivisions of the Kharatara and ā gacchas, many of which generated considerable debate around ritual prescriptions or questions of legitimacy.

The Kharatara gaccha arose out of the disgust felt by its founder for the corrupt practices of temple-dwelling monks. Its most prominent teacher was Jinadatta Sūrī (1075–1154) who became an energetic propagandist for the gaccha, even travelling to Muslim-dominated Sind in search of converts. Corruption in temples was a theme that preoccupied Śvetāmbara systematizers in the medieval period. There were numerous debates around the questions of the validity of temples and of the duty of monks to supervise them. It had become a great marker of prestige and piety for a Jain layperson to build or make a donation to a temple. As a result, a large number of temples were built, most of which were tended by appointed monks, much in the manner of the brahmin guardians of Hindu temples. Some Jains were infuriated by what they saw as the corrupt practices of the Jain temple monks who had given up the prescribed detachment and wandering ascetism in favour of life at temples complete with rituals involving music and dancing girls, and the use of garlands, fine clothes, betelnut, and lac to paint their hands and feet.[76] One argument, however, defended the temple-dwelling monks for preserving the temples that were neglected by kings and the laity, thus keeping the faith alive. Although the sources would lead one to believe that temple-dwelling monks were regularly worsted in public debate, it is more likely that there was a pragmatic acceptance of the need for certain monks to manage the sacred places while others maintained a wandering existence.

Another sect that evolved from the Śvetāmbara fold in the fifteenth century was that started by a wealthy layman, Loṅkā Śāh. This breakaway and short-lived faction argued against image worship and in fact rejected temples altogether. It has been suggested that Loṅkā, who lived in the sultanate capital of Ahmadabad and was acquainted with Muslims at the court, was influenced by the Islamic aniconic arguments to reject images.[77] Aniconicity, however, also has a scriptural base within the Jain doctrine itself, thus, Loṅkā may have merely been recommending a return to the fundamentals.[78]

While Islamic ideas may not have had a direct influence on the Jains, there was a shared substratum of religious practices in this period. The mid-sixteenth century author Surabhaṭṭa—not a Jain, but a brahmin—listed the degenerate practices of the Kalī age. Many of these were reminiscent of Jain injunctions against involuntary animal slaughter: 'People will take their meals at night (that is, instead of before sunset) and will use water without straining it.' He also opposed the cultivation of indigo, whose manufacture involves the death of tiny beings, the use of kilns for preparing mortar, and the felling of trees to supply timber for building houses. These are similar to prescriptions followed by Ismā'īlī-influenced sects such as the Biṣnoīs in Rajasthan.[79]

As Paul Dundas argues, it will only be possible to get a sense of Jain history if 'a wider range of source materials such as stories, legends, *belles-lettres*, clan and sectarian traditions, hagiographies and so on' are used in addition to the information from inscriptions and chronicles.[80] Thus, it might be worthwhile to examine more closely the biography of a prominent Śrīmālī Jain merchant-prince in Kachchh who lived in the thirteenth century. The *Jagaḍūcarita* is a tale that illuminates several aspects of the relationship between Jains and trade, the question of individual wealth, the duty of philanthropy, the constraints of the faith, ethics, and the lack of them in trade.[81] It also illustrates the complex relationship between trade and religious patronage in this period. The narrative consists of linked episodes from the life of Jagaḍū, most of which are intended to explain and celebrate his life as an exemplary philanthropist.

Jagaḍū's initial wealth, which enabled him to fulfil the religious duty of philanthropy, was obtained through the exploitation of some resource that pertained to livestock:

Once, while he was taking a walk near the town, he saw a shepherd tending his goats. In the herd he remarked a beautiful she-goat, from whose neck hung a Mani, i.e., either a fleshy excrescence, such as goats usually have, or more probably an amulet. Recognising that the Mani was one that would grant prosperity, he

> purchased the goat from the shepherd for a small sum. Jagadu took the goat home, took the Mani from its neck and worshipped it secretly, after which his riches increased greatly.

As Jains are prohibited from killing animals or profiting from their slaughter, this instance and its retrospective justification may be an indication that Jagaḍū's *maṇi* was actually a means of profiting from livestock. This is the first instance in the text of Jagaḍū's indulging in practices that are less than praiseworthy, but as they lead to an increase in his wealth and the expression of his proclivity for generosity, they are narrated without censure.

Another account of Jagaḍū's life similarly finds him profiting from the sale of beeswax, a forbidden substance for Jains.[82] The ethics of trade came up in another incident too. Jayantasiṃha, one of Jagaḍū's servants, sailed to the Persian Gulf with a load of merchandise to trade there. On arriving, his attention was drawn to a large stone lying on the shore and he ordered his servants to take possession of it. Meanwhile, the captain of a Turuṣka (Turk/Muslim) vessel from Cambay also noticed the stone and similarly ordered his men to remove it to his ship.[83] When Jayantasiṃha stopped him, the Turuṣka declared that the stone would belong to he who paid 1,000 *dināras* to the lord of the town. The two attempted to outbid each other for the possession of the stone, and finally Jayantasiṃha paid out three lakh dināras, placed the stone in his ship, and returned to Bhadreshvar. He delivered the stone to ḍū, confessing that he had lost much money in trying to preserve his master's honour. Unexpectedly, Jagaḍū was delighted and thanked him for upholding his honour even in a foreign land.

Jagaḍū was eventually rewarded for the mysterious stone when a aivite yogi revealed that it was filled with jewels.[84] This indicated, first, some source of wealth in the Persian Gulf for the control of which a large investment had to be made. This investment also had to be made in competition with merchants from Cambay, by now dominated by Muslim merchants. The fact that bribes were offered to the local ruler suggests that this 'stone' was a local mineral resource of great value. When the 'stone' was brought back to Bhadreshvar, Jagaḍū was pleased at the investment and also at the fact that his employee outbid the Cambay merchant. The Cambay trade was the dominant one in the region and it was a matter of satisfaction to have had the better of a Cambay merchant, both in the possession of a valuable commodity, and in terms of prestige and bidding power. This fortuitous investment, exploited with the help of Bhadra, thus made Jagaḍū richer and thus more meritorious, as he could engage more freely in charitable activity. He was also blessed by the god of the ocean that fortune would be faithful to him and all his ships would come safely to port. The ethics of trade are not in question here: wealth gained by mysterious means was acceptable if it was used in the service of charity and pious acts.

Due to the influence of his guru, Paramadeva of the Pūrṇimā gaccha, ḍū then led a pilgrimage to Shatrunjaya and Girnar with the Jain community of the town: 'the fourfold Samgha which included many monks of the Purnima Gachchha, came forth from Bhadresvarapura, "just as the pure doctrine issues from the mouth of a lord of sages"'. On his return, Jagaḍū constructed and endowed several Jain structures in and around the town, including temples, a well, a garden, and a hospital. He also restored a Śaivite temple and built a mosque for the local Ismā'īlī community.

The image of Jains in the history of Gujarat has been that of austere, vegetarian merchants, well-known for their ethics in business. The story of Jagaḍū demonstrates chinks in this image. Jains (even in the eyes of their laudatory chroniclers) were often less than austere and dabbled in business for which they were censured within their community. If they followed up their errors with sufficient penance and philanthropy, however, they could be rehabilitated and lauded in posterity. Moreover, Jagadu's career spanning business in livestock, precious goods, and horses demonstrates the various worlds a Jain merchant could travel on the way to becoming a magnate backed by the respectability of Jain *munis* and with ready access to royal courts. Indeed, the story makes a moral point of his rise from the simple world of shepherds and she-goats to one of glamour and service to royalty through the horse trade. Thus, in the fourteenth century the Śrīmālī Jains claimed kinship with the Rajput Paramāras and were part of a larger world of trade that depended on goatherds, Śaiva yogis, sea captains, and horse traders, all participants in an increasingly complex political economy.[85]

ISMĀᶜĪLĪS AND OTHER MUSLIMS IN A CHANGING REGION[86]

While there were many Muslims living along the Gujarat coast from an early period, evidence of Muslims settling in the hinterland appears from the thirteenth century onwards in inscriptions from Junagadh and Anhilvada.[87] By this time the Delhi sultanate was well established and Muslim merchants and missionaries had travelled into the interiors of Gujarat. A twelfth-century gravestone of the son of an Ismā'īlī dā'ī from Nagaur, now in Rajasthan but intermittently a part of the Gujarat kingdom, shows that there was a community of Ismā'īlīs here in the twelfth century. Meanwhile, Muslims had long been settled in Sind and had ruled parts of it since the eighth century. It is likely that there were settlements in the contiguous region of Kachchh too even before the Bhadreshvar settlement in the mid-twelfth century.

An early Muslim proselytizer was in hinterland Gujarat in the early thirteenth century, as is shown by the grave of Shaykh al-Mashā'ikh Arjun in Petlad dated 1236.[88] Traditional accounts hold that Māngrolī h (Sayyid Maḥmūd b. Hasan b. 'Alī) came to Saurashtra in the early eleventh century and converted local people in Mangrol.[89] Preachers continued to come to Gujarat in subsequent years. From the fourteenth century there was an influx of north Indian Muslims into Gujarat. Again, after the invasion of Tīmūr the elite fled the disintegrating Delhi sultanate and many came to Gujarat. An important Sufi order, that of the Rifā'īs, was established when Sayyid Aḥmad īr arrived in Ahmadabad in the fourteenth century.[90] The Uraizīs were found in Gujarat from the early fifteenth century when Sayyid Budha Ya'qūb, the descendant of a cavalry commander who planted the banner of Islam on the hill citadel of Ajmer (1165), arrived there.[91] The Sufi family that became closest to the sultans was that of the Bukhārīs, established by Sayyid Burḥān al-Dīn Quṭb-i 'Ālam, who came and settled in Patan with his mother at the age of ten in 1397. He moved to Ahmadabad when the city was founded.[92]

An Ismā'īlī mission was established in Gujarat in the reign of the imid caliph al-Mustanṣir (d. 1094). According to a version from the Musta'lī tradition, a dā'ī named 'Abd Allāh arrived in Gujarat and made his way to the capital, eventually winning over the ruler as a convert. ārī missionaries now began to travel to other parts of north India and the next major sites of Ismā'īlī settlement and activity were Gujarat, Kachchh, and Rajasthan. By 1500 pockets of Ismā'īlī influence were to be found all over north India, particularly in Sind, southern Punjab, Rajasthan, and Gujarat.

In the early period the Ismā'īlīs in western India were ethnic Arab or Persian merchant settlers as well as local converts from pastoralist, cultivating, or merchant groups. These included militarized peasants and pastoralists from north-west India, some of whom went on to become part of its emerging Rajput status hierarchy.[93] The early stories tell of vanquishing adversaries such as *jogī*s and Sufi pīrs. After the fall of Alamut to the Mongols in 1256, more Nizā ī missionaries came to

Sind and Gujarat, Uchch in particular becoming an important centre. While the Nizārī missionaries worked among the peasant and pastoralist groups, the Musta'lī influence seems to have been restricted to merchant groups who came to be called Bohras or Vohras. Although it appears that Musta'lī missionaries did not have had a wider influence, this has not yet been systematically researched.

This crucial phase of Nizārī activities from the twelfth to the fifteenth centuries has hardly been chronicled in non-Ismā'īlī historical records, the traditions in the South Asian Ismā'īlī devotional *ginān*s being almost the sole source of information about them. There are scattered mentions of 'heretical' and 'semi-Islamized' groups in the accounts of the Delhi sultans, some of whom were Ismā'īlīs.[94] Kachchh, with its proximity to Sūmrā-dominated lower Sind and its history of Ismā'īlī settlements from the twelfth century, was a natural home for Ismā'īlī groups. Maḥmūd Bīgara, the sultan of Gujarat, campaigned against the chieftains of the region in 1471 and compelled the Sūmrās and Soḍhās to submit. His injunctions to them included giving up matrimonial and other relations with Hindus and being instructed in (Sunni) Islam.[95]

Although the ginãns are virtually the only source of information about the activities of the mission in this period, it is clear that it was a time when considerable success was achieved. This is buttressed by new information about the da'wa and its converts from the compositions and traditions of pastoralist and occupational groups such as the noīs, Meghvāls, and Āhīrs. Many of these corroborate and reflect the themes in the ginãns and show that Ismā'īlī influence encompassed much wider circles than previously suspected. These compositions indicate that that the sects of Rāmdev, Jambha, Āī Mātā, and other such figures that appear to be manifestations of saint- and hero-worship within popular Hinduism were formerly part of the larger ārī da'wa in the subcontinent (sometimes called the Satpanth) and are still linked through the commonality of their compositions, rituals, and networks of pilgrimage.[96] Some of these sects thought fit to jettison or hide their Ismā'īlī affiliations later, but they were known in some cases to the Nizārī da'wa and later were revealed to ethnographers. As these shrines and compositions cannot be reliably dated, it is only through careful comparative study that they reveal patterns and trends. However, questions still remain. To what extent were Ismā'īlī groups in the pre-fifteenth century period linked to each other? Did individual preachers branch out into their own sects or did they maintain contacts with a central authority in Multan, Uchch, or Persia? While the 'official' branches of the Nizārī daʿwa were clearly closely linked, what was the nature of contact of the central daʿwa with the hero and saint cults, and their lay adherents?

Such sects, particularly those that demonstrate signs of 'syncretism', have often been dismissed as marginal to the history of religious identity in South Asia. They are seen as part of secret, low-status, cultic beliefs without much consequence for the history of either Hinduism or Islam.[97] However, it is now becoming clear that such sects commanded a widespread lay allegiance, whether covert or not. Further, medieval sectarian religiosity is closely bound with the processes of caste and state formation in western India. Several indications and illustrations of these processes may be discerned in the gināns and Satpanthī compositions.

Various Nizārī dāʿīs are believed to have worked in Gujarat, beginning with Satgur Nūr whose shrine is at Navsari in south Gujarat. Although he is a shadowy and semi-mythical figure, one tradition says his disciples included Kaṇbīs, Kolīs, and the coastal Kharvas.[98] Pīr Shams (13th/14th century?) was active in Sind and Punjab and is also believed to have carried the message to Kashmir and Bengal.[99]

Ṣadr al-Dīn, believed to have lived in the fourteenth century, is credited with converting members of the Lohāṇā merchant caste in Sind. His descendants continued the work of the Ismāʿīlī mission in Gujarat. In the early sixteenth century, there were several distinct āʿīlī centres in Gujarat. One location was Kachchh, where revenue from the surrounding regions was collected in order to be transmitted to the Imamate in Iran. Another Ismāʿīlī branch in eastern Gujarat, apparently repudiated by the imamate, was that of Pīr Ṣadr al-Dīn's grandson, Imām Shāh (d. 1513).

On the death of his father, Imām Shāh travelled to Kahak in Iran to seek permission to be appointed pīr in his father's place, but this was not granted. He returned to Sind and set out to seek his fortune in Gujarat like many other religious propagandists at the time. According to the tradition, he made his way to the capital, Ahmadabad, and stunned the sultan, Maḥmūd Bīgara, with miracles, including making a dead cat come alive.[100] The sultan gave him permission to settle in a village near Ahmadabad inhabited by Kaṇbīs and Kolīs, with whom he gained influence by bringing rain. By the time of his death in 1520, he had made converts and established his growing family in the village of Pirana.

Imam Shah's mission to Central Gujarat in the mid-fifteenth century fulfilled the objectives of the current Sunni ruler of Gujarat, ḥmūd Bīgara, by helping pacify the turbulent and rebellious inhabitants of the Sabarmati valley, in particular Kaṇbīs and Kolīs, by bringing them under organized spiritual authority. Although he was not an officially sanctioned pīr, Imām Shāh appears to have continued to send an annual tithe collected from his followers to Iran. His son, r Muḥammad Shāh, achieved even more success with the Kaṇbīs. His long narrative poem in Gūjarī, *Satveṇī jī vel* (sixteenth century), explains that large numbers came under his influence:

> Then I took over the order and stayed with the *kuṇbās* (Kaṇbīs); there were ten thousand devotees. I told them all the ways of the Satpanth, told them about the lineage of the Imam.[101]

The Kaṇbīs' affiliation with the Imāmshāhīs and the Nizārī tradition can also be seen as moves to realign their status in local society. Meanwhile, other groups of Kaṇbīs, who came to be known as the ā and Kaḍvā Pāṭīdārs, were aligning themselves to Vaiṣṇava groups around the same time, under the influence of Vallabhācarya and his followers.[102]

While attempts have been made to place the history of the Ismā'īlīs in the context of other Muslim groups functioning in South Asia, for example, the Sufis, who are believed to have been responsible for much of the conversion to Islam in the early period, little effort has been made to place the Ismā'īlīs in the religious context of their potential converts. The Ismā'īlīs were among a number of groups competing for followers, patrons, and resources. Thus, to understand their spread, it might be as useful to study the rise of Vaiṣṇavism as to study the Sufis. This would also go some way towards explaining the links between medieval Indian sectarian literature and Satpanthī compositions. Our understanding of Ismā'īlī history tends to be coloured by the experience of the Khojā community and its process of self-definition from the nineteenth century. However, Ismā'īlī history in South Asia extends over a much wider field. Although it was never a 'state' religion in India (apart from the short-lived Fāṭimid outpost in Multan), the history of the Ismā'īlīs is inextricably tied to politics and we may find that it revises our understanding of the process of medieval state formation, the rise of the Rajputs, the rise of sectarian traditions, and the widespread 'syncretic' traditions of the region.

The long history of Muslims' engagement with indigenous groups in north India is closely bound to the transformation and evolution of local polities and societies. As Ismā'īlī preachers established footholds all over the region between the ninth and the fifteenth centuries, the political landscape was transforming itself. Pastoralist chieftaincies were replaced by the Delhi sultanate whose armies were sent out over large parts of the subcontinent. Many local rulers were defeated and supplanted by governors from Delhi—as in Gujarat—while other chieftains continued in their holdings on payment of tribute.

Ismāʿīlism in western India has many of the characteristics of medieval belief systems that arose outside the purview of state patronage. This may have something to do with the fact that these beliefs were disseminated among merchants, pastoralists, peasants, and lower-status occupational castes over a wide geographical area. Conversion to āʿīlism was not a unitary phenomenon. There were several strands of it, and the literature reveals some of these tensions. The Ismāʿīlīs had to compete for resources with other proselytizing groups active in this period. When Imām Shāh arrived in Gujarat in the mid-fifteenth century, it is likely that a number of Ismāʿīlī traditions were already coexisting in Gujarat. While there might have been a millenarian dream that all converted groups would one day rise in unison, in practice they continued to evolve within their own social circumstances. At times there was some political organization, and accordingly some of the literature represents political aims; at other times it has a more didactic or devotional aspect.

Like other religious groups, the Ismāʿīlīs had political objectives. In some cases this may have taken the form of actual political mobilization, for example, the groups that marched to Delhi during the reign of Raẓiyya (r. 1236–40). It is evident that the dāʿīs were aware of the hierarchies within the local society they encountered—they approached powerful pastoralist groups in the countryside, some of which took on a militant character and posed a military threat to the towns and centres of power. In other cases political intervention was through access to rulers. In common with other sects who made attempts to influence rulers and those around them, the Satpanthī tradition has several examples of attempts to link up with rulers, their wives, and subordinates.[103]

Some of the groups who accepted the Ismāʿīlī message went on to undergo processes of Rajputization—this includes Jāts, Sūmrās, Bhaṭṭīs, and perhaps the Sammas. Other groups such as Kaṇbīs were left out of this process of upward mobility, becoming part of the continuum of armed peasants and pastoralists all over north India. Groups that responded to the Ismā'īlī message later found that this affiliation was damaging to their chances of rising in status and jettisoned traces of it. Nevertheless, several of them retained traces of previous practices, which included accommodation of or obeisance to Ismā'īlī beliefs.

The Ismā'īlī groups were part of a network of linked religious movements from medieval times and may have been a catalytic factor in the development of much of modern religious identity. They were part of a continuum of religious affiliation—internally contested and more often than not opposed by state authority, which made regular attempts to apply normative standards to it. Each of these traditions is a site of contestation: while they may represent spaces set aside from normative religious traditions, they also represent a history of intense and often violent struggle for power and resources. The millenarian aspects of some of the narrative ginān̄s reflect these social and political contests. Others, in their stories of conversion and mystical awakening, and the defeats of jogīs and rival pīrs, represent the struggle for followers, humiliate opponents, and find patrons. A common vocabulary of messianic themes, often featuring an martial, mounted avenger cast in the local idiom was common all over India, especially among sedentarizing pastoralist groups gradually being fitted into a caste order. These themes continued even in the colonial period.[104]

PILGRIMAGE

From the thirteenth century onwards, while monumental temple building was on the decline, networks of pilgrimage were being consolidated. In the early period the chief group for whom pilgrimage was important was the Jains. As a network of sacred sites associated with tīrthaṅkaras developed, groups of lay Jains travelled to them, often making donations for their upkeep. Although there was no scriptural injunction on Jains to conduct pilgrimages, these journeys became a means of linking members of the community, and combined recreational religious benefits for those who undertook them. The Jain interest in travel led to the composition of travel manuals such as the *Vividhatīrthakalpa* ('Guidebook to Various Pilgrimage Places'), which offered an account of the history and significance of the great Śvetāmbara holy places in Gujarat. Written in the early fourteenth century (after the Khaljī conquest of Gujarat), this volume contains information on over forty sites of pilgrimage.[105] For Jain grandees and merchants, it was meritorious to provide facilities for pilgrims at major shrines. On

Girnar, the Vāghelā minister Tejahpāla commissioned 'an excellent fort, monastery, drinking station, temple, and a beautiful garden, named Tejalapura after himself'.[106]

Among Hindu sacral sites was the pilgrimage circuit of Prabhasa, centred on the temple of Somanāth. As we have seen, the tenth century ruler Mūlarāja was said to have made weekly trips to Somanath until he decided to build his own shrine to Somanāth in Anhilvada. By the fifteenth century a new circuit of 'popular' devotional pilgrimage was beginning to grow around such sites as the Bahucarājī temple. Shrines of goddess worship were gaining prominence as sites for healing and fertility.

The rise of Vaiṣṇava bhakti in the fifteenth century saw a number of sacral sites such as Dvaraka, Dakor, and Sāmalājī being drawn into a Vaiṣṇava pilgrimage cycle. The Ḍankapura Māhātmya, a *tīrtha-ātmya* or praise-text associated with the shrine at Dakor, relates that the image of Kṛṣṇa as Raṇachoḍajī had lived in the house of the devotee Boḍāṇā for four hundred years and was enshrined in the temple only in 1556 by Nanda, a devotee from Cambay.[107] A great temple on the island of Jagat, in the Dvaraka region, attracted multitudes of pilgrims in the fifteenth century, many of whom ritually prostrated themselves as they approached the temple.[108] From the accounts of the temple, it is hard to gauge its denomination, although it became known as a Vaiṣṇava site in the sixteenth century. The sixteenth century saw the rise of the Dvaraka region as a Vaiṣṇava pilgrimage site and the Narayana Saroṿar temple was built in Kachchh.[109]

The Girnar mountain with its Jain, Muslim, Nāthpanthī, Śākta, and ṣṇava shrines was a sacred site of great antiquity, and was in the nineteenth century believed to be the resort of Aghorī ascetics and cannibals.[110] The region around Mount Girnar possesses important ṣṇava shrines including the Dāmodara temple and the Revati tank from the thirteenth century, the latter possessing images of twenty-four forms of Viṣṇu. On Mount Girnar is a temple of Ambikā, and nearby are the images of Pradyumna and Sāmba, the sons of Kṛṣṇa. In addition, the Cakratīrtha temple on Mount Girnar was formerly a temple of Vāmana, the dwarf-avatāra of Viṣṇu.

From the fifteenth century a network of shrines associated with Muslim pīrs and frequented by pastoralists and occupational groups became popular. Although it is hard to find contemporary evidence for the extent of these networks, many of them are associated with figures who lived in the fourteenth and fifteenth centuries. Some of these shrines are now associated with fairs and periodic markets, allowing adherents to perform pilgrimages while conducting business, a link that may well date back to our period.

A fair is held in Chaklasi in Kheda district of central Gujarat on the occasion of the death anniversary (*'urs*) of Amīr Sayyid Pīr who is believed to have lived there during the reign of Maḥmūd Bīgara. After his death his followers found a heap of flowers instead of his body. This is a hagiographical device common to narratives of many 'syncretic' saint figures, including Kabīr, that prevents conflict by allowing followers to share the saint's remains and conduct the death rituals of their choice, whether burial or cremation. The protagonist's legacy can thus be shared amicably by followers from various denominations.[111]

Some distance to the south is Amod, with another shrine frequented by Hindus as well as Muslims. This is the tomb of Quṭb h and four other soldiers of Maḥmūd Bīgara who died in battle with local rulers and were buried in a common grave over which five tombs were erected.[112] This is an example of the vogue for the Pāñc r, five saints, all over northern and western India. The significance of the number was related in terms of the Muslim and especially Shī'ī reverence for the family of the Prophet (comprising Muḥammad, 'Alī, asan, Ḥusayn, and Fāṭima), which finds equivalence with the Hindu theme of the five Pāṇḍava heroes and the older quintet of heroes of the Yādavas.[113]

There are several sites, especially in south and central Gujarat, dedicated to the commemoration of Bālamshā or Bālā Pīr, most of which claim to have originated during the sultanate period. In some cases, Bālamshā is associated with the famous Suhrawardī Sufi, Shaykh Muḥammad (Bahā' al-Dīn) Zakariyyā of Multan.[114] Fairs associated with these shrines invariably draw both Muslim and Hindu devotees, including Rajputs, Garāsiyās, Kolīs, Ṭhākarḍās, Naḍodās, Kumbhārs, Bharvāḍs, and 'Harijans' ('lower' castes), a mix, in other words, of pastoralist and occupational castes with diverse religious affiliations.

The *dargāh* of Bābā Ghor, the patron saint of the carnelian mines near Ratanpur in south Gujarat, is mentioned even in the fourteenth century by Ibn Baṭṭūṭa.[115] This Afghan adventurer-holy man is believed to have pioneered the agate mining industry of the region, which was already flourishing in the fourteenth century.[116] Subsequently, Bābā Ghor became the preceptor for the Sīdī community of northeast African origin and an annual fair dominated by the Sīdīs from all over Gujarat came to be held at the shrine.

Another shrine that became the focus of pilgrimage and an annual fair by the fifteenth century is that of Dāval Shāh Pīr, seen as a healer and a promoter of agriculture. The main shrine is at Amran in Saurashtra, but smaller commemorative shrines can be found at several other places in Saurashtra and Kachchh.[117] 'Dāval Shāh' was a courtier of Maḥmūd gara, a Qurayshī named 'Abd al-Laṭīf Malik Maḥmūd entitled Dāvar al-Mulk. He developed a reputation for justice towards the cultivators of his lands as a result of which people flocked to his territories: 'They say that he charged the cultivators of his estates only the small rates sanctioned by Muhammadan Law, and not an iota above.'[118] He did not permit his troops to plunder fields they passed through or even to graze their horses in them.

He was also a righteous and proselytizing Muslim. He was appointed thānadār of the region of Amran in Saurashtra and 'used often to engage in warfare with the unbelievers', eventually securing the submission of the volatile pastoralist groups of the Kachchh frontier.[119] He had a reputation as a healer during his own lifetime for curing a prince of the Deccan of leprosy. After he was killed by a local pastoralist chieftain in 1509, his tomb became a major site of pilgrimage:

> From that day to this the fame of the Malik as a martyr attracts numbers of believers from far and near to his shrine, and his miracles, after martyrdom, have been numerous. The blind are given eye-sight, the lame return whole, the barren are gladdened by the birth of children and few return disappointed from his shrine. Others having some desires to be obtained, put fetters on their legs with locks of iron joining the fetters. It has often happened that, when one of these has gained his desire, the lock has opened of itself, and the fetters have dropped.[120]

Intriguingly, the properties of the shrine also extended to money matters and transactions could be facilitated by the buried saint: 'Some people wishing for gold are given it by the saint by being directed to apply to a particular person at a given address for a certain sum. The man referred to as the giver is also described in a dream to pay the sum on appearance to the person described.'[121] In the nineteenth century the r retained his powers to intervene in pastoralist disputes at the frontier. One story from north Gujarat relates that thieves were stopped by a row of horses miraculously materialized by the pīr.[122] Here again, visitors at the fair and the shrine of the pīr included, in the 1960s, a range of groups: Muslims, brahmins, merchants, Pāṭīdārs, potters, and 'lower' castes.

At Matar in Kheda district is a fair associated with the dargāh of a r named Ātanshāh Pīr.[123] A local Rajput king named Bālangī had taken a vow to eat only after killing a Muslim daily. Ātanshāh, passing by, cursed Bālangī and in due course the latter was defeated by ḥmūd Bīgara and his palace destroyed. There is no other evidence about this fair or shrine but it is a stereotypical story that may be associated with Maḥmūd Bīgara's pacification and clearance of central Gujarat in the second half of the fifteenth century.

The Ismā'īlī preacher Imām Shāh, who established himself in a village near Ahmadabad on a charter granted by Maḥmūd Bīgara, was an important agent in the pacification of the 'turbulent' clans of central Gujarat in the mid-fifteenth century. He made converts from among the minor pastoralist groups and cultivators of the region as well among the Kolīs who had a reputation for thievery and plunder. One of these was Nāthākākā, a Kolī dacoit turned disciple of Imām Shāh whose grave is commemorated at a shrine and fair in Baroda district.[124]

Another dargāh that became the focus of pilgrimage was that of ī Pīr located at Banni on the edge of the Rann of Kachchh. Hājī Pīr was reputed to have been a soldier named 'Alī Akbar in the army of izz al-Dīn Muḥammad of Ghūr who invaded Gujarat in 1197. After giving up service, he settled in the village of Nara and served the local populace, laying down his life trying to recover cows driven away by dacoits.[125] Hājī Pīr is an early example from Gujarat of the crusading warrior-saints who were more common in north India and Bengal. In Gujarat his legend is similar to other pastoralist heroes who died rescuing cattle or in skirmishes with neighbouring clans.

Another warrior hero is Rāval Pīr in Kachchh, believed to have lived in the fourteenth century. When his mother Cāraṇ Deval prevented him from leading a celibate life, he became an ascetic. He was obliged to compete with the Muslim missionaries who were then active in Kachchh, and in one contest caused several to drown in the sea. He attached himself to a chieftain of the Dhal clan, caring for his horses and then assisting him to victory against the Rāṭhoḍs with the help of his miraculous powers. Before his death he built himself a grave and a stone horse near the place he used to graze horses and asked the chieftain to erect a tomb over it. This location became a popular annual fair, frequented by both Hindus and Muslims.[126]

The shrines of ghāzīs, holy warriors from invading Muslim armies who died in battle often became sites of healing and attracted a wide range of pilgrims of all denominations. One of these is the fair and shrine that commemorate Ja'far Muẓaffar, a general of Maḥmūd of Ghazna who died in battle at Somanath Patan in the eleventh century.[127]

The shrine of Dāval Shāh described earlier also belongs to this category. Perhaps the most prominent of these is the shrine of Mīrā Dātār r in Unava in north Gujarat. The tomb of one of Muẓaffar Shāh's generals who died in the fifteenth century, this soon became a site for the healing of mental illness and infertility.[128]

By the end of the fifteenth century a complex web of local and trans-regional tomb and saint shrines had developed all over Gujarat. As trade and settlement extended into new areas, some of these shrines began to attract pilgrims from distant places in the hope of cures or boons. Some of them became sites for large seasonal festivities, livestock fairs, or periodic markets, often on dates associated with death anniversaries or other festivals. Others remained local institutions for the benefit of the community. Many of these shrines became wealthy and influential on the proceeds of pilgrim traffic.

OTHER GROUPS, HEALING, AND MEDICINE

The most important feature of pastoralist religion was the worship of various forms of the goddess, usually as manifestations of Śakti. From the thirteenth century onwards, there are literary references to the *Devī ātmya* in Sanskrit poems such as the *Sūraṭhotsava* by Someśvara, the author of the *Kīrtikaumudi*.[129] That Śāktism was connected with royal power is indicated by the fact that Someśvara was the royal poet of the Caulukyas. By the fifteenth century, the Caṇdi episode of the *ī mahātmya* was translated into Old Gujarati by Śrīdhara as the *īkavitta*.[130] He also wrote a ballad, *Raṇamalla chanda,* describing the defence of Idar against Ẓafar Khān. The development of the *garbā* as both a poetic metre and folk dance is related to Śakti worship.

Many pastoralist clans owed allegiance to martial goddesses who were protectors in battle and guarantors of success in general. The Cauhāns and Jāḍejās, for example, evoked Āśāpurā Mātā as their champion. Others venerated Khoḍiyār or Śikotar. An important translocal site was that of Bahucarā in north Gujarat, visited and venerated by a variety of groups, especially Rajputizing pastoralists and bards, as part of an expanding pilgrimage network from the fifteenth century. Some of these goddesses required animal sacrifice. The Jādejā rulers of Kachchh, for example, sacrified buffaloes to Āśāpurā Mātā.[131]

The region between Multan in Punjab and Saurashtra is home to a number of temples of the sun built from the Gupta period to about 1400 CE. In fact, this belt, comprising southern Punjab, Sind, Rajasthan, and Gujarat, was the main location for the practice of sun worship in India, the other being Orissa. The prevalence of solar worship in Gujarat is indicated by the sun temples at Modhera in north Gujarat as well as in Somanath, Than, Dhamlej, and Chorvad in Saurashtra. Several instances of composite images dating from the fourteenth century have been found in Gujarat. These include those that combine Sūrya and Nārāyaṇa ṣṇu), and in one case the images of Brahma, Viṣṇu, Śiva, and Sūrya.[132]

One tradition of the origin of the Somanāth temple associates it with the cure of leprosy, a disease often associated with sexual practices. Soma, the moon, was married to twenty-five sisters, but favoured only one of them. Their father Prajāpati rebuked him, but was ignored. He then made the Moon's face leprous. The moon repented, but the curse could not be revoked. The only way to wipe out the sin would be to worship Śiva. Accordingly, the moon built the temple of Somānath, 'The Lord of the Moon'.[133]

Near the bottom of Girnar hill was a Muslim shrine that was reputed to have a beneficent effect on lepers.[134] The cure of leprosy and 'white leprosy' is attributed in the *Sāmba Purāṇa* to the worship of the sun. mba, the son of Kṛṣṇa, was afflicted by leprosy and was eventually cured by obeisance to the sun.[135] The shrine of Dvaraka was also associated with the cure of leprosy.[136] It is interesting in this context to find a legend that Rā Māṇḍalik, the Cūḍāsamā ruler of Junagadh, was endowed with the power to cure leprosy. His friend, the Vājā ruler of Somanath Patan (it is significant that the Śaiva temple of Somanath is not associated here with the cure of leprosy) was afflicted by leprosy and was advised by his priests to bathe in the Dāmodara *kuṇḍa* (tank) at Girnar. He bathed there in secret, but when Māṇḍalik heard of it, he went to meet his friend after hastily pouring Ganges water over himself. When he embraced the Vājā, the latter's leprosy was cured.[137]

Leprosy was a common feature of pre-modern life and was often more prevalent on islands and coastal areas.[138] Its symptoms were frequently confused with other skin diseases or with venereal diseases, and the terms used to describe them were often the same. Seeming cures for leprosy may partly have been due to the ability, found prescriptively in Arabic medical literature from the tenth century, to distinguish it from minor skin ailments. In Europe and the Islamic world the treatment for leprosy and subsequently for syphilis was the ingestion of mercury.[139] In medieval India mercury was an important ingredient in the alchemical experiments of the Nāthpanthīs and ntriks. It is likely that the Nāths, Tāntriks, and other related groups at Girnar and elsewhere had the reputation of being able to cure skin conditions such as leprosy.

The cult of Dattātreya in the medieval period was largely spread by the Mahānubhāva sect, which began in Gujarat in the late thirteenth century, but had its major impact in Maharashtra.[140] Even in Gujarat, the figure of Dāttatreya recurs in a variety of textual and sectarian traditions. These include the śakti-pīṭha or goddess temples, the Dasanāmī, Nāth and Aghora ascetic orders, Vaiṣṇavism, and Jainism.[141] In Jainism, Dattātreya is worshipped as Neminātha, a tradition paralleled in the Nāth literature in which Neminātha and Pārasnātha are regarded as sons of Matsyendranāth. Further, in the Jain *mahāpurāṇas*, Datta figures as seventh in the list of nine Vāsudevas.[142] After Neminātha's austerities on Girnar, his first convert was a king—Dattātri.[143] In yet another Jain text, Datta appears as the son of Kalkin, who is the last, promised manifestation of Viṣṇu in the brahmanical Purāṇas. The *atrunjaya māhātmya*, written after the twelfth century, foretells that Kalkin, the tenth incarnation of Viṣṇu, would be born to a mleccha and would cause much destruction and persecution of the Jains.[144] Kalkin's son and successor would be Datta, who would be instructed in the Jain doctrine and would spread it far and wide.[145]

Dattātreya often appeared to devotees in disgusting or shocking forms in order to test their true devotion. His guises included those of a low-caste hunter carrying meat, a drunk or sexually promiscuous ascetic, a Muslim soldier, or a faqīr. To the Marathi poet Eknāth whose guru Janārdana belonged to the Dattātreya community, the initial manifestation of the deity was in the form of a faqīr. However Janārdana may also have had a dual identity as an Ismā'īlī preacher.[146] The mythology of Dattātreya brings together disparate belief-systems, which, coincidentally, all have shrines in the Girnar hills. This blessing thus conferred the approval of all the sects that he represented, particularly in his most common manifestation, a Muslim holy man. Girnar was a multifaceted and complex pilgrimage centre, inhabited by a number of competing sects. The nearby Dātār hill had a small shrine of Jamial h near the summit, which was venerated by Muslims, Rajputs, and 'lower-class Hindus'. Jamial Shāh was said to have come there from Thatta in Sind, sent by his preceptor Pīr Paṭṭā in the reign of Māṇḍalik, that is, in the fifteenth century.[147]

Girnar was also associated with gold and it was believed that the river Suvar arekhā had alchemical powers.[148] This property also attracted religious figures of all denominations, including Tāntriks and others who dabbled in medicine and alchemy. The *Mir'āt-i Aḥmadī* relates the story of a dervish who had filled his gourd with water from a spring on the Girnar mountain:

> The Darvish descended and went to the town, and unwillingly stopped at the shop of one Raeka, a grocer, to whom he entrusted his gourd and went out to answer a call of nature. And it so happened that a drop of water from the hanging gourd oozed out, transmuting into gold the grocer's iron weight which was lying under it. The wondering Raeka understood the process, and quickly taking the golden weight and the gourd placed them in a safe corner, and then set fire to his shop. Soon the Darvish returned and asked for his gourd. The wily grocer, who was lamenting and crying out for help, exclaimed 'Cursed be thy gourd which brought this ruin on my shop. See how the flames are consuming everything. Woe is me; I am undone.'
>
> The Darvish, who was unaware of the mystic action of the water, went back to the mountain, hoping again to fetch water from the fountain; but to his surprise he saw no trace of it. Like the fountain of life it was hidden from his sight! It is said that Raeka built from that wealth the famous temple of the Shravaks. He left descendants, who are still found in this land, living as common men.[149]

Hero-gods and local deities, some of which have a dual identity as Hindu gurus and Muslim pīrs, avatāras, and non-Sanskritic legends, abound in the bardic chronicles. Apart from the surviving cults and sects, there are also forgotten ones. The worship of Rāmdev Pīr is still an important feature of 'popular religion' in Gujarat. Some cults, such as that of Rāmdev, were despised by Rajputs aspiring to brahmanical legitimization, connected as they were with the lower castes and reputedly *vāma-mārgī* (left-handed) Tāntric practices.[150] It is important that several chieftaincies in Gujarat, especially in Kathiavad, did not solely on brahmins for legitimation. Several clans such as the ūḍāsamās had originated outside the pale of brahmanical influence and owed allegiance to cults such as the aforementioned. Also, several clans were low-status pastoralists who adopted cults such as these because they were in a local idiom. In Rajasthan untouchables, Mers, ls, and even Jains became followers of Rāmdev Pīr.

In the fifteenth century, rājā of Bikaner and the governor of Nagaur, ḥammad Khān (an appointee and kinsman of the Gujarat sultan), both became disciples of Jambha, an Ismā'īlī-affiliated saint of the noīs, and had a dispute whether he was Hindu or Muslim. Jambha asserted that he was above all distinctions of sect and caste.[151]

such figure was Āī Mātā, said to be a follower of 'Shams Pīr', perhaps to be identified with the Ismā'īlī Pīr Shams, who was active in Gujarat in the fifteenth century. The term 'Āī', the equivalent of mother or grandmother,[152] referred in Gujarat to the powerful goddess of the raṇs.[153] In one version of her story, the Cāraṇi Āī/Āvaḍ was born to Mammad/Mamoud Gaḍhavī. The ruler of Sind, Umar, or Hamīr Sūmrā, a Rajput convert to Islam (perhaps Ismā'īlī), wanted to marry her. On being rebuffed, he threatened violence, but the goddess spoke through ḍ that the fall of the Sūmrās at the hands of the Sammas was already destined. Āvaḍ then led the Cāraṇs from Sind to Gujarat. A similar story of migration is also related by the Rabārīs.[154]

The relationship between Ismā'īlī-affiliated religious groups and their leaders with the Cāraṇs points to the formers' role not just as religious movements, but as conduits of information. As long as the pastoralist clans and immigrant adventurers were still mobile, as were the Ismā'īlī missionaries and pīrs, the Nāth yogis, the Bhāṭs, and the raṇs, religious affiliation was less codified and its expression more flexible and accommodative. The 'power' of the pīr, sant, or devī related largely to resource management, as miraculous granters of fertility, water diviners, defenders of cattle. This power may have been acknowledged without yet tying it down to a high-brahmanical or high-Sunni identity. With the sedentarization of many of the pastoralist clans by the end of the fifteenth century, the grant of tenures to many of them by the Gujarat sultans, especially under Maḥmūd Bīgara and his son Muẓaffar II and the establishment of a descent-based hierarchy increasingly based on genealogical legitimation, the liminal character of these cults began to decline. Some were absorbed over time into more defined traditions, such as those of the Sufis, Vaiṣṇavas, or orthodox Sunnis, a further tactic for survival.

CONVERSION

The religious marketplace of the period offered individuals and groups a range of religious choices. What evidence do we have for religious conversion in this period? Who were the instigators of such religious change? What were the groups or individuals being addressed? And, finally, how were these changes recorded?

Narratives of religious conversion, whether actual or claimed, may be divided into three rough categories. The most important of these was the conversion of a king or chieftain, the ultimate prize for the missionary and an event of significance in political terms. Proselytizing traditions often claimed, as a marker of legitimacy, to have won over the ruler of the territory in which they operated. It was usually representative kings associated with long periods of prosperity who became associated with conversion stories. At least four traditions claimed to have converted Siddharāja Jayasiṃha in the eleventh century: the Jains and three Muslim traditions.[155] Siddharāja was replaced only by Maḥmūd gara in the fifteenth century as the ultimate granter of legitimacy.[156] It is also a gauge of the cultural influence of the ruler that he passes into folklore or religious tradition as the ultimate guarantor of the faith being peddled even though there is no other evidnece of his interest in it.

In one version of the narrative, the king would be approached through his converted subordinates or wife and, after witnessing a miracle, would be persuaded to enter the fold. Mokal Siṃha (r. 1420–33), the ruler of Mevad, is believed to have supplicated before Rāmdev Pīr and granted him five *bighās* of land after witnessing the miraculous birth of his heir from an earthen pot.[157] Reasons of state meant that the ruler was sometimes obliged to be discreet about his new allegiance, an explanation offered by the tradition as to why official chronicles failed to mention the conversion. Thus, a Bohra tradition claims that Siddharāja Jayasiṃha was persuaded to embrace Islam, but kept this a secret.[158] Some of the Jain chroniclers of the Caulukyas claim, for example, that most of the rulers, not merely Kumārapāla, were converted to Jainism.[159]

In some narratives, the king was approached through the medium of his wife. This is an indicator of the importance of the queen and her natal family in alliance-dominated early Rajput politics. In some cases tradition does not go so far as claiming that the ruler was actually converted, confining themselves to gaining legitimacy by the use of his name. An example of this is the Satpanthī tradition about a marriage alliance between the family of Imām Shāh and Maḥmūd Bīgara. The tradition also claims that Imām Shāh performed a miracle before ḥmūd, who offered him gifts including a bullock cart.[160]

The Caulukyas in the twelfth and thirteenth centuries held to Śaiva religious observance manifested by patronage of Śaiva monastic institutions, land grants to monasteries and Śaiva temples, prominent aiva ascetics at court, and sacrifice as a ritual of kingship. They also extended patronage to Vaiṣṇava, mother goddess, and Jain temples and institutions at times, although this was usually as a manifestation of royal patronage than an indication of a change in primary allegiance. Only in the case of Kumā ala can we be fairly sure that the primary allegiance of the Caulukya ruler did change from Śaivism to Jainism. This was accompanied by greater patronage to Jain institutions and a disavowal of sacrifice. However this change in patronage did not last long and did not transform the basic nature of Caulukya religiosity. Kumārapāla's successor, Ajayapāla seems to have reverted to traditional aiva practice and all his successors followed suit.[161]

The second kind of conversion episode is that of the religious reaffiliation of entire cohesive clans or groups. In stories of this kind the entire group is impressed by a missionary and agrees to give him their allegiance. It is also seen among merchant or peasant groups. One example of this is the conversion of the Kaṇbīs from central Gujarat. A group of Kaṇbīs was on their way to Kashi on pilgrimage when they encountered Imām Shāh at Pirana. The pīr offered to facilitate their pilgrimage and, accordingly, when they awoke the next morning, they found themselves miraculously transported to their destination. On their return they pledged their allegiance to the Satpanth.[162] Similar stories appear in the Vaiṣṇava tradition of Vallabhācārya.[163]

Another instance of this kind was the conversion of the Ker clan in Kachchh. Formerly Hindus and led by the pious Jām Jakharo Gangā Jaliyo who bathed daily in Ganges water, they were converted to Islam by Bāuddin (Bahā' al-Dīn) Pīr, who lived, according to tradition, in the thirteenth or fourteenth century. In the nineteenth century they retained Rajput names, intermarried with the Jaḍejas, and refrained from dining with other Muslims, but exchanged daughters with the Muslim Pīrzādas of Sind.[164]

The invasion of 'Alā' al-Dīn Khaljī's armies at the end of the thirteenth century is associated with several groups' conversion to Islam. One of these was the Kamāliās, worshippers of the goddess Bahucarājī in north Gujarat. Their name derives from the word *kamāl* or perfect, given to their headman on his conversion.[165] One version of the 'conversion' story goes as follows: 'Alā' al-Dīn's army was encamped at Varkhadi in north Gujarat after desecrating the temple of Siddhpur. The goddess Bahucarā produced countless magical chickens which were consumed by the army. In the morning she took the form of a chicken and crowed, at which the eaten chickens replied and tore their way out of the soldiers' bellies. 'Alā' al-Dīn, distressed at the decimation of his army, begged the goddess' forgiveness and promised not to destroy any more temples. As for the chickens that had emerged from the soldiers, the goddess turned them into the cross-dressing and Islamized

Kamāliās, whose men were ordered to grow a moustache on one side of their face and to wear bangles on one arm.[166]

A transfer of religious allegiance was also carried out by certain militarized clans, many of whom had a pragmatic affiliation to religion. This includes the Molesalām garāsiyās, militarized pastoralists who converted to Islam during the reign of Maḥmūd Bīgara but retained many Rajput customs. The Molesalām Rāṭhoḍs of Bharuch district, for example, claimed they are descended from Yādava Rajputs converted to Islam by Maḥmūd in 1486.[167] Several similar groups had already converted to varieties of Islam in the fourteenth century. These include the Sammas of Sind and Kachchh, and branches of the Khokhars, Makvāṇās, and Paramārs in Gujarat and Saurashtra.[168]

A third kind of conversion narrative is that of individuals or groups who converted for reasons of personal conviction, career enhancement, or as a consequence of military defeat. One such instance is that of the brothers Sādhu and Sahāran, peasants from the Thanesar region who joined Fīrūz Shāh's retinue and converted to Islam. Their descendants were the sultans of Gujarat.[169] Another example is the alleged conversion of Rā Māṇḍalik, the Cūḍāsamā ruler of Junagadh, after his defeat by Maḥmūd Bīgara: 'The Sultan recited the creed of Islam, the Rao repeated it and saved himself from the flame of the Sultan's wrath which was like the fire of hell.'[170] Although Rā Māṇḍalik may have accepted Islam only after his defeat, he had apparently already been impressed by it: 'After his conversion the Rao used to say: "Before I met the king Shah Shamsuddin Bukhari ... had attracted me towards Islam. Now by the kindness of the Sultan I am exalted by the profession of the faith with the tongue while believing in it with the heart."'[171] There are also some instances of the conversion to Islam of the children or wives of defeated Hindu chieftains. The Paṭāi Rāval of Champaner was defeated and captured in 1483–4, but refused to embrace Islam. After his execution, his son was adopted by one of the sultan's courtiers and brought up as a Muslim, eventually attaining the title of Niẓām al-Mulk.[172]

The more common form of 'conversion' that can be gleaned from the labyrinth of sectarian politics in this period is one of multiple affiliations of a group or leader to a number of sects. One of the commonest ways in which this happened was the accretion of sectarian affiliations along migratory routes. Most of the goddess affiliations were picked up by various Rajput chieftains in this manner as is evident from the stories of Khoḍiyār and Āī with respect to the migratory histories of the Sammas. The same was true of affiliations with the hero cults of mdev or Gugā, or with certain charismatic Nāth holy men. It seems that these affiliations were not so much conversions to one particular faith, but the effect of the ritualization of politically or economically pragmatic relationships established with certain social groups that helped set up a kingdom or principality. The sectarian organizations could then claim to have 'converted' a military leader to assert the symbolic importance of such affiliation in the religious world of pastoralist kingdoms.

The variety of religious choices available inevitably led to competition between adherents and leaders of sects over converts, religious sites, and sources of legitimation. This is the main reason for the plethora of tales of contest in the religious literature of the period. Certain sites were particularly potent sources of sanctity. The Girnar hill was one of these. A range of religious groups—Jain, Śaivite, Nāth, Vaiṣṇava, and Sufi—established settlements on or near the hill. The Abu hill was also a site long considered sacred. It was the mythical birthplace of the Rajput clans. In the thirteenth century important Jain temples were built there and it became one of the most important Śvetāmbara sites of pilgrimage in western India. However, the importance of the site for Hindus meant that there was a contest over space here.

Many conversion narratives include competitions between religious figures. It is interesting that Śaivite yogīs or 'jogīs' are the most common antagonists of both Jain and Muslim proselytizers. The Nizārī Ismā'īlī preacher Satgur Nūr faced off against the king's magician, Jāniā jogī: he made the temple's stone idol speak and bring water from the tank for the pīr to wash his face, then caused the jogī's staff to fly into the air.[173] The processes of interaction between various forms of Hinduism and of Islam are more complex than would be described by either of these categories and little investigation has been done of their 'popular' or 'transitional' forms. The role of Ismā'īlīs in this interaction and their relationship with other religious groups, pastoralism, 'lower' castes, Tāntrism, and the dissemination of information had implications for political formations, especially in Gujarat.

While Sufism and Ismā'īlism were two distinct traditions, there are also significant links between them. There has been some study of the role of the Sufis in the interaction with the indigenous religious traditions.[174] While Ismā'īlīs at times took on Sufi garb and terminology to escape persecution, the relation between them was not always harmonious. Some Sufi orders regarded the Ismā'īlīs as dangerous heretics who should be eliminated. They compelled Nizārī converts to revert to Islam, witnessed in the role of the Bukhārī Sufi Shāh 'Ālam in reconverting the 'heretic' tribes of Junagadh and Kachchh. By the end of the fifteenth century there was some decline in the influence of Ismā'īlīs in Gujarat. Shrines of Ismā'īlī pīrs were taken over, others were appropriated as Sufi pīrs, as in the instance of Ḥasan Kabīr al-n being listed in a Suhrawardī hagiography as Ḥasan Daryā. Similarly, Lāl Shāhbāz Qalandar is claimed both by the Suhrawardīs and the Ismā'īlīs. As the latter are rarely present in the sources of Sunnis or Ithnā 'Ashariyyas, it has been inferred that 'whenever an Ismā'īlī appeared in a Muslim guise, he was identified with a Sufi dervish or a Qalandar'.[175] It is not impossible that some of the early Muslim missionaries to Gujarat were in fact Ismā'īlīs, for example, Shāh 'Alī Sarmast who rode on a lion and used a snake as a whip, mentioned in the *Tuḥfat al-qārī* of Manṣūr b. Muḥammad (1707).[176]

For the Ismā'īlīs, the key became to adapt to the currents of the times—whether this took the form of Sufi garb or terminology, local Hindu religious concepts as a translated vocabulary, or secrecy and circumspection. In theory at least, their missionary efforts were secret and individualized and not public or mass.[177] Converts were supposed to be made by 'choosing an influential person belonging to a specific social group who would later convert his fellows'.[178] Preaching was highly organized and texts often used the secret Khojkī script, derived from commercial shorthand and introduced by Pīr Ṣadr al-Dīn in the fifteenth century.[179] However, the use of the local idiom and traditional concepts that enabled the Ismā'īlīs to infiltrate and win believers later led to the decline of their influence when groups rising in the status hierarchy adopted 'orthodox' Sunni or Hindu vocabularies and rituals.

SECT AND RELIGION IN THE SULTANATE

The complex dynamics of fissioning pastoralist clans in search of territory and wealth made this region ripe for exploitation by sectarian leaders in search of followers and converts. Within pastoralist clan politics, marriage and conquest through alliance could lead to intricate networks of sectarian affiliation. In this phase sectarian ideologies developed through pragmatic alliances between militant pastoralist groups patronizing equally militant sectarian groups. Multiple sectarian affiliations were, therefore, commonplace. Certain groups were able to shift allegiances or strike up unlikely mercenary ties with others, thereby changing the sectarian map, while others retained their original affiliations and evolved other sect-based territorial and economic quests. The sectarian history of Gujarat in the fifteenth century is that of groups at various points on this complex maze of clan and sectarian politics.

That the process was deeply contentious, if not always violent, is evident from the sheer proliferation of cults and sects. The relationship between political and religious spheres is made clear by the number of martyrs—both Hindu and Muslim—who became deities or intercessors and the increasing political power of 'honour' groups such as the Cāraṇs. Cāraṇ women were raised to godhood based on feats of honour involving clan rivalries. The displeasure or departure of the raṇ-goddess could augur bloody defeats for the kingdom that depended on her favour.[180] The millenarian tone of such stories and poetry present a picture of honour-based communities desperate for survival in an unstable ecological zone. The sacrality of such heroes and goddesses was established as a result of the intersection of pastoralist codes of honour and the militancy created by clan splitting. The large numbers of saint-warriors who combined healing or fertility-granting powers with military valour in this period (such as Rāmdev Pīr) indicate a link between clan politics and religion. The prominence of thpanthī ideologues with their aggressive mix of renunciation and wealth-generating alchemy is another hint of the warrior-ascetic ideals that were required for political success. The stakes were high and so was the intensity of religiosity. In the more stable fifteenth century the proliferation of militant cults began to give way to more settled shrine and pilgrimage-based religiosity.

As pastoralists entered Gujarat, sectarian groups could link themselves to one or another of its branches. Groups such as the Sammas, for example, repeatedly changed their affiliations during their resettlements from Sind to Kachchh and Saurashtra when they came into contact with missionaries or local cults (see Chapter 3). Competing proselytizers tended to invoke each other's terminology. Most groups in this period used simple poetic verses dealing with similar issues to convey their message, differentiated only by sectarian motifs that would be recognizable by adherents.[181] This allowed them to simultaneously disseminate difference and similarity with other sectarian beliefs and customs. What really worked were the 'miracles' that brought practical benefits to the community. A missionary's success in recruiting converts or getting patrons often depended on securing the material and physical well-being of the target clan, lineage, or individual. Accordingly, sect leaders were often facilitators of water, wealth, and territory or claimed abilities to heal, and demonstrated their skill in contests with other proselytizers.

Gujarat was also a religious marketplace in another sense. Here, players could choose from a range of options depending upon their needs. Given the mobile nature of the economy, merchants often had multiple sectarian affiliations. Jagaḍū's biography shows how many affiliations he accumulated due to the favours done to him by holy men before settling for a respectable Jain identity towards the end of his life. As a notable of Bhadreshvar, he paid his dues by making donations to all the religious institutions of the town, thereby ensuring that he would have the goodwill of the groups who could assist him in trade and politics.

The notion of a religious marketplace is also demonstrated by the proliferation of sectarian shrines at a site like Girnar. Such clustered shrine sites were restricted to certain regions or particularly important spots on trade routes. The proliferation of sects in the period under survey is a proof of Gujarat's dynamic trading ethos that flourished despite political instability. Over time, sects that had carved out a following by offering a millenarian rhetoric to militant lineages and clans in search of territory and wealth became prosperous and sedentary, shed their millenarian edge, and settled down to business. The Satpanthī ā'īlīs, for example, restricted proselytization after the death of Imām h in 1512.[182] The hectic sectarian activity and religious conversion began to die down by the late fifteenth century as the religious map of modern Gujarat was finally settled into place.

The sultans contributed substantially to the stabilization of the religious marketplace. Most importantly, they put an end to the endless clan fissioning by settling the lineages into stable principalities so that the unstable peripatetic plunder-based pastoralist politics of the pre-fifteenth century that were intimately linked to the sectarian dynamic were now finally subdued. Second, by ensuring safe routes they enabled religious sects to settle down at places where they could expect a regular flow of pilgrims. At important shrine sites like Somanath and Girnar, the returns from pilgrimage could be very substantial indeed. Finally, by regularizing trade, they ensured that mercantile communities remained prosperous and could provide sustained patronage to the denominations of their choice. This meant that sects did not need any longer to engage in aggressive competition for converts for sheer economic survival. Moreover, city merchants depended on a complex network of trade and affiliations, and a civic atmosphere was created within which merchants donated money to institutions belonging to a variety of denominations. Over time, the stabilization and expansion of a resident population coupled with the dynamic trading ethos would give these institutions long-term stability.

The stabilization of the religious marketplace paved the way for the rise of Vaiṣṇavism, Sufism, and the ethos of bhakti. The genealogy of a notable in the Mansa inscription of 1526 demonstrates the move of a Vāghelā lineage from a pastoralist militant identity towards a mercantile Vaiṣṇava one.[183] This was also when the great Gujarati Sufis established themselves as a logical outcome of the process of settling down and the formation of an imperium in the region. The Sufis and bhakti Vaiṣṇavism brought prestige of the kind that early Ismāʿīlism or the Nāthpanthīs could not offer. Ismāʿīlism itself underwent a transformation when the Satpanthīs of Pirana established or claimed marital relationships with the sultans. The sultans married into Sufi families as well. Bhakti as an inter-sectarian ideology was intimately related to the world of the merchant in Gujarat, and began to be codified in the form of written texts. The ideology of bhakti was in keeping with the multi-ethnic cosmopolitanism of the towns. Thus, what might have begun as a militant sectarian ideal to oppose the cultic opponent through a competitive enunciation of ideal devotionalism was finally assimilated into a pragmatic ideology of religious co-existence for the sake of keeping the motors of trade running smoothly. The imputed 'syncretism' of bhakti, therefore, refers to the two phases of cultic religiosity in Gujarat—the first when the similarities between deities or gods was used to prove that a particular cult was the culmination of all other religious beliefs and the second in which sects emphasized the sameness of religious beliefs for reasons of maintaining social order.

This did not mean that the rest of the cultic spectrum in Gujarat disappeared. On the contrary, sects coexisted in multiple niches, a scenario made possible by the overall prosperity of the region. In Gujarat, perhaps more than in any other region of pre-modern India, sects had a remarkable propensity to survive and flourish. This is because the wealth from trade allowed communities to support those of their choice. The fifteenth century's stable religious marketplace allowed more information about religious options to circulate in the public domain, through texts, oral compositions, performers, and missionaries as villages and towns became linked through better roads and improved security. It was now possible to belong to a dominant religious identity while dabbling in others: the lay followers of 'syncretic' cults made choices of this nature. Women, for example, were now able to patronize fertility-granting shrines without the participation of their husbands.[184] People visited shrines with a reputation for curing leprosy or blindness regardless of their other religious affiliations. Over this period it may be noticed that devotion and its manifestation became a cultural trait as more people began to take part in it publicly. While religion had previously been restricted to the royal temple cults on the one hand and the observance of life-cycle rituals in the domestic sphere on the other, it now became increasingly and inclusively public. Festivals were celebrated in public, and large numbers of people went on pilgrimage and visited public shrines.

The religious options being offered were over time subsumed within a regional identity. Thus, 'imported' options, whether Ismā'īlism from Sind or revivalist Vaiṣṇavism from south India, had to be translated into the local idiom, both linguistically and culturally. Religious movements were also now incorporated within the history of the region. Thus, the goddess Khoḍiyār, the guarantor and protector of the ūḍāsamās was not just a manifestation of the transregional goddess akti but also a figure who was granted a part in the history of the region.[185] Trans-regional themes were now given a local manifestation and were incorporated into historical narratives. This trend was manifested in the appendices to the Purāṇas composed from this period to celebrate and mythologize shrines, temples, and priesthoods.[186] By the fifteenth century religious options operated within a distinctly Gujarati cultural ecumene.

The fifteenth century marks a watershed in the religious history of Gujarat. The older remnants of *Purāṇic* Vaiṣṇavism, courtly Jain and aiva religiosity, and Ismā'īlī sectarian religion were swept away and were replaced by new forms of religiosity. These centred on new forms of temple building in the Jain case, bhakti-oriented sectarian activities in the case of Vaiṣṇavism, and more organized Ismā'īlī and Sufi sectarian activities. However, the religious marketplace of the fifteenth century was prosperous enough to accommodate a host of religious affiliations as there was an expansion in the kinds of patrons for religious sects. Indeed, by the late fifteenth century all the major religious organizational streams that proved to be subsequently significant were in place.

The pacification of the Gujarat countryside by the sultans had an enormous impact on the relationship between religion and politics. If the period between the thirteenth and fifteenth centuries was marked by uncertainties of migration, conversion, and struggles over resources, the fifteenth century was about the making of a stable polity based on the settling of pastoralist clans and their participation in sultanate politics, the rise of religious activity as a lucrative economic sphere, and the interconnections between various regions and economies tilting towards the sultanate centre. The pre-fifteenth century political and religious scenario saw pastoralist bands with local religious affiliations move into Saurashtra. This led to violence and competition as the references to clan fission and sectarian struggle indicate. By the fifteenth century the clans had settled down into proto-courtly polities. Correspondingly, conversion and inter-sectarian struggle seem to have been slowed down as well. The bardic literature was finding its way into texts like *Velī Kṛṣṇa Rukmini* that mixed the bardic with the Purāṇic and new bhakti Vaiṣṇava idioms to legitimize the rise of a courtly Rajput society.[187] Goddess worship was being converted to organized sectarian activity and links were being forged with Vaiṣṇava ideology indicating a more flexible clan ideology that stressed the values of pacification and political power rather than mobile warfare and political brigandage. The parcelling of territories amongst the clans had allowed them to settle down as feudatories of the sultans. Over time the Rajput polities came to control Vaiṣṇava shrines such as the one at Dakor. It is interesting that here Kṛṣṇa is worshipped in the form of Rāṇachoḍajī—the one who leaves the battlefield—perhaps a remark on the pacification of the Rajputs.[188]

The fifteenth century marks the beginning of a new and more complex religious marketplace in Gujarat that ensued from the pacification of the region. The hallmark of this religious marketplace was organization towards the unified economic and political context of the sultanate.

ṣṇava shrines in Gujarat were now being rendered subsidiary to that of Dvaraka. Later, this phenomenon permitted Raṇachoḍajī of Dvaraka to appear in Dakor as a manifestation of the same godhead in the sixteenth century. The links between the pastoralist clans made the connections between shrines more fruitful in terms of religious patronage and paved the way for the formulation of an interlinked hierarchy of deities under the larger rubric of Vaiṣṇavism, Śaivism, or Śāktism. Although each clan had its own kul-devī, over time, most of them came to be seen as emanations of the transcendent goddess.

In every case shrines benefited from a steep rise in the number of patron groups as a result of pacification and the ensuing prosperity that ensued. New social groups like the Pāṭīdārs cleared land under the sultan's peace and organized their own religious activities. The Bhāṭiā merchant group (that had aspirations to Rajput status) assumed a more florid and eroticized style of Kṛṣṇa bhakti in the late fifteenth century. Similarly, goddess shrines were patronized by Rajputs and celebrated in bardic poetry. As artisanal, agrarian, and military groups became prosperous, they became patrons of various sects too. The rise of women as patrons added another level to the patronage of religious activity.

However, increased organized religiosity should not lead to the assumption that religious identities were becoming fixed. In the late fifteenth century the Pāṭīdārs of central Gujarat adopted the new wave of Kṛṣṇa bhakti as well as the Satpanthī Ismā'īlī sect in Pirana. The Rajputs patronized a range of sectarian activities from Nāth yogis and mother goddess cults to forms of Vaiṣṇavism. Sects served to organize social functions and groups that were fundamental to the functioning of politics. Thus, if marriage brought in Kṛṣṇa or a version of the mother goddess into a Rajput household, it was politic for the clan leader to accept and honour the deity in order to signal good political relationships between the families.[189] If soldiers were organized around the worship of a goddess or if the financing of war and conscription were performed by the Nāths, then clan leaders were obliged to act as patrons for these cults.[190] Equally, a Sufi pīr could gain the patronage of a Rajput household if he had blessed the women of the house with children or had brought rain to an arid region.[191] The Sufi pīr could additionally depend on the piety of local villagers to sustain a *khānqah* on an everyday basis. The *malfūz* literature on the lives of the Sufis is replete with stories that demonstrate the saint's charismatic hold over and economic dependence on local populations.[192]

Moreover, when shrines expanded or changed denominational affiliation, earlier forms of worship were accommodated within the new order. This could happen in two ways. One was the incorporation of the deity into the dominant cosmology as happened with the evolution of Ismā'īlī devotionalism.[193] In the case of Sufi belief, the interface with bhakti devotionalism is well documented. Or, as in the case of Dvaraka or Dakor, earlier religious factions were accommodated within the new management of shrines.[194] In Dvaraka, Śaivite Sankaracharyas remained leaders of the maṭha (the monastery) while the temple became the centre of Vai ava devotionalism in Gujarat.[195] Or as in the case of

Girnar, a single site could become the literal exemplification of the religious marketplace. The general reputation of the site as a sacred site meant a variety of cults could benefit from its aura of sacrality. A discourse of harmony would have been attractive to pilgrims rather than one of in-fighting and bitterness. Thus, it is not surprising that in Girnar Dattātreya was claimed by Śaivites, Vaiśnavas, Jains, as well as Ismā'īlīs.

The religious marketplace in Gujarat was thus characterized by a mix of the formal and informal organization. At the very bottom were small devotional cults restricted to the community context and organized by kinship ties. Above this were levels of sectarian organization up to the regional sect. Of course, the dominant patronage context made a shrine Jain, Vaiṣṇava, Ismā'īlī, or Sufi, but shrines that transcended particularist affiliation may have attracted more followers and pilgrims. Often an extraordinary deed by a charismatic religious leader in matters of childbirth, health, or ecological cycles ensured cross-belief patronage and the rise of subsidiary shrines at the local and trans-local levels. For example, while the main shrine of Rāmdev Pīr was in Runicha in Rajasthan, countless subsidiary shrines that claimed to offer his miraculous powers came up all over Gujarat. The same is true of other fifteenth century pīrs such as Geban Shāh, Bālā Shāh, Mīrā Dātār, and so on.[196] The religious marketplace thus consisted of a number of coexisting and overlapping systems of practice that allowed for competition and coexistence.

The economic prosperity of Gujarat in the fifteenth century resulted in a complex religious marketplace that over time developed a discourse of mutual existence that is noticeable in the bhakti poetry or Sufi doctrine of the sixteenth century. However, competition was necessary, especially when it came to roping in important patrons or when it came to raising the level of shrine importance through miracles. The politics of the sultanate was related to religion in two ways. First, at a general level, all patrons of regional importance, starting from the sultan all the way down to petty feudatory and merchant, had to act as patron to a variety of religious activities that reflected patronage to subordinate power centres—wives, soldiers, artisans, saints, holy men—who ensured the stability of the polity. Second, social groups like the Pāṭīdārs began to appear as religious patrons in order to reflect their social and political power in the historical context of the pacification and settlement of fifteenth-century Gujarat. The balance between these sects and shrines was always negotiated and sometimes precarious. But as long as the sultans kept the trade routes pacified, opened up new economic vistas, and ensured peace and prosperity, this ever-burgeoning religious marketplace would remain peaceful, reflecting a political consensus between social groups that made up the sultanate.

Exercising religious options was only possible in a situation where there were many migrants and identities could be reinvented and realigned along the way. This socio-cultural world was obliged to be flexible and accommodative: identities could not be too fixed because the entire edifice of religion, trade, and politics was conceptually and institutionally dynamic. But this did not mean that identities were floating or unanchored. From the point of view of the religious individual, it was possible to remain affiliated to various sects while maintaining a dominant religious identity. The sects, on the other hand, could go on believing that they were unified and exclusive. They could not, however, restrict the movement of their adherents. That need was obviated by the levels of prosperity they could achieve by serving the sultanate's ideology of trade. For the Gujarat sultans in the fifteenth century, the question was to determine how this complex and dynamic society could be regulated, pacified, and administered without losing the dynamism that generated its prosperity. This question will be dealt with in the final chapter.

NOTES

1. F. Mallison (1980), 'The Cult of Sudāmā in Porbandar-Sudāmāpuri (II)', *JOIB*, 29(3–4), p. 220, fn. 17.
2. Desai, 'Muslims in the 13th century'.
Epigraphia Indica: Arabic and Persian Supplement; Hultszch, 'A Grant of Arjunadeva,' p. 242f; Sircar, *Select Inscriptions*, Vol. 2, p. 402–8; Sircar, 'Veraval Inscription,' p. 141ff.
4. On kul-devīs, see Lindsey Harlan (1992), *Religion and Rajput Women: The Ethic of Protection in Contemporary Narratives*, Chapter 3. Also see Tambs-Lyche, *Power, Profit and Poetry*, p. 32–5.
5. Rangarajan, *Spread of Vaiṣṇavism*, p. 33.
6. Ibid., p. 36. For reflections of the professionalization of architecture, see Patel, *Building Communities in Gujarat*, in particular Chapter 1.
7. Majumdar, *Chaulukyas of Gujarat*, p. 288.
8. Ibid., p. 294, citing the play *Moharājaparājaya*. The four carnivorous sects were the Kaula and Kāpālika, both Śaiva sects, the Rahamāna (unidentified, but perhaps Muslims), and the Ghaṭacaṭaka (agnostics).

9. Ibid., p. 290.
10. Ibid., pp. 290–1.
11. Georg Bühler (1877), 'Eleven Land-grants of the Caulukyas of Anahilvad', *IA*, 6, pp. 82–3.
12. Majumdar, *Chalukyas of Gujarat*, p. 292.
13. Ibid., p. 293.
14. Ibid., p. 294.
15. The lower status of temple officials was seen also in contemporary Jainism, where there was a conflict between the temple-dwelling and reforming ascetics. Dundas, *The Jains*, pp. 136–7. Later too temple-dwelling brahmins have had a lower or 'fallen' status. See D.F. Pocock (1981), 'The Vocation and Avocations of the Guggali Brahmans of Dvaraka,' *Contributions to Indian Sociology*, 15, p. 321.
16. Majmudar, *Cultural History of Gujarat*, p. 233.
17. Shastri, *HIG*, p. 56; Hariśaṅkar Prabhāśaṅkar Śāstrī (1972), 'Prabhās-na vājā rājā śivarāja-nā samay-no saṃvat 1451 (ī.s. 1395)–no ek aprasiddha śilālekha. [An Unpublished Inscription from VS 1451 (AD 1395) of the Time of the Vājā Ruler Śivarāja of Prabhās]', *Svādhyāya*, 9(2), p. 228.
18. Burgess and Cousens, *RLARBP*, p. 56.
19. C. Vaudeville (1999), 'The Cowherd God in Ancient India', in Vasudha Dalmia, ed., *Myths, Saints, and Legends in Medieval India*, p. 18.
20. Rangarajan, *Spread of Vaiṣṇavism*, p. 4, citing H.C. Raychaudhuri (1936) *Materials for the Study of the Early History of the Vaiṣṇava Sect*, p. 173.
21. Rangarajan, *Spread of Vaiṣṇavism*, p. 2.
22. Ibid., pp. 3, 36.
23. Ibid., p. 4.
24. Vaudeville, 'Cowherd God', p. 19.
25. Ibid., p. 26.
26. Ibid., p. 9.
27. Ibid., p. 10.
28. G. S. Ojha and Georg Bühler (1888), eds, *EI*, Vol. 2, p. 439.
29. Rangarajan, *Spread of Vaiṣṇavism*, p. 10.
30. J. Kirste (1892), 'Inscriptions from Northern Gujarat', *EI*, Vol. 2, Shastri, *HIG*, p. 43.
31. Vaudeville, 'Cowherd God,' p. 32.
32. P. Peterson (1905), *A Collection of Prakrit and Sanskrit Inscriptions*, p. 11.
33. K.M. Munshi (1935), *Gujarāta and its Literature: A Survey from the Earliest Times*, p. 116.
34. Ibid., p. 122.
35. Ibid., p. 123.
36. N.M. Thoothi (1935), *The Vaishṇavas of Gujarat: Being a Study in Methods of Investigation of Social Phenomena*, p. 67.

37. See, for example, Anncharlott Eschmann, Hermann Kulke, and Gaya Charan Tripathi, eds (1978), *The Cult of Jagannath and the Regional Tradition of Orissa.*
38. Rangarajan, *Spread of Vaiṣṇavism*, p. 27.
39. Ibid., p. 31.
40. Majmudar, *Cultural History of Gujarat*, p. 202. For an analysis of the appearance of Kṛṣṇa-Rāṇachoḍa in Dakor, see F. Mallison (1991), 'Lorsque Raṇachoḍarāya quitte Dwarka pour Dakor, ou Comment Dvārakānātha prit la succession de Ḍaṅkanātha', in *Devotion Divine: Studies in Honour of Charlotte Vaudeville*, eds, Diana Eck and Françoise Mallison.
41. Rangarajan, *Spread of Vaiṣṇavism*, p. 35.
42. Munshi, *Gujarata and its Literature*, p. 119.
43. Padmanābha (1953), *Kānhaḍade prabandha (15th Century)*, verses I. 15–17.
44. Ibid., verse I.86.
45. Ibid., verse I.142–3.
46. Ibid., verses II.132–5.
47. Ibid., verse II.138.
48. Ibid., verse II.135.
49. Majmudar, *Cultural History of Gujarat*, p. 212–13.
50. D.R. Bhandarkar (1912), 'Anâvâḍâ Stone Inscription of Sâraṅgadeva, VS 1348 (1291 AD),' *IA* 41, p. 21.
51. Vaudeville, 'Cowherd God,' p. 31, fn. 18.
52. Rangarajan, *Spread of Vaiṣṇavism*, p. 22.
53. A considered analysis of Narasiṃha's achievements is in Sitanshu Yashaschandra (2003), 'From Hemacandra to *Hind Svarāj:* Region and Power in Gujarati Literary Culture', in *Literary Cultures in History: Reconstructions from South Asia*, ed. Sheldon Pollock, pp. 583–9.
54. Françoise Mallison (1986), *Au point du jour: Les Prabhātiyāṃ de Narasiṃha Maheta, poète et saint vishnouite du Gujarāt (Xve siecle)*, p. 24; C.R. Naik (1964), 'Cultivation of the Persian Language and Literature by the Nagaras of Gujarat', *JOIB* 14, p. 125–6.
55. Pocock, 'Vocation and Avocations of the Guggali Brahmans'.
56. Marco Polo (1993 rpt), *The Travels of Marco Polo*, trans. Henry Yale.
57. Ahmad, *Indo-Arab Relations*, p. 27.
58. Dundas, *The Jains*, pp. 135.
59. Majumdar, *Chaulukyas of Gujarat*, p. 116.
60. Toshikazu Arai (1998), 'Jain Kingship in the *Prabandhacintāmaṇi*', in J.F. Richards, ed., *Kingship and Authority in South Asia*, p. 113.
61. Majumdar, *Chaulukyas of Gujarat*, p. 324; E.K. Burgess and James Burgess (1902), 'Translation of Arisiṃha's Sukritasankirtana (VS 1285)', *IA* 31.
62. Misra, *Rise of Muslim Power*, pp. 68–9, citing *Samrā rāsu* and

Nābhinandanjinoddhāra prabandha written by Kakkāsūri of the Ukeśagaccha (1336).

63. For example, the inscription of Śāh Jesal from Cambay in 1309 to mark the building of a temple and hospital during the reign of Alp Khān in Gujarat. Jinavijayaji, *PJLS*, 2, p. 447, Shastri, *HIG*, No. 1, p. 3. Or the inscription of 1345 from Himmatnagar in north Gujarat, recording the installation of an image. K.G. Krishnan, ed. (1987) *ARIE for 1976–77*, App. B, No. 58.
64. Lālacandra Bhagavān Gāndhī (1939), *Jinaprabha-sūri ane Sultān Muhammad Tughluq*.
65. The *Bombay Gazetteer* reports only one group of Jain cultivators in Gujarat—the Panca Osvāls of Kachchh—in the nineteenth century. Campbell and Kirparam, *Gujarat Population*, p. 99.
66. V.K. Srivastava (1997), *Religious Renunciation of a Pastoral People*, p. 65.
67. Campbell and Kirparam, *Gujarat Population*, Vol. 2, p. 496.
68. See Lawrence A. Babb (1998), 'Rejecting Violence: Sacrifice and the Social Identity of Trading Communities', *Contributions to Indian Sociology*, 32.
69. Campbell and Kirparam, *Gujarat Population*, Vol. 2, p. 485.
70. Dundas, *The Jains*, p. 215.
71. Ibid., p. 212.
72. Deyell, *Living Without Silver*, p. 247; Khare, 'Dravyapariksha of Thakkura Pheru', p. 25.
73. Dundas, *The Jains*, pp. 51–2.
74. Sarvāṇanda. *Jagaḍūcarita*, p. 21.
75. Dundas, *The Jains*, p. 221.
76. Ibid., pp. 136–8.
77. Majmudar, *Cultural History of Gujarat*, p. 208.
78. Dundas, *The Jains*, p. 249. See also Peter Flügel (2000), 'Protestantische und Post-Protestantische Jain Reformbewegungen: Zur Geschichte und Organisation der Sthanakvasi I', *Berliner Indologische Studien* 13–14, (15).
79. Kṛṣṇarām Biśnoi (1996), *Guru Jambheśvar: vividh āyām*, p. 21, Khan, *Conversion and Shifting Identities*, p. 65.
80. Dundas, *The Jains*, p. 113.
81. Sarvāṇanda. *Jagaḍūcarita*, p. 33.
82. Hemacandra argues that those who eat honey are worse than butchers. Dundas, *The Jains*, p. 177.
83. Cambay was routinely known as an Arab port due to the numbers of foreign merchants settled there. See Chapter 2 in this volume. Turuṣka was a common appellation for Muslims, it did not necessarily denote ethnic Turks. See Chattopadhyaya, *Representing the Other*, p. 40.
84. The tale indicates that Jagaḍū received some assistance from local Śaivite yogis in exploiting the resource that the stone contained, possibly a valuable mineral or a marine commodity such as ambergris, often found in the Persian Gulf.

85. Campbell and Kirparam, *Gujarat Population*, Vol. 2, pp. 469–502, 496.
86. Parts of this section appear in Samira Sheikh (2007), 'Religious Traditions and Early Ismā'īlī History in Western India: Some Historical Perspectives on Satpanthi Literature and the Ginā ns', in *Ginā ns: Texts and Contexs: Essays on Ismaili Hymns from South Asia in Honour of Zawahir Moir*, eds, Tazim Kassam and Françoise Mallison.
87. Desai, 'Muslims in the 13th century Gujarat,' p. 355.
88. Desai, *Arabic, Persian and Urdu Inscriptions*, No. 1865.
89. Sayyid Imāmuddin Dargāhvāla (1973), *Gujarāt-nā auliyā*, Vol. I, pp. 9–11.
90. James McNabb Campbell, ed. (1899), *Gujarát Population: Musalmáns and Pársis: Gazetteer of the Bombay Presidency*, Vol. 9, Part 2, p. 6 fn.
91. Ibid.
92. Ibid.
93. On this phenomenon, see Kolff, *Naukar, Rajput and Sepoy.*
94. On the rebellion of Nūr Turk in the reign of Raẓiyya see Jūzjānī, *Ṭabaḳāt-i Nāṣirī*, p. 646–7. Fīrūz Shāh claimed to have suppressed rebel sects including the Shī'ī Rāfiẓīs and other 'heretics'. Fīrūz Shāh, 'Futuhāt-i Fīrūz Shāhī', in Elliot and Dowson, *History of India*, Vol. 3, p. 377–8.
95. Sikandar, *MS*, p. 127.
96. Khan, *Conversion and Shifting Identities*.
97. Aziz Ahmad (1964), *Studies in Islamic Culture in the Indian Subcontinent*, p. 140.
98. Nāñjīyāṇī, *Khojā vṛattānt*, p. 158.
99. The dates of this semi-legendary figure are discussed in Kassam, *Songs*, pp. 93–4. According to Daftary, he must have lived in the fourteenth century. Daftary, *Ismailis*, p. 478.
100. Nāñjīyāṇī, *Khojā vṛattānt*, p. 216–8.
101. Nūr Muḥammad Shāh (1962), *Satveṇī-jī vel*, p. 222.
102. F. Mallison, 'Early Kṛṣṇa *Bhakti* in Gujarat', p. 51.
103. As witnessed in the stories of Surjādevī, Rānī Rūpānde, and Kākā Akelā and his wife, the gardeners of the king's minister and several others. See Kassam, *Songs of Wisdom*, p. 102; Khan, *Conversion and Shifting Identities*, pp. 86–7. It is significant that many of these stories have the queen being converted secretly to the faith, eventually convincing her husband through her steadfastness. Similar tales testifying to the influence of the queen in insinuating religious change in royal households are seen in the adoption of gurus and mother goddess cults. See Harlan, *Religion and Rajput Women*, Chapter 3, especially pp. 100–101.
104. See, for example, the messianic theme in Sumit Sarkar (1989), 'The Kalki-Avatar of Bikrampur: A Village Scandal in Early Twentieth Century Bengal', in Ranajit Guha, ed., *Subaltern Studies VI*. Many of the so-called 'subaltern' protests of the colonial period featured a messianic theme,

usually missed or glossed over by historians seeking only an anti-colonial or nationalist agenda.

105. John Cort (1990), 'Twelve Chapters from *The Guidebook to Various Pilgrimage Places, the Vividhatirthakalpa of Jinaprabhasuri*', in Phyllis Granoff, ed., *The Clever Adulteress and the Faithful Wife, and Other Stories from the Jain Tradition*, p. 245.
106. Ibid., p. 257.
107. Rangarajan, *Spread of Vaiṣṇavism*, p. 34.
108. Tūnī, *TMS*, p. 176.
109. Rangarajan, *Spread of Vaiṣṇavism*, p. 29.
110. J.W. Watson (1880), *The Statistical Account of Junagadh: Being the Junagadh Contribution to the Kathiawar Portion of the Bombay Gazetteer*, p. 87.
111. Khan, *Conversion and Shifting Identities*, p. 70; Trivedi, *Census of India*, p. 200.
112. Trivedi, *Census of India*, p. 162.
113. The Yādava heroes were Kṛṣṇa, Balarāma, Satyaki, Pradyumna, and Aniruddha. For reflections on equivalence between Hindu and Muslim categories, see Stewart, 'In Search of Equivalence', pp. 260–87.
114. Trivedi, *Census of India*, p. 55.
115. Ibn Baṭṭūṭa, *Riḥla*, p. 212.
116. Helene Basu (1995), 'Muslim Shrines as Boundary Markers of a Cult Region: The Network of Sidi Saints in Western India', in Makhan Jha, ed., *Pilgrimage: Concepts, Themes, Issues and Methodology*, p. 65; Peter Francis, Jr. (1986), 'Baba Ghor and the Ratanpur Rakshisha', *JESHO*, 29(2), p. 200.
117. Trivedi, *Census of India*, p. 21.
118. Sikandar, *MS*, trans., p. 82.
119. Ibid., p. 83.
120. Ibid., p. 84.
121. Ibid.
122. Trivedi, *Census of India*, p. 87.
123. Ibid., p. 112.
124. Ibid., p. 147.
125. Ibid., p. 39.
126. Khakhar, *Report on the Architectural and Archaeological Remains*, p. 25.
127. Trivedi, *Census of India*, p. 35.
128. Beatrix Pfleiderer (1984), 'Mira Datar Dargah: The Psychiatry of a Muslim Shrine,' in Imtiaz Ahmad, ed. *Ritual and Religion among Muslims in India*, p. 201.
129. Majmudar, *Cultural History of Gujarat*, p. 223.
130. Ibid., p. 224.
131. Khakhar, *Report on the Architectural and Archaeology Remains*, p. 13.

132. Rangarajan, *Spread of Vaiṣṇavism*, pp. 36–55.
133. Wilberforce-Bell, *History of Kathiawad*, p. 60.
134. Watson, *Kathiawar*, pp. 408–9.
135. R.C. Arora (1971), 'The Magas, Sun-Worship and the *Bhaviṣya Purāṇa*', *Purāṇa*, 3(1), p. 47–76; Hazra, *Studies in the Upapurāṇas*, p. 76.
136. A. Rigopoulos (1998), *Dattātreya: The Inmortal Guru, Yogin, and Avatāra*, p. 39.
137. Desāi, *Saurāṣṭra-no itihās*, p. 113.
138. Kenneth F. Kiple, ed. (1993), *The Cambridge World History of Human Disease*, p. 410.
139. Roy Porter and W.F. Bynum, eds (1993), *The Companion Encyclopedia to the History of Medicine*, p. 562.
140. Yashavant A. Raikar (1962), 'Sri Chakradhara: A Medieval Saint from Gujarat', *JOIB*, 12.
141. Rigopoulos, *Dattātreya*, pp. 89–109.
142. Ibid., p. 98, p. 106, No. 40.
143. Amarjī, *Ta'rīkh-i Sorath*, pp. 47–8, note.

Mleccha is literally translated as 'barbarian', but in the post-12th century period, was often used in Sanskrit texts for Muslims. This Jain rendering of Kalki/Kalkin as a barbarian or Muslim has intriguing parallels with the Ismā'īlī rendering of the *Dasāvatāra*, in which the tenth avātara of Viṣṇu is homologous with the promised Mahdī. See G. Khakee (1981), 'The "Das Avatara" of Pir Shams as Linguistic and Literacy Evidence of the Early Development of Ismailism in Sind', in *Sind through the Centuries*, ed., Hamida Khuhro,

145. C.L. Lassen (1873), 'Papers on Satrunjaya and the Jains III', *IA*, 2, pp. 195–6.
146. H. van Skyhawk (1989), 'Sufi influence in the *Ekanāthī-bhāgavat*', in R.S. McGregor, ed., *Devotional Literature in South Asia, Current Research, 1985–1988*, p. 77–8, fn. 23.
147. Watson, *Kathiawar*, pp. 408–9. Pīr Paṭṭa or Paṭho is identified in Sind with the Nāth tradition and is also called Gopīcand. He is also claimed by the Suhrawardī tradition. Khan, *Conversion and Shifting Identities*, pp. 52–3. According to another tradition, he is said to have come to Kachchh from Sind. His grave in Shikarpur is on the place where he used to tend his cattle, where he miraculously brought fresh water out of the ground. Khakhar, *Report on the Architectural and Archaeological Remains*, p. 34.
148. Khan, *Mir'āt-i Ahmadī: Supplement*, trans., p. 213.
149. Ibid., pp. 213–14. This account is significant also because it bears out the historical relationship between the pastoralist Raikas (also known as Rabārīs) and the Śrāvaks or Jains. An ethnographic account of this

relationship is found in Srivastava, *Religious Renunciation*. In the Baroda state the Rabārīs were reported as belonging to the Ramānandī, Bījmārgī and Ismā'īlī Satpanthī sects. G.H. Desai (1912), *Glossary of Castes, Tribes and Races in the Baroda State*, p. 83.

150. Khan, *Conversion and Shifting Identities*, p. 79.
151. Ibid., p. 189.
152. Tambs-Lyche, *Power, Profit and Poetry*, p. 180.
153. Khan, *Conversion and Shifting Identities*, p. 186, fn. 1.
154. Tambs-Lyche, *Power, Profit and Poetry*, pp. 181–5.
155. Misra, *Muslim Communities*, pp. 9–10.
156. Kumkum Sangari (2000), 'Tracing Akbar: Hagiographies, Popular Narrative Traditions and the Subject of Conversion', in *Mapping Histories: Essays Presented to Ravinder Kumar*, ed., Neera Chandhoke, pp. 61–103.
157. Khan, *Ramdev Pir*, p. 81.
158. Misra, *Muslim Communities in Gujarat*, p. 10.
159. Dundas, *The Jains*.
160. Misra, *Muslim Communities in Gujarat*, pp. 59–60.
161. An intriguing and uncorroborated tradition relates that more than one Caulukya rulers converted to Islam. In this account, the most enthusiastic Muslim was Ajayapāla (1174–7), the anti-Jain successor of Kumarapāla, who apparently left only one temple standing in his dominions. Campbell, *Gujarat Populations*, p. 5, fn.1; James Tod (1829–32), *Travels in Western India: Embracing a Visit to the Sacred Mounts of the Jains, and the Most Celebrated Shrines of Hindu Faith between Rajputana and the Indus, With an account of the Ancient City of Nehrwalla*, pp. 184, 191. The only evidence to corroborate this is that contemporary inscriptions repeatedly refer to Ajayapāla by the epithet *niṣkalaṅkāvatāra*, the untainted future avatāra of Viṣṇu who will appear as the destroyer at the end of the Kaliyuga. See inscriptions of Brahmanwada (1175) and Patan (1199) in G.V. Acharya, *Historical Inscriptions of Gujarat* (1933, 1935, 1942), Vol. 3, nos.157B, 158. This term is often used in Ismā'īlī traditions to denote the qā'im or messiah. See D.-S. Khan (1997), 'The Coming of Nikalank Avatar: A Messianic Theme in Some Sectarian Traditions of North-western India', *Journal of Indian Philosophy*, 25, p. 403.
162. Misra, *Muslim Communities in Gujarat*, p. 60.
163. See Bhagavānjī Prāṇvallabh (1881), *Corāśī vaiṣṇav-nī vārta*, Girdhārīlāl Hargovinddās Śāh and Kalyāṇjī Raṇchoḍjī Vyās (1917), *Basobāvan vaiṣṇav-nī vārtā (252 Narratives of Vaiṣṇava Devotees for the Puṣṭimārga Sect)*.
164. Khakhar, *Report on the Architectural and Archaeological Remains*, p. 20. Bahā' al-Dīn Pīr is usually identified with the Sufi shaykh Bahā' al-Dīn Zakariyyā of Multan, a figure often credited with conversions.
165. Campbell, *Gujarat Population*, p. 82.

166. Bhudharlāl Gangjī Bookseller (1919), *Sri Bahucarājīno itihās*, p. 12.
167. Campbell, *Gujarat Population*, p. 68.
168. Ibid., pp. 65–9.
169. Sikandar, *MS*, pp. 1–2.
170. Sikandar, *MS*, trans., p. 57.
171. Ibid.
172. Sikandar, *MS*, p. 136.
173. Misra, *Muslim Communities in Gujarat*, p. 11.
174. Richard M. Eaton (1974), 'Sufi Folk Literature and the Expansion of Indian Islam', *History of Religions*, 14(2), p. 119.
175. Khan, *Conversion and Shifting Identities*, p. 37.
176. M.I. Dar (1953), 'Gujarat's Contribution to Gujari and Urdu', *Islamic Culture*, 27, p. 24.
177. MacLean, *Religion and Society*, p. 149.
178. Khan, *Conversion and Shifting Identities*, p. 39.
179. Ali Asani (1987), 'The Khojkī Script: A Legacy of Isma'ili Islam in the Indo-Pakistan Subcontinent', *Journal of the American Oriental Society*, 107(3), p. 440.
180. See the story of Khoḍiyār in Tambs-Lyche, *Power, Profit and Poetry*, p. 78.
181. This is one reason for the apparent similarity of religious compositions across sectarian boundaries, often ascribed to 'syncretism'.
182. Campbell, *Gujarát Population*, p. 41.
183. Shastri, *HIG*, pp. 63–4. For details, see Chapter 5 in this volume.
184. For example, the queen of the ruler of Mevad visited the shrine of Rāmdev Pīr to conceive a child without the knowledge of her husband. Khan, *Conversion and Shifting Identities*, p. 97.
185. Tambs-Lyche, *Power, Profit and Poetry*, p. 37.
186. See Mehta, 'Kaumārikā Khaṇḍa'; Mehta and Kantawala, 'Two Legends from the Skanda Purāṇa'.
187. L.P. Tessitori, ed. (1919), *Bardic and Historical Survey of Rajasthan: Velī Krisana Rukamaṇī rī Rāṭhoḍa Rāja Prithī Rāja rī Kahī*. This fifteenth-century text links the mythological story of Kṛṣṇa and his wife Rukminī to the historical Rajput hero Pṛthvirāja Cauhāṇ, one of the early examples of a Kṛṣṇa legend being used to legitimize a Rajput theme.
188. F. Mallison (1983), 'Development of Early Krishnaism in Gujarat, Viṣṇu-Raṇchoḍ-Kṛṣṇa', in Monica Thiel-Horstmann, ed. *Bhakti in Current Research, 1979–1982: Proceedings of the Second International Conference on Early Devotional Literature in New Indo-Aryan Languages, St. Augustin, 19–21 March 1982*.
189. Harlan, *Religion and Rajput Women*, p. 76. The fifteenth-century Kṛṣṇaite poet Mīrā brought Kṛṣṇa as her personal deity into her marital home. The affinal family first rejected the new deity, but were eventually

converted. Nancy M. Martin (1999), 'Mira Janma Patri and Other Tales of Resistance and Appropriation', in Rajendra Joshi and N. K. Singhi, eds, *Religion, Ritual and Royalty*, p. 230.

190. D.P. Khakhar (1878), 'History of the Kânphâṭâs of Kachh', *IA*, 7.
191. Khan, *Conversion and Shifting Identities*, p. 101.
192. Z.A. Desai (1991), *Malfuz Literature: As a Source of Political, Social, and Cultural History of Gujarat and Rajasthan*, p. 22.
193. Kassam, *Songs of Wisdom*, p. 65.
194. Mallison, 'Development of Early Krishnaism in Gujarat', p. 76.
195. Pocock, 'Vocation and Avocations', p. 325.
196. Trivedi, *Census of India*, Table I.

5

Court and State

Evolution of a Regional Consensus, c. 1390–1511

By the early fifteenth century the Delhi sultanate hardly existed. While it had great prestige in name and the sultan of Delhi was still the ruler of India, in actuality it was a provincial kingdom, and poorer in resources than the sultanates of the Deccan and Gujarat. The Gujarat sultanate, on the other hand, was growing and becoming more powerful. It differed from earlier regional state formations in north India in many ways: in the size of the kingdom, bringing about unity where there had been multiple locations of political authority and facilitating connectivity within the region and with the world outside. It was the site for the formation of a regional culture as well as a deepening and diversifying literary culture that was evolving a variety of new genres and registers. Finally, the sultanate was able to facilitate more extensive trading networks than ever before.

The state depended for its prosperity on the prevalence of trade, but there was a continuing tension between the contrasting impulses of mobility and settlement. As described in Chapter 2, the early sultans built widely, but had to keep moving to ensure that the trade routes and strategic forts were well secured. They needed to establish general security to enable the population to be mobile and productive; hence, roads had to be kept safe and groups had to be induced to clear and move into new territories and live in the new forts and settlements. The early sultans presided over a loose but functional system of alliances. In the fifteenth century they were able to enforce this system because of access to military resources and their financial ability to the most munificent employers of manpower in South Asia. The social and political consensus they presided over was not entirely sustained by military threat. It worked because traders, military and landed intermediaries and religious figures decided it was in their interest to support the sultans and this, in effect, brought cohesion to the region they ruled.

The dominance of the marketplace allowed groups to negotiate their social and political identities and express them in cultural forms. Moreover, the mobility and diversity of the economy allowed players to choose more freely: people could bargain better since they had some choice in opting for more advantageous clients or patrons. However, trade was a fragile system, and monetary and commodity networks required flexible arrangements between partners. Paradoxically, the very fragility of trade may have contributed to a relatively stable polity in Gujarat because so much was at stake. As the sultans could raise the stakes and make the system lucrative for many, the polity was simultaneously more flexible and more stable than elsewhere.

We find here that the regional identity of sultanate Gujarat did not come about through recourse to homogeneous ethnic or cultural values. Instead, it came together despite multiple group interests that nevertheless functioned with a degree of flexibility and unison that allowed the state to survive. In other regions this political reality tended to be masked by other processes. In Gujarat, political and cultural power that non-brahmin communities derived from trading wealth allowed multiple voices to be heard simultaneously and yet in dialogue with one another.

THE ARMY AND MILITARY CONTROL

One complaint against Farḥat al-Mulk, the last governor of Tughluq Gujarat before Ẓafar Khān, was that he was friendly with the locals and tolerated idolatry.[1] While this may have been a retrospective smear to discredit him, it shows that he was becoming a threat to central authority on account of the fact that he had set down local roots. All the sources report that a section of the populace was discontented and had complained to Delhi about him. A delegation also came to complain to Ẓafar Khān who had been sent out from Delhi and was encamped near Nagaur. According to Firishta, Farḥat al-Mulk had an army of 10,000 to 12,000 men, mostly Hindus. On receiving information about this force, Ẓafar Khān was obliged to raise an army locally (in north Gujarat) and enlisted 4,000 cavalry.[2] Although Farḥat al-Mulk joined battle with Ẓafar Khān's forces near Patan, he was defeated and killed.

What happened to the army subsequently? Vital to the success of the Gujarat sultans, the army was perhaps the most important segment of the administration. How were the sultans able to organize it, recruit and pay soldiers, and arrange for military supplies?

Ẓafar Khān's ability to rapidly raise local levies bears out the observation that north India possessed thousands of fighting peasants and professional soldiers in search of employment in this period.[3] After the initial successful battle against Farḥat al-Mulk, he went about consolidating his forces. In 1394 news arrived that Muḥammad Shāh, the sultan of Delhi, had died. Soon after this, Ẓafar Khān heard that the chieftain of Idar had 'placed his foot outside the circle of obedience and fealty'.[4] He was again obliged to assemble an army with fighting men and elephants to besiege the fort of Idar. The troops proceeded to plunder the countryside around, eventually leading the chieftain to sue for peace.

By now a fighting force had been assembled and Ẓafar Khān made a rapid campaign to Saurashtra by way of Jhalavad along the route running west of Patan. He overran the chieftaincies of Jhalavad and Junagadh, and compelled the payment of tribute, then marched to Somanath, where he destroyed the temple, built mosques, and established a military post. The following year the army had to be reassembled to take on another siege, this time in Mandalgarh after the ruler had failed to pay tribute and had, during Farḥat al-Mulk's reign, expelled Muslims from his territories.[5] As Kolff has pointed out, it is misleading to search for a standing army in this period: Niẓam al-Dīn relates that again on this occasion 'Ẓafar Khān collected the army of Gujrat'.[6] The army was convened from armed peasants and professional soldiery whenever the need arose. In order that his peasant soldiers could return to their lands at the end of the campaigns of the past three years, Ẓafar Khān ordered that his troops should be excused from service for a year.[7]

In 1403 Ẓafar Khān called back his army, distributing a year's pay among them, to march on Idar again.[8] The chieftain fled and Ẓafar n was able to install a military post in the fort. Soon after this was another campaign towards Somanath, where the 'Hindus and *kāfirs*' had regrouped.[9] On the advance of Ẓafar Khān's army, the local forces, probably led by the Vājā chieftain Bharam or Brahmadāsa, met them 'by way of the sea'.[10] They were defeated and retreated to the island fort of Diu, which was also taken after a few days siege.

Also in 1403, Ẓafar Khān's son, Tātār Khān, demanded an army to intervene in the unsettled politics of Delhi. When his father relented and made over the army to him, Tātār Khān assumed the title of Sultan ḥammad Shāh, rewarded courtiers, and collected a large army to march towards Delhi, but before he had gone very far, he suddenly died. Ẓafar Khān then assumed royal titles in 1407.

When Aḥmad Shāh became sultan in 1411, it is clear that a number of employers were in contention for the large pool of manpower that was available in Gujarat. These included courtiers of the former governor, Afghan mercenaries, as well as local chieftains. Soon after his accession, Aḥmad Shāh faced a challenge from a relative who was supported by Afghans and Hindu chieftains. When they were defeated, their army came over to him.[11] Over the next decade the troops of defeated rivals began to come into his employment as his campaigns demonstrated that he was emerging as the most successful warlord of the region. His only challengers now were the sultans of Malwa and the Deccan, and hill chieftains who possessed a military advantage through their control of strategically located forts.

From about 1425, Aḥmad Shāh introduced a regularized system of pay for his soldiers: half in cash and half from grants of land in their native territories. According to the seventeenth-century writer Sikandar, the reason for this was that if the pay had been all in cash, as while paying mercenaries from other regions with no ties to the land, it would not last, and, moreover, 'the soldiers would be badly equipped and careless in protecting the country'. However,

> if half the pay were given by a grant of land [*jāgīr*] from that grant they [the soldiers] would obtain grass, firewood, milk and butter-milk and if they engaged in agriculture and building houses they would derive profit and would strive to protect the country with their heart and life.[12]

This had the additional advantage that itinerant soldiers would be induced to settle and cultivate wasteland. Several other provisions were made which ensured that:

1. Soldiers would receive the cash component of their pay monthly and without delay wherever they might be posted. This would ensure that they would remain at their posts and, if called up for active duty, would not be obliged to borrow money.

2. If soldiers were on a distant expedition and the revenues from their lands could not reach them, they could draw half their pay in cash from the treasury. This would ensure that they would not be obliged to borrow money to obtain weapons, and would also allow their families to subsist on the proceeds of their lands.
3. The treasurer should be one of the royal slaves, while the paymaster a free man 'in order that they may not combine and stretch forward the hand of treachery and peculation'.[13] The same means of preventing corruption was also extended to the '*āmil*s or district revenue officials.

Later, Maḥmūd improved on these provisions by ensuring that the rs granted to his soldiers would pass on to the descendants of those who were killed in service. 'Whoever had a jāgīr it was confirmed to his son and he who left no son, half of his jāgīr was given to his daughter, and he who left no daughter had his dependents provided for in a fitting manner.'[14] He also ensured that his soldiers never had to borrow money at interest and appointed a separate treasurer to advance money to whoever needed it.[15]

These arrangements for soldiers were among the factors that made the sultans of Gujarat among the most generous employers of the time.[16] They also ensured the soldiers' loyalty against rival employers such as rebellious courtiers and Rajput chieftains. These measures proved to be a profitable investment in the long term. According to Sikandar, revenue assessors during the reign of Bahādur Shāh in the sixteenth century found that returns from these districts had in some cases increased tenfold and in no case were they less than double.[17]

A number of Arab and Abyssinian mercenaries and adventurers found employment at the Gujarat court, more here than in north India where Persian, Afghan, and Central Asian mercenaries were more common. Most importantly, the sultans were able to command allegiance from several chieftains and their clans, from professional mercenaries, some of foreign origin and others who were soldiers recruited from peasant or landed communities, by generous gift-giving and the lavishness of their resources.

HORSES, ELEPHANTS, BOATS

Military resources were the sultans' trump card. They had the advantage of being able to secure supplies of war horses from the overland route from Central Asia as well as by the sea route. Sikandar mentions ā ā ī merchants bringing Iraqi and Turkish horses to sell in

Gujarat.[18] The Kāṭhī horses of Saurashtra were also reckoned highly. With the immense resources from their prosperous province, the sultans could import war elephants from Malwa and as far off as Ceylon.[19] The fifteenth century was the period when the war elephant became crucial to army strategy and the rise to prominence of the Malwa sultans and the Gajapatis (Lords of the Elephants) of Orissa was due in large measure to their access to areas where wild elephants could be captured and trained. The long tussles that the Malwa sultans waged for the control of areas such as Kherla, Jājnagar, Sarguja, and Gondwāna were almost solely due to the abundance of wild elephants found in these forested areas.[20] According to the *Mir'āt-i Aḥmadī*, elephants were also to be found in the mountainous region between Gujarat and Malwa.[21]

The sultans were also able to secure supplies of swords and other weaponry. Gujarati swords were well known even in the Arab world, but Maḥmūd Bīgara possessed a wide range of weaponry. Other weapons were used too. Firishta reports that during the siege of Mandalgarh in 1395, Ẓafar Khān used battering rams and catapults, and had underground passages dug to force entry into the fort.[22]

On occasion the sultans could commandeer boats and engage in warfare by sea.[23] The first instance of an engagement by sea was during afar Khān's second campaign to Somanath and Diu when the local chieftains attacked by sea and then were beaten back to the island of Diu. Nicolò Conti, who visited Cambay in Aḥmad Shāh's reign, said that Cambay shared in equipping the fleet of the Gujarat kingdom and that Aḥmad Shāh sent seventeen vessels to recover the islands of Bombay and Salsette which had been seized by the Bāhmanīs in 1429.[24] Later, Maḥmūd Bīgara also conducted several naval campaigns. He was able to call up boats from his ports for an expedition to finish off the pirates of the Dvaraka region and made them 'chase and capture the vessels of the enemy'.[25] Soon after, he sent out vessels to punish Malabar pirates who had been harassing the ports of Gujarat.[26] He was thus able to secure boats even away from the areas of direct influence. In 1507–8 there was a famous naval battle at Chaul in which the flotilla commanded by Malik Ayāz, assisted by boats sent by the last mluk sultan of Egypt, Qānṣawh al-Ghawrī, and the Ottoman governor of Bahrayn defeated the Portuguese—their only defeat in Indian waters.[27] In the sixteenth century the sultan of Gujarat was called the Lord of the Sea.[28]

ICONOCLASM: CUTTING THE ROOTS OF POLITICAL HINDUISM

While Muslim iconoclasm and political control are the usual reasons offered for the decline in monumental temple architecture, it has been noticed that there had been a fall in temple building throughout the thirteenth century. What is more interesting, however, is the abrupt disappearance, in the wake of the Turkic invasion, of the Caulukya model of grants for the upkeep of temples and monasteries. The fact that an entire bureaucratic system and language of parcelling out land could be wiped away before the sultanate armies had captured a dozen towns may indicate that the land-grant system as well as Caulukya/Vāghelā sovereignty were only a rhetorical fiction by the late thirteenth century.

As Richard Eaton has pointed out, temple desecrations were usually political acts. As was the case during the Khaljī invasion of Gujarat, they 'typically occurred on the cutting edge of a moving military frontier'.[29] The generals were usually well informed about what temples to target, in this case going for the royal temples in Anhilvada Patan, Siddhpur, and Somanath, bringing down the shell and removing or destroying the icons within. Although the Jain temple complex of Shatrunjaya was also desecrated, the governor of Gujarat, Alp Khān, soon realized that alienating the prosperous Jain community had been an impolitic act and made provision for its reconstruction.

Once political power had been established, there are no further instances of desecration until the end of the fourteenth century, by which time independent chieftains throughout Gujarat and Saurashtra had been consolidating their territories and building temples. As the last governor Ẓafar Khān proceeded to re-establish sultanate rule over Gujarat, he again targeted the royal temples of chieftains. These included those of Idar, Junagadh, and Diu as well as Somanath, the destruction of which bore ideological weight for both Muslims and Hindus.

Subsequently, too, political factors predominated when the Gujarat sultans attacked temples: 'Wherever any one was headstrong he [Aḥmad h] cast down his stronghold, and he overthrew temples and built mosques in their stead.'[30] Aḥmad Shāh was particularly zealous in this regard. According to Firishta, he appointed a courtier, Malik Tuḥfa Tāj al-Mulk, to destroy temples and establish Muslim authority throughout Gujarat.[31] While breaking idols was considered meritorious for the sultans, temples were clearly associated with political assertion. Malik fa's exertions did not end idolatry but put an end to the local political units of '*mehwās*' and '*girās*'.[32]

If a chieftain was willing to be cooperative, accept sultanate overlordship, and become an ally, the temples in his territories were not harmed. In the case of a Hindu chieftain of Sirohi who asked Quṭb al- n Aḥmad for assistance in recovering the fort of Abu, the sultan campaigned against Rānā Kumbha and restored him to his lands. Again, Rā Māṇḍalik of Junagadh was permitted to rule his territories until he became 'arrogant' and visited his temples 'in great state and with a golden umbrella over him'.[33]

Richard Eaton's path-breaking article documenting and analyzing instances of temple desecration and analysing them probably underestimates the number of 'desecrations' in Gujarat from our period. While he rightly lists only those instances clearly documented in the Persian chronicles or inscriptions, there were probably a handful of other instances that are less well documented. Hindu chieftains were aware that setting up a royal temple would be seen as a gesture of insubordination that could lead to violent consequences. An epigraph of 1417–18 from the mountainous region near Bharuch makes this clear. It records the building of a temple by one Vīj in the reign of king Śaktisiṃha who ruled over a town named Vāpī on the peak of the Vindhya mountain which was hidden from the coming *yavana-* (the Muslim forces).[34] In some cases the 'infidels' did win back a captured temple. A mosque inscription of 1430 from Vijapur in north Gujarat mentions that the building was originally built by Hindus. After the establishment of Muslim rule, it was used as a place of prayer by the Muslims, was destroyed by the Hindus thereafter, and was renovated by Sarkhail Bahādur.[35]

REVENUE AND ADMINISTRATION

The ostensible reason for sending Ẓafar Khān to replace Farḥat al-Mulk as governor of Gujarat was that the latter had 'spent the revenue of a number of years of the *khāliṣa* [crown] lands of the Sultan, for his own needs and purposes, and had not remitted one *dīnār* to the treasury'.[36] He was urged, accordingly, to deliver whatever was left of the khāliṣa revenues to Ẓafar Khān and then proceed to Delhi. Ẓafar n's task was to reclaim control over the crown-controlled lands and collect their revenues. Although he succeeded in establishing a tenuous military control over most of urban eastern Gujarat, many of the defeated minor chieftains of the region turned to plunder and robbery on being deprived of their lands.

When Aḥmad Shāh came to the throne in Patan, his first act was to confirm the administration in its position: 'He conferred honours on the nobles and the chief men of the kingdom, the great men of the city and the chiefs of various groups; and gave a share of his gifts to all sections of the people.'[37] He also reinforced the established administration: 'He kept the officers and writers charged with matters connected with the revenue in their former positions; and made great exertions in the matter of increasing the cultivation, and in the building up of the country and the administration of justice.'[37] However, he was still faced with controlling the rebellious dispossessed chieftains of the region: 'Anarchy increased, confusion prevailed, the decay of cultivation became visible, and the ryots were distressed.'[39]

According to the *Mir'āt-i Aḥmadī*, Aḥmad Shāh was responsible for the origin of the vāṇṭā system of revenue collection in which chieftains who had been defeated were restored partial control of their lands. The ṭā or 'part' was one-fourth of the land that the chieftain had formerly controlled. The other three-fourths were adjudged crown property. This system was created to pacify defeated chieftains who were becoming rebellious and plundering roads and villages:

> Those whose duty it was to advise, in their foresight put an end to these calamities, and exacted from the zamindar of every village security to discontinue his opposition. Three parts of the land of each village, under the denomination *tal pat*, were acknowledged as the property of the king, and one portion was given to the zamindars under the denomination of *wanta*, and they were engaged to furnish guards and protection to their own villages and were to hold themselves in readiness for the service of the king whenever called upon. As these people, without paying obedience to the prince, did not see it possible to establish themselves, they attended to make their submission and engaged to pay the crown a *salami* from their *wanta*. From this time 'salami', and 'peshkash' became established against them.[40]

This arrangement enabled the sultans to claim a large portion of the captured territories to be directly administered, while the rest was controlled by chieftains who had been rendered submissive and had agreed to pay tribute from the proceeds of their lands. Some of these chiefs converted to Islam and were guaranteed their possessions on payment of a tribute.[41] The system also ensured that the sultans had a loyal or contracted base in the countryside from which to draw military manpower.

There were still several chieftains who had not been alienated from their lands in the fifteenth century. The territory controlled by these chieftains was called the 'grās' or 'mouthful', from which the term siyā' or 'garāsiyā', often used for chieftains before the sixteenth-century popularity of the term 'Rajput', was derived.[42] The latter were nominally subject to the payment of an annual tribute that often had to be extracted by force personally by the sultans.[43] The sultans did not interfere with internal administration within the chieftains' territories. The latter continued to collect revenues from the land, usually in kind, as well as other cesses and dues from trade and transit.

Directly administered territories, from which the local chieftain had been comprehensively alienated, were administered in two ways. From Aḥmad's time, but more so during the reign of Maḥmūd gara, territories were assigned to courtiers to administer as military assignments or iqtā‘ from which they were also expected to raise troops. Alternatively, a paid official would be stationed in the chief town or fort of the region to administer it and collect revenues, supported by troops sent from Ahmadabad. In addition, military outposts or thānas were set up in charge of subordinate officers who were also responsible for raising local levies.

These territories were assigned a hierarchy of officials responsible for collecting the state's share of the produce with the help of village headmen or other intermediaries. They also produced reports on the collections which were sent to the treasury officer and accountant who were, on Aḥmad Shāh's orders, alternately a free man and a slave so that their interests would not coincide and lead to dishonesty.

In territories granted as iqṭā‘, the proceeds of the land were expected to support the courtier and his contingents of troops for a fixed duration. However, many of these military grants or jāgīrs became long-standing holdings of the courtiers in question, at times becoming hereditary. There are instances of Maḥmūd confirming the son of a courtier in his father's rank and military territories.[44] Military assignees were prevented from over-taxing their territories by appointed civil officials who also assisted in administration.[45] The policy of granting long-term iqṭā‘s and jāgīrs encouraged courtiers to put down roots and develop economic interests in the regions under their control.

The settlement of land was instrumental in the stabilization of that other source of wealth—trade. An inscription struck in 1525 to mark the construction of a step-well by Dhārājī, a notable from Mansa in north Gujarat, provides an idea of the process by which erstwhile marauding pastoralist groups were settling down to a mercantile identity by the fifteenth century.[46] Given that the donor Dhārā had adult grandchildren in 1525, it can be safely assumed that he belonged to a generation that was active under the sultanate of the fifteenth century. The inscription, which begins by acknowledging the auspicious reign of Muẓaffar Shāh II, is partially in Sanskrit verse and the rest follows in Gujarati prose. It lists the descendants of a junior or allied branch of the erstwhile military-pastoralist family of the Vāghelās who had ruled Gujarat in the thirteenth century. The text is long and well-formulated, and indicates a literate culture and audience.

The composition of this history of a minor notable in Sanskrit verse is a legitimizing gesture by an upwardly mobile clan with a pastoralist past. The clan had settled in Mansa in north Gujarat (they earlier belonged to the village of Uganij) and were fairly prosperous in 1525. In a Sanskrit quartet in the middle of the inscription, Dhārā claims to be a devotee of Hari (Viṣṇu), a warrior and king. Another verse in Sanskrit indicates that he was also a prosperous merchant of the town. This verse praises the sea and honours Varuṇa, the sea god, as the guarantor of his well-being, indicating that his wealth was achieved through the sea trade. However, the family seems to have aligned itself seamlessly with other sectarian groups too. The names of Dhārā's sons from one wife—Mīyā Śrī Phatūlā, Keṣṇājī, Bhābhujī, Arjanjī, and Bhīmjī—are a combination of Vaiṣṇava and Islamic names. One grandson from Dhārā's daughter Rājbāī was named Malik Śrī āmal Malik Savāī, clearly a rendering of a sultanate title. The sons from his other wife had Vaiṣṇava names: Rāmjī, Lakhmaṇjī, and āyaṇjī. Given that Dhārā was a devotee of Hari and his offspring were named after avatāras of Viṣṇu, it is clear that he was claiming a ṣṇava identity. This did not prevent at least one son and a daughter being allied to a Muslim identity.[47] The donation stakes a claim for higher ritual and cultural status showing off Dhārā's position as chieftain, merchant, and Vaiṣṇava. The route to this status was two-fold: through Dhārā's own success as a merchant with the blessings of Varuṇa and through the employment of his offspring as servants of the sultans.

The inscription brings together the themes being discussed in this and the previous chapter—the stabilization of pastoralist clans under the sultanate—which, in this case, is linked to the point made in the previous chapter of the stabilization of sectarian identities under formal institutionalized religious practices such as Vai avism.

Step-well inscriptions from the later part of Maḥmūd Bīgara's reign indicate a growing link between the state, pastoralist chieftains, and trade.[48] Most step-well inscriptions struck by traders do not fail to mention the chieftain in charge of the locality and the reign of the sultan in which the well was built. One such inscription that survives was engraved in 1480 in Sanskrit and Gujarati, and comes from Gosa in Porbandar *taluka*.[49] The inscription records the building of a step-well by Muñjā, son of Sūrā of the vāṇiā caste, in the reign of Sultan ḥmūd and during the time of the Jethva ruler Vikramait. Two years later four Sanskrit inscriptions were struck in a well in Rampura in Vadhvan district that record the reign of Sultan Maḥmūd (*pātasā śrī Mahimūda*) as well as that of the local chief Rāṇā Vāghjī in addition to mentioning the officers in charge of the district—Paramār Lakhdhīr, Paramār Hādā, and *Khānśrī* Alūkhān. The well was built by Rāṇībāī and Valhāde, wives of the merchant Vīṇā of the Śrīmāla caste and resident of Jhanjhnagar (Jhinjhuvada). In this inscription a picture emerges of the administrative hierarchy—from the Rajput or Muslim official upwards through the local Rajput overlord to the sultan—that was being acknowledged for facilitating the wealth made by a merchant. It also reflects the way in which the Rajput clans were being accommodated within the administrative and fiscal hierarchies of the sultanate.

This mode of inscription making, mostly on the walls of step-wells, continued throughout the remaining reign of Maḥmūd and during the reign of his successors. A 1482 step-well inscription of Cambay struck by Dhanad, a Mer, begins by praising the reign of the sultan, yet again demonstrating the conversion of erstwhile militant pastoralist groups into urban notables during the reign of Maḥmūd.[50] An inscription in Arabic from 1495 describes Somanath as having been converted into a Muslim city and records the building of a mosque by Hamīr, son of Rāwat, a 'humble slave' of the governor.[51] A Sanskrit step-well inscription of 1498 from Bhoj in Baroda district gives a list of donors. These included Kāja from the Cāhamāna lineage, variously described as merchant and king, and other men from mercantile castes, their wives, and daughters.[52] Kāja seems to have been in charge of at least eighty-four villages that were under the administration of Bhūpanārāyaṇ, a minister described as a 'wise trader from the Disāval caste'. As in the case of Dhārā in the 1525 inscription, this is an example of how a 'princely' Rajput chieftain was, by the end of the fifteenth century, also a trader with administrative and revenue-collecting powers. The mention of a minister and other notables of the 'estate' shows how the sultans had left the administrative structure of such areas to the clans. As long as the revenues were ploughed back into the development of the sultanate, clan hierarchies were reinforced.

In 1499 one of the most famous step-wells of Gujarat, the Adalaj near Ahmadabad, was built under the patronage of Rāṇī Rūdādevī, wife of another Vāghelā chieftain.[53] The inscription (mostly in Sanskrit with a few lines in Gujarati) records the building of the well at a cost of 500,000 ṭankās. Significantly, the inscription records the lineages of both her husband's and father's family, but does not fail to mention the reign of Maḥmūd Bīgara. The Rajput clans seem to have accepted the role of arbiters of the sultanate economy that was burgeoning due to the rapid expansion of trade, especially during Maḥmūd Bīgara's reign. Such step-well inscriptions come from all over Gujarat and show the ubiquity of the process of accommodating erstwhile pastoralist clans into the new economy. The fifteenth century had thus seen the pacification of militant pastoralist groups, the Rajputs of the future, and their settlement into an accommodative triangular relationship between the sultan, the trader, and the chieftain. In certain areas, as seen from the example of Dhārā and Kāja, the roles of merchant and chieftain were hardly distinguishable.

ALLIANCE, MARRIAGE, AND LEGITIMATION

As pastoralists became merchants and traders became courtiers in fifteenth century Gujarat, it is worth while recalling the lineage of the sultans who presided over Gujarati society. The story of their ancestors, the brothers Sādhu and Sahāran, and the promise of the kingdom of Gujarat to their descendants is related in the *Mir'āt-i Sikandarī*. The brothers were inhabitants of a village in the qaṣba of Thanesar in the late fourteenth century. Once, when Sultan Fīrūz Shāh of Delhi was a prince, he had been hunting in the region and had become separated from his companions. As night fell, he spied a village and approaching, saw several men sitting on its outskirts. The prince alighted and asked one of the men to help him pull off his boots. This man happened to be gifted in the science of physiognomy and foretold future greatness for the stranger from the lines on his feet, declaring that he was either a king or would shortly become one. The sultan spent the night in the brothers' home where their sister caught his fancy and a marriage was soon contracted.

Sādhu and Sahāran attached themselves to the prince's retinue and followed him to the capital. Eventually, they converted to Islam and āran received the title of Wajīh al-Mulk. Shortly there after, the brothers became disciples of the saint Makhdūm-i Jahāniyān[54], who prophetically promised the kingdom of Gujarat to Ẓafar Khān, the son of Wajīḥ al-Mulk, to reward him for providing food for the dervishes at his abbey.

The saint sent for the donor Muẓaffar Khān, who, coming, kissed the ground before him. The saint said: 'Oh! Muẓaffar Khān, the return for this feeding of my derwishes is the kingdom of the whole of Gujarat which in reward of this handsome deed, I grant thee. May it be auspicious to thee!'

Muzaffar was appropriately grateful and returned home to relate his good fortune to his wife, a woman of sharp wit and solid sense.

She heard his account with pleasure, but said: 'thou art now verging on old age—if thou attainest to the rule of Gujarat—how long wilt thou reign? So hie back the presence of the saint and tell him to pray that, the kingdom may continue in thy family for generations. Today the sun of the kindness of the saint hath dawned on thee, and I doubt not, but that whatever request thou makest shall be complied with.' Muẓaffar Khān went forth with delicate perfumes, sweet smelling flowers, delicious fruits, and pretty betel-leaves and placed them before the holy man, who pleased at this elegant tribute, said: 'Thou hast brought us perfumes!' He gave a handful of dates from out of the tray presented by affar to him, saying: 'According to the number of these dates, shall thy children rule over Gujarat!' Some say the number of dates was twelve or thirteen; others that it was not more than nine or ten. God knows best.[55]

This story provides the sultans of Gujarat with two significant legitimizing forces—a marriage alliance and employment with the Delhi sultan followed by the blessings of a prominent Sufi. This was just as well, because the brothers had a rather ambiguous origin in the community Tāk or Tānk, which 'is hidden (concealed) from the history of the Hindus'.[56] Formerly, the Tāks and the Khatrīs were related 'as brothers', but the former developed an affinity for wine and were expelled from the caste. In due course, their laws and customs diverged and became distinct. In common with groups such as the Kaṇbīs and ts, this is an explanatory narrative of former entitlement followed by involuntary exclusion from the kṣatriya status coveted by middle-ranking peasant/pastoralist groups of the period.

Sikandar then lists the ancestors of the sultans before they converted to Islam, a conventional list that leads back to Rāma in an attempt to associate the lineage with divine or kṣatriya origin.[57] It is interesting

Table 5.1: The Sultanate Family in the Fifteenth Century

Sultans	Wives	Sons	Reign
ran alias h al-Mulk	?	Zafar Khan, later Muẓaffar I	
affar I	?	1. Tātār Khān, later Muḥammad I 2. Fīrūz Khān 3. Haibat Khān 4. Shīr Khān 5. Sa'ādat Khān 6. Mehtah Khān	1407–10
ammad I	?	1. Aḥmad I 2. Latif Khan	1403 (before his father Muẓaffar)
mad I	?	1. Fatḥ Khān, later Muḥammad II	1411–42
ammad II	1. d.o. Rā'i Quṭb of Mahā'im 2. Bībī Mughalī, d.o. Jām of Sind (Makhdūma-i Jahān), mother of Fatḥ Khān (Maḥmūd I) 3. Hans Bā'i, daughter of Rā'i Har of Idar	1. Quṭb al-Dīn Aḥmad II 2. Fatḥ Khān, later Maḥmūd I 3. Ḥasan Khān	1442–51
b al-Dīn mad II	1. Rani Rūp Manjarī 2. d.o. Shams Khān of Nagaur	Dā'ūd	1451–8
d			Briefly in 1458
mūd I gara	1. Rani Rūp Manjarī (from harem of Quṭb al-Dīn Aḥmad II), son Muḥammad Kālā 2. Rānī Pīraī (Sabrā'ī), mother of Āpā Khān 3. Rani Hīrābāī, mother of Khalīl Khān, later Muẓaffar II	1. Muḥammad Kālā 2. Āpā Khān 3. Aḥmad Khān 4. Khalīl Khān, later Muẓaffar II	1458–1511
affar II	1. Chief wife Bībī Rānī, son was Sikandar Khan 2. Lakshmībā'i, a Gohilānī, mother of Bahādur Khān 3. Rājbā'i, d.o. Rānā Mahipat, mother of Laṭīf Khān 4. Slave women	1. Sikandar Khān 2. Bahadur Khān 3. Laṭīf Khān 4. Chānd Khān 5. Nāṣir Khān 6. Ibrāhīm Khān, Others	1511–26
Subsequent sultans			Until 1584

: Compiled from epigraphic and textual sources including the *Mir'āt-i Sikandarī, abaqāt-i Akbarī Ẓafar al-wālih* that the seventeenth-century *Mir'āt* is the only surviving history of the sultanate, including the court-commissioned Sanskrit eulogy, the *javinoda*, in which an attempt is made to discuss its pre-Muslim origins. The sultans themselves do not seem to have been eager to claim Rajput status or even to acknowledge their earlier history. It is possible that Sikandar's frankness on the convert origins of his subjects is because of his separation in time from them. Although they were conquered by his Mughal patrons, he was obliged to treat them with honour as their chronicler. It is also possible that by the early seventeenth century when he wrote, convert origins no longer needed to be suppressed and prevalent conjecture as to the origins of the sultans could be included in the tale. Or the acknowledgement of legitimizing genealogies that had much in common with those employed by the Rajputs could be an indication of the peculiarly accommodative polity that Gujarat was. There was a genuine attempt at the level of the court ideology to link up with the politics of the Rajput chieftains who were now the mainstay Gujarat's administrative and economic stability. Indeed, the stabilization of Saurashtra through the formulation of stable Rajput polities (now defined through fledgling court societies and primogeniture) was the greatest achievement of the Gujarat sultans, an achievement that distinguished them from previous polities and one that made the Gujarat sultanate more prosperous than its predecessors.

Association of a lineage with Rāma is a trait of groups aspiring to high-status Rajput Sūryavaṃśa status, but there no evidence in later years that the Tāk community ever achieved it.[58] The cursory reference to Rāma has led modern writers to refer to the Tāks as Rajputs and to the Gujarat sultans as descendants of Rajput converts, even though the reference to Rāmacandra may have been a retrospective attempt in the seventeenth century to assign the sultans a creditable lineage.[59] However, says Sikandar, 'Whatever and whoever they were, they were a goodly race of men, having pure and virtuous souls, and they performed meritorious actions and gave numberless endowments, and showed good qualities and amiable traits in connection with God's creatures.'[60]

What was important for Fīrūz Shāh was not the ancestry of his new allies, but their ability to provide manpower. The Tāk community were peasants or pastoralists in the late fourteenth century, and the brothers Sahāran and Sādhu were men of influence in their village who 'could at a call summon thousands of horse and foot'.[61] From the perspective of the Tāks, offering women and military allegiance to the sultans represented a potent means of upward mobility. The transformation of the Tāk peasants into independent sultans within a generation is a prime example of the benefits that manpower-rich groups derived from association with the sultanate. In their turn, the sultans of Gujarat went on to provide legitimacy for a range of transforming groups in Gujarat.

As with the Tāk peasants, there were two chief means of becoming associated with the legitimacy derived from the sultanate.[62] The first was to offer military alliance to the sultans. As shown previously, Ẓafar n's talent was in raising military levies, and inducing a range of chieftains to accept his 'legitimacy' and put their manpower in his service. The second way of hitching group or personal advancement to the sultans was to make or claim to have made marriage alliances. This remained important in a transforming pastoralist society heavily based on alliance politics. Concurrently, it also became an important ideological trope to decline marriage alliance with the Muslim sultans, a refusal that also implied a rejection of the prospects of political advancement by those means, and a declaration of military confrontation.

In the early period groups later described as Rajputs included a large number of warrior-ascetics seeking to make advantageous alliances and secure patrons. Alliance was a significant theme in politics and influence was derived less from descent or the control of land than from negotiation and brokerage. As the sultans of Gujarat and their courtiers were able to command more military resources than petty clanships in Gujarat and Malwa, the only way for chieftains to exist was to maintain a situation in which, by negotiation, they were allowed to retain virtual autonomy in return for nominal subject status and payment of tribute. Conflict was avoided as far as was possible, except for occasional skirmishes and recalcitrance in tribute paying, which was more a manner of asserting autonomy than any design to overthrow the sultanate power.

For chieftains in this period, the existence of the sultanate as patron and paramount employer came to be accepted as part of the order of things.[63] Alliance, marriage, and patronage were part of a dialogue of reciprocal reliance between sultanate and chieftains. In the larger picture, brotherhoods were identified in terms of their ties and allegiance to the paramount local ruler.[64] While kinship and descent were the organizing principle of power within the family, clientship determined access to land and positions of authority outside its ambit. Several clans developed a relationship with the sultans which acknowledged them as overlords and employers.

Between the thirteenth and fifteenth centuries several pastoralist bands were able to achieve and pass on to their heirs a measure of landed status, enhanced by agricultural expansion, military opportunities, and demographic growth during the sultanate period. This period was characterized by 'the complementarity of asceticism and settled life and by alliance politics as expressed in marriage links'.[65] Marriage had a particular importance in this alliance-based political system. While it united a woman with her husband's family, it also created a political alliance.[66] Women did not simply relocate from one clan to another on marriage, they remained members of both clans but with a changed

[67] The basic loyalties of the chieftain were defined by his 'brotherhood' as well as his relations by marriage. An alliance-seeking warrior, often a dispossessed younger son seeking better prospects abroad, could on occasion contract a marriage at a distance from his natal territory. In these circumstances the in-laws were vital for him to achieve legitimacy in the region. Legitimation then proceeded through the religious affiliation of the natal clans of the women who often retained their own deities and values. While women were generally expected to adopt the kul-

ī of the husband's family after marriage, there are several instances in which the goddess of the woman's natal clan took a place in the husband's family.[68] Later, with the decline in importance of kinship and alliance, there was a tightening of patriliny, loss of importance of the queen's natal lineage, and corresponding loss of political influence of the queen.

Who did the sultans marry? The first marriage alliance we encounter is in 1431. After Aḥmad Shāh had defeated the Bāhmanī ruler, he had his son Fatḥ Khān married to the daughter of the Rā'i of Mahaim, one

'i Quṭb.[69] In 1442 Muḥammad Shāh married Bībī Mughalī, daughter of the Samma Jām Jūnā of Sind, another daughter, Bībī Turkī, being wed to the Sufi Shāh-i 'Ālam.[70] This alliance with the ruler of Sind was an acknowledgment of the close ties between the two regions and proved politically significant subsequently.

In 1446, soon after the birth of his son, Muḥammad marched on

'i Har of Idar who submitted and offered his daughter in marriage.[71] 'That lady owing to her great beauty kept Muḥammad Shāh bound to her by her personal charm.'[72] She used her influence with the sultan to get the fort of Idar restored to her father Rā'i Har. According to Firishta and Badā'ūni, she was also responsible for poisoning him to death on the instigation of some of his officers.[73] This is the first instance of alliance with the family of a local chieftain, but it did not succeed in cementing the latter's loyalty to the sultan.

Quṭb al-Dīn Aḥmad married the daughter of Shams Khān of Nagaur, thereby consolidating the family connection between them. (Shams n was the grandson of Shams Khān Dandānī, brother of Ẓafar Khān). However, when Quṭb al-Dīn died, it was again suspected that his wife had poisoned him. The amīrs put Shams Khān to death and the sultan's mother (Muḥammad Shāh's wife) handed his daughter over to her slave girls 'who tore her to pieces, and thus killed her with torment'.[74]

While Quṭb al-Dīn was ruling, his stepmother Bībī Mughalī took refuge with her sister and brother-in-law Shāh 'Ālam, as she was afraid the sultan had designs on her young son's life. The sultan sent his chief wife Rāṇī Rūp Manjarī, a disciple of Shāh 'Ālam, to find and fetch the boy, Fatḥ Khān. She saw the boy sitting beside Shāh 'Ālam and grasped his hand to take him away. Shāh 'Ālam remarked: 'You take Fatḥ Khān's hand today, but a day will surely come when he will take yours.'[75] This came to pass after the death of Quṭb al-Dīn when Fatḥ Khān married his stepbrother's widow. Meanwhile, Bībī Turkī died and Shāh lam then married her sister, the former queen Bībī Mughalī.[76]

After the unsatisfactory and brief rule of Dā'ūd, Fatḥ Khān, Quṭb al-Dīn's younger brother, was sought to be made sultan. He was the son of Makhdūma-i Jahān, a senior wife of Muḥammad Shāh, otherwise known as Bībī Mughalī, the daughter of the Samma Jām Jūnā of Sind.[77] She was reluctant to consent: 'Please keep your hands off my son; for he has not the strength to bear this heavy burden.'[78] In spite of her misgivings, this boy went on to become Maḥmūd Shāh 'Bīgara', the most influential ruler of Gujarat. His mother's clan was important to him: he was advised on his campaign to Junagadh by his maternal uncle, Tughluq Khān, who presumably knew the area.[79] In 1472 the sultan marched against a reported insurrection on the borders of Sind, but the rebels scattered when his army came close. Some of his officers averred that this was a good opportunity to take control of the region and appoint a governor there, but the sultan refused: 'As the Makhdūma-i Jahān was descended from the sultans of Sind in the line of chieftainship and royalty, the consideration of the rights of relationship was incumbent upon him; and it appeared very far from kindliness and humanity to seize their territory.'[80]

Maḥmūd had several wives.[81] One of these was Rāṇī Harbāī or Hirabāī, daughter of the Tāh Rāṇā, a Rajput zamīndār from the bank of the Mahindri.[82] She was the mother of Khalīl Khān, the future ẓaffar II, and died soon after giving birth. The child was brought up by Maḥmūd's stepmother, Hans Bā'ī, a widow of Muḥammad (perhaps the daughter of the Idar king). Another wife was Rānī Rūp Manjarī who had formerly been married to his elder brother Quṭb al-Dīn, and came to him after the latter's death. Yet another was Rānī Pīrāī (Sabrā'ī). After the conquest of Champaner in 1484, the two daughters of the captured Paṭāi Rāval were sent to the harem. Traditions of the Imām hi family near Ahmadabad also relate that one of the daughters was given to Maḥmūd, but there is no confirmation of this alliance and it may be only a legitimizing claim made by the Imām Shāhīs.

It is significant that in this period the sultans contracted marriages largely with the daughters of local chieftains and with a branch of their own family at Nagaur. One of Maḥmūd's daughters was married Ādil Khān who was a contender for the control of Asir and Burhanpur. There are no alliances contracted with the contemporary sultans of Malwa, Delhi, or the Deccan, nor with Hindu chieftains from further afield. The only extra-territorial marriage alliance we come across in this period was with the daughters of the Jām of Sind. In a landscape in which marriage was a vital means of negotiating status, the restricted circle of alliances must have reflected the Gujarat sultans' social status in the fifteenth century.

LANGUAGE AND LITERATURE: GUJARATI AND GŪJARĪ

The sultans actively patronized learning and literature in Arabic and Persian, perhaps more than other contemporary courts. The Gujarat sultans, especially Maḥmūd, became important patrons of Arabic learning and gave Sufis and scholars court patronage and grants of land. As upstart Muslim sultans surrounded by Muslim kingdoms, patronage to religious scholarship was an easy way of legitimizing their claim to be better Muslims than their neighbours. There was considerable competition to attract famous scholars to the court. The Gujarat sultans were also recent converts to Islam, unlike the Bāhmanīs of the Deccan and the Ghūris of Mālwā, and were therefore all the more anxious to prove their orthodox credentials. When Ẓafar Khān departed from Delhi on his way to Gujarat, he was accompanied by a large number of *'ulama*, as the previous governor, Farḥat al-Mulk, had been accused of condoning idolatry. The pacification of Gujarat also inclued dispatching religious scholars to different towns to back up temporal authority.

The orthodox Sunni 'ulama attached to the court carried out administrative and judicial functions. However, the representatives of several Sufi orders were well established and deeply influential in Gujarat when Ẓafar Khān came to the region. Some of the adepts of these orders came to take an active role in the politics of the time and were selectively conciliated and rivalled by the sultans. The discourses of prominent Sufis such as Shaykh Aḥmad Khattū, Quṭb-i 'Ālam Bukhārī and his son Shāh 'Ālam were faithfully recorded by their disciples and some have survived. Some of the Sufis were themselves scholars and writers, in Arabic, Persian and Gūjarī. Additional information about the Gujarati Sufis can be found in the numerous *kiras* (biographies) that were compiled later.

Even before the advent of the sultans, Gujarat was becoming a centre for Arabic theological learning. Several commentaries on important theological works were written there. At least sixty works in Arabic and Persian on different religious subjects that were written in Gujarat between 1400 and 1550 are still extant.

Little is known of the scholars of the reign of Ẓafar Khān/Muẓaffar h. One writer who is known to have come to Gujarat at this time was Makhdūm 'Alī, prolific in the fields of theology and mysticism. He wrote Persian commentaries on works of Ibn al-'Arabī and Suhrawardī and died at Bombay in 1431–2.[83] But the only texts that survive from the era of Muẓaffar I are the works of Shaykh Shihāb al-n Qawām who lived in Nagaur in the reign of Ẓafar Khān. He was a physician of Islamic medicine who also knew the Ayurvedic system, and wrote a versified description of diseases and their treatment in Persian, *Shifā' al-maraḍ*. He also wrote a lexicon, the *Farhang-i Shihābī*.[84]

The next sultan, Ahmad Shah, was himself the author of a collection of Persian verse. When he founded the city of Ahmedabad, he composed *ṣīda* or ode in praise of the Bukhārī Sufi of Ahmedabad, Burḥān al-n Quṭb-i 'Ālam (the Pole of the World). The poem begins thus:

ḥān, the Proof, our polar star;
Our pattern and our guide.
The Proof, in whose convincing truth
We, and all men, confide.[85]

After reciting the qaṣīda, the sultan asked for a reward. 'My father's father has already blessed you', said the Sayyid, recalling Makhdūm-i āniyān's prophetic gift of Gujarat to Ẓafar Khān. '"But", replied the sultan, "that blessing is for the kingdom and my family. I now want a blessing for this new city." "This city will last for ever by the favour of God, the Merciful", said the Sayyid.'[86]

Aḥmad Shāh's reign was chronicled by the poet Hūlwī Shīrāzī. A scholar and poet, Maulānā Yaḥyā Gujarātī, is known to have composed the chronogram to mark the completion of the congregational mosque in the new city of Ahmadabad in 1414.[87] A renowned scholar and grammarian from Egypt who came to the court of Ahmad Shāh was Badr al-Dīn Muḥammad al-Damāmīnī. He is known to have completed three works in Arabic, dedicated to Aḥmad Shāh, during his sojourn in Gujarat. One of these works was the *'Ayn al-ḥayāt*, which was an abridgement of the famous Book of Animals, the *Ḥayāt al-ḥayawān*, of the Egyptian theologian al-Damīrī.[88] His other two works were a commentary on the *Tashīl al-fawā'id wa-takmīl al-maqāṣid* of Ibn Mālik, a manual of grammar that had a great reputation in the Islamic world, and a commentary on Ibn Hishām's *Mughni'l-labīb*, a famous work on syntax.[89] Sayyid Nūr al-Dīn Aḥmad of Shiraz was another scholarly visitor to Gujarat, and Ibn al-Jazarī of Syria sent a representatve to present his *Ḥiṣn al-ḥaṣīn* to Aḥmad Shāh.

The rule of Maḥmūd Bīgara has records of several scholars. One of these was Abū Bharochī, who prepared a translation into Persian of Ibn al-Jazarī's *Ḥiṣn al-ḥaṣīn* at the request of the sultan.[90] Ibn al-Jazarī was a Syrian scholar who lived in Damascus through the siege by ūr and his prayer book, inspired in a dream by the Prophet, was a collection of *hadīth* used for prayer.[91] Bharochī's translation, *Fatḥ-i mubīn*, evidently became popular, judging from the number of surviving manuscripts.

An Arab scholar who lived at Maḥmūd Bīgara's court was Ibn Afrash, who translated the *Shifā' bi-ta'rīf ḥuqūq al-muṣtafā'*, a biography of the Prophet by the Andalusian Māliki jurist Qāḍī 'Iyāḍ into Persian.[92] Ibn Afrash mentioned in his translation that although the sultan was all but unlettered, he was discerning in matters of history, law, poetry and biography. Later, Sikandar also attested to his skills.

> Although the sultan had not cultivated the traditional sciences, he had learnt so much of the theological sciences, the verses of the poets, the biographies of the saints and the chronicles and history, that all but the learned in the assembly would think that he was an *'ālim* and a *faqīh*.[93]

Another scholar who came to Bīgara's court was the Egyptian īḥ al-Dīn Muḥammad al-Mālikī (Ibn Suwayd), a pupil of the renowned traditionist al-Sakhā ī (1427–97). Maḥ ūd bestowed the title of *malik al-muḥaddithīn* (Master of Traditions) on this scholar, who died at Ahmedabad in 1522.[94] Yūsuf b. Aḥmad Sijzī was another scholar who was engaged by Maḥmūd Bīgara in his enthusiastic pursuit of commissioning translations of renowned Arabic works. Yusuf was entrusted with the task of translating into Persian the famous biographical dictionary of Ibn Khallikān, which he completed around 1489 as *Manẓar al-insān fi-tarjumāt wafayāt al-a'yān* and dedicated it to his patron.[95] The *'urs* or death anniversary of Sayyid Yūsuf is still observed in Ahmadabad.[96]

Other than the religious subjects, texts on music, medicine, farriery, philology, astrology, and astronomy also survive from the Gujarat sultanate. One of the earliest Persian treatises on Indian music, *Ghunyāt al-munya* was written in Gujarat in the 1370s, commissioned by Malik ū Rija, a governor of Gujarat.[97] Famous musicians from Gwalior came to the Gujarat court in the sixteenth century, and there are several references to court theatricals and musical performances.[98]

Outside the direct patronage of the court, several literary dialects were employed in medieval Gujarat. These included versions of Apabhraṃśa, inflected to suit the religious, ethnic, or regional identity of patron and writer. Prominent amongst these was the Jain version of Apabhraṃśa, elaborated to its greatest extent by intellectuals affiliated to the Caulukyas and Vāghelās in the twelfth and thirteenth centuries. Long after the demise of the Vāghelās, Jain Apabhraṃśa continued to be used by community intellectuals. Other Apabhraṃśas shaded into versions of Old Gujarati and Rajasthani, languages which possess a substantial repertoire of poetry, plays, and chronicles.[99] Of course, Sanskrit, Jain Sanskrit, Persian, and Arabic were also used for non-court literary production in Gujarat.

Genealogist and performative communities such as the Cāraṇs, āṭs, and Langhās who were patronised by the emerging pastoralist chieftaincies of Gujarat produced genealogies and other compositions in their own literary-performative dialects—Ḍiṅgaḷa amongst others. One such text is the *Raṇamalla chanda* by the poet Śrīdhara, written in the late fourteenth century. This text uses a number of Persian-derived words that must have entered the vocabulary by this time.[100] Later historical ballads in Gujarati such as the *Kānhaḍade prabandha* (1456) also used vocabulary derived from Persian and Arabic. These genres of poetry were distinguished from other kinds of compositions partly by a distinct vocabulary, but also by specific prosodic, declamatory and musical forms.[101] The antiquity of these dialects as they have been recorded in recent times is difficult to determine. This is partly because of the paucity of manuscript material from before the eighteenth century, as bardic groups tend to copy (and often telescope) worn-out manuscripts and discard older ones. These dialects were also trans-regional, being comprehensible to knowledgeable audiences all over Gujarat, Rajasthan, and Malwa.[102]

The earliest Gujarati works, as opposed to those in Jain Apabhraṃśa, are usually dated to the fourteenth century.[103] A prominent example of a transforming linguistic style is found in the Apabhraṃśa poem *deśarāsaka*, written probably in the fourteenth century by a Muslim writer Abdala Rahamāna ('Abd al-Raḥmān).[104] This is a love poem, combining the message-poem and rāsa genres, which anticipates a later vogue for Kṛṣṇaite Vaiṣṇava-inflected love poetry in fifteenth-century Gujarat.[105] A popular genre of poetry was the rāsa—erotic songs that often accompanied goddess worship or other religious festivities. Such song lyrics were often set to music and accompanied by dancing. Also popular were the *bārahmāsā* poems that had narrative descriptions of the seasons. The rāsas celebrating the spring were known as *phāgus*, which became a popular genre, including important compositions such as the *Sthūlibhadraphāga* (1324) and the *Vasantavilāsa* (early fifteenth century). Many rāsa, phāgu, and bārahmāsā poems dealt with the heroine's *viraha* (separation from the beloved), a motif that was later elaborated by Vaiṣṇava poets. The rise in popularity of these compositions is related to the revival of interest in Kṛṣṇa worship in Gujarat, and many of the compositions are inflected by a Kṛṣṇaite Vaiṣṇava theme. A phāgu by Natarśī (c.1439) expresses this:

> The sylvan goddess came and besought the Lord. 'The ten quarters have assumed new forms; Kāmadeva is coming to embrace you, Kṛshṇa, Lord Murāri, pray come.'
>
> Having heard this, the Lord was pleased and looked at his friends; and with his friends, the Yādava went to the forest.[106]

It has been argued that Narasiṃha Mahetā was the first in Gujarat to begin writing 'Gujarati poems in Gujarati'.[107] A poet who wrote without the usual courtly patronage, Narasiṃha's compositions voiced a new sensibility and became widely popular. He was also a product of the new political order of late fifteenth century Saurashtra. Now, the Cūḍāsamās and their patronage of Sanskrit represented an *ancien regime* to which Narasiṃha and his brand of popular non-brahmanical Kṛṣṇa-worship were firmly opposed. Yashaschandra argues that

Narasiṃha's 'relationship with the [Cūḍāsamā] state was not one of client and patron, but rather one of victim and victimizer ...'[108] Through his poetical narratives, Narasiṃha carved out an independent sphere for the Gujarati poet, one that belonged to the world of congregational and personal devotion, the ethics of trade and traders, and the rapidly urbanizing ethos of the late fifteenth century sultanate. The traditional religious and literary vocabulary represented by the Cūḍāsama state, already politically neutralized by sultanate power and abandoned by raṇī legitimation, was further archaised by Narasiṃha's poetic oeuvre. This transformation was revolutionary for Gujarati poetry and society.

It is not often appreciated just what a melting pot Gujarat was under the sultans in the fifteenth and early sixteenth centuries. Merchants and migrants had settled in Gujarat for centuries. When the Delhi sultanate achieved control of the trade route from north India to the sea, fortune-seekers poured into Gujarat. The governorship of the region was the most prized position in the administration, often virtually auctioned by the sultans, but there were good pickings to be had for almost everyone who tried his hand at trade, war, or preaching. It has been surmised that a lingua franca known as Gūjarī was evolved by this diverse and polyglot population: a language, basically north Indian in structure, that had been developing in the region for the past couple of centuries to facilitate commercial and social transactions.[109] However, this language did not yet have a literature.

After Tīmūr's invasion of Delhi in 1398–9, the Delhi sultanate sank into deep crisis and the balance of power began gradually to shift towards the south—to the new sultanates of Malwa, Jaunpur, Gujarat, and the Deccan. More fortune-seekers came to Gujarat, including the fugitive Delhi sultan himself, as the last governor of Tughluqid Gujarat struck out on his own in the first decade of the fifteenth century. Over the next half-century, the new sultans of Gujarat succeeded in regulating the trade and politics of the region, reining in freebooters, suppressing rebellion, and ensuring a relatively secure environment for trade. Theirs was a deeply eclectic court and had fewer elite tendencies than, say, the contemporary Dakkhanī courts, which espoused a largely Persianate culture. The necessity for the sultanate to enforce a pragmatic, trade-promoting consensus permitted a variety of religious formations to flourish. None of this was hindered by the prosperity of the region and the ready availability of patrons, around the court and elsewhere.

By the first decades of the fifteenth century there had been little development in the field of Hindavi poetry. While texts were produced in other north Indian vernaculars or trans-regional languages, Indo-Muslim literature continued to be in Persian. It is significant then that the first effusion of Indo-Muslim vernacular composition took place not in north India, but in Gujarat, with the poetry of the Ahmadabad-born Sufi, Shaykh Bahā' al-Dīn Bājan. Along with Persian verses, he wrote Hindi poems in a verse form called *jikrī* (based on the Arabic *dhikr*, remembering) which became popular with later Gujarat Sufis.[110] Significantly, Shaykh Bājan mentioned that his jikrī verses (presumably unlike his Persian ones) were sung and set to music, a useful reminder that much of vernacular poetry at the time was performed or sung in public.

Poems that have been composed by this *faqir* are called *jikri* in the Hindvi tongue, and the singers of Hind play and sing them upon instruments, observing the discipline of the ragas.[111]

In practice, Gūjarī was not usually distinguished from Hindavi as a separate language. Indeed, many saints and poets composed in both jarī and Hindavi. In *Rāval deval* attributed to Shaykh Bājan, there is little to distinguish it as a composition in Gūjarī:

We do not go to the king's palace (*rāval*) or temple (*deval*)
We wear rags and eat dry bread
The practice of us, the dervishes, is this,
We search for water and mosque,
In the pleasant cool shade we sit
And eat whatever others give us.[112]

Gujarati words such as 'rāval' and 'deval' create a referential atmosphere to the immediate Gujarati landscape against which such a poem would have been recited. Moreover, the poem's metre and other musical specificities might have made it recognizable as a jarī composition.

Gujarat was becoming a magnet for Sufis and other Muslim preachers from north India and Sind. By the mid-fifteenth century more poets like Qāḍī Maḥmūd Daryā'ī (1415–1534) and Shaykh 'Alī Jīv Gāmdhanī (d. 1565) were beginning to write in the vernacular popularized by Shaykh Bājan, only now it was generally called Gūjarī. Other prominent Sufis such as Shaykh Aḥmad Khattū (d.1446) and Shāh lam Bukhārī (d.1531)—both closely associated with the Gujarat sultans—also used it to preach in, utterances and compositions that were later anthologized by their followers.[113] In 1434 Faẓl al-Dīn Balkhī of Kadi in north Gujarat composed a lexicon, *Baḥr al-faẓā'il* (The Ocean of Virtues), which included a section on the Hindavi words used in contemporary poetry.[114] The fifth sultan of Gujarat, Quṭb al-Dīn Aḥmad is believed to have composed poetry in Gūjarī.[115] Earlier, Ismā'īlī preachers such as the shadowy Pīr Shams and Satgur Nūr, generally dated between the twelfth and fourteenth centuries, used the language for their compositions. In the sixteenth century, the Ismā'īlī preacher r Muḥammad Shāh also wrote in a language he identified as Gūjarī and Hindī.[116]

The first mention of the term Gūjarī was probably in Amīr Khusrau's list of the languages of India in *Nūh sipihr*.[117] However, the term appears as the description of a particular text only in the fifteenth century, under the sultans of Gujarat. Although its practitioners continued at times to call the language they used Hindi or Hindavi, at this time it was usually called Gūjarī, the version of the general north Indian lingua franca that pertained to and had distinguishing characteristics specific to Gujarat but was distinct from Gujarati. There are several explanations of the origin and function of this name. One is that it was a remnant of the tongue of the Gujar pastoralists who began to settle all over the plains of northern and western India from the first century CE.[118] This would explain why it has features similar to Punjabi and Sindhi. Another etymology suggests that Gūjarī was the tongue employed for haggling and bartering at periodic markets, *guẓargāh*, the likes of which were—and are—common in Gujarat and Rajasthan. These markets were colloquially called 'gujarī' or 'gūjarī'.[119] Gūjarī bears, like Hindavi and Gujarati, traces of the language of pastoralist north-western India that also appear in ballads and bardic narratives. It was equally a marketplace patois evolved in a region where merchants from many countries transacted business. Nevertheless, its *literary* form, as opposed to its spoken one, should be associated with the Indo-Muslim culture presided over by the sultans of Gujarat from the fifteenth century.

There has been little notice taken of the sultanate contribution towards vernacularization in recent analyses of that phenomenon. In jarī we have an instance of vernacularization proceeding through an Indo-Muslim literary dialect, a representation of an Indo-Muslim *spoken* dialect. How then did an immigrant patois become a literary dialect? And further, why did this transition take place within the wider circles of the Gujarat sultanate to the extent that, by the sixteenth century, Gūjarī was widely used as a literary and spoken Indo-Muslim dialect, helping link the Gujarat court with the other Indo-Muslim courts of north India and the Deccan?

The rise of Gūjarī was a function of the complexity of the religious market in sultanate Gujarat in which preachers and missionaries competed for converts and resources. Gujarat was a place where, in order to be influential, preachers needed to communicate with a diverse population in an idiom that would be familiar to them. Associated with an evolving court, itself presiding over an emerging political and economic consensus of considerable prosperity and inventiveness, jarī was a lingua franca, a language for a region of migrants to communicate with each other. Pīr Mashā'ikh, a Gūjarī poet and Ismā'īlī preacher, expressed it succintly in the seventeenth century:

The yokels who live in the wilderness
Will not understand without Gujarī
I must make books thus
I must take on their speech so that they understand.[120]

While Gūjarī may have been the only way to communicate with yokels for a seventeenth-century writer, earlier it was also associated with a certain local feeling. Khūb Muḥammad Chishtī (1539–1614) wrote:

Like the speech
Flowing from my mouth:
Arabia and Iran join in it
To become one

The speech that flows
From the heart,
The speech of Arabia and Iran:
Listen, listen to the speech
Of Gujarat.[121]

This verse sums up some of the context for the evolution of Gūjarī: it was the speech of Gujarat tinged by the speech of Arabia and Iran.

This dialect of the bazaar, the Sufi's hospice, and the army was soon elevated by its association with the court into a literary language. This process of 'elevation' was part of the larger reinvention of cultural institutions—in literature, theatre, and music—carried out at the Gujarat court.[122] The court cast around for available cultural forms and then made them official by patronizing them. Gūjarī became emblematic of the linguistic public culture of the Gujarat sultanate, but remained whimsical and flexible, and was not subjected to classicising impulses.

Thus Gūjarī was granted a certain legitimacy when Quṭb al-Dīn Aḥmad, the fifth sultan, composed a *dīvān* in Gūjarī as well as when court-affiliated Sufis adopted the language for their discourses.

A metaphor for the cultural process operating here may be found in the story of the gardener Hālu related in the *Mir'āt-i Sikandarī*. Sultan ḥmūd had commissioned a man from Khurasan to lay out an artful garden in his new town of Champaner. The Khurāsānī built a beautiful garden and adorned it with fountains and waterfalls, features previously unknown in Gujarat. The delighted sultan rewarded him lavishly. Soon a Gujarati carpenter named Hālu came forward and claimed that he could do an even better job. In due course, he built an even more beautiful and ingenious garden. On being questioned how he had learnt these skills, he replied: 'I disguised myself as an ignorant labourer and worked for the man from Khurāsān, and partly by watching what he did and partly by my own skill, I acquired the knowledge.' The author of the chronicle, the seventeenth century writer Sikandar, sums up what was happening:

> Most of the elegant arts and crafts that are now common in Gujarat were copied from men of skill and genius from other countries, and Gujarat like an accomplished person became a collection of merits gathered from different sources. It was in the time of this great Sultan [Maḥmūd] that the people of Gujarat learned arts and wit—else before his time they were very simple homely folks indeed.[123]

Literary and performative dialects were evidently intelligible to their audiences. However, their use was largely restricted to professional groups or trained writers. 'Gujarati' literature, in the sense of written versions of a widely *spoken* tongue, may be traced, arguably, no earlier than the fifteenth century, and the emergence, for the first time, of compositions whose provenance had little or nothing to do with government patronage.[124] These were compositions emerging from religious orders patronized by merchant and occupational groups, and an increasingly prosperous peasantry. Chief among these orders were forms of Vaiṣṇavism and Satpanthī Ismā'īlism. While it is not clear whether these compositions were written or textualized in their earliest phase in the fifteenth century, their redactions even a century later, as with the compositions of Narasiṃha Mahetā, make it clear that this was a different order of texts.[125] For the first time, religious and sectarian compositions were emerging from the laity, not from a literati or professional group such as brahmins or bards specially trained in the production of religious literature and the use of a suitable language. This trend soon became widespread, with vernacular compositions emerging—and eventually becoming textualized—from previously excluded groups such as women, and occupational and 'lower' castes.[126] Correspondingly, the performance—recitation, dramatization, or singing—of such compositions also tended to be carried out by the laity itself in exclusive gatherings, *satsang*s or *jamā'at*s, rather than by professional performers, priests, or bards.

Gūjarī, similarly, could potentially be used by a lay population. It did not require particular training and was never part of a curriculum. While it was employed by some sultans and courtiers, it was chiefly the language of Sufis. Muslim mystics of various kinds, including Ismā'īlī ones, used Gūjarī for their compositions not as literary conceits but out of the necessity of communicating with their followers. Gūjarī never developed tendencies towards classicization or standardization, as Urdu eventually did. This may have been because of its location within a particularly practice-oriented society, where refined vernacular language training was not part of a grooming repertoire for the sons of the courtiers or merchants. It remained the idiom of Sufis and Muslim mystics, providing them with a language to communicate with their followers and potential converts, and, while the Gujarat sultanate existed, with the court.

THE SULTANATE: STRUCTURE AND LEGITIMACY

The court was where the sultan was and it travelled with him on his military expeditions and from capital to new capital. By the mid-fifteenth century, an administrative structure of governance, military control and fiscal regulation was beginning to emerge but there is little evidence of the elaborate bureaucratization seen in sultanates that presided over a predominantly agrarian order.[127] Nor is there much evidence of elaborate courtly ritual in the fifteenth century. The accession of each sultan was marked by lavish gift-giving, but this was not accompanied by court ceremonial of the kind witnessed by Baṭṭūṭa at the Tughluqid court.[128] We do not elaborate receptions for foreign ambassadors in the sources. This was a trading sultanate ruling a civic world.

Over the course of the fifteenth century, power came to be seen as deriving from the sultan and his immediate family. This was contested at first, as when Muẓaffar Shāh and Aḥmad Shāh were opposed by locally powerful factions for the control of the whole of Gujarat, but by the mid-fifteenth century there was no real opposition to the existence of the dynasty. Nevertheless, the sultan's person was not sacralized. In the chronicles, the sultans emerge as accessible to courtiers, employees, Sufis, and even common people.[129] The first figure who emerges from the chronicles as larger-than-life is Maḥmūd Bīgara but even he is a benevolent, folkloric figure from the point of view of later chroniclers. One anecdote relates that a peasant soldier returned from his village with a gift of the freshest grasses for Maḥmūd's favourite horse:

The Sultan smiled his thanks, encouraged whereby the unsophisticated countryman proceeded to give an account of a *koli* woman in his village, who, he said, used to bear a son every year. This year, said he, her husband was dead, and if the Sultan was so inclined, she was worth bringing to the royal harem to multiply heirs for the throne. The Sultan laughed, and the more he did so, the more the yokel began to assert the truth of the story, swearing that the woman had given birth to seven sons in seven years.[130]

Maḥmūd was illiterate but had a deep interest in religion. His learning was described by the chroniclers in a style that anticipates another unlettered monarch, Akbar:

Though illiterate, the Sultan's mind from his constant association with learned men was stored with such a rich stock of useful knowledge, colloquial and historical (both sacred and profane), legal, poetical and biographical that, except scholars, nobody in speaking with him could say that he was unlettered.[131]

Elsewhere, he was represented as a pious paternal figure: 'The existence of the Sultan was, one would say, for the happiness of his people. There was not a man who had the load of an injustice or injury on his heart, and everyone was blessed with happiness and liberty.'[132] After a gruelling set of campaigns in which he lost many soldiers, his attendants found him deeply distressed. When asked the reason for his grief, he explained:

I should indeed be a thoughtless and unworthy man if after arriving here in safety and comfort I do not enquire after and make provision to assuage the grief of the widows and families of those who have for ever marched away from this transitory world. It matters little if we delay for two or three days to enter the city, but to enter it without enquiring after and comforting and cooling the ardour of the grief of those whose dear ones have not returned, would be far from considerate or humane.[133]

In the course of the fifteenth century the sultanate generally came to be accepted as the paramount power. Texts and inscriptions throughout the region mention that they were composed during the reign of one of the sultans or their local subordinates. This was the case even with texts composed in a Jain or Sanskritic idiom. In 1413, an early Vaiṣṇava text from Talaja mentions that it was composed when Malik Śrī Usmān, the local sultanate official, and Raol Śrī Sāraṅgajī, the chieftain, were in power in Ghogha.[134] A heavily illuminated copy of the Old Gujarati poem *Vasantavilāsa* was composed in the reign of b al-Dīn Aḥmad Shāh. The poet Gaṅgādhara, who arrived at the court of Champaner from Vijayanagara, claimed as his highest achievement to have vanquished the poets of the Ahmadabad court.[135] Thus, ultimate local legitimacy was derived from the court of the sultan.

Maḥmūd Bīgara's reign carried this tendency even further, so that legitimacy was now vested not merely in the dynasty, but in the person of the sultan. His emergence as the prototypical benevolent monarch of folklore is related first to the length of his reign of over half a century. Second, it has to do with his reign being viewed as proverbially prosperous, a veritable golden age, by contemporaries as well as subsequent chroniclers. Maḥmūd was the first ruler after the twelfth-century Caulukya ruler Siddharāja Jayasiṃha to be viewed as the fount of legitimacy and justice in this fashion. Over his long reign, he was seen as having delivered peace and prosperity to his people.

> Now followed a period of such peace and prosperity that no eye had seen nor ear heard; the soldier was independent and in comort, the dervish careless of all but the worship of the Almighty, the merchant happy in his trade and profit, and the whole country full of peace and tranquillity, and free from anxiety and danger.[136]

The segmentary lineage state posits a quasi-autonomous centre whose administrative structure is repeated at the periphery at every segment of lineage power. Thus, the centre has limited territorial sovereignty, and power diminishes towards the periphery and does not possess a monopoly on force. The structure is held together by ritual sovereignty. However, the Gujarat sultans were the sole sovereign force in Gujarat and there was no ritual sovereignty holding the centre to the periphery. As Maḥmūd Bīgara's career shows, the sultanate was maintained by force and by setting up a relatively complex bureaucratic hierarchy fuelled by a dynamic trade economy. B.D. Chattopadhaya has shown that even Rajput polities in this period were not held together by ritual sovereignty.[137] The sultans were a far more forceful centralizing power than the Caulukyas. Their principal achievement lay in curbing the powers of their courtiers and the fissiparous potential of clan politics amongst the pastoralist bands. Once the pastoralist bands had been reduced to subsidiary positions under a Muslim sultan, they were denied access to the central ruling lineage, which meant that they could not play the intimate marriage- and alliance-based politics of the clan. Their only chance would have been the overthrow of the sultans through force, and this was ruled out as the sultans had a much greater hold over military resources and personnel.

This form of politics was based on the centralization of imperial power around the charismatic figure of the sultan and his court, backed by a strong army that owed allegiance to the sultan rather than to feudatories. The sultanate was gained through military conquest and was maintained through military power. The sultanate's ideology was not in the main about clan politics, redistribution of resources, or religious patronage in the manner of the Hindu polities of the preceding period. The sultan was the fount of political sovereignty, not the clan. Also, it needs to be emphasized that the Gujarat sultanate, like other pre-Mughal Islamic states, was based on a constant readiness for war.[138] Military garrisons from the central army were placed in strategic locations to balance the regional forces of courtiers and clans. Finally, the military nobility was part of a centralized impersonal military bureaucracy, not of a set of interlinked clan polities. The sultan's power was unchallenged and stood above everyone. Indeed, the history of Rajput polities after the onset of Muslim rule is marked by a running tension between the centrifugal potential of clan politics and the attempt to emulate Islamic kingship through the centralization of power.

The Gujarat sultanate depended on loose alliances through which it would control but not destroy the mobile identities of its participants. Mobile groups such as pastoralist chieftains and mercenary warriors were sought to be drawn into the sultanate and pacified. It was rare for a repository of manpower or resources to be alienated completely from his base; thus, after a chieftain was defeated, he or his descendants were handed back a portion of their lands.[139] Merchants continued to be patronized, as did carrier communities. However, central rule did not mean that the centre took over all power. This was still a rudimentary court, and it depended on the loyalty of subordinates and courtiers. But the sultans did ensure that the military power of the chieftains was curbed, be they Muslim or Hindu. They absorbed many of the mercenary armies into the sultanate forces and allowed the chieftains to set up stable principalities that were fuelled by returns from trade and cultivation of land. This put an end to the cycles of loot and plunder that inevitably followed the entry of pastoralist groups into the region and their subsequent political and economic manoeuvres. The generous salaries and perquisites offered by the sultans to the soldiers in the army made it possible for the system to function more or less smoothly. And this again was made possible as long as the state coffers were stable enough, well oiled by the rich Gujarat trade.

The sultans were now seen as the primary guarantors of prosperity and security in the region. This also enabled migrant groups to evolve long-lasting networks of trade and kinship. Many more were now settling in Gujarat, and prosperity was now perceived to permeate to all levels of society through new prospects for employment and trade. The prosperity and expansion of the social order led to the expansion of existing institutions and the development of new ones as the increasingly complex system became self-sustaining. As people struck deep roots and became committed to their long-term prospects in the region, their kin and professional ties widened, and economics and language began to intersect. Peripheral regions were drawn into the widening networks of communication and trade. The new literary languages such as Gujarati and Gūjarī represented the codification of the laity's language into written form, and texts in these languages now circulated for education and edification. This was a region self-consciously thinking about itself as a region.

As the sultanate changed from a randomly tribute-exacting agency to a sustained administrative order, returns were felt all the way down the infrastructure. Apart from the overt protection and patronage to the Sunni orthodoxy and the Sufi orders, there was little state discrimination between other groups. They were put down only when they became a political threat. Thus, the Ismā'īlī pīr Imām Shāh was allowed to proselytize right next to the capital as long as he did not become a political threat. However, the Sūmrās on the Kachchh border represented a political challenge and had to be put down. Similarly, Vaiṣṇava merchants did not represent a political threat and could be allowed to build step-wells. Temples were another matter as they had a reputation of becoming a centre for disaffection and political challenge. By the mid-fifteenth century the intense competition for religious converts was beginning to ease as newly prosperous groups formed sustainable kin and professional networks. The variegated religious marketplace within which proselytizers vied for converts began to give way to a scenario in which cultural concordances could take place and groups could make a variety of religious choices, often opting for 'syncretic' practices or new congregational forms of personal worship such as bhakti or Satpanthī Ismā'īlism.

NOTES

1. According to Firishta, Farḥat al-Mulk 'became desirous of establishing his independence; and in order to gain popularity for the furtherance of that object, he encouraged the Hindoo religion, and thus rather promoted than suppressed the worship of idols'. Firishta, *History of the Rise of Mahomedan Power,* Vol. 4, p. 1. Sikandar mentions only that he had rebelled and that there were complaints about his tyranny. Sikandar, *MS,* trans., p. 5.
2. Firishta, *History of the Rise of Mahomedan Power,* Vol. 4, p. 2. None of the other sources indicate that Ẓafar Khān left Delhi with a substantial army.
3. Kolff, *Naukar, Rajput and Sepoy,* p. 98.
4. Aḥmad, *TA,* trans., p. 177.
5. Firishta, *History of the Rise of Mahomedan Power,* Vol. 4, p. 3.
6. Aḥmad, *TA,* trans., pp. 178–9, Kolff, *Naukar, Rajput and Sepoy,* p. 44.
7. Aḥmad, *TA,* trans., p. 180.
8. Ibid., p. 181.
9. According to Sikandar, this was in 1397–98. Sikandar, *MS,* trans., p. 7.
10. Aḥmad, *TA,* trans., p. 181. Epigraphic records indicate that Vājā chieftains controlled the territory around Somanath although the port town was probably run by merchant groups as it had been in the thirteenth and fourteenth centuries.
11. Sikandar, *MS,* trans., p. 11.
12. Ibid., p. 20.
13. Ibid., p. 21.
14. Ibid., p. 64.
15. Ibid., p. 47.
16. Kolff, *Naukar, Rajput and Sepoy,* p. 65.
17. Sikandar, *MS,* p. 58. According to the *Mir'āt-i Aḥmadī,* after the reign of Muẓaffar II (1511–1525), the army increased in size and courtiers began to permit revenue farming on their lands. This produced much higher returns, but as a consequence the careful checking of accounts was abandoned, leading to confusion. James Bird (1835), *The Political and Statistical History of Gujarat,* p. 192; Campbell, *Gazetteer,* p. 210.
18. Sikandar, *MS,* p. 154.
19. Digby, *War-horse and Elephant,* p. 61.
20. Ibid., pp. 72–3. citing Ibn Baṭṭūṭa, *Riḥla,* p. 77.
21. Khān, *Mir'āt-i Aḥmadī: Supplement,* trans., p. 118.
22. Firishta, *History of the Rise of Mahomedan Power,* Vol. 4, p. 3.
23. Bayley, *Local Muhammadan Dynasties,* p. 386. The Sangars of Kachchh

were known for their skill in shipbuilding during the sultanate. Majmudar, *Cultural History of Gujarat*, p. 75.

24. Major, *India in the Fifteenth Century*, p. 28.
25. Sikandar, *MS*, trans., p. 62.
26. Ibid., p. 63.
27. The Mamlūk force included royal slaves and soldiers commanded by Ḥusayn Mushrif al-Kurdī. The Mamlūk and Gujarati forces were victorious in 1508 but were then summarily defeated by the Portuguese near Diu in February 1509. See P.M. Holt (1960), 'Ḳānṣawh al-Ghawrī', *Encyclopaedia of Islam*, Vol. 4, p. 551.
28. Majmudar, *Cultural History of Gujarat*, p. xiv.
29. Eaton, 'Temple Desecration', p. 108.
30. Sikandar, *MS*, trans., p. 17.
31. The destruction of (rival) temples was carried out by Hindu rulers too. Chattopadhyaya cites the *Rājataraṅginī* on the 'appointment of a *devotpātananāyaka*, an official in charge of uprooting images of gods from temples and of confiscation of temple property, by an early medieval ruler of Kashmir.' Chattopadhyaya, *Making of Early Medieval India*, p. 201, citing *Rājataraṅginī*, Vol. 7, pp. 1146–8.
32. Firishta, *History of the Rise of Mahomedan Power*, Vol. 4, p. 10. According to Commissariat, 'The term "gras" (lit. a mouthful) has been used from time immemorial throughout Gujarat and Kathiawar to indicate the lands and villages given for their subsistence to junior members of the Rajput ruling families that came and settled down in the land, and these cadets came to be called "grasias" or "garasias". In course of time *gras* came to mean a hereditary landed patrimony, large or small, and even to-day it is the commonest word in Kathiawar in connection with land administration. In the decline of Mughal power during the eighteenth century, when the Maratha incursions were in operation, the term acquired for a time another connotation, and came to signify, under the form of *toda-gras*, the blackmail which turbulent robber chiefs levied from villages exposed to their attacks as the price of their protection and forbearance.' M.S. Commissariat, *History of Gujarat*, Vol. 1, pp. 80–1. Also see Desai, *Glossary of Castes, Tribes and Races*, Vol. 2, p. 102; Watson, *Kathiawar*, pp. 315–26.
33. Sikandar, *MS*, trans., p. 55.
34. Shastri, *HIG*, No. 107.
35. Desai, *Arabic, Persian and Urdu Inscriptions*, No. 2144.
36. Aḥmad, *TA*, p. 175.
37. Ibid., p. 189.
38. Ibid.
39. Forbes, *Ras Mala*, Vol. 2, p. 270.
40. Ibid., pp. 270–1.
41. Ibid., p. 270.

42. Campbell, *Gazetteer*, p. 89.
43. Majmudar, *Cultural History of Gujarat*, pp. 118–19.
44. Sikandar, *MS*, trans., p. 65.
45. Campbell, *Gazetteer*, p. 211.
46. Shastri, *HIG*, pp. 63–6.
47. Mīyā Śrī Phatūlā's wife was Bībī Śrī Lālājī and their sons had Islamic names: Alījī, Rājejī, and Cāndajī. Ibid., pp. 64–5.
48. See section on Architecture and Politics in Chapter 2 in this volume.
49. Diskalkar, *IK*, No. 85.
50. Pravīṇ Candra Parīkh and Bharatī Shelat (1991), *Gujarāt-nā abhilekho: svādhyāya ane samīkṣā*, pp. 94–101; Shastri, *HIG*, No. 14–15.
51. Oza, *Corpus Inscriptionum Bhavanagari*, pp. 28–30.
52. M.N. Katti, ed. (1998), *ARIE for 1986–87*, R.N. Mehta and S.G. Kantawala (1979), *Svādhyāya*, 16, pp. 192–6; Shastri, *HIG*, No. 19A.
53. Burgess and Cousens, *RLARBP*, pp. 301–11; Shastri, *HIG*, pp. 19–23.
54. Jalāl al-Dīn Ḥusayn al-Bukhārī, known widely as Makhdūm-i Jahānīyān Jahāngasht, lived in Sehwan in the fourteenth century and was a preceptor of Firūz Shāh.
55. Sikandar, *MS*, trans., pp. 3–4.
56. Sikandar, *MS*, p. 4.
57. Sikandar, *MS*, trans., p. 1.
58. In the nineteenth century they are generally recorded as being of 'low caste'. W. Crooke (1896), *The Tribes and Castes of the North-western Provinces and Oudh*, Vol. 1, pp. 192, 271, Vol. 2, pp. 224, 254, 264, 370, Vol. 3, pp. 107, 169, Vol. 4, pp. 334, 360–1.
59. Misra, *Rise of Muslim Power*, pp. 137–8.
60. Sikandar, *MS*, trans., p. 4.
61. Ibid., p. 2.
62. The third means was in the field of religion. As ultimate legitimacy derived from the king, a claim by a proselytizer to have converted the ruler was particularly significant. See Chapter 4 for details.
63. Kolff, *Naukar, Rajput and Sepoy*, p. 100.
64. Ziegler, 'Rajput Loyalties', p. 225.
65. Kolff, *Naukar, Rajput and Sepoy*, p. 83.
66. Ziegler, 'Rajput Loyalties', p. 225.
67. Tambs-Lyche, *Power, Profit and Poetry*, p. 74.
68. Ibid.
69. Aḥmad, *TA*, p. 219.
70. After the death of Muḥammad Shāh and then Bībī Turkī, Shāh-i 'Ālam married the sultan's widow, Bībī Mughalī, the mother of Maḥmūd I. This event is played up by Sikandar, a follower of Shāh 'Ālam's family, in projecting them as a parallel and equal centre of power to the sultans. Sikandar, *MS*, trans., p. 38.

71. Firishta, *History of the Rise of Mahomedan Power*, trans., Vol. 4, p. 65.
72. Aḥmad, *TA*, p. 224, Sikandar, *MS*, trans., p. 23.
73. Firishta, *History of the Rise of Mahomedan Power*, trans., Vol. 4, p. 76.
74. Aḥmad, *TA*, p. 235, Sikandar, *MS*, trans., p. 40. The *Muntakhab al-tawārīkh* describes eunuchs tearing the woman into pieces, while Firishta says that it was later proved that Shams Khān (and presumably his daughter) were not guilty of having poisoned the sultan. Firishta, *History of the Rise of Mahomedan Power*, trans., Vol. 4, p. 71.
75. Sikandar, *MS*, trans., p. 37.
76. This is a manifestation of the Bukhārī Sufis' claims of parallel power to the sultanate and to their own semi-royal status. This claim to political significance is made only in the chronicle by their follower, the seventeenth century writer Sikandar.
77. Sikandar, *MS*, p. 103. Although her son Fatḥ Khān came into power only in 1459, Makhdūma-i Jahān, the widow of Muḥammad Shāh, is recorded as having commissioned a mosque to be built in 1454 during the reign of her stepson. See Burgess and Cousens, *RLARBP*, p. 292; Chaghatai, *Muslim Monuments of Ahmadabad*, Vol. 16, pp. 53–4.
78. Aḥmad, *TA*, p. 237.
79. Ibid., p. 256; Tūnī, *TMS*, p. 146.
80. Aḥmad, *TA*, p. 259.
81. He is also credited with strong 'virile powers'. 'The women of his country were too weak for him; and, after cohabitation with several of his wives, he used to derive satisfaction only from a young and strapping Abyssinian lass.' Sikandar, *MS*, trans., p. 42.
82. Ibid., p. 48.
83. M.H. Siddiqi (1985), ed., *The Growth of Indo-Persian Literature in Gujarat*, 'Introduction', p. xi.
84. Nabi Hadi (1995), *Dictionary of Indo-Persian Literature* (1995), p. 490.
85. Khān, *Mir'āt-i Aḥmadī: Supplement*, trans., p. 27.
86. Ibid., p. 25.
87. Hadi, *Dictionary*, p. 624.
88. L. Kopf (1960), 'al-Damīrī', *Encyclopaedia of Islam*, Vol. 2, p. 107.
89. Siddiqi, *Growth of Indo-Persian Literature*, 'Introduction', p. x.
90. Ibid., p. xviii, also Hadi, *Dictionary*, p. 31.
91. M. Benecheb (1960), 'Ibn al-Djazarī', *Encyclopaedia of Islam*, Vol. 3, p. 753.
92. M.A. Quraishi (1972), *Muslim Educational and Learning in Gujarat (1297–1758)*, p. 29.
93. Sikandar, *MS*, p. 109.
94. Siddiqi, *Growth of Indo-Persian Literature*, 'Introduction', p. x.
95. Hadi, *Dictionary*, p. 628.
96. Z.A. Desai (1989), 'The Major Dargahs of Ahmadabad', in C.W. Troll,

Ghunyat al-munya (1971), ed., Shahab Sarmadee, p. 3.

98. See Françoise 'Nalini' Delvoye (1994), 'Indo-Persian Literature on Art-Music: Some Historical and Technical Aspects', in *Confluence of Cultures: French Contributions to Indo-Persian Studies*, ed., Françoise 'Nalini' Delvoye; and Françoise 'Nalini' Delvoye (2000), 'Indo-Persian Accounts on Music Patronage in the Sultanate of Gujarat', in *The Making of Indo-Persian Culture: Indian and French Studies*, eds, Muzaffar Alam, Françoise 'Nalini' Delvoye, and Marc Gaborieau.
99. Vaudeville, *Myths, Saints, and Legends*, pp. 274–5.
100. Majmudar, *Cultural History of Gujarat*, p. 312.
101. Balavant Jānī (2000), *Svādhyāya ane saṃśodhan*, p. 40; Gordon Ross Thompson (1987), 'Music and Values in Gujarati-speaking Western India', p. 113.
102. Majmudar, *Cultural History of Gujarat*, p. 309.
103. K.M. Munshi locates the earliest Gujarati works in the late twelfth century. However, many of the recognizable features of modern Gujarati only entered texts from about 1400. Munshi, *Gujarāta and its Literature*, pp. 85–6.
104. Abdul Rahmān (1998), *The Saṃdeśarāsaka of Abdul Rahman*, p. xii.
105. Ibid., p.xi. The editor remarks: 'This genre is associated, in ways that deserve further exploration, with the worship of Kṛṣṇa as the god who offers humankind his grace in return for its devotion.' See also Mansukhlal Jhaveri (1978), *History of Gujarati Literature*, p. 12.
106. Munshi, *Gujarāta and its Literature*, p. 91.
107. Yashaschandra, 'From Hemacandra to *Hind Svarāj*', p. 584.
108. Ibid., p. 585. For the transformation of Cūḍāsama political power, see Chapter 3 in this volume.
109. Munshī 'Abbas 'Alī, *Qissa-i ghamgīn*, quoted in S.R. Faruqi (2001), *Early Urdu Literary Culture and History*, pp. 111–12.
110. Desai, *Malfuz Literature*.
111. Cited in Faruqi, *Early Urdu Literary Culture*, p. 72.
112. Ibid.
113. Desai, *Malfuz Literature*, p. 43.
114. Dar, 'Gujarat's Contribution to Gujari and Urdu', p. 22.
115. Desai, *Malfuz Literature*, p. 45.
116. Zawahir Moir (2006), 'The Gujari Ginans of Nur Muhammad Shah', unpublished paper. The Ismā'īlī preachers represent the link between the Indo-Muslim vernacular world of the sultanate courts and the balladic tradition of the martial pastoralist groups of western India: they participated in and helped to constitute both worlds. See Khan, *Conversion and Shifting Identities*.
117. Dar, 'Gujarat's Contribution to Gujari and Urdu', p. 19.
118. Faruqi, *Early Urdu Literary Culture*, p. 65.
119. Ambāśaṅkar Nāgar and Alābakhsh Shaikh, eds (1991), *Gujarāt kī hindustānī*

120. Ibid., p. 46.
121. Faruqi, *Early Urdu Literary Culture*, p. 97.
122. Delvoye, 'Indo-Persian Literature on Art-Music, p. 115.
123. Sikandar, *MS*, trans., p. 61.
124. Yashaschandra, 'From Hemacandra to *Hind Svarāj*', p. 585.
125. See Mallison on the early textual versions of Narasiṃha Mahetā's compositions and the problems of dating them. Mallison, *Au Point du Jour*, pp. 24–6.
126. Some of the groups who employed these compositions as religious literature became secretive about their affiliations, rites, and membership, and eventually may also have developed a dedicated cultic and partially secret mystic vocabulary accessible only to the initiated. Khan, *Conversion and Shifting Identities*, pp. 49, 78, 91; Nirañjan Rājyaguru (1995), *Bījamārgī gupta pāṭ-upāsana ane mahāpanthī santonī bhajanvāṇī*, pp. 3–4.
127. Jackson, *The Delhi Sultanate*, Chapter 3.
128. Ibn Baṭṭūṭa, *Riḥla*, p. 91.
129. Of the texts contemporary to Maḥmūd, only the Sanskrit eulogy *Rājavinoda* ritually praises him in a traditional idiom.
130. Sikandar, *MS*, trans., p. 70, Sikandar, *MS*, p. 140.
131. Sikandar, *MS*, trans., p. 49.
132. Sikandar, *MS*, pp. 140–1.
133. Sikandar, *MS*, trans., p. 64.
134. Peterson, *A Collection of Prakrit and Sanskrit Inscriptions*, p. 87.
135. Gaṅgādhara (1973), *Gaṅgadāsa-pratāpavilāsa-nātakam*, p. vii.
136. Sikandar, *MS*, trans., p. 45.
137. Chattopadhyaya, 'Origin of the Rajputs', p. 133.
138. Digby, *War-horse and Elephant*, p. 41.
139. Examples include the Paṭāī Rāval of Champaner, the Jhālās, and the Vaghelās. Sikandar, *MS*, trans., pp. 41, 47, 60.

Afterword

The fourteenth and fifteenth century were times of turbulence and suited military and religious entrepreneurs. There were many groups vying for power. Religious groups vied for patrons and converts. As organizers of manpower, religious leaders were often political power-brokers too. Although the sultans were Sunnis, and some of them aggressively so, it suited them to parcel out territory to those who could claim to pacify turbulent groups, whether these were aspirant courtiers, Rajputs, mercenaries, or religious leaders. As the sultans emerged at the top of the military tree and became the most prolific customers and employers in the region, the sectarian landscape also began to stabilise.

Gujarat had been a consistently urbanised and prosperous region since early historic times. As it was always on a cultural frontier, there was scope for migrants to reinvent their identities and stay mobile. For states starting up in this region, the challenge was always to maintain the dynamism of trade and derive maximum benefit from it while maintaining order and security. The Gujarat sultanate was the first state in the region to make the transition from a tribute-exacting economy to a structured semi-bureaucratic system with relatively fixed and predictable returns accruing from land revenue and trade. Over the fifteenth century, an administrative infrastructure was extended all over the region in an attempt to systematize governance and facilitate trade.

By Maḥmūd Bīgara's time, the sultanate represented the overarching were now conjoined linguistically and discursively. It was now commonsensical to acknowledge the linking of sultanate, region and language as representing similar values. The greatest achievement of the sultanate was therefore twofold. Firstly it settled the frontiers of Gujarat, a constant source of political and economic instability for dynasties that had ruled earlier. Most dynasties fell as a result of their inability to absorb pastoralist groups making inroads into the region, most notably from the west. Even if they managed to convert pastoralist groups to vassaldom, they were unable to curb their military autonomy. This the sultans did. The sultan's achievements in the fifteenth century can be measured by the fact that by the sixteenth century, garāsiyā and Rajput groups had set up imitative courts and households within sultanate territories. They were even able to generate sub-clans in the regular manner of Rajput segmentation without challenging the ultimate power of the sultans.

Secondly, the sultanate managed to regularize trade in a complex society that was rapidly becoming sedentarized and urbanized. This process now included all parts of the region that we now recognise as Gujarat, unlike earlier polities that had consisted of a settled core and wide unsettled hinterland. This was the first polity that depended on an understanding of the intermeshing of pastoralist clan politics, trade, and sectarian religion. The sultans and their administrators recognized that the prosperity generated through trade would help pacify pastoralist groups and curb the militancy of sectarian religiosity. The slow, fixed, and uneven returns from a predominantly agrarian economy would not have served the purpose. Only a well-managed and constantly expanding trading empire could meet the challenge of the results of prosperity itself—expanding populations, increasing stratification in society and newer upwardly mobile social groups with economic and political aspirations. It was to facilitate this that ḥmūd Bīgara constantly toured his territories, marrying the women of pastoralist chieftains, subduing pirates and intransigent pastoralist groups and imposing the peace of the region. He was busy ensuring the symbolic presence of the sultan across the region in ways that would convince one and all of the benefits of belonging to the Gujarat sultanate.

The legacies of the Gujarat sultanate continue to pervade Gujarat. Anyone who explores the religious landscape of Gujarat with some care will notice the proliferation of religious options, even today. The grand temples and great mosque-tomb complexes of the medieval period are only part of the story. There are scores, if not hundreds, of local goddesses, pīrs, saints, heroes, and *satis* commemorated everywhere in small wayside shrines, in fairs, markets, shops, and homes. The stories of these shrines and their adherents record struggles and accommodations, patronage and politics that speak as tellingly of antiquity as of Gujarat today.

Why does a society that offers such a profuse and multilayered array of religious options, erupt regularly into sectarian violence? The tapestry of social relations in Gujarat has not necessarily been one of harmonious coexistence, but it has been one of largely pragmatic pluralism. How did such a plural society become home to discourse of violent Hindu exclusivism, to the extent of condoning ethnic cleansing? How can a society made up of avowed migrants—hardly any caste or religious group in Gujarat will admit to indigenous origins—retreat into conspiracy theories about 'outsiders'? Most intriguingly, how do dominant discourses of pacifism, pragmatism, and vegetarianism—think Gandhi and the Jains—coexist with the kind of martial aggression that we saw in 2002?

While there are many answers to these questions in the analyses of contemporary historians and anthropologists, few of these address the underlying loops of memory and relations of power that have evolved over centuries. The more I explored these issues, the more I was convinced that some answers lay in the long-term history of Gujarat, in the legacy of half-forgotten and selectively remembered relations between the powerful and those seeking power, between rulers, merchants, herders, farmers, and religious professionals. Answers also lay in the links between histories that have, in the last century, been wrenched apart and stripped of context. How many in Gujarat, apart from a handful of specialists, remember that Maḥmūd Bīgara and Narasiṃha Mahetā were near contemporaries? In the historiography, the sultanate belongs to a Persianate world rendered alien by language and religious denomination, while the father of Gujarati poetry belongs to a timeless narrative of Hindu devotional sensibility. This polarization is deeply unproductive for a historian. The first task has been to get these histories to talk to one another.

Bibliography

Abbās 'Alī, Munshī. 1975. *Qissa-i ghamgīn*, ed. S.C. Misra. Baroda: M.S. University.

Adriaensen, R., H.T. Bakker, and H. Isaacson, eds. 1998. *The Skandapurāṇa*, Vol. 1. Groningen: Egbert Forsten, 1998.

mad b. Muḥammad Muqīm, Niẓām al-Dīn Haravī. 1927–35. *Ṭabaqāt-i Akbarī*, trans. Brajendranath De and M. Hidayat Hosain as *The Ṭabaqāt-i-Akbarī of Khwājah Niẓāmuddīn Aḥmad*, 3 Vols. Calcutta: The Asiatic Society of Bengal.

Ahmad, Aziz. 1964. *Studies in Islamic Culture in the Indian Subcontinent*. Oxford: Clarendon Press.

Ahmad, S. Maqbul. 1969. *Indo-Arab Relations: An Account of India's Relations with the Arab World from Ancient upto Modern Times*. Bombay: Popular Prakashan.

Alam, Muzaffar. 1998. 'The Pursuit of Persian: Language in Mughal Politics', *MAS*, 32(2), pp. 317–49.

Altekar, A.S. 1924–5. 'A History of Important Ancient Towns in Gujarat and Kāṭhiawaḍ', *IA*, 54 (Supplement), pp. 1–54.

Amarjī, Ranchodjī. 1882. *Ta'rīkh-i-Sorath. A History of the Provinces of Sorath and Hālār in Kāthiāwād*, translated by E. Rehatsek, revised by J.W. Watson, edited by James Burgess. Bombay and London: Education Society Press & Thacker.

Annual Report on Indian Epigraphy for 1961–62. 1966. New Delhi: Department of Archaeology, Archaeological Survey of India.

—— *1963–64*. 1967. New Delhi: Department of Archaeology, Archaeological Survey of India.

Appadurai, Arjun. 1977. 'Kings, Sects and Temples in South India, 1350–1700', , 14(1), pp. 47–73.

Arai, Toshikazu. 1998. 'Jain Kingship in the *Prabandhacintāmaṇi*', in J.F. Richards, ed., *Kingship and Authority in South Asia*. New Delhi: Oxford University Press, pp. 92–132.

Arora, R.K. 1971. 'The Magas, Sun-Worship and the *Bhaviṣya Purāṇa*', *Purāṇa*, 13(1), pp. 47–76.

Arrianus. 1912. *The Periplus of the Erythraean Sea: Travel and Trade in the Indian Ocean by a Merchant of the First Century*, trans. W.H. Schoff. New York: Longmans Green.

Asani, Ali S. 1987. 'The Khojkī Script: A Legacy of Ismaili Islam in the Indo-Pakistan Subcontinent', *Journal of the American Oriental Society*, 107(3), pp. 439–49, reprinted in Ali Asani, *Ecstasy and Enlightenment: The Ismaili Devotional Literature of South Asia*. London and New York: I.B. Tauris, 2002. pp. 100–23.

Aubin, Jean. 1964. 'The Secretary of Maḥmūd Gāvān and his Lost Chronicle', *Journal of the Research Society of Pakistan*, 1(2), pp. 9–13.

——— 1966. 'Indo-islamica I. La vie et l'oeuvre de Nimdihi', *Revue des Etudes islamiques*, 34, pp. 61–81.

Babb, Lawrence A. 1998. 'Rejecting Violence: Sacrifice and the Social Identity of Trading Communities', *Contributions to Indian Sociology*, 32, pp. 387–407.

Bakkarī, Sayyid Muḥammad Ma'ṣūm. 1938. *Ta'rīkh-i ma'ṣūmī (1019 AH)*, ed. U.M. Daudpota. Bombay: Maṭbā-yi Qayyima.

Baranī, Ḍiya al-Dīn. 1860–62. *Ta'rīkh-i Fīrūz Shāhī*, eds, Sayyid Aḥmad Khān and W. Nassau Lees, as *The Táríkh-i-Feroz-sháhí of Ziaa al-Din Barni, Commonly Called Ziaa-i Barni*. Calcutta: Asiatic Society of Bengal.

Barbosa, Duarte. 1918–21. *The Book of Duarte Barbosa: An Account of the Countries Bordering on the Indian Ocean and their Inhabitants, Written by Duarte Barbosa, and Completed about the Year 1518 AD, Including the Coasts of East Africa, Arabia, Persia, and Western India as far as the Kingdom of Vijayanagar*, trans. Mansel Longworth Dames, 2 Vols, Vol. 1, London: Hakluyt Society (repr. Asian Educational Services: New Delhi, Madras, 1989).

Barnes, Ruth. 1997. *Indian Block-Printed Textiles in Egypt: The Newberry Collection in the Ashmolean Museum*, 2 Vols. Oxford: Clarendon Press.

Basu, Helene. 1995. 'Muslim Shrines as Boundary Markers of a Cult Region: The Network of Sidi Saints in Western India', in Makhan Jha, ed., *Pilgrimage: Concepts, Themes, Issues and Methodology*. New Delhi: Inter-India Publications, pp. 157–69.

ṭṭūta, Ibn. 1953. *Riḥla*, trans. Mahdi Husain as *The Rehla of Ibn Battuta (India, Maldive Islands and Ceylon)*. Baroda: Oriental Institute (repr., 1976).

Beal, Samuel. 1884. *Si-yu-ki: Buddhist Records of the Western World, translated from the Chinese of Hiuen Tsiang (AD 629)*, 2 Vols. London: Kegan Paul, Trench, Trübner (repr. as *Chinese Accounts of India: Translated from the Chinese of Hiuen Tsiang*, Calcutta: Susil Gupta, 1958).

Benecheb, M. 1960. 'Ibn al-Djazarī', *Encyclopedia of Islam*, 2nd ed., Vol. 3. Leiden: Brill, p. 753.

Bhandarkar, D.R. 1912. 'Anâvâḍâ Stone Inscription of Sâraṅgadeva (Vikrama) Saṃvat 1348', *IA*, 41, pp. 20–1.

noi, Kṛṣṇarām. 1996. *Guru Jambheśvar: vividh āyām [Guru Jambheśvar: Various Aspects]*. Delhi: BR Publishers (Hindi).

Blochmann, H. 1875. 'Inscriptions from Ahmadâbâd', *IA*, 4, pp. 367–68.

Bookseller, Bhudharlāl Gaṅgjī. 1919. *Śrī Bahucarājī-no itihās [The History of Śrī Bahucarājī]*. Mehsāṇā-Bahucarājī: Author, 1919 (Gujarati).

Briggs, G.W. 1938. *Gorakhnath and the Kanphata Yogis*. London: Oxford University Press.

Bühler, Georg. 1877. *Eleven Land-grants of the Chaulukyas of Aṇhilvâd*, reprinted from *IA*, Bombay: Education Society's Press.

Bühler, Georg, E.K. Burgess, and James Burgess. 1902. 'Translation of Arisimha's Sukritasankirtana (VS 1285)', *IA*, 31, pp. 477–95.

Bukhārī, Sayyid Maḥmūd. 1964. *Ta'rīkh-i salāṭīn-i Gujarāt*, ed., S.A.I. Tirmizi. Aligarh: Muslim University.

Bukhārī, Sharaf al-Dīn. 1985. *Ṭabaqāt-i Gujarāt*, ed., M.H. Siddiqi. Baroda: M.S. University.

Burgess, James. 1876. *Report on the Antiquities of Kutch and Kathiawar, being the Result of the Second Season's Operations of the Archaeological Survey of Western India 1874–75*. London: India Museum (repr., Jam Shoro, Pakistan: Sindhi Adabi Board, 1991).

—— 1900, 1905. *The Muhammadan Architecture of Ahmadabad*, 2 Vols. London: W. Griggs & Sons.

Burgess, James and Henry Cousens. 1897. *Revised Lists of Antiquarian Remains in the Bombay Presidency*. Bombay: Archaeological Survey of India.

Campbell, James McNabb, ed. 1899. *Gujarát Population: Musalmáns and Pársis—Gazetteer of the Bombay Presidency*, Vol. 9, part 2. Bombay: Government Central Press (repr. as *Muslim and Parsi Castes and Tribes of Gujarat*, Gurgaon: Vintage Books, 1990).

Campbell, James McNabb and Bhimbhai Kirparam, eds. 1901. *Gujarát Population: Hindus*, 2 Vols, *Gazetteer of the Bombay Presidency*, Vol. 9, part 1. Bombay: Government Central Press, 1901 (repr. as *Hindu Castes and Tribes of Gujarat*, Gurgaon: Vintage Books, 1988).

Chaghatai, M.A. 1942. *Muslim Monuments of Ahmedabad through their Inscriptions*. Poona: Deccan College Research Institute.

Chakravarti, Ranabir. 2002. 'Nakhuda Nuruddin Firuz at Somanath: AD 1264', in *Trade and Traders in Early Indian Society*. Delhi: Manohar, 2002, pp. 220–42.

Chattopadhyaya, B.D. 1993. 'Historiography, History and Religious Centers: Early Medieval North India, circa AD 700–1200', in Vishakha N. Desai and Darielle Mason, eds, *Gods, Guardians and Lovers: Temple Sculptures from North*

Chattopadhyaya, B.D. 1993. *The Making of Early Medieval India*. New Delhi: Oxford University Press.

1993. 'Origin of the Rajputs: The Political, Economic and Social Processes in Early Medieval Rajasthan', in *The Making of Early Medieval India*. New Delhi: Oxford University Press, pp. 57–88.

1998. *Representing the Other? Sanskrit Sources and the Muslims (8th–14th century)*. New Delhi: Manohar.

Cohen, Richard J. 1999. 'The Apabhraṃśa *Cariu* as Courtly Poem', in Alan W. Entwistle, Carol Salomon, Heidi Pauwels and Michael C. Shapiro, eds, *Studies in Early Modern Indo-Aryan Languages, Literature and Culture*. New Delhi: Manohar, pp. 101–14.

Commissariat, M.S. 1938. *A History of Gujarat, Including a Survey of its Chief Architectural Monuments and Inscriptions*, Vol. 1: *From* AD *1297–8 to* AD *1573*. Bombay and New York: Longmans Green.

Cooke, H.R., Rev. J. Wilson, and Col. A. Walker. 1875. *Repression of Female Infanticide in the Bombay Presidency: A Compilation Report, Setting out Briefly all the Measures Taken to Repress the Crime in Gujarat and some of the Neighbouring Native States, and the Result of those Measures*. Bombay: Government Printing Press.

Cort, John E. 1990. 'Twelve Chapters from *The Guidebook to Various Pilgrimage Places*, the *Vividhatīrthakalpa* of Jinaprabhasūri', in Phyllis Granoff, ed., The *Clever Adulteress and the Faithful Wife, and Other Stories from the Jain Tradition*. Oakville, Ont.: Mosaic Press, pp. 245–90.

Cousens, Henry. 1931. *Somanātha and Other Mediaeval Temples in Kāṭhiāwād*. Calcutta: Government of India, Central Publication Branch.

Crooke, W. 1896. *The Tribes and Castes of the North-Western Provinces and Oudh*, 4 Vols. Calcutta: Office of the Superintendent of Government Printing.

al-Dabīr, Hajjī 'Abd Allāh. 1970–74. *Ẓafar al-wālih bi muẓaffar wa-ālihī: An Arabic History of Gujarat*, trans. M.F. Lokhandwala, 2 Vols. Baroda: Oriental Institute.

Daftary, Farhad. 1990. *The Ismā'īlīs: Their History and Doctrines*. Cambridge: Cambridge University Press (2nd rev. ed., 2007).

Dalal, C.D., ed. 1920. *Prācīna gurjara kāvya-saṅgraha: A Collection of Old Gujarati Poems from the 12th to the 15th Centuries*. Vol. 1. Baroda: Oriental Institute (repr. 1978).

Dar, M.I. 1953. 'Gujarat's Contribution to Gujari and Urdu', *Islamic Culture*, 27, pp. 18–36.

1959. *Literary and Cultural Activities in Gujarat under the Khaljis and the Sultanate*. Bombay: Bazm-i Isha'at, Ismail Yusuf College.

Dargāhvālā, Sayyid Imāmuddīn. 1973. *Gujarāt-nā auliyā [Saints of Gujarat]*, Vol. 1, Navsari: Author, 1973 (Gujarati).

Das, Veena. 1977. *Structure and Cognition: Aspects of Hindu Caste and Ritual*. Delhi: Oxford University Press.

Daudpota, U.M. 1970. 'Sind and Multan', in Mohammad Habib and K.A. Nizami, eds, *The Delhi Sultanat (*AD *1206–1526)*, 2nd ed., 1993. New Delhi:

Delvoye, Françoise 'Nalini'. 1994. 'Indo-Persian Literature on Art-Music: Some Historical and Technical Aspects', in Françoise 'Nalini' Delvoye, ed., *Confluence of Cultures: French Contributions to Indo-Persian Studies*. New Delhi: Manohar (repr., 1995), pp. 93–130.

2000. 'Indo-Persian Accounts on Music Patronage in the Sultanate of Gujarat', in Muzaffar Alam, Françoise 'Nalini' Delvoye, and Marc Gaborieau, eds, *The Making of Indo-Persian Culture: Indian and French Studies*. New Delhi: Manohar, pp. 253–80.

Desai, G.H. 1912. *Glossary of Castes, Tribes and Races in the Baroda State*. Baroda: Census Office.

āi, Śambhuprasād Haraprasād. 1991. *Saurāṣṭra-no itihās [History of Saurashtra]*, 3rd ed. Rajkot: Pravīṇ Prakāśan (Gujarati).

Desai, Z.A. 1956. 'On Karakhdi Bilingual Inscription of 1340', *Bulletin of the Baroda Museum and Picture Gallery*, 12, pp. 33–5.

1960. 'Muslims in the 13th Century Gujarat, as Known from Arabic Inscriptions', *JOIB*, 10(4), pp. 353–64.

1962. 'Arabic Inscriptions of the Rajput Period from Gujarat', *Epigraphia Indica, Arabic and Persian Supplement: 1961*. Delhi: Manager of Publications, pp. 1–24.

1965. 'Kūfī Epitaphs from Bhadreshwar in Gujarat', *Epigraphia Indica: Arabic and Persian Supplement*. Delhi: Manager of Publications, pp. 1–8.

1982. *Persian and Arabic Epigraphy of Gujarat*. Baroda: M.S. University.

1985. *Corpus of Persian and Arabic Inscriptions in the Museums of Gujarat*. Vadodara (Baroda): Director, Department of Museums, Gujarat State.

1989. 'The Major Dargahs of Ahmadabad', in C.W. Troll, ed., *Muslim Shrines in India: Their Character, History and Significance*. Delhi: Oxford University Press, pp. 76–97.

1991. *Malfuz Literature: As a Source of Political, Social, and Cultural History of Gujarat and Rajasthan*. Patna: Khuda Bakhsh Oriental Public Library.

1999. *Arabic, Persian and Urdu Inscriptions of West India: A Topographical List*, New Delhi: Sundeep Prakashan.

Deyell, John. 1990. *Living Without Silver: The Monetary History of Early Medieval North India*. New Delhi: Oxford University Press.

Dhaky, M.A. 1961. 'The Chronology of the Solanki Temples of Gujarat', *Journal of the Madhya Pradesh Itihas Parishad*, 3, pp. 45–8.

Digby, Simon. 1971. *War-Horse and Elephant in the Dehli Sultanate: A Study of Military Supplies*. Oxford: Orient Monographs.

1979. 'Muḥammad bin Tughluq's Last Years in Kāthiāwār and his Invasions of Thattha', *Hamdard Islamicus*, 2(1), pp. 79–88.

1986. 'The Sufi Shaikh as a Source of Authority in Mediaeval India', *Puruṣārtha: Islam et Société en Asie du Sud: Études Réunies par Marc Gaborieau*, 9, pp. 57–77.

1995. 'Illustrated Muslim Books of Omens of Gujarat or Rajasthan', in John Guy, ed., *Indian Art and Connoisseurship: Festschrift for Douglas Barrett*. Ahmedabad, New Delhi: Indira Gandhi National Centre for the Arts in association with Mapin, pp. 343–60.

2004. 'Before Timur Came: Provincialization of the Delhi Sultanate through the Fourteenth Century', *JESHO*, 47(3), pp. 298–356.

Dikshit, K.R. 1970. *Geography of Gujarat*. New Delhi: National Book Trust.

Diskalkar, D.B. 1938. 'Some Unpublished Inscriptions of the Chaulukyas of Gujarat (contd.)', *Poona Orientalist*, 2(4), pp. 222–33.

1938–41. *Inscriptions of Kathiawad*. Poona: reprinted from *New Indian Antiquary*.

Dundas, Paul. 2002. *The Jains*, 2nd ed. London and New York: Routledge.

Durlabharām, Uttamarām. 1877. *Ṭoḷakanibandha [Essay on the Ṭoḷakas]*. Ahmedabad: Author, (Gujarati).

Eaton, Richard M. 1974. 'Sufi Folk Literature and the Expansion of Indian Islam', *History of Religions*, 14(2), pp. 117–27 (repr. in *Essays on Islam and Indian History*, New Delhi: Oxford University Press, 2000, pp. 189–202).

1993. *The Rise of Islam and the Bengal Frontier, 1204–1760*. Berkeley: University of California Press (repr., New Delhi: Oxford University Press, 1997).

2000. 'Temple Desecration and Indo-Muslim States', in *Essays on Islam and Indian History*, New Delhi: Oxford University Press, 2000, pp. 94–132.

Elliot, H.M., and John Dowson. 1867. *The History of India as told by its own Historians*, 7 Vols. London: Trübner & Co. (repr. Allahabad: Kitab Mahal, 1969).

Enthoven, R.E., and S.M. Edwardes, eds. 1909. *Imperial Gazetteer of India*, Provincial Series, *Bombay Presidency*, Vols 1 and 2. Calcutta: Superintendent of Government Printing.

Eschmann, Anncharlott, Hermann Kulke, and Gaya Charan Tripathi, eds. 1978. *The Cult of Jagannath and the Regional Tradition of Orissa*. New Delhi: Manohar.

Faruqi, Shamsur Rahman. 2001. *Early Urdu Literary Culture and History*. New Delhi: Oxford University Press.

Firishta, Abu'l-Qāsim. 1829. *Ta'rīkh-i Firishta*, trans. John Briggs as *History of the Rise of the Mahomedan Power in India till the Year 1612*, 4 Vols. London: Longman, Rees, Orme, Brown and Green (repr. New Delhi: Oriental Books Reprint Corp., 1981).

Flügel, Peter. 2000. 'Protestantische und Post-Protestantische Jaina-Reformbewegungen: Zur Geschichte und Organisation der Sthānakvāsī I', *Berliner Indologische Studien*, 13–14, pp. 37–103.

Forbes, Alexander Kinloch. 1856. *Râs Mâlâ. Hindoo Annals of the Province of Goozerat in Western India*, 2 Vols. London: Richardson Brothers (repr. Gurgaon: Vintage Books, 1993).

Francis, Peter, Jr. 1986. 'Baba Ghor and the Ratanpur Rakshisha', *JESHO*, 29(2), pp. 198–204.

Gai, G.S., ed. 1990. *Annual Report on Indian Epigraphy for 1974–75*, New Delhi: Archaeological Survey of India.

ndhī, Lālacandra Bhagavān. 1939. *Jinaprabha-sūri ane sultān muhammad tughluq* [*Jinaprabha-sūrī and Sulṭān Muḥammad Tughluq*]. Lohawat-Mevāḍ: Śrī Jinahari Sāgar Sūri Jñāna Bhaṇḍār, (Gujarati).

gādhara. 1973. *Gaṅgadāsa-pratāpavilāsa-nāṭakam*, eds, Bhogilāl Jayacandbhāi Sāṇḍesarā and Paṇḍit Amṛtlāl Mohanlāl Bhojak. Baroda: Oriental Institute.

Goitein, S.D. 1954. 'From the Mediterranean to India: Documents on the Trade to India, South Arabia, and East Africa from the Eleventh and Twelfth Centuries', *Speculum*, 29(2–1), pp. 181–97.

Gordon, Stewart. 1994. 'Bhils and the Idea of a Criminal Tribe', in *Marathas, Marauders and State Formation in Eighteenth Century Central India*, Delhi: Oxford University Press, 1994, pp. 151–62.

——— 1994. *Marathas, Marauders and State Formation in Eighteenth Century Central India*. Delhi: Oxford University Press.

Habib, Mohammad, and Khaliq Ahmad Nizami, eds, 1982. *The Delhi Sultanat (AD 1206–1526)*, 2nd ed., Vol. 5, part II, *A Comprehensive History of India*. New Delhi: Indian History Congress, People's Publishing House (repr. 1993).

Hadi, Nabi. 1985. 'Tārīkh-i Ṣadr-i Jahān or Tārīkh-i Maḥmūd Shāhi', in M.H. Siddiqi, ed., *Growth of Indo-Persian Literature in Gujarat*. Baroda: M.S. University, pp. 46–51.

——— 1995. *Dictionary of Indo-Persian Literature*. Delhi: Indira Gandhi National Centre for the Arts and Abhinav Publications.

al-Hamdani, Abbas H. 1956. *The Beginnings of the Ismā'īlī Da'wa in Northern India*. Cairo: Dār al-Ma'arif.

Harlan, Lindsey. 1992. *Religion and Rajput Women: The Ethic of Protection in Contemporary Narratives*. Berkeley: University of California Press.

Hasan, Farhat. 2004. *State and Locality in Mughal India: Power Relations in Western India, c. 1572–1730*. Cambridge: Cambridge University Press.

Hazra, R.C. 1958. *Studies in the Upapurāṇas*, 2 Vols. Calcutta: Sanskrit College.

Heitzman, James. 2000. *Gifts of Power: Lordship in an Early Indian State*. New Delhi: Oxford University Press.

Hemacandra. 1915. *Dvyāśrayakāvya*, ed., A.V. Kathavate, 2 Vols. Bombay: The Department of Public Instruction.

——— 1938. *Kavyānuśāsana*, ed, R.C. Parikh and R.B. Athavale, 2 Vols. Bombay: Śrī Mahāvīra Jain Vidyālaya.

Holt, P.M. 1960. 'Ḳānṣawh al-Ghawrī', in *Encyclopaedia of Islam*, 2nd ed., Vol. 4. Leiden and London: Brill, Luzac, p. 551.

Hultszch, E. 1882. 'A Grant of Arjunadeva of Gujarat, dated 1264 AD', *IA*, 11, pp. 241–45, 377.

Ibrahim, Farhana. 2009. *Mobility, Territory and Memory: The Making of a Region in Western India*. New Delhi: Taylor & Francis.

Ismail, Ch. Mohammad and Munshi Fazil. 1921–22. 'Two Inscriptions from the

Epigraphia Indo-Moslemica. Calcutta: Government of India Central Publication Branch, pp. 2–5.

Ivanow, W. 1948. 'Satpanth', in W. Ivanow, ed., *Collectanea*. Leiden: The Ismaili Society, E.J. Brill, pp. 1–54.

Jackson, Peter. 1999. *The Delhi Sultanate: A Political and Military History*. Cambridge: Cambridge University Press.

Jain-Neubauer, Jutta. 1981. *The Stepwells of Gujarat in Art Historical Perspective*. Delhi: Abhinav Publications.

Jain, V.K. 1990. *Trade and Traders in Western India, 1000–1300*. New Delhi: Munshiram Manoharlal.

Janaki, V.A. 1980. *The Commerce of Cambay from the Earliest Period to the Nineteenth Century*. Baroda: M.S. University of Baroda.

, Baḷavant. 2000. *Svādhyāya ane saṃśodhan [Study and Research]*. Gandhinagar: Gujarat Sahitya Academy (Gujarati).

, Varṣā Gaganvihārī. 1992. *Saurāṣṭra-nā pāḷiyā, ī.s. 1500 sudhi [Hero-stones of Saurashtra, to CE 1500]*. Ahmedabad: Author (Gujarati).

Jayasiṃha Sūri. 1920. *Hammīra-mada-mardana*, ed., C.D. Dalal, Baroda: Central Library.

——— 1926. *Kumarapālabhūpālacaritram mahākāvyam*, ed., Kṣāntivijaya Gaṇi, Bombay: Nirṇayasāgar Mudraṇa.

Jhaveri, Mansukhlal. 1978. *History of Gujarati Literature*, New Delhi: Sahitya Akademi.

ānī, Minhāj al-Dīn Abū 'Umar 'Uthmān b. Sirāj al-Dīn. 1872–81. *Ṭabaqāt-i Nāṣirī*, trans. H.G. Raverty. Calcutta: Asiatic Society of Bengal.

Kassam, Tazim R. 1995. *Songs of Wisdom and Circles of Dance: Hymns of the Satpanth Ismā'īlī Muslim Saint, Pīr Shams*. Albany: SUNY Press.

Katti, M.N., ed. 1998. *Annual Report on Indian Epigraphy for 1986–87*, New Delhi: Archaeological Survey of India.

Khakee, Gulshan. 1981. 'The "Das Avatara" of Pir Shams as Linguistic and Literacy Evidence of the Early Development of Ismailism in Sind', in Hamida Khuhro. ed., *Sind through the Centuries*. Karachi: Oxford University Press, pp. 143–55.

Khakhar, D.P. 1879. *Report on the Architectural and Archaeological Remains in the Provinces of Kachh*. Bombay: Government Central Press.

——— 1878. 'History of the Kânphâṭâs of Kachh', *IA*, 7, pp. 47–53.

n, 'Alī Muḥammad. 1927–28. *Mir'āt-i Aḥmadī: A Persian History of Gujarat*, ed., Syed Nawab Ali. Baroda: Oriental Institute (Persian).

——— 1928. *Mir'āt-i Aḥmadī: Supplement*, trans. Syed Nawab Ali and C.N. Seddon. Baroda: Oriental Institute.

——— 1930. *Khātima-yi Mir'āt-i Aḥmadī*, ed., Syed Nawab Ali. Baroda: Oriental Institute (Persian).

——— 1835. *Mir'āt-i Aḥmadī*, trans. James Bird as *The Political and Statistical History of Gujarat*. London: Richard Bentley (repr. New Delhi: Asian

1965. *Mir'āt-i-Aḥmadī: A Persian History of Gujarat*, trans. M.F. Lokhandwala. Baroda: Oriental Institute.

Khan, Dominique-Sila. 1997. 'The Coming of Nikalank Avatar: A Messianic Theme in Some Sectarian Traditions of North-Western India', *Journal of Indian Philosophy*, 25, pp. 401–26.

1997. *Conversion and Shifting Identities: Ramdev Pir and the Ismailis in Rajasthan*. Delhi: Manohar.

Khare, G.H. 1966. 'Dravyapariksha of Thakkura Pheru—A Study', *Journal of the Numismatic Society of India*, 28, pp. 25–37.

Kiple, Kenneth F., ed. 1993. *The Cambridge World History of Human Disease*. Cambridge: Cambridge University Press.

Kirste, J. 1892. 'Inscriptions from Northern Gujarat', *EI*, 2, pp. 24–34.

Kolff, Dirk H.A. 1990. *Naukar, Rajput and Sepoy: The Ethnohistory of the Military Labour Market in Hindustan, 1450–1850*. Cambridge: Cambridge University Press.

Kopf, L. 1960. 'al-Damīrī', *Encyclopaedia of Islam*, 2nd ed, Vol. 2. Leiden: Brill, p. 107.

Krishnan, K.G., ed. 1986. *Annual Report on Indian Epigraphy for 1977–78*, New Delhi: Archaeological Survey of India.

ed. 1987. *Annual Report on Indian Epigraphy for 1976–77*, New Delhi: Archaeological Survey of India.

ed. 1987. *Annual Report on Indian Epigraphy for 1978–79*. New Delhi: Archaeological Survey of India.

Lambourn, Elizabeth. 2001. 'A Collection of Merits': Architectural Influences in the Early Friday Mosque and Kazaruni Tomb Complex at Cambay, Gujarat', *South Asian Studies*, 17, pp. 117–49.

Lassen, C.L. 1873. 'Papers on Satrunjaya and the Jains III', *IA*, 2, pp. 193–200.

Ludden, David. 1985. *Peasant History in South India*. Princeton, N.J.: Princeton University Press.

MacLean, Derryl N. 1989. *Religion and Society in Arab Sind*. Leiden: E.J. Brill.

Macmurdo, James. 1834. 'Dissertation on the River Indus', *JRAS*, 1, pp. 20–44.

1977. *The Peninsula of Gujarat in the Early Nineteenth Century (Journal of a Route through the Peninsula of Guzeraut in the year 1809 and 1810)*, ed. S.C. Ghosh, New Delhi: Sterling.

Mahetā, R.N. 1979. *Cāmpāner: ek adhyayana [Cāmpāner: A Study]*, Baroda: M.S. University, (Gujarati).

Mahetā, R.N., and S.G. Kāṅṭāvālā. 1979. 'Bhoj-nī vāv-no śilālekha [An inscription from the step-well at Bhoj]', *Svādhyāya*, 16(2), pp. 192–6 (Gujarati).

Majmudar, M.R. 1965. *Cultural History of Gujarat (From Early Times to Pre-British Period)*. Bombay: Popular Prakashan.

Major, R.H., ed. 1857. *India in the Fifteenth Century, Being a Collection of Narratives of Voyages to India in the Century Preceding the Portuguese Discovery of the Cape of Good Hope; from Latin, Persian, Russian and Italian Sources.* London: Hakluyt Society.

Majumdar, A.K. 1956. *The Chaulukyas of Gujarat.* Bombay: Bharatiya Vidya Bhavan.

Mallison, F. 1980. 'The Cult of Sudāmā in Porbandar-Sudāmāpuri (II)', *JOIB*, 29(3–4), pp. 216–23.

1983. 'Development of Early Krishnaism in Gujarat, Viṣṇu-Raṇchod-Kṛṣṇa', in Monika Thiel-Horstmann. ed., *Bhakti in Current Research, 1979–1982: Proceedings of the Second International Conference on Early Devotional Literature in New Indo-Aryan Languages, St. Augustin, 19–21 March 1982.* Berlin: Dietrich Reiner Verlag, pp. 245–55.

1986. *Au point du jour: les Prabhātiyāṃ de Narasiṃha Mahetā, poète et saint vishnouite du Gujarāt (Xve siecle)*. Paris: Ecole Française d'Extrême-Orient.

1989. 'Hinduism as seen by the Nizārī Ismā'īlī Missionaries of Western India: The Evidence of the *Ginān*', in G.D. Sontheimer and Hermann Kulke, eds, *Hinduism Reconsidered.* New Delhi: South Asia Institute, pp. 93–103.

1991. 'Lorsque Raṇachoḍarāya quitte Dwarka pour Dakor, ou Comment Dvārakānātha prit la succession de Ḍaṅkanātha', in Diana Eck and Françoise Mallison, eds, *Devotion Divine: Studies in Honour of Charlotte Vaudeville.* Paris: Forsten, École Française d'Extrême-Orient, pp. 196–208.

1995. 'Early Kṛṣṇa *Bhakti* in Gujarat: The Evidence of Old Gujarati Texts Recently Brought to Light', in Alan W. Entwistle and Françoise Mallison, eds, *Studies in South Asian Devotional Literature, Research Papers 1988–1991*. Delhi: Manohar, pp. 50–64.

2003. 'Saints and Sacred Places in Saurashtra and Kutch: The Cases of the Naklaṃki Cult and the Jakhs', in Phyllis Granoff and Koichi Shinohara, eds, *Pilgrims, Patrons, and Place: Localizing Sanctity in Asian Religions.* Georgetown: University of British Columbia Press, pp. 332–49.

Mallison, F. and Z. Moir. 1996. '"Recontrer l'Absolu, O Ami": Un Hymne Commun aux Hindous Tantriques et aux Musulmans Ismaeliens du Saurashtra (Gujarat)', *Puruṣārtha*, 19, pp. 265–76.

Martin, Nancy M. 1999. 'Mira Janma Patri and Other Tales of Resistance and Appropriation', in Rajendra Joshi and N. K. Singhi, eds, *Religion, Ritual and Royalty.* Jaipur: Rawat Press, pp. 227–61.

al-Mas'ūdī, Abu'l-Ḥasan 'Alī. 1841. *Murūj al-dhahab wa ma'ādin al-jawhar*, trans. Aloys Sprenger as *El-Mas'údí's Historical Encyclopaedia.* London: Oriental Translation Fund.

Mehta, R.N. 1965. '*Kaumārikā Khaṇḍa*—A Study', *JMSUB*, 14, pp. 39–48.

Mehta, R.N., and S.G. Kantawala. 1973. 'Two legends from the *Skanda Purāṇa*—a Study', *Purāṇa*, 15(1), pp. 124–32.

Merutuṅgācārya. 1933, 1936, 1955. *Prabandhacintāmaṇi*, ed. Jinavijaya Muni, 3 Vols. Santiniketan, Calcutta and Ahmedabad: Singhi Jain Series.

1901. *Prabandhacintāmaṇi, or Wishing-stone of Narratives*, trans. C.H. Tawney. Calcutta: Asiatic Society.

Minorsky, V. 1937. *Ḥudūd al-ʿĀlam: 'The Regions of the World': A Persian Geography 372 AH–982 AD*. London: Luzac (2nd rev. ed., C.E. Bosworth, 1970).

Misra, S.C. 1963. *The Rise of Muslim Power in Gujarat: A History of Gujarat from 1298 to 1442*. London: Asia Publishing House.

1964. *Muslim Communities in Gujarat: Preliminary Studies in their History and Social Organization*. New York: Asia Publishing House.

Moir, Z. 2006. 'The Gujari Ginans of Nur Muhammad Shah', unpublished paper.

Munshi, K.M. 1935. *Gujarāta and its Literature: A Survey from the Earliest Times*. London and New York: Longmans Green.

1952. *Somanatha: The Shrine Eternal*. Bombay: Bharatiya Vidya Bhavan.

1958. *Glory that was Gurjara-deśa*, 2 Vols, Bombay: Bharatiya Vidya Bhavan.

Nadwī, Sayyid Sulaymān. 1929. *Arab-o-hind ke taʿalluqāt [Relations between the Arab Lands and India]*. Allahabad: Hindustani Akaydami (Urdu).

gar, Ambāśaṅkar and Alābakhsh Shaikh, eds. 1991. *Gujarāt kī hindustānī kāvyadhārā*. Ahmedabad: Gujarat Vidyapith (Hindi).

Naik, C.R. 1964. 'Cultivation of the Persian Language and Literature by the Nagaras of Gujarat', *JOIB*, 14, pp. 125–33.

Nanavati, J.M., R.N. Mehta, and S.N. Chowdhary. 1971. *Somnath, 1956: Being a Report of Excavations*. Ahmedabad and Baroda: Department of Archaeology, Gujarat State; Department of Archaeology and Ancient History, M.S. University of Baroda.

ñjīyāṇī, Sacedīnā. 1892. *Khojā vṛattānt [Account of the Khojas]*. Ahmedabad: Author (Gujarati).

Narang, Satya Pal. 1972. *Hemachandra's Dvyāśrayakāvya: A Literary and Cultural Study*. New Delhi: Munshiram Manoharlal.

Nazim, M. 1937. 'Inscriptions from the Bombay Presidency', in G. Yazdani, ed., *Epigraphia Indo-Moslemica (1933–34), Supplement*. Delhi: Manager of Publications, pp. 1–61.

Nazim, Muhammad. 1931. *The Life and Times of Sulṭān Maḥmūd of Ghazna*. Cambridge: Cambridge University Press (repr. New Delhi: Munshiram Manoharlal, 1971).

mdihī, 'Abd al-Karīm. 16th century. *Ṭabaqāt-i Maḥmūd Shāhī*. Cambridge University Library, Ms. Eton (Pote) 160.

r Muḥammad Shāh, Sayyid. 1962. *Satvenī-jī vel*, ed., Laljī Devarāj. Bombay: Laljī Devarāj (Gujarati).

Ojha, G.S. and Georg Bühler, eds. 1888, 1892–4. *EI*. Calcutta: Superintendent of Government Printing, 2 Vols.

Oza, Vajeshankar Gourishankar. 1887 [1885?]. *Bhāvanagar prācina śodha saṅgraha*, Vol. 1. Bhavnagar: Daravāri chāpakhānāmānī chāiyuin (Gujarati).

, ed. 1889. *Corpus Inscriptionum Bhavanagari: Being a Selection of Arabic and Persian Inscriptions Collected by the Antiquarian Department, Bhavnagar State*

Bhavnagar, Bombay: Education Society (repr. New Delhi: Kumar Brothers, 1971).

Padmanābha. 1953. *Kānhaḍade prabandha (15th century)*, ed. K.B. Vyas. Jaipur: Rājasthān Purātattva Mandir.

1991. *Kānhaḍade prabandha [India's Greatest Patriotic Saga of Medieval Times]*, trans. V.S. Bhatnagar. New Delhi: Aditya Prakashan.

kh, Pravīṇcandra and Bhāratī Shelat. 1991. *Gujarāt-nā abhilekho: svādhyāy ane samīkṣā [Inscriptions of Gujarat: Study and Analysis]*. Ahmedabad: B.J. Institute (Gujarati).

Parmar, Bhabhooti Mal N. 1990. *Cultural and Critical Study of Srimala Purana*. Jodhpur: J.S. Gahlot Research Institute.

Patel, Alka. 2004. *Building Communities in Gujarāt: Architecture and Society during the 12th through 14th centuries*. Leiden and Boston: Brill.

Patel, Alka. 2004. 'Architectural Histories Entwined: The Rudra-Mahalaya/ Congregational Mosque of Siddhpur, Gujarat', *The Journal of the Society of Architectural Historians*, 63(2), pp. 144–63.

el, Ḍāhyābhāi Lakṣmaṇdās. 1906. *Vaḍnagarā kaṇbīnī utpatti ane temno ācār-vicār [The Origin of the Vaḍnagarā Kaṇbīs and their Customs]*. Ahmedabad: Author (Gujarati).

el, Gokaḷdās Somābhāi and Aśokbhāi Gokaḷdās Paṭel. 1986. *History of the Pātīdārs of Gujarat*. Ahmedabad: Author (Gujarati).

Pearson, M.N. 1976. *Merchants and Rulers of Gujarat: The Response to the Portuguese in the Sixteenth Century*. New Delhi: Munshiram Manoharlal.

Peterson, P. 1905. *A Collection of Prakrit and Sanskrit Inscriptions*. Bhavnagar: Bhavnagar Archaeological Department.

Pfleiderer, Beatrix. 1984. 'Mira Datar Dargah: The Psychiatry of a Muslim Shrine', in Imtiaz Ahmad, ed., *Ritual and Religion among Muslims in India*. New Delhi: Manohar, pp. 195–234.

Pocock, D.F. 1981. 'The Vocation and Avocations of the Guggali Brahmans of Dvaraka', *Contributions to Indian Sociology*, 15, pp. 321–36.

Pollock, Sheldon. 1998. 'India in the Vernacular Millennium: Literary Culture and Polity, 1000–1500', *Daedalus* 127(3), pp. 41–73.

Polo, Marco. 1993. *The Travels of Marco Polo*, trans. Henry Yule. New York: Dover.

Porter, Roy and W.F. Bynum, eds. 1993. *Companion Encyclopedia to the History of Medicine*. London and New York: Routledge.

Pramar, V.S. 1985. 'The Effects of Trade and Urbanization on the Architecture of Gujarat', in V.K. Chavda, ed., *Studies in Trade and Urbanization in Western India*. Baroda: M.S. University, pp. 85–93.

āṇvallav, Bhagavānjī. 1881. *Corāśī vaiśṇav-nī vārtā*. Amdāvād: Bukselar Maganlāl Varajbhuṣaṇ (Gujarati).

Prasad Sahai, Nandita. 2006. *Politics of Patronage and Protest: The State, Society, and Artisans in Early Modern Rajasthan*. New Delhi: Oxford University Press.

Puri, B.N. 1986. *The History of the Gurjara Pratihāras*, 2nd rev. ed. Delhi: Munshiram Manoharlal.

Purohit, Narasiṃharām Durlabharām. 1877. *Audicya ṭoḷakiyā jñātinī sthiti [The Condition of the Audicya Ṭoḷakiyā Caste]*. Amdāvād: Candrodaya Press (Gujarati).

ni', Mīr Sayyid 'Alī. 1942. *Ta'rīkh-i Muẓaffar Shāhī*, ed. and trans. into Gujarāti by Sayyid Abū Ẓafar Nadwī and C.R. Naik. Ahmedabad: Gujarat Vernacular Society.

Quraishi, M.A. 1972. *Muslim Education and Learning in Gujarat (1297–1758)*. Baroda: Faculty of Education and Psychology, M.S. University.

Rabitoy, Neil. 1974. 'Administrative Modernization and the Bhats of British Gujarat, 1800–1820', *IESHR*, 11(1), pp. 46–73.

Rahmān, Abdul. 1998. *The Saṃdeśarāsaka of Abdul Rahman*, trans. C.M. Mayrhofer. Delhi: Motilal Banarsidass.

Raikar, Yashavant A. 1962. 'Śrī Cakradhara: A Mediaeval Saint from Gujarāt', *JOIB*, 12(2), pp. 113–18.

jyaguru, Nirañjan. 1995. *Bījamārgī gupt pāṭ-upāsana ane mahāpanthī santonī bhajanvāṇī [The Secret Worship of the Bījamārga and the Devotional Compositions of Mahāpanthī Saints]*. Gandhinagar: Gujarat Sahitya Academy (Gujarati).

Rangarajan, Haripriya. 1990. *Spread of Vaiṣṇavism in Gujarat up to 1600 AD (A Study with Special Reference to the Iconic Forms of Viṣṇu)*. Bombay and New Delhi: Somaiya Publications.

Rawlinson, H.G. 1924. 'Alexander Kinloch Forbes: A Memoir', in H.G. Rawlinson, edn, *Râs Mâlâ: Hindoo Annals of the Province of Goozerat in Western India*. London: Humphrey Milford, pp. ix–xvii.

Raychaudhuri, H.C. 1936. *Materials for the Study of the Early History of the Vaiṣṇava Sect*, 2nd rev. edn Calcutta: University of Calcutta.

ādā, Vikramsiṃh Bharatsiṃh. 1995. *Cūḍāsamā rājavaṃśa-no itihās, cūḍāsamā rājavaṃśa-nī praśasti kavitā, cūḍāsamā, sarvaiyā ane rāyjādā śākhā-nāṃ itihās sāthe [The History of the Cūḍāsamā Dynasty, its Eulogy, with the History of the Cūḍāsamā, Sarvaiyā and Rāyjādā Branches]*. Rajkot: Dr. Vikramsinh B. Rayjada (Gujarati).

Richards, J.F., ed. 1998. *Kingship and Authority in South Asia*. Delhi: Oxford University Press.

Rigopoulos, A. 1998. *Dattātreya: The Immortal Guru, Yogin, and Avatāra: A Study of the Transformative and Inclusive Character of a Multi-faceted Hindu Deity*. Albany: State University of New York Press.

Rocher, Ludo, ed. 1986. *The Purāṇas*. Wiesbaden: Otto Harrassowitz.

Sachau, E. 1910. *Alberuni's India: An Account of the Religion, Philosophy, Literature, Geography, Chronology, Astronomy, Customs, Laws and Astrology of India about AD 1030*. London: Kegan Paul, Trench, Trübner (repr., 1964).

Sandesara, B.J. 1953. *Literary Circle of Mahāmātya Vastupāla and its Contribution to Sanskrit Literature*, ed. Muni Jinavijaya. Bombay: Bharatiya Vidya Bhavan.

Sandesara, B.J. and P.N. Mehta, eds. 1964. *Mallapurāṇam: A Rare Sanskrit Text on Indian Wrestling Especially as Practised by the Jyeṣṭhimallas*. Baroda: Oriental Institute.

Sangari, Kumkum. 2000. 'Tracing Akbar: Hagiographies, Popular Narrative Traditions and the Subject of Conversion', in Neera Chandhoke, ed., *Mapping Histories: Essays Presented to Ravinder Kumar*. New Delhi: Tulika, pp. 61–103.

Sankalia, H.D. 1949. *Studies in the Historical and Cultural Geography and Ethnography of Gujarat: Places and Peoples in Inscriptions of Gujarat: 300 BC–1300 AD*. Poona: Deccan College.

Sarkar, Sumit. 1989. 'The Kalki-Avatar of Bikrampur: A Village Scandal in Early Twentieth Century Bengal', in Ranajit Guha, ed., *Subaltern Studies* 6. New Delhi: Oxford University Press, 1989, 1–53.

Sarmadee, Shahab, ed., 1971. *Ghunyāt al-munya*. New Delhi: Asia Publishing House.

1978. *The* Ghunyat-ul-Munya*: The Earliest Known Persian Work on Indian Music*, Bombay: Asia Publishing House, 1978.

āṇanda. 1892. *Jagaḍūcarita*, ed. Georg Bühler as *The Jagaḍûcharita of Sarvâṇanda, A Historical Romance from Gujarât*. Vienna: Sitzungberichte der Kais. Akademie der Wissenschaften in Wien.

strī, Bhadraśaṅkar Jayaśaṅkar. 1930. 'Khambhāt-nī vaḍvā-nī sundar vāv-no prācīn praśasti lekha [An Ancient Inscription from the Beautiful Step-well at Vaḍvā in Khambhāt]', *Buddhiprakāś*, 77(1), pp. 27–32 (Gujarati).

strī, Hariprasād. 1955. 'Aḍālaj-nī vāv-no śilālekh, V.S. 1555 [The Adalaj Step-well Inscription, VS 1555]', *Buddhiprakāś*, 104(1955), pp. 19–23 (Gujarati).

strī, Hariśaṅkar Prabhāśaṅkar. 1972. 'Prabhās-nā vājā rājā śivarāja-nā samay-no saṃvat 1451 (ī.s. 1395)-no ek aprasiddha śilālekha [An Unpublished Inscription from VS 1451 (1395 CE) of the Time of the Vājā ruler Śivarāja of Prabhās]', *Svādhyāya*, 9(2), pp. 227–31 (Gujarati).

strī, Revāśaṅkar. 1922. *Unevāl jñāti-no itihās [History of the Unevāl Caste]*. Ahmadabad: Śrī Unevāl Sevā Samāj (Gujarati)

Shackle, Christopher and Zawahir Moir. 1992. *Ismaili Hymns from South Asia: An Introduction to the Ginans*. London: SOAS (rev. edn, Richmond, Surrey: Curzon, 2000).

Shah, A.M. and R.S. Shroff. 1959. 'The Vahīvancā Bāroṭs of Gujarat: A Caste of Genealogists and Mythographers', in Milton Singer, ed., *Traditional India: Structure and Change*. Philadelphia: The American Folklore Society, pp. 40–70 (repr. Jaipur: Rawat Publishers, 1975).

Shah, U.P. 1960. *Sculptures from Śāmalājī and Rodā*. Baroda: Government Press.

Shastri, H.G. 1979. *Historical Inscriptions of Gujarat*, Vol. 4, *The Sultanate Period*. Bombay: Forbes Gujarati Sabha (Gujarati with Sanskrit and Gujarati inscriptions).

Sheikh, Samira. 2007. 'Religious Traditions and Early Ismā'īlī History in Western India: Some Historical Perspectives on Satpanthī Literature and the Gināns', in Tazim Kassam and Françoise Mallison, eds, *Gināns: Texts and Contexts: Essays on Ismaili Hymns from South Asia in Honour of Zawahir Moir*. New Delhi: Matrix, pp. 149–67.

—— 2008. 'Alliance, Genealogy and Political Power: The Cūḍāsamās of Junagadh and the Sultans of Gujarat', *Medieval History Journal*, 11(1), pp. 29–61.

Shokoohy, Mehrdad. 1986. *Rajasthan*. London: Lund Humphries.

Shokoohy, Mehrdad, Manijeh Bayani-Wolpert, and Natalie Shokoohy. 1988. *Bhadreśvar: The Oldest Islamic Monuments in India*. Leiden: E.J. Brill.

Siddiqi, M.H., ed. 1985. *The Growth of Indo-Persian Literature in Gujarat*. Baroda: Department of Persian, Arabic and Urdu. Baroda: M.S. University of Baroda.

Sikandar b. Muḥammad. 1886. *Mir'āt-i Sikandarī*, part trans. by E. C. Bayley in *The Local Muhammadan Dynasties: Gujarát*. London: W.H. Allen (rev. ed., Nagendra Singh, Delhi: S. Chand, 1970).

Sikandar b. Muḥammad, Manjhu Gujarātī. 1961. *Mir'āt-i Sikandarī*, ed. S.C. Misra and M.L. Rahman as *The Mir'āt-i-Sikandarī: A History of Gujarat from the Inception of the Dynasty of the Sultans of Gujarat to the Conquest of Gujarat by Akbar of Shaikh Sikandar ibn Muḥammad urf Manjhu ibn Akbar*. Baroda: M.S. University.

—— no date (1890s). *Mir'āt-i Sikandarī*, trans. Fazlullah Lutfullah Faridi as *Mirati Sikandari*. Dharampur: Education Society's Press (repr Gurgaon: Vintage Books, 1990).

Singh, R.L. 1971. *India: A Regional Geography*. Varanasi: National Geographic Society of India.

Sinha Kapur, Nandini. 2002. *State Formation in Rajasthan: Mewar During the Seventh-Fifteenth Centuries*. New Delhi: Manohar.

Sircar, D.C. 1942, 1983. *Select Inscriptions Bearing upon Indian History and Civilization from 6–18th Century* AD, 2 Vols. Calcutta: University of Calcutta (Vol. 1), and New Delhi: Motilal Banarsidass (Vol. 2).

Sircar, D.C. 1961–2. 'Veraval Inscription of Chalukya Vaghela Arjuna, 1264 AD', *EI*, 34(3), pp. 141 ff.

Sirhindī, Yaḥyā b. Aḥmad b. 'Abd Allāh. 1932. *Ta'rīkh-i Mubārak Shāhī*, trans. K.K. Basu. Baroda: Oriental Institute.

Someśvaradeva. 1883. *Kīrtikaumudī*, ed., A.V. Kathavate as *Kīrtikaumudī: A Life of Vastupāla, a Minister of Lavaṇaprasāda and Vīradhavala Vāghelā*. Bombay: Government Central Book Depot.

Spate, O.H.K. and A.T.A. Learmonth. 1967. *India and Pakistan: A General and Regional Geography*. London: Methuen.

Spencer, George W. 1968. 'Temple Moneylending and Livestock Distribution', *IESHR*, 5(3), pp. 277–93.

Sreenivasan, Ramya. 2007. *The Many Lives of a Rajput Queen: Heroic Pasts in India 1500–1900*. Seattle: University of Washington Press.

Srinivasan, P.R., ed. 1986. *Annual Report on Indian Epigraphy for 1975–76*. New Delhi: Archaeological Survey of India.

Srivastava, Vinay Kumar. 1997. *Religious Renunciation of a Pastoral People*. Delhi: Oxford University Press.

Stein, Burton. 1977. 'Circulation and the Historical Geography of Tamil Country', *JAS*, 37(1), pp. 7–26.

1985. 'State Formation and Economy Reconsidered: Part One', *MAS*, 19(3), pp. 387–413.

Stewart, Tony K. 2001. 'In Search of Equivalence: Conceiving Muslim-Hindu Encounter through Translation Theory', *History of Religions* 40(3), pp. 260–87.

Stietencron, Heinrich von. 1966. *Indische Sonnenpriester: Sāmba und die Śākadvīpīya-Brāhmaṇa*. Wiesbaden: Otto Harrassowitz.

Subhan, Abdus. 1960. 'Malik Ayāz', *Encyclopaedia of Islam*, 2nd edn, Vol. 6, p. 269.

ā, Jīvarām Durlabhajī and M.M. Vyās. 1917. *Śrī girinārāyaṇ jñāti-nī unnati tathā utpatti [The Progress and Origin of the Śrī Girinārāyaṇ Caste]*, Bombay: Authors (Gujarati).

Talbot, Cynthia. 2001. *Precolonial India in Practice: Society, Region and Identity in Medieval Andhra*. New Delhi: Oxford University Press.

Tambs-Lyche, Harald. 1997. *Power, Profit and Poetry: Traditional Society in Kathiawar, Western India*. New Delhi: Manohar.

Tessitori, L.P., ed. 1919. *Bardic and Historical Survey of Rajasthan: Velī Krisana Rukamaṇī rī Rāthorā Rāja Prithī Rāja rī Kahī*. Calcutta: Asiatic Society.

Thapar, Romila. 1981. 'Death and the Hero', in S.C. Humphreys and Helen King, eds, *Mortality and Immortality: The Anthropology and Archaeology of Death*. London: Academic Press, pp. 293–315.

2004. *Somanatha: The Many Voices of a History*. New Delhi: Viking Penguin.

Thattawī, Mīr 'Alī Shīr Qāni'. 1971. *Tuḥfat al-kirām*, ed., Sayyid Ḥusām al-Dīn Rāshidī. Hyderabad (Pakistan): Sindī Adabī Board.

Thompson, Gordon Ross. 1987. 'Music and Values in Gujarati-speaking Western India', PhD, University of California, Los Angeles.

Thoothi, N.A. 1935. *The Vaishṇavas of Gujarat: Being a Study in Methods of Investigation of Social Phenomena*. Calcutta and London: Longmans Green.

Tirmizi, S.A.I. 1968. *Some Aspects of Medieval Gujarat*. Delhi: Munshiram Manoharlal.

1993. 'Gujarat and Khandesh', in Mohammad Habib and K.A. Nizami, eds, *The Delhi Sultanat (AD 1206–1526)*. New Delhi: Indian History Congress, People's Publishing House, pp. 846–98.

Tod, James. 1829–32. *Annals and Antiquities of Rajast'han, or the Central and Western Rajpoot States of India*, 3 Vols. London: Smith, Elder & Co (repr., Delhi: Low Price Publications, 1990).

1839. *Travels in Western India: Embracing a Visit to the Sacred Mounts of the Jains, and the Most Celebrated Shrines of Hindu Faith between Rajpootana and the Indus, with an Account of the Ancient City of Nehrwalla*. London:

W.H. Allen & Co., 1839 (repr., New Delhi: Munshiram Manoharlal Publishers, 1997).

Trivedi, R.K. 1965. *Census of India: 1961*, Vol. 5, *Gujarat*, Part VII-B, *Fairs and Festivals*. Delhi: The Manager of Publications.

, 'Abd al-Ḥusayn. 1988. *Ta'rīkh-i Maḥmūd Shāhī*, ed. S.C. Misra. Baroda: M.S. University.

Udayarāja. 1956. *Rājavinodamahākāvyam or Maḥmūda-suratrāṇa-carita*, ed., G.N. Bahura. Jaipur: Rajasthan Oriental Research Institute.

Vallabhajī, Ācārya Girjāśaṅkara. 1933, 1935, 1942. *Gujarata-nā aitihāsika lekho [Historical Inscriptions of Gujarat]*, 3 Vols. Bombay: Śrī Forbes Gujarati Sabha (Gujarati).

van Skyhawk, H. 1989. 'Sufi Influence in the *Ekanāthī-bhāgavat*', in R.S. McGregor, ed., *Devotional Literature in South Asia, Current Research, 1985–1988*. Cambridge: Cambridge University Press, pp. 67–79.

Vaudeville, C. 1999. 'Braj Lost and Found', in Vasudha Dalmia, ed., *Myths, Saints and Legends of Medieval India*. New Delhi: Oxford University Press, pp. 47–71.

1999. 'The Cowherd God in Ancient India', in Vasudha Dalmia, ed., *Myths, Saints and Legends in Medieval India*. New Delhi: Oxford University Press, pp. 17–46.

1999. *Myths, Saints and Legends in Medieval India*, ed. Vasudha Dalmia, New Delhi: Oxford University Press.

Velankar, H.D. 1953. 'Maṇḍalīka, the Last Great King of Independent Saurāṣṭra', *Bhāratīya Vidyā*, 14, pp. 36–61.

1954. 'Maṇḍalīka Mahākāvya of Gaṅgādhara Kavi', *Bhāratīya Vidyā*, 15(1), pp. 35–57.

1954. 'Śrī-gaṅgādharakavi-kṛta śrī-maṇḍalīka-mahākāvyam', *Bhāratīya Vidyā*, 15(2), pp. 13–40.

s, Kalyāṇjī Raṇchoḍjī. 1917. *Basobāvan vaiṣṇav-nī vārtā [252 anecdotes of Vaiṣṇava devotees for the Puṣṭimārga sect]*, 3rd ed. Ahmedabad: Prajāhitārtha Mudralaya.

, Mīr Abū Turāb. 1909. *Ta'rīkh-i Gujarāt*, ed., E. Denison Ross. Calcutta: The Asiatic Society of Bengal.

Watson, J.W. 1875. 'Sketch of the Kathis, Especially those of the Tribe of Khachar and House of Chotila', *IA*, 4, pp. 321–6.

1876. *History of Gujarát (Musalmán Period, AD 1297–1760)* in James McNabb Campbell, ed., *Gazetteer of the Bombay Presidency*, Vol. 1, part 1. Bombay: Government Central Press [repr. as *History of Gujarat (Ancient, Medieval, Modern)*, Gurgaon: Vintage Books, 1986].

1880. *The Statistical Account of Junagadh: Being the Junagadh Contribution to the Kathiawar Portion of the Bombay Gazetteer*. Bombay: Government Central Press.

____ 1884. *Gazetteer of the Bombay Presidency*, Vol. 8: *Kathiawar*. Bombay: Government Central Press.

Wilberforce-Bell, H. 1916. *History of Kathiawad from the Earliest Times*. London: W. Heinemann.

Williams, L.F. Rushbrook. 1958. *Black Hills: Kutch in History and Legend*. London: Weidenfeld and Nicolson.

Wink, Andre. 1990, 1997, 2004. *Al-Hind: The Making of the Indo-Islamic World*, 3 Vols, Vol. 1: *Early Medieval India and the Expansion of Islam, Seventh to Eleventh Centuries*, New Delhi: OUP; Vol. 2: *The Slave Kings and the Islamic Conquest, 11th-13th Centuries*, Leiden: Brill; Vol. 3: *Indo-Islamic Societies, 11th–13th Centuries*, Leiden: Brill.

Wood, John R. 1984. 'British Versus Princely Legacies and the Political Integration of Gujarat', *JAS*, 44(1), pp. 65–99.

Yagnik, Achyut and Suchitra Sheth. 2005. *The Shaping of Modern Gujarat: Plurality, Hindutva and Beyond*. Delhi: Penguin Books.

Yashaschandra, Sitanshu. 2003. 'From Hemacandra to *Hind Svarāj*: Region and Power in Gujarati Literary Culture', in Sheldon Pollock, ed., *Literary Cultures in History: Reconstructions from South Asia*. Berkeley: University of California Press, pp. 567–611.

Yazdani, G., ed. 1916. *Epigraphia Indo-Moslemica* (1915–16). Delhi: Department of Archaeology.

Yazdani, G. and R.G. Gyani. 1944. *Important Inscriptions from the Baroda State*, Vol. 2: *Muslim Inscriptions*. Baroda: Baroda State Press.

Zaki, M. 1987. *Arab Accounts of India (During the Fourteenth Century)*. Delhi: Idārah-i Adabiyāt-i Delli.

Ziegler, Norman P. 1998. 'Rajput Loyalties during the Mughal Period', in J.F. Richards, ed., Kingship *and Authority in South Asia*. Delhi: Oxford University Press, pp. 242–84.

Index

107–09, 111, 118–19, 125n36, 158, 161, 172–3, 208, 211, 213–14. *See also* Cāraṇs, Bhāṭs, genealogists

Rajpipla, 72, 106
Rajput, 3–6, 13–19, 21, 36, 41–2, 54–5, 58*n*73, 68–70, 81, 82, 87, 95*n*15, 102, 104, 106–8, 119, 126*n*48, 130, 139, 142, 147–8, 151, 155–6, 160–6, 172–3, 183*n*187, 189, 194, 196–7, 200–1, 203, 216–27, 220, 225–6
Pūrbiyā Rājpūts, 12
Rajputization, 43, 139, 152, 158
Rakhyal, in Ahmadabad, 73
ma, Rāmacandra, 58, 198, 200
mānuja, 138
mdev Pīr, 149, 161, 163, 166, 168, 174, 183*n*184
achoḍa. *See* Kṛṣṇa
amalla chanda, 158, 208
mal (ruler of Idar), 72
Rann of Kachchh, 27, 29–33, 36–8, 102, 113, 157
Ranpur, 103–4
, love song genre, 208
rakūṭas, 49, 52, 78
Rasulabad, 10
Ratanpur, 155
hoḍs, 157
Dhandhal, 102
of Idar, 67–9
Molesalām, 165
val Pīr, 156
ādā, Vikramsiṃh, 125*n*30
iyya (ruler of Delhi, r. 1236–40), 152, 179*n*94
Red Sea, 46–7
Reva Kantha, 72
ī. *See* Sufis
ūḍādevī, Rāṇī, 197
Rudramahālaya temple, 31, 75, 131
Runicha, 174
p Manjarī, Rānī, 199, 202
Russian, 46–7

Sabarkantha, 136
Sabarmati river, 27–9, 33, 67–9, 72, 101, 103, 151
Sādhu, also known as Wajīḥ al-Mulk, 165, 197, 201
Ṣadr al-Dīn, Pīr, Ismā'īlī *pīr*, 167
Sahāran, 165, 197, 201
Śāh Jesal, 89, 178*n*63
Śaivite, Śaivism, 7, 20, 35, 49, 51, 82, 120, 130, 132, 135–7, 146–7, 164, 166, 172–4, 178*n*84
Śakadvīpa (Persia or Afghanistan), 49
Śakas, 37, 39
Śakti. *See* goddess worship
Salsette, 190
Sām, Jām, 110
Sāmalājī, 135–6
Samarkand, 110
Sāmba (son of Kṛṣṇa), 109–10, 154, 159
Sāmba Purāṇa, 48, 59*n*100, 159
Sambhar, 29
Saṃdeśarāsaka, 208
Sammas, 37–9, 102, 106, 109–11, 115, 119, 121, 152, 162, 165–6, 168, 202–3
Samrā Śāh, 89, 141
Sana, in Yemen, 125*n*30
Sangana, pirate chieftain, 117
Sanskrit, 4–8, 14, 41, 55*n*2, 65, 75–9, 88, 95*n*6, 97*n*51, 106–7, 111, 118–9, 125*n*25, 126*n*49, 127*n*53, 135, 158, 181*n*144, 195–7, 200, 207–8, 224*n*129
sanskritized, 25, 41, 58, 111
Sanskritic, 14, 20, 82, 112, 117, 124, 131, 216
Sāntal, 137–8
Santo Stefano, Hieronimo di, 85
Sāraṅgadeva (Vaghela ruler, r. 1274–96), 137–8
Sarangpur, in Ahmadabad, 84
Sārasvata-maṇḍala (area of north Gujarat), 29

SOAS Studies on South Asia: Understandings and Perspectives

Daud Ali	*Invoking the Past: The Uses of History in South Asia*
Michael Anderson and Sumit Guha, eds	*Changing Concepts of Rights and Justice in South Asia*
Nigel Crook, ed.	*The Transmission of Knowledge in South Asia: Essays on Education, Religion, History and Politics*
C.J. Fuller, ed.	*Caste Today*
Julia Leslie and Mary McGee, eds	*Invented Identities: The Interplay of Gender, Religion and Politics in India*
Christopher Pinney and Rachel Dwyer, eds	*Pleasure and the Nation: Public Culture in Contemporary India*
Peter Robb, ed.	*The Concept of Race in South Asia*
Peter Robb, ed.	*Meanings of Agriculture: Essays in South Asian History and Economics*
Burton Stein and Sanjay Subrahmanyam, eds	*Institutions and Economic Change in South Asia*

SOAS South Asian Texts Series

Michael Hutt	*Modern Literary Nepali: An Introduction*
Christopher Shackle and Javed Majeed	*Hali's Musaddas: The Flow and Ebb of Islam*
Christopher Shackle and Zawahir Moir	*Ismaili Hymns from South Asia*
Christopher Shackle and Rupert Snell	*Hindi and Urdu since 1800*
Rupert Snell	*The Hindi Classical Tradition*